Absolute Efficiency

PART ONE:

A Guide to Operational Efficiency in the Theme Park Industry

Neil Wilson

Theme Park Press
The Happiest Books on Earth
www.ThemeParkPress.com

Editor: Bob McLain
Layout: Artisanal Text
ISBN 978-1-68390-310-9
Printed in the United States of America
Theme Park Press | www.ThemeParkPress.com
Address queries to bob@themeparkpress.com

"Curiosity leads us forward"
—Walt Disney

I wrote this book for anyone who's curious about how theme parks can get rid of their queues.

I dedicate this book to my Mum and Dad, who have always been happy to stand in line with me.

Contents

Introducing Operational Efficiency

Introduction

When I told one enthusiast about this book, they said to me, "I don't care about why the queues are long. *That's not my problem*. I just expect to have a decent number of rides". That's a reasonable opinion. The park worries about managing the queues, and the guests can concentrate on having fun. You pay your money, you buy your ticket, and you expect a certain number of rides in return. If you don't want to know how parks manage their queues, then I'm afraid this isn't for you. It's going to be a technical look at how parks can reduce their waiting times.

I have tried to make this book interesting as well as useful, and avoid using unnecessary jargon or acronyms. I don't want to lose readers along the way. I have also included a glossary at the back. At the same time, Youtube's full of videos aimed at the 'casual' visitor, who's looking for a little background knowledge on their favourite ride or park. In this book we're going to dig deeper and consider how the most successful theme parks manage their crowds.

I understand that most visitors aren't interested in learning about operational efficiency. I also know that there's a large body of enthusiasts who are fascinated by efficiency, hourly capacities and how parks move their queues. We will meet some of these enthusiasts shortly. If you're a theme park manager, it's your job to manage the queues and keep them as short as possible. This book will help you do that.

For those of you who work in the industry, managing the queues can be a difficult and thankless jobs.

We have the guest who arrives two hours after the park opens, slowly walks to the ride at the back of the park, stopping for selfies along the way, before realising they had their map upside down and walking back to the entrance. Then they go looking for a coffee, before realising that it's lunch time. After lunch they spend half an hour in a queue, before deciding that they "can't be bothered", at which point they head off to spend another half hour wandering around aimlessly. Guest Services know these people well.

There's a type of manager who walks around the park banging a clipboard telling everyone to work faster. They're masters at stating the obvious. "The park's really busy today", they bark, as sweat pours off the operator's face. Perhaps it's all they know, or it's just the easiest option. Then there are the managers who don't even visit the park, and spend all their time sitting in the office looking at spreadsheets. "It looks like we're doing okay", they say, optimistically. They might get a different view if they stepped out the office, or looked on Trip Advisor.

There's the enthusiast who spends a lot of time on message boards moaning about the waiting times, often looking at the queue time apps when they're not even at the park. When someone tries to explain why the queues are so long, they're not interested. Perhaps it spoils 'the magic' for them. Maybe they lack the curiosity. Some people just want to moan.

Whoever you are, you've picked up a book called 'Absolute Efficiency: Part One – a guide to operational efficiency in the theme park industry'. Hopefully you're reading this book, because you want to know why some theme parks have long queues, and what they can do about it. This book has lots of practical advice and case studies. We will be visiting many parks around the world to see how they do it, including some of the busiest and best regarded, as well as those that struggled with the challenges they faced.

Parks we'll visit include; Disney, Universal, Sea World, Dollywood, Silver Dollar City, Legoland California, Knott's Berry Farm, Hard Rock Park, Hershey Park, Kentucky Kingdom, Holiday World, Silverwood, Waldameer, Magic Springs, Leolandia, Liseberg, Walibi Belgium, Europa Park, Parc Astérix, Efteling, Phantasialand, The Milky Way, Oakwood, Alton Towers, Blackpool Pleasure Beach, Thorpe Park, Paultons Park, Warner Bros World and Ferrari World. Aside from an extensive look at Hong Kong Disneyland and Disney Shanghai, this book is dominated by parks in the United States and Europe. That's based on where my own experiences are, and it doesn't mean that parks in other regions aren't doing clever things. Indeed, the TEA (Themed Entertainment Association) estimates that in 2019 Chimelong Ocean Park attracted 11,736,000 visitors[1]. Presumably they've had to be very good at managing their crowds.

Some of the ideas might only work at the larger parks and chains. Fast Pass and My Magic Plus could be examples of that. However, most of the ideas can be scaled up or down, for parks big or small.

The secret to efficient operations, is to give your staff plenty of coffee. No, I'm joking. Originally, I was going to write a book about 'the guest experience'. I noticed that there were quite a few books about customer service, but very little had been written about the other qualities that make a strong all-round experience. There would have been a chapter about music in theme parks, landscaping, cleanliness, uniforms, and one about managing the queues. When I started writing it, I realised pretty quickly that managing the queues was a massive subject that deserved its own book. Then I realised that there was too much for one book. Rather than diluting the content, I thought I'd rather focus on a few aspects of reducing queuing, rather than trying to cover every idea in less detail.

Friendly, helpful and knowledgeable staff are vitally important. I don't think it should ever be seen as a choice between good manners and keeping the queues moving. I've spent a lot of time reading guest feedback, particularly on Trip Advisor, and what strikes me is that long, slow moving queues

---

1   2019 Theme Index, Themed Entertainment Association, http://www.
teaconnect.org/images/files/TEA_369_717589_200717.pdf

are the biggest source of complaints. Even above rude staff. Yet there are numerous books about guest service, and nothing about managing the lines. I hope this book can shed some light on what is an often-misunderstood area of theme park management.

We'll begin this book by looking at a cross range of views about queuing, including enthusiasts', employees' and the wider publics'. I'll ask why efficiency's important. We'll discuss what are acceptable queue lengths for a theme park to have.

Having set the scene, we move through three sections, each looking at a different area of managing queues. In the first one, we look at ways to even out the peaks and troughs, so that visits are shifted from busier days to quieter days. We will look at communication and how parks can nudge people towards the quieter days. We will consider how events can be used to drive attendance towards the slow periods. October used to be the lightest month for attendance, but Halloween changed that. We will also discuss some lesser known events, like Universal's Mardi Gras or the growing number of food and drink festivals. We'll look at what makes a successful event, both for the guests, and the bottom line. We'll talk about pricing and how that can encourage people to pick the quieter days to visit. This includes promotions, like Disney's free Dining Plans and Europa Park's bring a friend at Christmas. It also covers tiered and dynamic pricing. Theme parks typically get very crowded when they open a new attraction, so we'll explore ways to manage that. Parks often have big peaks when the weather's likely to be good, so we'll discuss weather proofing, in terms of design and operations. There can be a sizeable difference in how busy a park is at a weekend or school holiday compared to term time. We'll consider ways to grow a park's attendance by attracting the kinds of people who visit in the week. We'll finish the first section by discussing how parks can make sure they're staffed properly at peak times.

The second section focuses on how we can make sure our visitors are evenly spread out around our parks, rather than clustered together in one area. We'll discuss park layouts and how they encourage guests to circulate around the site. In particular, we'll look at Disney's hub and spoke layout. We'll consider how parks can expand without being too disruptive to the guest flow and other design considerations, like where to place the entrance to the park or the exit of a show. We'll look at where to place your biggest rides to handle the crowds most effectively. We'll talk about timed tickets (virtual queues) to manage the flow at an attraction through the day. We'll look at how you can help guests plan their day by advertising the wait times. We'll also talk about how we can make sure the advertised waiting times are accurate and other subtle design features that encourage guests to plan their day. To complete this second section, we examine guest flow through the day. How can we make sure our park's busy from opening to close, rather than all the visitors coming for the middle period?

The third section looks at park capacities, how they're set and how they can be raised. We'll discuss the safety issues around a park's capacity, including the number of toilets and fire regulations, particularly around building occupancy. We'll look at how quickly guests can access drinking water, and the ability to deal with security and first aid incidents. We'll cover Blue Routes that get emergency vehicles quickly to areas of the park, and crowd control. In particular, we'll look at bottle necks, and use Disney's Project Star Dust as a case study. We'll then look at how we can manage the guest experience in a crowded environment and why there might be times to limit the capacity, even when it's safe to let in more people. I'll illustrate how these techniques work in practice by placing some parks 'under the spotlight'. We consider the challenges faced by Geauga Lake. We'll find out how the attendance was able to suddenly shoot up at Paultons Park and Island of Adventure without their guest satisfaction falling. We go back in time to the early days of amusement parks when Coney Island handled Disney World level crowds. We'll take a trip to Holiday World in Indiana, to see how you run a successful theme park in a sparsely populated area. We'll look at Dollywood to see how a top regional park finds that balance between guest satisfaction and profitability. We'll follow Hong Kong Disneyland's journey from a new park and how its capacity has grown over time. We'll finish this section by considering how typical Hong Kong Disneyland's story is of a Disney park.

There are plenty of things we won't be discussing. We won't be looking at queue design and theming, or how to prevent queue jumping. We won't be talking about 'throughputs' – the number of people who can ride an attraction each hour. We won't be exploring single rider queues, handling loose articles, the design of ride vehicles and their restraints. We won't be looking in detail at different types of rides, or how to encourage your staff to work quicker through training, motivation and management. All of these things are important, and very worthy of a sequel. I decided that I didn't want this book to become too long. I do most of my reading on trains and public transport, so I know that big heavy books make good doorstops, but they're not the most practical for actually reading. I could have diluted some of the examples and skimped on the details to cover a broader range of factors, but I think the detail's important. A lot of managers know about things like single rider queues and queueline entertainment. It's the detail that tells you how to make them work effectively.

I have got a couple of personal reasons for writing this book. During my lifetime I've seen a big chunk of the UK parks close: Frontierland, The Rotunda, American Adventure, Camelot, Loudon Castle, Pleasure Island, Spanish City, Granada Studios, Crinkley Bottom, Pleasurama, Ocean Beach, Grove Land... to name a few. Some of the UK parks have ended up in the absurd situation where they're inundated with complaints about the queues, but then they close because they're losing money. That doesn't seem right to me. I hope there might be something in this book that helps some of the UK parks to manage their queues more effectively.

I've seen managers waste a lot of time ineffectually wandering around telling everyone to work faster, which lowers morale and encourages staff to cut corners, potentially risking the safety of themselves, their colleagues and the guests. In this book, I want to show that it doesn't have to be like that. While there's no doubt that energised and well-trained staff do make a difference to how quickly the queues move, I want to give managers a tool kit that doesn't involve barking at the staff to work faster.

This book features my own experiences from working at parks, including Alton Towers, Chessington World of Adventures, Dreamland, Europa Park and Epcot. I have also been privileged to visit many other fantastic attractions. For all other information I've given my sources in footnotes.

Because this is the first book on the subject, most of my sources are online, although I've used a few books, like In Service to the Mouse and The Wonderful World of Customer Service at Disney. They include podcasts (particularly the Season Pass Podcast and Attractions Pros), various Youtube channels, including Expedition Theme Park, Coaster Studios and Theme Park Worldwide, industry websites including Bloo Loop, TEA (Themed Entertainment Association) and IAAPA (International Association of Amusement Parks and Attractions), various fan sites including RCDB (Roller Coaster Data Base), Theme Park Insider, Theme Park University, Theme Park Tourist, Towers Street, Ultimate Roller Coaster, Roller Coaster Philosophy and Coaster Kingdom, other media such as the BBC (British Broadcasting Corporation) and the New York Times and numerous official parks' sites. Much of this information might not be completely new, but by gathering it all up together and presenting the best practices for reducing queues, hopefully it will provide a useful service for the industry.

I have done my best to make sure that all the information is accurate and presented in a balanced way. Researching a book of this nature can be tricky. Managers are often keen to big up any changes they've made, while employees lower down the company can be tempted to exaggerate how many guests they managed to serve. Manufacturers tend to give optimistic estimations of what their rides can achieve, because they're making a sales pitch. Ex-employees don't always accurately remember facts and figures, journalists mis-interpret information or get their facts muddled, and often it's tricky to link cause and effect when a park's satisfaction rating improves or their attendance increases. By considering a wide range of parks and a lot of sources, I hope that my findings and conclusions are able to ride through these distortions to provide some genuinely useful insights. My goal is to show how the most successful theme parks manage their crowds safely and efficiently.

I am always grateful for additional views or corrections. If readers want to respond to any of my points, or add additional information, please get in touch:

forneilwilson@gmail.com

My aim is to make this book, and any future books, as helpful as I can. It has been a personal learning curve. I've discovered a lot more about a subject I was already interested in. Let's work together, to make the theme park industry the very best it can be.

A Fascination with Queues

On the surface throughputs and operational efficiency might appear to be something quite technical that theme park managers would worry about, but are too geeky for most enthusiasts to take an interest in. However, there have been some fairly lengthy discussions in online message boards about the throughputs on certain rides. Youtube channel Coaster Studios have made a regular feature out of comparing the throughputs on different rides. A couple of enthusiasts made an app for measuring throughputs, and another group of enthusiasts created a game that simulates being a ride operator. One of the challenges is to get a certain number of riders through your attraction. Ride reviews and trip reports, comment on how quickly the lines move and how efficient the staff are. Whilst it's not hard to find complaints about slow staff, most staff find long queues stressful and can be competitive about their throughputs.

Most of this book looks at ways for managing queues more effectively. But before we dive into this, let's have a quick tour around the enthusiast community and beyond. How much do people really care about the queues? I mean, people don't like queuing, but are they that bothered? Before I start suggesting my ideas for reducing the queues, what does the public blame and what are their solutions?

Coaster Studios

At the time of writing (December 29th, 2018) Coaster Studios has 116,744 subscribers. The channel was created in 10th December 2012 and has had 48,129,026 views for their 1,677 videos. That's an incredible number of views, meaning that collectively their videos have been watched almost as many times as there are people living in the UK. Whilst the stats are currently slightly behind the UK's biggest theme park Youtube channel, Theme Park Worldwide (currently 66,371,994 views), Coaster Force (450,975,504 views) and Theme Park Review (972,421,522 views), it is currently one of the most popular Youtube channels dedicated to theme parks.

Coaster Studios runs several popular features. These include reviews of theme parks, reviews of roller coasters, cinematic montages of theme parks where various clips are put to music, 'parodies' (which are spoof reviews of well-known roller coasters) and their Testing Theme Park Operations series of videos. At the time of writing this series contains 21 videos out of the 1,677 videos on the channel. That's only about 1.25% of the channel's total output. However, these videos have promoted a lot of discussions about efficiency with many ex-staff chipping in with their views.

To show the level of interest in their videos, here's a summary of the number of views they've got (again, the time of writing is 29th December

2018). Some videos are more recent than others, which partly explains why some videos have a lot more views than others, plus it is an American channel although they do have a reasonable coverage beyond the US. I've shown the number of views these videos have to indicate the level on interest in theme park throughputs. On average each video on Coaster Studios had 28,699 views at the time of writing, so you can see from the following table that the operations series of videos are amongst their most popular. These videos aren't simply getting a lot of views because the channel does, and people click on them by accident. The videos comparing ride throughputs are one of the biggest draws for the channel.

Video Name	Park	Views
Does Europa Park have the world's fastest operations?	Europa Park (Germany)	76,916
Does Six Flags America have the worst operations in the world?	Six Flags America (Maryland)	261,762
How bad are La Ronde's operations?	La Ronde (Quebec, Canada)	164,957
How bad are Thorpe Park's operations?	Thorpe Park (UK)	21,530
How fast are Phantasialand's operations?	Phantasialand (Germany)	8,032
Are Hershey Park's operations really good or really bad?	Hershey Park (Pennsylvania)	17,921
So how bad are Dorney Park's operations?	Dorney Park (Pennsylvania)	30,596
How fast are Cedar Point's operations?	Cedar Point (Ohio)	204,744
How fast are Six Flags Magic Mountain's operations?	Six Flags Magic Mountain (California)	69,036
How fast are Six Flag's Great Adventure's operations?	Six Flags Great Adventure (New Jersey)	87,460
How fast are Kings Island's operations?	Kings Island (operations)	54,719
So how fast are Carowind's operations?	Carowinds (North Carolina)	50,075
How bad are Knott's Berry Farm's operations?	Knott's Berry Farm (California)	80,348
How bad are Elitch Garden's operations?	Elitch Gardens (Colorado)	31,584
So how fast are Port Aventura's operations?	Port Aventura (Spain)	36,099
Just how fast are Dollywood's operations?	Dollywood (Tennessee)	61,680
So how good are Busch Gardens Williamsburg's operations?	Busch Gardens Williamsburg (Virginia)	77,315
So how bad are Kennywood's operations?	Kennywood (Pennsylvania)	26,867
Just how fast are Walt Disney World's operations?	Walt Disney World (Florida)	46,622
So how bad are Waldameer Park's operations?	Waldameer Park (Pennsylvania)	9,656

The average throughput video has 70,896 views compared to an average of 28,699 for the channel. The fact that some of the most popular videos on one of the biggest theme park channels are comparing throughputs, shows the level of interest in them. When I started working in the industry, I'd never have guessed that one day over 260,000 people would have watched a video about how quickly Six Flags America loads their roller coasters. Whilst this book is aimed at theme park professionals, it is quite possible that some enthusiasts will also read it, looking to broaden their understanding of throughputs and ride capacities.

So, we've said that the Coaster Studios series on roller coaster operations shows the level of interest in throughputs, but how do these videos work? Each one is presented by channel owner Taylor Bybee. The episode starts with a disclaimer saying he understands that safety is the top priority and that he's not trying to put pressure on parks to cut corners with safety. Along the way he also makes a few other acknowledgements. These include pointing out that the nature of some rides makes it easier to get good throughputs than others, that the dispatches on a roller coaster won't always be the same and that sometimes coasters have short queues meaning there isn't the same need to push trains out quickly.

In each video he tries to visit as many of the park's coasters as he can to measure their dispatches. He doesn't include kiddie coasters. On each one he starts a clock counting when a train begins loading and stops it when the train is ready to dispatch. He doesn't time how long it is between when one trains is dispatched and when the next one parks in position, which does take longer on some coasters than on others.

The clock starts off green, changes to yellow after 60 seconds and to red after 120 seconds. When the clips are fast forwarded and set to chirpy music, they're fun to watch. After each coaster dispatch a word or short phrase pops up on the screen to give his reaction, for example, "Unbelievable", "Fantastic", 'Okay", "Could do better".

Ride Sims

Ride Sims is a popular website that allows you to operate virtual versions of real theme park rides. It's browser based, meaning it doesn't need to be downloaded, and it's made using Adobe's Flash, the same programme used for famous games like Angry Birds and Farmville.

The original Ride Sims had around 1,240,000 plays and ran from 2012-2016[2]. After a couple of years 'SBNO' (standing but not operating) Ride Sims relaunched with Ride Sims 2.0 at the end of 2018. To make it more competitive and game like, they introduced a new feature where players could compete to see who could get the highest hourly throughput with their virtual 'peeps'. They explained it on their Facebook page, "We know that with Ride Sims V1.0, to get onto the leader boards really came down to how long you played for. So we wanted to add more challenge for our operators. Along with your usual score, you will be able to compete for the highest hourly peep through-put."

Specific challenges include 'Dispatch 200 fully loaded logs on Ripsaw Falls', 'handle 1000 peeps on Taron', 'handle 50 priority peeps on Phantom Manor'

---

2   Ride Sims Facebook page, August 12th 2016

and 'handle 50 slow load [disabled] peeps on Phantom Manor'. Players get ranked in a league table based on their throughputs. Geekism is a Youtube channel that reviews strategy and simulation games for adults. They say, "The whole point of this, the actual game element, is to really up your throughput and get as many people through the gates as possible per hour"[3]. If the real ride has a single riders queue, so does the version on Ride Sims. You can transfer trains on and off the track. It only lets you have one train in a block section at a time. Broadly speaking, it gives you the main variables that real parks have when they're looking at throughputs.

My IT skills are near non-existent. I can just about manage turning my computer off and on again, so I'm easily impressed by other people's IT skills. But Ride Sims is an incredible achievement. It looks like a professional video game with detailed graphics. Perhaps not surprising, considering it was worked on by people who've become influential in the industry, such as John Burton, who became a creative lead for Merlin Magic Making. It includes some fantastic details, such as letting players choose the time of day. Rides can be affected by adverse weather and technical difficulties. A dispatch might be delayed by a guest not having their restraint down properly. If you take the Walt Disney World Monorail simulator as an example, as you skip between the different stations it plays the music you'd hear at that station, and the game automatically plays the right safety announcements at the right times.

They have an active fan community on social media who suggest rides they'd like to operate and new features they want to see added. Following feedback, you couldn't just open the Matterhorn Bobsled in their simulator, you had to do a series of pre-start tests without guests. For people who haven't worked in a theme park themselves, it must be a really interesting insight into how operations actually work. Best of all, it's free. What kind of throughputs will you get?

Other video games

There has been a string of simulations games where players run their own theme park. Perhaps the first one that became a mainstream success was Bullfrog's Theme Park in 1994, but other earlier basic simulations did exist. As computers have become more powerful and the games have got more sophisticated, players have had increasing control over the throughputs and the efficiency of their parks.

When Roller Coaster Tycoon 2 was released in 2002, it had several developments over the original, which was released in 1999. This included allowing players to add block section to rides and run the ride in 'block mode', making it harder for trains to crash into each other. They also gave the guests improved AIs (artificial intelligence), meaning they didn't just walk around randomly anymore. This meant you could build wider paths

3   Ride Sims 2 first look gameplay, Geekism, https://www.youtube.com/watch?v=ShKaI097Kzw

at busier locations in the park without the guests getting confused. All the Roller Coaster Tycoon games gave you the option to decide how regularly a mechanic inspects the ride, and the more frequently the ride's inspected, the less likely it is to break down. This gives players a crude understanding of preventative maintenance. You chose how frequently a mechanic was scheduled to inspect the ride, but you also chose how many mechanics were hired and how big an area they covered. Without enough mechanics in the right places, the maintenance schedule couldn't be fulfilled. In Roller Coaster Tycoon 3 they introduced the option to train staff, which would make them more efficient, quicker and perform better. With Roller Coaster Tycoon 3 you can give staff more training at any point, but Planet Coaster took it a stage further. Now you can't train an employee up to the next level until they've been working at the previous level for a certain length of time. We can raise staff morale by paying them more, which will also cause them to work faster and more efficiently.

I grew up playing the Roller Coaster Tycoon games, and although at the time I hadn't worked in a theme park myself, looking back they did give me a broad understanding of the different challenges associated with running a theme park.

In 2018 Parkitecht came out, which compared to other games focussed more on the management side and less on the design side. You could build backstage routes to get staff around the parks quicker, for example trash could be moved around backstage rather than through the guest areas. On the flat rides, guests would have to walk between the entrance/exit and the attraction. If we take a slide/Helter Skelter as an example, it's best to place the exit on the attraction's perimeter as close to the bottom of the slide as possible. That way it takes less time for the guest to leave the ride area and for the next one to slide down. If you cluster your food outlets near your food depot in a food court, it's easier keeping them stocked up. If a ride has a long queue, then it's a good idea to place a toilet near the exit.

To really understand operational efficiency, getting a job working in a theme park is a great education. But video games can give people a decent starting point.

Virtual Queue Line

In 2020 April Fools Day was a lower key affair than normal because of the Coronavirus. However, the Theme Park Guide created a fake website called 'Virtual Queue Line'[4]. For a long time, enthusiasts have been able to watch POV (point of view) videos filmed from the front of different roller coasters. This means you can enjoy them from the comfort of your own home and see what a roller coaster's like at a park you've never visited. Originally these were on VHS, then they switched to DVDs. Finally, as broadband spread, we often saw these videos posted online, most commonly on Youtube.

4   Virtual queueline, Theme Park Guide, http://queue.themepark-guide.biz/queue_line.html?queueTime=15&ride=Nemesis

Virtual Queue Line let us watch POV videos from different roller coasters. However, rather than clicking on the ride and watching it straight away, you had to wait the time you'd have waited in the queue if you'd actually visited the park. It was an impressive amount of effort for an April Fools, and it captured the slightly eccentric fascination that many enthusiasts have with queuing and throughputs.

Throughput Calculator

Sam Gregory and David Fairbairn created a Throughput Calculator app (see facing page) for mobile phones.[5]

While standing in a queue, you can use the Throughput Calculator to work out how many people are riding an attraction each hour. According to Sam they choose green and black to style it on 'retro' technology. You tell it how many seats there are and then press 'dispatch' each time a train's sent (or passes any particular point in the ride). Each time a train's dispatched it recalculates the throughput based on all the dispatches so far, so the reading gradually becomes more accurate as any anomalies get averaged out. Towers Street users suggested ideas to develop the app further, for example allowing users to submit the throughputs they've recorded for rides so that you could crowd source statistics for different rides around the world. Although his app was developed for other enthusiasts, I wonder whether any managers have found it useful. They certainly should do.

Queue Times.com

These days a lot of theme parks have mobile apps (cell phones), so that guests can view the current waiting times as they walk around the park. There are various reasons for this, including managing expectations (you know you'll

---

5   Sam, Throughput Calculator, Rest of the World Parks and Attractions, Towers Street Forum, https://towersstreet.com/talk/threads/throughput-calculator.914/

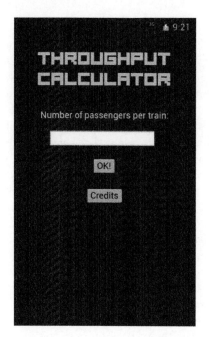
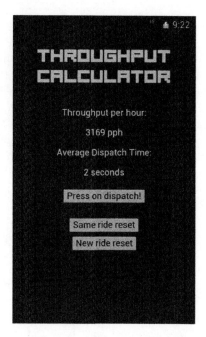

be waiting for half an hour before you step into the line), to help guests plan their day (you won't join a 60 minute queue, if you want to see a show in 45 minutes) and to move guests to quieter areas of the park (you can see if the queues in another area of the park are shorter). We discuss phone apps as a queue management tool later in this book.

Often you can only use the app when you're at the park. They don't want people sitting at home and seeing what the queue times are. If they're really long it might put people off visiting. They don't want people to use the information to make fraudulent complaints, claiming they were at the park when they weren't, and they don't want theme park enthusiasts mocking them for their long queues when they weren't even there.

Then in 2014 Zachary Bull created queue-times.com. It's a website that allows anyone, anywhere, to view the waiting times at different parks, regardless of whether or not they're actually there. His website takes its information from the official apps. He created his website after visiting a theme park and being frustrated by how long the queues were[6]. At the time of writing (July 29th 2019) his website includes 81 theme parks and 5191 rides and to date it has delivered 547,952,439 different waiting times for these rides. Zachary created his website while studying engineering at Cambridge University.

Theme parks covered by his site include many of the big Western theme park chains (Disney, Universals, Six Flags, Cedar Fair, Merlin Entertainments, Herschend Entertainment, Sea World Parks and Resorts) as well as several independent parks (including Port Aventura, Blackpool Pleasure Beach, Efteling, Europa Park and Phantasialand).

---

6   About queue times, https://queue-times.com/pages/about

Coaster Kingdom

I was 10 when my parents got our first computer. It was Windows 95. If you wanted to use the Internet you had to unplug the phone, and plug the computer into the phone socket, and wait for the computer to dial into the Internet. Older readers will remember the noise it made. You couldn't use the phone and the Internet at the same time, which wouldn't have mattered if most people had mobiles. We didn't have Youtube channels. You had to leave it a couple of minutes if you wanted to download a photo. This was a long time before broadband. Youtube wasn't founded until 2005 and Facebook goes back to 2004.

What we used to have were website and forums, that were far more text based than most of what you see online today. Perhaps my favourite was the British website Coaster Kingdom, that reviewed parks and rides. In their reviews, they often commented on how quickly the lines moved. It was from reading Coaster Kingdom that I first started thinking about throughputs and efficiencies. At the time, as a 10-year-old, I never imagined that one day I'd be working in theme parks, and the one responsible for managing their queues.

When I'm considering the waiting times, I often think about Coaster Kingdom's review of Wild Wasser 3, a travelling log flume from the German fair circuit (wasser means 'water' in German).

"Wildwasser doesn't have a queue in the theme park sense of the word. Sure, it has a pathway full of people that leads to the station, but the ferocious efficiency of the staff, coupled with the vast number of boats the ride can handle, means that all you really do is join a line of people who are continually advancing at a perfectly normal walking pace. Even if the queue area is full to bursting, the throng moves at a speed that means you'd get on the ride no later than if the place were deserted. You almost don't get a chance to notice the fact that the station is, again, fully themed, with animatronic figures sitting on the roof, and western lanterns hanging from the ceiling. For the more observant rider, it also bears the name of the ride's owner, Joachim Löwenthal, a man who should be very proud of his charge"[7].

I'd be so chuffed if somebody one day wrote that about one of the rides I was managing. At the end of 2017 Wildwasser 3 was retired from travelling. In 2018 it found a permanent home at Skyline Park near Munich, which is owned by the Löwenthals. It replaced the park's smaller, but still impressive, pirate themed log flume, that was sold to Eifel Park (also in Germany).

Since this is a book about efficiency, it's worth mentioning that Wildwasser 3 was unusual, if not unique, because it had two bases (sometimes known as frames, or 'spiders', because when viewed from above the crisscross of metal struts looks like a spider's web). This meant they could start building the ride up in one area while still dismantling it in another. Whilst the flume was being dismantled at one fair the base was already being built up at the next one. This reduced the turnaround time between each location, and maximised the amount of fairs it could attend.

---

7   Wild Wasser (3), German Fairs, Coaster Kingdom, http://www. s104638357.websitehome.co.uk/html/wildwasser_main.htm

The German website Coasters and More explains why this was important, by describing the assembly for another large German coaster that used to travel; Euro Star[8]. Euro Star was a four abreast inverted coaster, meaning the trains hang below the track. It had four inversions. Their description is a little technical, but the key point is that rides have to be completely flat. If they're not, the ride might not work, or it could damage some of the parts.

"It has the be precisely aligned in order that the whole ride stands straight and the static and dynamic forces are safely led into the ground. For this purpose sophisticated laser leveling instruments are used to ensure that all support points are on the same level. The steel sole is variably underpinned depending on the evenness of the ground. Like for all mobile rides wooden beams and planks of different thickness are used for this task.

The further assembly is pure routine: Piece for piece the respective next supports are installed and the next track segment is mounted thereupon, resulting in an inherent stability making the single segments standing free. Due to the conical design of the connections the mutual elements are automatically adjusted correctly before they are fixed in position by large bolts. For the supports the rather unusual H-profiles were used. The Stengel engineering office had adopted them only once before for the transportable Münchner Bahn by Schwarzkopf, a ride debuting on the Oktoberfest in 1982."

Static rides are either placed on completely flat concrete pads, or the supports rest on footers dug into the ground. Travelling rides sit on uneven land, where digging holes and pouring concrete into them isn't an option. To keep the base (spider) level, they put pieces of wood underneath it. It's a bit like having a wonky chair at home, and you put a folded piece of paper under one leg to stop it rocking around. In the UK these pieces of wood are called packing, because you pack them underneath the ride. Building a large base for a mobile ride, and constantly adjusting it to keep things flat, is a time-consuming process. This is why having a second base was important for the world's largest travelling log flume.

I don't have time to cover project management in this book, but it's an area I'd like to include in a sequel. It's always worth reducing the construction time for a ride, particularly as time is money. The longer it takes to build a ride, the longer you have to pay the staff for and the longer you have to hire plant equipment like diggers and dumper trucks. Most rides only get built up once. When you're building a ride up several times a year in different locations, the logistics and the efficiency become particularly important.

These days review sites have mostly been replaced by Youtube channels and Facebook groups, but reviews of rides and attractions still tend to comment on how efficient they are.

---

8   Euro Star – the full story, Coasters and More, http://www.coas-tersandmore.de/rides/eurostar/eurostar_eng.shtml

Online discussions

On theme park message boards, throughputs tend to provide a lively discussion. There was a lot of enthusiasm when Alton Towers added a single rider queue to Nemesis, and just as much disgruntlement when they removed a lot of their single rider queues (some people did point out that it might be a good thing, if it lifts the overall throughput of an attraction). Since then, when fan forums (such as Towers Street) have threads where people post their 'wish lists', bringing back the single rider queues is one of the most frequent suggestions.

Trip reports often refer to throughputs, efficiency and 'operations'. How quickly the queues move, often gathers more focus than how long the waiting actually was. Construction topics about rides that haven't yet opened are likely to gather considerable debate about what the throughput is likely to be. Here's one comment about a British roller coaster, "The staff literally swan around, push a harness down, do a little dance about how they love not being efficient, put another harness down, go for a poo break, close another bar, then 10 minutes later you get dispatched. But seriously, the worrying thing is that I'm only exaggerating a little bit!!"[9] I share this, not because I necessarily agree with the judgement. Throughputs are complicated. But it's one of the comments that made me laugh.

Theme Park History is one of the major theme park channels on Youtube. At the time of writing (April 2020) they have 84,000 subscribers. The creator was asked in a Q&A what he thinks makes a great theme park. He answered, "It's got to have a lot of different types of attractions to it. It has to have pretty good theming all around the park itself. If there is one universal theme it sticks throughout the park and nothing sticks out like a sore thumb. And probably most important of all, no long wait times for any attractions.... when I choose a park for the entire day I want to be able to enjoy it, not get stuck waiting very long times to ride any attraction"[10]. The enthusiast community can be a hard bunch to please, but when it comes down to it, long, slow moving queues are often what turns a smile into a frown.

It's not just enthusiasts who like to chip in on the issue. On social media there are often plenty of ex-staff ready to give their views, usually bemoaning that the current staff aren't as fast as they were. A guest wrote a long comment on one park's Facebook page about the throughputs on their rides. In the interest of fairness, I haven't named the park, the rides nor the people posting. Clearly when people have a discussion on Facebook, they're not expecting their comments to be suddenly printed in a book.

"Having been visiting for years and years one massive thing we have noticed is the total lack of urgency loading and un-loading rides.

Everyone can accept queueing for 45-60 or so minutes in the summer, but it's soul destroying and makes me so frustrated to see staff chatting, messing

---

9   User Danzibarr, Coaster Force forum, https://coasterforce.com/
forums/threads/kumalis-second-train.32428/page-2

10   Theme park history presents the 75k Q&A spectacular part 2: electric boogaloo, Theme Park History, https://www.youtube.com/watch?v=PN-DzlsfN1k

NEIL WILSON   19

around together (not for visitors benefit) and paying no attention to fully filling the ride.

The [name of ride] today (and every day to be honest) is painfully slow. The disabled/wrist band entrance is killing the throughput and today despite an hour queue whilst I was waiting in the station I saw 4 sets of two seats go out empty and no one was bothered. That's 8 sets of seats minimum not including single riders in 5 trains!"

This was followed by a succession of comments from ex-staff, including, "When I worked on it, we would have been shot if we were that slow! (Totally understandable too! Also, I remember trialling pre-batching and we all said it was too slow.) Still my favourite theme park, still my favourite ride, just needs a little bit of TLC with regards to operations. Maybe bring some of the old 3 train [name of ride] crew back?"

"I still remember us getting them out in 25 seconds on 3 trains! You couldn't even play the auto-announcements now in that time. Shall we go back and show them what a real dispatch is?"

"OMG I miss the old days too guys! The amount of fun we used to have! We really did smash the 3 train operation too, doing it quickly but safely too. I can remember us all working so hard and constantly shouting get up the stairs! Was such a great ride to operate too and always had an awesome bunch of work colleagues! I do miss those days."

From reading a lot of comments by ex-staff, there clearly is a sense of pride in getting people on and off the rides more quickly, as well as a bit of rivalry. When I told friends that I was writing a book about efficiency, they would say things like, "I was the fastest member on my team. It wasn't official, but I think everyone knew it", and, "Although the other teams wouldn't admit it, we clearly were the fastest". I'd congratulate them on their dedication and assure them that I took their claims completely at face value. "So, er, will you mention me in your book?". "I'll certainly think about it", I'd say. "Your anecdote about how you were the fastest person in your team is incredibly interesting. I'm sure my readers would love to hear about it. It's just so difficult trying to fit everything into one book".

The reassuring thing about all of these stories, is that people clearly do care about efficiency and want to do their bit. Or at least, they want people to think that they did their bit. In the long run though, petty rivalries, mundane anecdotes where the storyteller is always the hero, and people putting each other down, isn't a great way to run an attraction. In these books, I'm going to be advocating for a different way of tackling queues, where people work together and think long term.

Lampooning the queues

American stand up Jim Gaffigan summed up how a lot of people imagine theme parks with his comic analysis[11]. "There's pressure to have fun on

---

11   Jim Gaffigan Disney, Paul Rose, Youtube, https://www.youtube.com/watch?v=eYacdfsORec

your vacation, but at Disney it's like a desperation. You see it on the faces of parents. They're like, this was an enormous mistake. It was either this or send you to college. I stood in line for an hour and fifteen minutes for the Dumbo ride. After a minute I was like, I'm the Dumbo. I'm waiting to see myself. At the end of the line there's just going to be a mirror and some guy going – Dumbo."

UK comedian Rob Beckett took his kids to Legoland Windsor. He said, "You can't explain to a two-year-old why you're queuing, because the answer is, you shouldn't be, you're wasting your life"[12].

In 2008 Universals Florida converted Back to the Future [simulator] into The Simpsons ride. It was complimented by a Kwik-E-Mart gift shop and a few side shows. In 2013 this was expanded into a full Springfield area. Springfield being the fictional home of the Simpsons. As part of the area they opened a second ride, Kang and Kodos' Twirl 'n' Hurl. It was themed to the aliens who appear in every one of the Treehouse of Horrors episodes. There was one of these in each series of The Simpsons from the second onwards, shown once a year around Halloween. They often parody horror and supernatural films and take place outside the usual Simpsons universe.

The Simpsons area has various jokes taking the mick out of the theme park industry, particularly on The Simpsons ride, which includes a pastiche of attractions at Disney World and Sea World. A sign in the Kwik-E-Mart says 'Today's merchandise at tomorrows prices'. Another says 'Professionally shot priced souvenir photos'. The queue for Kang and Kodos' Twirl 'n' Hurl includes a few jokes about how theme park guests must enjoy queuing. One says, "Clearly humans like waiting in line. You will be happy to know that there is much more line to come".

When comedians lampoon theme parks, the queues are often what they go for. If you ask people to think of a negative stereotype about theme parks, queues and break downs are what they think about. When people actually are stuck in a two-hour line, they probably won't see the funny side. Luckily, Kang and Kodos' Twirl 'n' Hurl has one of the shortest lines at the park.

Guest Feedback

It's pretty well known that queues are the biggest source of complaints about theme parks. Steve Brown is the CEO of Accesso, a theme park technology company. He says, "In every survey I've ever seen across my career, and I've seen a lot of them, the number one reason [why people don't like visiting theme parks] is that they don't like waiting in line. Number two is how much it costs. Always in that order. If you can address the number one objection that consumers have to doing something, why would you not address it?"[13].

12   Rob Beckett's tips for visiting Legoland with a young family, Hugh Fort, Berkshire Live, https://www.getreading.co.uk/whats-on/family-kids-news/rob-becketts-tips-visiting-legoland-18891852

13   Steve Brown talks about virtual queuing, episode 149, The Attraction Pros Podcast, http://attractionpros.com/podcast-details/

Nick Varney, the CEO of Merlin Entertainments, made the same point in his keynote speech at IAAPA (International Association of Amusement Parks and Attractions)[14].

The more casual reviewer on Trip Advisor or Google Reviews is less likely to use words like 'throughput', or to comment on single rider queues. But, the pages for some parks do frequently make comments like, "they seemed to be short staffed", "they need more staff to make the queues move quicker", "the staff seemed to be very slow at loading the rides". The wider public don't necessarily think about queues in quite the same language that we will in this book, but it is very much on their minds.

At the time of writing Trip Advisor lets you search reviews of an attraction for key words, but when you do a key word search it only brings up the first 1,000 reviews containing that word. A number of major theme parks with low Trip Advisor scores clock up 1,000 reviews containing the word 'queue' in less than a year. In contrast, at the time of writing Magic Kingdom has 63,605 reviews, but to find 1,000 reviews mentioning the word queue you have to go back 2.5 years. Legoland Windsor has 17,890 reviews, but has had 1,000 reviews mentioning the word queue in little less than one season. Chessington has 7,754 reviews, including 1,000 reviews mentioning the word 'queue' in less than a year. Not all of these use it in a negative context. Some say things like, "We went in half term so queues were to be expected", or even, "the queues were well themed". Nonetheless, there is clearly a link, that the more guests comment on the queues, the lower the park's rating tends to be.

The word queue is often mis-spelt, for example as 'cue'. My rudimentary analysis wouldn't have picked up on any reviews using a mis-spelling of the word queue. It is also didn't pick up on all the alternative ways of phrasing it like, "the lines moved very slowly", or, "there were long waits". Americans are more likely to say 'line', which may make my comparison between Legoland Windsor, Chessington and Magic Kingdom a little unfair. However, I did also search for the word 'line', and even factoring in the results from this search, queues are referred to relatively infrequently in the Magic Kingdom reviews.

It is clear when queues are long and slow moving, a lot of reviews will comment on it. Just as helpful and friendly staff are one of the biggest criteria for parks with high ratings, long waits and closed attractions are one of the hallmarks of parks with low guest satisfaction. I have no doubt that the queues are one of the biggest concerns for a lot of visitors. The Walt Disney Company wrote as such in their 1999 annual report, "We've found over the years that lines are the single most mentioned criticism of our parks"[15]. This was the year they introduced Fast Pass, a virtual queuing system designed to reduce the time that guests spent in line.

I thought it was important to include this chapter near the beginning of the book. It shows that there is a strong interest in queues and waiting times,

14   Mark Locker, attraction.io – Mobile apps and the art of the possible, Bloo Loop V Expo 2020

15   Annual report 1999, The Walt Disney Company, https://thewaltdisneycompany.com/app/uploads/2015/10/1999-Annual-Report.pdf

from enthusiasts, employee and from the broader public. And yet very little has been written about what parks can actually do to reduce their waiting times and to manage their queues more effectively. At some parks, their only strategy is to send a supervisor round with a clipboard telling their staff to work faster. I believe that this is by far the largest piece of research on the subject, and that is why I published it.

What do the staff think?

There is sometimes the perception that the employees don't care how long and slow the queues are. Unfortunately, some genuinely don't, and I hope to talk about motivating and engaging staff in a sequel to this book. In some cases, they were always the wrong people for the job. In other cases, they started off enthusiastically behind the cause, but something took away their passion. I'm sure most of us who've worked in theme parks can think of a time when a customer or a manager was mean to us, and it took our enthusiasm out of the job. What you can't do is allow the rot to set in. When staff stop caring about the job, you've lost the battle. When staff stop caring it's bad for safety, service, efficiency, cleanliness and any other area of operations that you can think of. Having a workforce who feel engaged is surely the foundations that everything else is built on.

Luckily, my experience from working in the industry, is that most staff do care about the queues. Often more deeply than the customers realise. And there are plenty of reasons for them to care.

Most people find dealing with a long queue stressful. They say happy staff, happy customers, but the reverse can also be true. If most of the customers are unhappy because the queues are long, it's hard for the staff to feel as positive. Emotions are contagious. It also means we end up dealing with a lot more complaints. Lacking control is stressful, and when our queues become overly long, we don't feel that we're in control. We can also feel hugely out-numbered by the hundreds of waiting, and often angry, guests.

Most of the problems that staff have to deal with wouldn't occur if the waiting times were short. That's not to say the queues are directly causing the problems, but they do create the conditions for them. Very little queue jumping would happen if the lines were short. This includes people jumping over fences or pushing past people, but also the more subtle forms of queue jumping, for example people abusing parent passes and disabled access schemes. When parents get to the front of the queue and are told their child's too short, they're a lot angrier when they've been waiting for two hours rather than fifteen minutes. Groups of people are less likely to come down the single rider line and refuse to split up when the main line's short. The shorter the lines, the less likely people are to smoke in them. When the ride breaks down and you have to evacuate the queue, it's a lot harder when some of the people have been standing there for three hours. When the park closes, people are more likely to start jumping the fences to get an extra ride when they've only been on a few rides. When the lines are really long, people might legitimately need to leave their place to go to the toilet.

Most of the guest complaints and conflicts that staff have to deal with do have at least some relationship to how long the waiting times are. I often look at complaints and arguments and think, "If the queue was a quarter of the length, that probably wouldn't have happened". Few staff enjoy being ranted at, threatened, abused, talked down to and told how to do their job. In the end staff get burned out from all the abuse and start to resent the customers, but that's not the same as saying that they don't care about the queues.

It frustrates me when I meet managers who seem to have this binary view that you either have good customer service or short waits. You can't have your cake and eat it. Yes, we can! When the waiting times are short the staff deal with happy customers, who treat them respectfully and who act with consideration for those around them. It's much harder to motivate your staff and deliver good service when things are inefficient.

I love motivating staff! When I was managing a rides', team I spent a lot of my own time and money on socials, award night, incentive schemes and fun morning briefings. One manager started telling me about his theory on transformative leadership and that you don't need fun and games to motivate staff. But these things do motivate people. I know they do, because I spent six years as a frontline employee before I became a manager, and I know what motivated me.

But I have also learned over the years that these things are the icing on the cake, and not the cake. They jazz the job up, but the job has to be inherently enjoyable and rewarding if you want the staff to be happy. If the hours are really long, people don't get proper breaks, it's really tough to get time off, and you spend all day dealing with complaints, conflict and people being nasty, it's hard to enjoy your job. A tub of sweets next to the clocking out machine and a certificate aren't going to change that.

The roller coaster designer John Wardley often emphasises in his interviews that we all work in the entertainment industry. When people apply to work in a theme park, that's often what they want to do; entertain people. When the guests aren't being entertained, the staff get frustrated.

Long queues aren't good for the managers either. When the queues are long, staff are more likely to abuse their positions and try jumping the queues when they visit on their days off (something most parks don't allow, and quite frankly shouldn't). Most managers have better things to be doing with their team than deal with staff who abused their position. When staff try to jump the queues, it puts their peers in a difficult position, who don't want to fall out with a colleague, but also don't want to get into trouble themselves. They may well resent it if they follow the rules when they visit. Complaints about queues are always very frustrating to deal with, and usually involve us being told how to do our job, by people whose sole expertise is spending 60 minutes in a queue line. They may even mention that they visited Disneyland once, and then they really are an expert! "I visited Disneyland once" [it was probably Disney World, but they call it Disneyland]". "Oh really? You're an expert then. Thank you for telling me how to do my job. I've only spent ten years doing it".

There is a strong interest in managing the queues. There are also a lot of people who seem to think that they're the only ones who care about them. This means that enthusiasts, the public, frontline staff and managers can waste a lot of time preaching to the converted, and treating each other like idiots. As we say in England, there's no point in telling people how to suck eggs. If we believe that we're the only ones who care, we assume that the queues would move quicker if only the people we're working with started making more of an effort. When you've got minimum wage, zero-hour contract, seasonal staff, some of them will care more than others. But I think it's also a problem that some parks are inefficient, not because they don't care, but because they don't know any better.

Pulling back the curtain

It's clear that there's a big public interest in efficiency and how attractions manage their queues. However, it's not something the parks generally talk about. Disney Imagineer Joe Rohde spoke about the way that Disney designs their areas to maximise guest flow. He says, "We don't want them [the guests] knowing how hard we've worked on the invisible function of that space. We want them inside of a story"[16]. This could sum up most aspects of efficiency. If you're a regular guest walking around a theme park, you don't want to be thinking about how they've designed the layout to maximise the guest flow. If you're about to board a roller coaster, you want to think about the journey you're about to go on, not about the way they've designed the architecture of the station and the trains to reduce the loading times. Behind the scenes good theme parks and managers spend a lot of time finding ways to reduce waiting times and helping the guests to experience more attractions, but the guests aren't supposed to notice these things. That's the magic of the theme park industry.

One manager told me that a good theme park is like the proverbial swan, where guests don't notice the legs flapping around under the water. Just as the swan appears to effortlessly glide through the water, the best theme parks can keep their queues steady and fast moving, and it all looks like it's happened by chance.

There are strong views and considerable interest about queuing, including amongst enthusiasts, the broader public and theme park staff. Most of the ideas tend to circulate around throughputs (also known as hourly capacities in America). When I was researching this book, it struck me that while throughputs clearly do affect the queues, there are many other factors that are rarely mentioned.

What is an acceptable waiting time?

It's impossible to say precisely what is an acceptable waiting time for an attraction, because it's subjective with a lot of variables. Queues are as old

---

16   Layout, Joe Rohde, Imagineering in a Box, https://www.khanacademy.org/humanities/hass-storytelling/imagineering-in-a-box

as the industry. In 1884 people were waiting up to three hours on peak days for Coney Island's Switchback Railway, which had a top speed of 6mph[17]. The Switchback Railway is often seen as the first 'proper' roller coaster, rather than a slide or railway. Although historian Jeffrey Stanton says that there were earlier patents for 'inclined railways' [roller coasters] and at least a few of them were built. They just weren't as well documented as The Switchback Railway[18].

In 1980 John Broome introduced a pay one price (POP) model to Alton Towers, the first time it was used in the UK. In the same year he also introduced a major roller coaster to grab the national interest. Corkscrew was the third coaster of its kind in Europe, following Super Wirbel at Holiday Park (Germany) [Wirbel is German for a vortex] and Tornado at Walbi Belgium. It was the UK's first roller coaster with a corkscrew and the first with two inversions. That year Alton Tower's visitor number doubled, despite the entry charge. Former Alton Towers archivist Les Davies remembered, "People were trying to climb over the fences and demanding to be let in. One car left, and another one would be let in. It was unbelievable. There was something like a 6 to 9 hour queue just for the Corkscrew. The roads were completely blocked back to Derby and Stoke. The police were ringing up saying they had shut the M6 and the M1[19]. We closed about 1 o'clock, we'd estimated 40,000 [visitors in the park] with people still outside"[20]. Six to nine hour queues continued on peak days during the 1980 season.

Europa Park is well known for their efficiency and fast-moving queues. Owner Roland Mack did an interview with Swiss website 20 Minuten. He said that they always aim to keep the longest queues to under 30 minutes[21]; "This is usually accepted by customers and that does not lead to negative comments. And we usually do that. Hardly any other park can do that." Whilst they don't always succeed, Europa Park is well known for their rapid throughputs and short queues.

A similar question to what's an acceptable waiting time, is how many attractions does the average guest expect to experience? In August 2020 Theme Park Inside asked their readers that very question. Here are their responses[22]:

---

17   Coney Island the People's Playground, Michael Immerso, p. 39.

18   History of early roller coasters 1870-1886, Jeffrey Stanton, Westland, https://www.westland.net/coneyisland/articles/EarlyRollerCoasters-1870-1886.htm

19   Motorways/freeways

20   Tales from the Towers: How Corkscrew catapulted Alton Towers to prominence, Nick Sim, Theme Park Tourist, https://www.themeparktourist.com/features/20130814/13810/tales-towers-how-corkscrew-catapulted-alton-towers-prominence, We discuss capacities later in this book. Alton Towers now has a lot more rides but a lower capacity. Health and safety has come a long way since 1980.

21   Interview with Roland Mack, 20 Minuten, 2019, https://m.20min.ch/finance/news/story/was-wollen-sie-vom-europa-park-chef-wissen--18145267

22   How much are you willing to pay for a theme park ride?, Robert Niles, Theme Park Insider, https://www.themeparkinsider.com/flume/202008/7642/

How many attractions do you reasonably expect to experience in a day at the park?

1-5:
3%

6-10:
37%

11-15:
39%

16 or more:
20%

(943 votes)

There is some movement within these bands. For instance, a guest would be happier with 10 attractions than 6, or with 15 attractions than 11. Some attractions are worth a longer wait than others. Someone might be happy with 8 major rides like big roller coasters and dark rides, but less happy with 8 roundabouts. In the comments section some people pointed out that it's not just about the attractions, but the experiences between the attractions. At some parks they're happier to spend time wandering around looking at the theming and soaking up the atmosphere. A couple of people in the comments said that for them the cost of the park had a baring, including the cost of tickets and the cost of parking (if it isn't free). If it's a very cheap park that's clearly priced as a part day park, most people will be happier with fewer rides. In my experience, if it's pitched as a full day out, then most people won't be happy to get on fewer rides just because the ticket price is lower. People expect cheaper parks to have smaller rides, less theming, and lower budgets for things like sound systems and horticulture. However, they don't expect to have to wait longer just because it's a cheaper park or a park that does a lot of discounting.

Theme Park Insider is read by theme park enthusiasts, who may or may not be industry professionals. Their readership isn't typical of the wider population. I have sometimes heard it said that the typical visitor expects to get on at least 7 rides when they visit a theme park, probably under the assumption that most of them are track rides (coasters, dark rides and water rides), rather than roundabouts. I think enthusiasts generally expect to get on more rides than the wider public, because enthusiasts know how to get the most out of their day. Guests visiting as large groups or with young children might also expect to get on fewer rides, just because everything takes longer, which isn't the park's fault.

Will Koch[23], former owner of Holiday World (Indiana), was interviewed by the Season Pass Podcast shortly before he died. He told them, "We keep the

---

23   Koch is pronounced 'Cook'.

lines as short as we can every day. We never think that standing in line's a good thing"[24]. His point is that they don't have a target for what is an acceptable waiting time. Even if the park is very quiet, they will still run all the coasters with the maximum number of trains. Their view is that you should always do what you can to keep the queues moving quickly.

This type of thinking helped Holiday World to become one of the most respected theme parks in the world. In 2009 they won a record six Golden Ticket Awards[25], but if I were to list all the awards they've won over the years, I'd need several pages. In 2009 Roller Coaster Philosophy wrote, "Is Holiday World the most universally loved small park in existence? Besides Knoebels, I cannot think of another park that has as large of an adoring fan base with virtually no critics anywhere"[26].

Holiday World is now one of the biggest independent parks in the US. It gets over a million visitors a year, despite being over an hour's drive from the nearest place of any size. It's just over an hour from Evansville (population 117,000) and Louisville (population 767,000). Their biggest competitor is Kentucky Kingdom. What Holiday World has shown is that people will travel a significant distance when you offer them the right experience.

This is a straightforward concept, but one that gets lost in a lot of parks. At one seaside amusement park a Dodgems had 24 cars and 12 of them weren't working. The operations team asked the engineers whether they'd had a chance to look at the broken cars. "There's not much point at the moment", they said. "We'll probably try and fix a few of them closer to the summer when it gets busier". This was a very different way of thinking to Holiday World, where they always try to run the rides at their maximum capacity. Not only did the seaside amusement park go bankrupt, but it became one of the biggest financial disasters in the history of the theme park industry.

Parks can get very scientific about tracking guest satisfaction using data. Touchscreens and mobile phone apps can allow parks to track guest feedback in real time and see how things like the weather, queue lengths and ride availability are affecting their feedback scores. I have heard a theory that most guests will be open to giving a reasonable feedback score (depending on other factors such as the quality of food, friendliness of the staff etc) once they've been on seven rides. You can spend a lot of time and money trying to collect and analyse this kind of data. In the end the parks that always do what they reasonably can to reduce their waiting times, are likely to be the ones that get the best guest feedback.

---

24   Will Koch interview, episode 8, Season Pass Podcast, https://hwcdn. libsyn.com/p/7/7/8/778038ba84d5d9ef/Vintage_Season_Pass_8. mp3?c_id=32763542&cs_id=32763542&destination_id=16678&expiratio n=1560081231&hwt=7c62719022067b21de4572d7ca48294d

25   Park wins record six 'golden ticket awards', Paula Werne, Holiday World blog, https:// www.holidayworld.com/holiblog/2011/03/09/park-wins-record-six-golden-ticket-awards/

26   Holiday World, Roller Coaster Philosophy, http://www.roll-ercoasterphilosophy.com/2009/holiday-world/

Whilst the simple answer might be, keep your queues as short as possible, I do understand that some theme parks might be looking for some more practical answers. What is a good level of ride availability? How many rides should your park have? What kind of throughputs do you need to be looking at?

There are a lot of variables here, so it's difficult to give one set of figures that every park should aim for. If a park's open year-round, people generally accept that some rides will be closed for scheduled maintenance, at quiet times of year. Aside from the two Disney parks in Paris, Efteling's the only major European park that's open every day of the year. They do have scheduled closures in the winter for maintenance, but aim to have no more than two major rides closed and no more than three rides in total closed. When parks keep their own records of ride availability, they may choose not to include rides closed for scheduled maintenance in the statistics. Some theme parks operate in harsher climates than others, where the weather will cause more closures, and some parks operate in regions with more stringent safety regulations, which leads to more closures and involves longer procedures before the ride can be re-opened.

Taking action

It's also easy for things like bad weather or stringent safety standards to become an easy excuse for poor availability. If your rides close often due to adverse weather, you need to look at whether they can be adapted to make them less weather dependant, and you need to think carefully about what kind of rides you add in the future.

If the issue is safety, then you need to look at the root causes of the downtime (sometimes called 'root cause analysis'). If rides are frequently being emergency stopped, why is that? Theme parks often tell guests that if they lose loose articles on ride, they have to come back at the end of the day to collect them. Sending staff into an area with moving trains is often too dangerous (although parks might do it for slow moving scenic rides), and shutting a ride to collect something someone's dropped leads to a lot of closures and downtime. In the UK, the HSE (Health and Safety Executive) started advising theme parks to close rides down when guests lose loose articles, rather than telling them to come back at the end of the day. This was because they had concerns about guests climbing over fences to collect loose articles and being hit by the ride. Safety regulation can put theme parks in a position where their hands are tied. Although the HSE issues guidance rather than laws, theme parks are generally expected to follow it. This is why it's difficult to suggest a single set of figures for theme parks around the world to aim for. However, if something like this happens, you need to look at solutions to minimise the disruption. Can you do more to communicate to guests the importance of securing loose articles? Are there ways to safely retrieve more loose articles without staff needing to enter the restricted area, for example with an extra-long litter pick?

If you want to give yourself something to aim for, I'd suggest four things:

- Try to improve each element by 10%. That tends to give you targets that are ambitious but manageable. Suddenly deciding you're going to go from 85% availability to 95% isn't necessarily going to give your staff something they believe in. But if you say you're going reduce downtime by 10%, you might aim for 86.5% availability. Once you've achieved that, you can set another target.

- When you're setting targets, involve the people who will need to hit them, like the engineers or the operations team. There's not much point in setting targets if people don't buy into them.

- Be aware of unintended consequences, for example rides being kept open when it isn't safe to hit an availability target, or procedures not being followed to hit a throughput target. Targets should be based around changes to systems, rather than putting people under pressure to work faster. For example, you decrease downtime by keeping more spare parts at the ride, rather than telling your engineers to just do their job quicker.

- Bench mark against competing theme parks in your region. Is there another theme park of a similar size? How many rides do they have? Visit them and spend the day measuring the throughputs on their rides to see how they compare to yours. To get figures on ride availability you might need to talk to the park and see whether they're willing to share the information. Trade bodies such as IAAPA[27] might also have anonymised figures they're able to give you.

Generally, I'd say that you want to aim for at least 95% ride availability. For number of rides there are lot of variables, such as how many days a year your visitors are distributed over and how big the rides are. For throughputs it depends more on the daily attendance figures than on the yearly attendance figures. Two parks might have similar attendance figures, but if one of them's open for twice as many days a year as the other, they won't need the same throughputs and capacity to keep queues down to the same length.

Away from rides, people are generally willing to wait for food if it's fresh. Cinnabon are the world leading retailer of cinnamon rolls, and many theme parks have their franchises. There are currently over 1,200 outlets in 48 countries. Their rolls bake in 14 minutes rather than the traditional 30, because founder Rich Komen believed that 14 minutes was the longest that guests would wait in line[28]. He wanted to make sure that if they ran out of rolls, they could bake more before people got bored and walked away. This was based on how he observed American behaviour in the early 1980s, before he founded Cinnabon in 1985. His meticulous efforts to measure guest behaviour are reminiscent of Walt Disney, who also liked watching guests, and timing things like how long a guest would walk to use a bin rather than dropping their rubbish (litter) on the floor. Keeping the baking times short helped to

---

27   International Association of Amusement Parks and Attraction, founded in 1918, this is the global body for the amusement industry and has over 5,000 members from over 100 countries.

28   Scents from a mall: The stick untold story of Cinnabon, Seattle Met, https://www.seattlemet.com/articles/2017/10/23/scents-from-a-mall-the-sticky-untold-story-of-cinnabon

keep them a little doughy in the middle, so they weren't as dry as traditional cinnamon rolls could be. Komen preferred this texture.

American restaurant chain Waffle House was founded in 1955, the same year as Disneyland opened. They now have about 2,100 restaurants in 25 States. One of Waffle House's service standards, is that there can be a maximum of eight minutes between when a server takes a guest's order and when they begin eating[29]. Their slogan was 'Good food fast', and it can still be seen printed outside their first restaurant in Georgia, which has been pre-served as a museum with the original façade. Waffle House made its success by applying fast food principles to a table service restaurant.

The quality of the waiting environment will also affect how long guests are happy (or willing) to stand in a line. The queuing experience is important, and one I hope to explore further in a future book. I believe that shorter queues, and the perception of shorter queues, are one of the most important competitive advantages that a theme park can have.

Redistributing Guests Between Days

Redistributing crowds

What do you do when your park can't handle the volume of visitors? Open more attractions? Improve the throughputs on the ones that you've already got? Both of these are obvious things to do, and both of them will help a theme park to entertain a bigger audience. But it's not always that simple.

Adding more attractions can require a significant investment and greatly increases your fixed costs. What happens if you sign off a big development, and then the park's attendance declines? Suddenly you've made a large capital investment and you can't sustain it. What happens if your attraction has big peaks and troughs? It's like building a church for Easter Sunday. You might not have the space to keep on growing across a bigger site, and packing more and more into the same plot of land comes with all kinds of challenges. If the park is already causing congestion problems on local roads, then the local planning bodies might not even give you planning permission to keep on increasing your capacity.

As a park you might have a reasonable degree of control over what happens within your park, but often parks have limited influence over the transport infrastructure surrounding it. This can be a problem for several British parks, such as Legoland and Alton Towers. Alton Towers has a stunning location straddling a valley with a gothic mansion in the centre. The park is built into what was originally the grounds of the stately home. Whilst a park might be able to do some things around local transport, such as laying on shuttle buses, and working with local authorities to improve roadways, the scope to do these things can be limited. Transport infrastructure is hugely

---

29   Meet the short-order cooks so good Waffle House officially calls them Rock Stars, Theodore Ross, Medium, https://medium.com/s/story/meet-the-short-order-cooks-so-fucking-good-waffle-house-officially-calls-them-rockstars-caf47c31912

expensive and there is often opposition to having more of the countryside tarmacked over.

There are numerous reasons why Disney parks have been so successful. One factor that can be overlooked, is that they're all well connected by transport. Disneyland Paris gets about 65% of its visitors by train[30], which compares to 3-4% at Europa Park (Germany's biggest theme park). Europa Park are hoping that one day they will be able to get their own train station, or at least upgrade their nearest station (Ringsheim) so that the long ICE (Inter City Express) trains can stop there.

If we analyse why Disney parks get so many visitors, some of it would have to come down to the strength of their brand and some of it would be due to the quality of their attractions. It helps that Disney Parks have strong transport connections, including being at the junction of multiple motorways, having their own train stations and being near major airports. When Disney has been considering the location for new resort, a pre-requisite has often been strong support from the government, including financing upgrades to the transport infrastructure around the park. Part of the reason why they chose Paris as the location for their European resort, was that it would have the necessarily infrastructure to get people to the park when it opened. No other brand has the cultural cache that Disney has, and most parks will only attract a small fraction of the visitors that Disney can. Major improvements to public transport quickly become hugely expensive, so often you end up with a situation where neither the park nor the government is able or willing to make the investment.

It must be stressed that while good public transport can help a park to expand its visitor base and increase the pool of people in a 30 minute and 120 minute travelling distance (which is often seen as an important statistic when feasibility studies are being done for new theme parks), you can't expect anyone to invest in a hugely expensive upgrade to transport that's only going to be needed on 15 particularly busy days each year. Part of the reason that governments have been happy to invest heavily in transport for a new Disney resort, is because they know it will be open 365 days a year and will be reasonably busy for most of that. No public body would want to invest in such infrastructure that will spend most of its time as a barely used white elephant.

Ways to increase visitor numbers without adding to local congestion include:

- Spreading your attendance out between more days
- Having longer opening hours so that the guests are less likely to all want to arrive and leave at the same time.
- Adding accommodation, which also shifts the patterns of when people travel to and from the park.

---

30   Europa Park's Roland Mack reflects on 70 years in the amusement business, Bloo Loop, https://blooloop.com/features/roland-mack-70th-birthday-europa-park/

An alternative to increasing the park's capacity, is to simply move guests from visiting at busy times to less busy times. The starting point for that is to open for more hours. The question is, are you better off opening for longer hours on the same number of days, or opening with the same hours on more days?

Opening for longer hours

This helps in two ways. Even if the queues don't go down, if you're open for more hours, people can still get more rides done. Secondly, if you're open for longer hours, there's more chance that the people who will be there when you open might not be the same people who are there when you close. Of course, there will normally be a lot of overlap in the middle of the day, so it's not quite like having two covers (sittings) in a restaurant, but it does at least mean that guests can have a few hours at the beginning and end of the day when only a portion of the guests will be in the park.

If you open the entire park for longer hours there is an advantage in better capacity. It also tends to mean a significant rise in food revenue, with people staying for evening meals. If people are there for the evening it encourages people to stay in onsite accommodation, and if they're out in the park until a reasonable time, there is less pressure to provide additional evening entertainment at the hotels.

Opening an entire theme park is expensive and can be logistically challenging, particularly if you don't have that many engineers. A lot of regional American parks have long hours over a limited number of days, but it must provide challenges with staffing and make them very reliant on students. There can also be safety concerns if staff end up working very long shifts. Parks like Disney and Universals can get around it by having more than one shift, but this wouldn't be practical at a lot of seasonal, regional parks. Other parks with long opening hours, such a Europa Park, have tended to give people four-day weeks (rather than a standard five-day week), so that staff don't accrue so many hours and get burned out.

There are two alternatives to opening the whole park for longer. The first, is that you open a limited selection of rides outside the main opening hours for ERT (exclusive ride time, known as Extra Magic Hours at Disney). This works by opening a small number of rides (maybe even just one major roller coaster), and only a limited number of people get access to it (often people staying in the park's accommodation. Perhaps annual pass holders, or people who've paid extra). How does this help? When parks chose the rides to offer ERT, they tend to be ones that get the longest queues, such as the newest roller coaster. Hopefully, once the ERT is over, the people who've been able to do these popular rides already move onto less popular rides that typically aren't so busy at the beginning of the day.

The fundamental principle here is similar to timed ticketing options (such as Fast Pass) where you encourage guests to ride quieter less popular rides when the queues build up. With a timed ticket you ride something with a short queue (like a roundabout) while you wait for your time slot at a major ride. With ERT the message is, 'you can ride the most popular ride before everyone else enters the park with little queuing, and then go and ride something less popular while other people have a turn'.

The other advantage is that offering ERT to a select group of guests, gives them an incentive to do whatever it is they need to do to join this 'select group'. That might be staying in the park's own accommodation rather than nearby accommodation (that's often cheaper), buying an annual pass (or upgrading to a premium annual pass), or paying extra for their entry ticket.

The engineers will prepare the rides on ERT first and then move onto the other rides that are opening later. If they had to prepare all the rides for the ERT time it'd mean the engineers would have to start earlier. Since the engineers typically start at least three hours before a park opens to inspect everything and then get involved in shutting the park down, moving the opening for the whole park forward could be difficult. ERT seems like a cost effective way of extending the park's opening hours for some guests and making the lines shorter for everyone else when it does fully open.

An alternative option is to do staggered openings, where you open a few areas at the start of the day, or half the park, but open the rest later in the day. Let's say your park opens at 9:30am. You could open the front two areas at 9:30. It's less expensive than opening the entire park at 9:30, and generally a lot of guests won't arrive as soon as the park opens. It's harder to do a staggered close or ERT at the end of the day. Phantasialand has done ERT at the end of the day for hotel guests, where they completely empty the park out, and then the hotel guests come back in through their dedicated hotel entrance.

Some cultures are more susceptible to visiting in the evenings than others, perhaps due to weather/climate and other factors, such as how far the typical guest travels to the park and what percentage are day visitors vs holiday makers (vacationers). If a park wants to start opening into the evenings, they may need to make a significant investment in lighting. At some parks, such as Tivoli Gardens in Copenhagen, the illuminations around the park are a major selling point. They also might need to look at their food offering, and potentially provide higher end catering options and more indoor restaurants.

Even in the 1890s Coney Island was ending the day with fireworks. Disney realised pretty quickly that if they wanted people to stay for the evenings, then they needed to provide reasons for them to do so. Fireworks, illuminated fountain shows, projection mapping shows and The Mainstreet Electrical Parade have all been part of the arsenal that's helped them to do this. However, all of these things are hugely expensive, and won't be worth it for many parks. For example, when Disney introduced Fantasmic to the River of America at Disneyland in 1992, it cost $35 million just to set the production up[31].

Aside from using nighttime entertainment to redistribute visitors from the day time to the evening, they also increase dwell time (how long a

---

31   In service to the mouse, Jack Lindquist, p. 207.

guest spends in the park) giving them more time to spend money, particularly on evening meals. At Disney, the sit-down restaurants switch their menus between lunch and dinner, with the dinner menus having a higher pricing point.

When Star Wars Land opened at Walt Disney World in 2019, it stretched the point on how parks can extend their opening hours to help them cope with bigger crowds. For the first three days after Star Wars Land opened on August 29th, the whole park opened at 6am for any guest 'brave enough to visit'. Between September 1st and November 2nd, Star Wars Land, Toy Story Land and selected other attractions opened from 6am – 9am for Extra Extra Magic Hours for hotel guests (as the time there were around 36,000 hotel rooms). During this period Animal Kingdom and Magic Kingdom also opened from 7am – 8am for Extra Extra Magic Hours.

We move onto dynamic pricing later, but many 'amusement park' style attractions offer cheaper entry in the evenings. This includes Adventure Island (UK) and Fun Spot (Orlando). Fun Spot's cheaper evening tickets have become so popular that they're actually busier in the evenings than during the day, with some guests choosing to visit after going to one of the larger parks (such as Universals) beforehand[32].

For parks looking to manage their crowds with longer opening hours, the challenge is to make sure that the guests are reasonably well spread out through the day. There's little point in opening 9am-11pm if most of the guests visit 11am-6pm. In the chapters on 'evening entertainment' and 'morning entertainment', we consider some ways to help with that.

Crowd Calendars

To those of us who've worked in the industry, it may seem obvious that we have these big fluctuations in how busy the parks are. We know when to visit if we want to avoid the crowds. Crowd calendars help to inform those who are less knowledgeable about the industry. If allows everyone to make better decisions about when they visit.

Let me tell you a story about Winter Wonder (UK), that highlights why we need crowd calendars. Winter Wonderland in Hyde Park, London, is typically open for six weeks, with some estimates suggesting it gets over five million visitors. It's the UK's biggest Christmas event, and features a German style Christmas market, a fun fair with major rides from around Europe, a circus, an ice show, a rink for public skating, ice sculptures and various other attractions.

For the last few years, the biggest ride has been München Looping (Olympia Looping). It's marketed as the world's largest travelling coaster, and although 'largest' depends on how you measure it, it is certainly the longest travelling coaster at 4,101 ft. At 106.7ft tall it also has an impressive height

---

32   Dynamic pricing, Jodi Helmer, Fun World Magazine, June 2019, https://www.iaapa.org/news/funworld/dynamic-pricing

that towers over all the fairs it visits[33]. It travels using 50 wagons/lorries and 20 shipping containers[34] and takes ten people a week to build up. It was such a complex project they started planning it in 1983 and the ride didn't premier until the Munich Okobterfest in 1989.

I've heard quite a few people talk about how much money Olympia Looping must make. One friend wrote on Facebook, "There's 28 riders per train and ride tokens cost £9 per person. Let's say there's an average of 24 people on per train. Each train is making £216. They can run this on 5 trains, meaning that they can have £1080 worth of riders sitting on it at any one time. In an hour each train will complete 16 cycles! That's about £17,000 an hour. If this beast runs on 5 trains for 12 hours its making over £180,000 a day. Winter Wonderland runs for 46 days! So, this roller coaster has the potential to generate revenues in excess of £7,000,000 this Christmas. Yesss, pick that jaw up from off the floor! You'll catch flies!"

Now, as other people pointed out in the comments, putting on an event like Winter Wonderland in central London is hugely expensive, including a significant advertising budget and set up costs as well as lots of cleaners, security and auxiliary staff. This has to be paid for out of the fees that the rides pay to rent their pitch. The Royal Parks, who own and run Hyde Park, also make a profit. Bringing a ride to Winter Wonderland is particularly expensive for the showmen, because they're not allowed to bring caravans to it, meaning a lot of them have to put their staff up at hotels, which is not cheap in London. Travelling rides are generally expensive to keep and tour. Being the world's largest travelling coaster, the cost of bringing 70 lorry loads across the channel to Britain all the way from Germany is in itself not cheap. To put it into perspective, the cross-channel ferry Spirit of Britain holds 180 lorries and 1,059 cars[35]. Bringing Olympia Looping across represents about a fifth of a cross channel ferry.

Nonetheless, even taking into account the high cost of bringing a ride like Olympia Looping, if it took anywhere near £7 million, then that would surely be more than a healthy profit. Now, I'm not saying that Olympia Looping doesn't make a healthy profit. If it wasn't making money, I doubt the Barth family would have kept it operating since 1989, but as I point out elsewhere in this book, big travelling rides are in decline and at least in Europe they're all family businesses. Rides such as Euro Star, Doppel Looping, Dreier Looping and the log flume Wild Wasser Bahn III have all retired, and whilst impressive new rides are often being built, they tend to be smaller than the aforementioned. This isn't just true in Germany, where the rides I've listed come from. In the UK showman are moving their focus away from mobile rides towards static attractions, including operating several seaside amusement parks: Fantasy Island, Barry Island and Pleasureland.

---

33 Statistics courtesy of Roller Coaster Data Base, https://rcdb.com/13819.htm

34 Official Olympia Looping website, http://olympialooping.com/#facts

35 Dover Ferry Photos Forum, MV Spirit of Britain – past and present, http://www.doverferryphotosforums.co.uk/mv-spirit-of-britain-past-and-present/

It seems clear that travelling rides aren't the gold mine that some people imagine them to be. This is partly down to the cost of running rides, but also because a lot of people visit these fairs at a peak time, such as a Saturday night with good weather, and assume that this is roughly how busy the fairs always are. The fact that people are often oblivious about these swings in demand and the fluctuations in waiting times, makes it important for parks to promote when the waiting times are likely to be shorter. We will discuss how they can do that shortly. Before we talk about the solutions, I want to give a few more examples of how big the problem is.

It's rare for parks to advertise figures about daily attendance. We know that parks have big peaks and troughs by tracking the waiting times and anecdotal evidence from both the guests and the employees. The State Fair of Texas is unusual in that they do publish the daily attendance on their website[36]. In 2019 they attracted over 2.5 million visitors across its 24 days. This works out at an average of about 104,000 a day. However, this reflects a range. Their quietest day was Monday 30th September, when they had 40,229 visitors. Their busiest day was Saturday 12th October when they had 226,094 visitors. This means that the busiest day of the Fair has 5.6 times as many visitors as on the quietest day. According to Sea World Orlando, their attendance varies between 5,000 on the quietest days and 30,000 on the peak days[37]. "That gives you some order of magnitude of how low the attendance can go and we still feel good about operating", says Sea World CEO Marc Swanson.

Most people realise that some days are going to be busier than others, but do they realise how big the differences are? You want to give your guests the information they need to make informed decisions about when to visit. This is what a crowd calendar does. Remember, the customer might not always be 'right', but it is your job to help them make better decisions. The customers aren't experts on operational efficiency. But you are, and it's your job to guide them away from the queues. Quite a few of the ideas in this book will help your guests to make better decisions about when they visit and how they plan their day. This is something to bear in mind when you're dealing with complaints. It can sometimes feel like the customers have deliberately gone looking for the longest queues, but no one actually does that. Ask yourself, "Is there something more we could have done to help this guest?"

World of Universal is an American vacation website, primarily focused on Universals theme parks (hence the name). They provide a range of unofficial advice for visiting the Universal parks, including their 12-month crowd calendar. Every day is colour coded either green, amber or red depending on how busy they expect the parks to be. The idea is that guests can try to avoid going

36   Daily attendance, State Fair of Texas, https://bigtex.com/about-us/daily-attendance/

37   Can theme parks make money at reduced capacity?, Brady MacDonald, Bloo Loop, https://blooloop.com/features/theme-parks-reduced-capacity/

November 2020

Sun	Mon	Tue	Wed	Thu	Fri	Sat
1 Fair	2 Slow	3 Slow	4 Slow	5 Slow	6 Slow	7 Slow
8 Slow	9 Slow	10 Slow	11 Slow	12 Slow	13 Slow	14 Slow
15 Slow	16 Slow	17 Slow	18 Fair	19 Fair	20 Fair	21 Busy
22 Busy	23 Busy	24 Busy	25 Busy	26 Busy	27 Busy	28 Busy
29 Busy	30 Fair	1 Fair	2 Slow	3 Slow	4 Slow	5 Slow
6 Slow	7 Slow	8 Slow	9 Slow	10 Slow	11 Fair	12 Fair

Universal crowd calendar

on the red days, and if possible, plan their visit for one of the green days, when the park should be quieter with shorter queues[38].

Efteling (the largest theme park in the Netherlands), uses a similar, but official design on their website[39].

Zachary Bull's website Queue Times also provides a forecast for each park (at the time of writing, that's all 94 of them) predicting how busy they will be over the next seven days. He explains his methodology, "The site uses machine learning (specifically Gradient boosting regressors) to come up with crowd calendars. The model currently includes time of the year, park opening times and weather. The predictions are therefore based on past data, so accuracy tends to improve the longer a park has been on the site for."[40]

More parks could create something similar, to guide guests towards their less busy days. At a regional park it is harder to predict when it will and won't be busy. Weather is likely to have a bigger bearing on busyness, as people can move day trips more easily than the days in a holiday (vacation) booked months in advance. Later in this section we'll look at weather proofing. The more you weather proof your attraction, the less likely guests are to move their visits around weather forecasts, and the more accurate a crowd planner is likely to be. Most parks won't be able to use all the ideas in this book, but some of the ideas do work best when they're combined together.

38   World of Universal Crowd Calendar, https://worldofuniversal.com/uocrowdcalendar/

39   https://www.efteling.com/en/park/opening-hours

40   About Queue Times, queue times, https://queue-times.com/pages/about

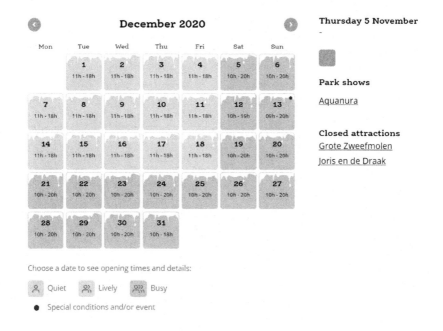

Efteling crowd calendar

At a park where most visitors come from the same country, people are more likely to know when it will or won't be busy. Parks with a large international base (either because they're significant parks with a resort element, or because they're near a border between countries) are less likely to know. When you're visiting a park in another country it's easy to unwittingly visit on a public holiday and find the park's a lot busier than you expected. For example, in the UK our public holidays (bank holidays) tend to be on a Monday, so you get a long weekend, whereas in other parts of Europe they float around and can be on any day of the week. Efteling gets a lot of international visitors, and I'm sure many of them have found their planner useful.

What's obvious to someone working in the industry isn't always obvious to a more casual visitor. For example, a guest might visit at the end of October expecting the park to be quiet, because it's getting colder and the park's preparing to close for the winter. They might not realise that the days leading up to Halloween are the busiest in the year.

Advertising a crowd calendar has three advantages:

- Guests might switch their visit from a busier day to a quieter day.

- It helps to manage expectations. If a guest is choosing to visit on one of the busiest days of the year, at least they know this before they leave home.

- If you can predict how busy the park will be, it helps you set your staffing levels. At Disney there is a tradition of management jumping into frontline roles for the busiest days, which has the double effect of increasing staff to handle the larger crowds, and also encouraging management to stay connected with the frontline staff and the guests.

How many categories a crowd calendar needs depends on your spread of visitors. A park where the queues are sometimes 3-hours long might need more categories than a park that never has queues longer than 30 minutes. A good crowd calendar should give enough information to help people plan their visits around the worst crowds. If the longest queues at the start of the summer are 60 minutes and at the end they're 3 hours, it isn't helpful if every day of the summer is labelled as 'busy'. Luckily, not too many parks do get 3 hour queues. If the ones that did used more of the ideas from this book, they probably wouldn't either.

I haven't seen any figures to suggest how effective crowd calendars can be. It will depend on how accurately you can predict the busyness and how much flexibility your guests have in when they visit. One of the advantages is that they are a cheap option, compared to putting on events, building more rides etc. If you're going for 'the low hanging fruit' first, the kind of 'cheap' options you might consider could include putting a crowd calendar on your website, a promotion at quiet times, free birthday badges and better wayfinding. These ideas are all covered further on. If your park is seriously overcrowded or has major capacity issues, then they won't be enough. You're going to have to dig deeper if you want to make a difference.

Using Events

Crowd calendars let people make better informed decisions about when they're going to visit. Events give them another reason to visit at a quieter time of year.

Liseberg (Sweden) have been consistently getting around 3 million or more guests a year for a couple of decades. By 2015 they were looking for ways to reduce the waiting times. In the period 2015-2018 Liseberg didn't grow its annual attendance, but by developing their Halloween and Christmas events they were able to move quite a few visits from the summer season, when they traditionally had most of their visitors, to other times of year, which tended to be quieter. As well as making the queues shorter, it also 'hedged' the risk, meaning that if they had a wet summer it wouldn't have such a damaging impact on the year's profit.

If you're looking at using events to shift crowds, there is a difference between a very short event like a concert that may only last for one day, and something longer like a Christmas event or a Halloween event. The problem with one- or two-day events, is that you can have a massive spike in guests that goes beyond what a park might even get on a public holiday with good weather. I wouldn't want to deter parks from things like concerts, which can be a lot of fun and profitable. But I know from my experiences at Dreamland (UK) that if a big one-day concert suddenly brings in triple the attendance, it's very challenging to cope with it. However, most successful events in the industry did start off small, and then grew over a number of years.

Mickey's Not So Scary Halloween Party started off as a one-night event at Magic Kingdom (Disney World) in 1995[41]. It was a family friendly answer to Halloween Horror Nights that Universal started in Orlando in 1991. Due to the popularity of the event, the one-night party was gradually expanded with additional nights. In 2019 it ran for 36 nights starting on August 16th. Celebrating Halloween in mid-August does feel odd, but it came to the classic conundrum that Disney couldn't work out a way of increasing the capacity of the event, so the only way to bring it to more people was to add additional nights. They could have started 36 nights before Halloween and done it every day. The problem is that the event starts at 7pm, meaning the park has to close at 6pm to handle the transition. It's unusual for Magic Kingdom (the world's most visited theme park) to close at 6pm and they only really do it when there's an evening event on. They wouldn't want to close at 6pm every day for over a month, so starting in August was the only option.

When Andreas Anderson announced to the board at Tivoli Gardens his plan for a Halloween event, there was resistance[42]. Tivoli Gardens is a Danish icon and many of his colleagues saw Halloween as too American. However, they went ahead with a family friendly event with Halloween theming around the park, and it was an immediate success. October used to be a quiet month for a lot of theme parks in the western hemisphere, when it's typically cold and the weather's unpredictable. Now for many parks it's become their busiest time of year. One manager at Europa Park told me that he thinks their busiest day on record was October 31st, 2014, when the park had 62,000 visitors. Generally, over 35,000 is considered busy and over 45,000 is considered very busy. Over 45,000 visitors and the longest queues can hit 90 minutes.

Merlin has also had a lot of success with their Halloween events. In 2015 guest numbers at Alton Towers' Halloween event Scarefest represented 12% of their total attendance. By 2018 it had risen to 16%[43]. This means that 336,000 people attended their Halloween event[44]. In 2018 Scarefest ran for 19 days, giving an average of 17,684 guests a day[45]. The rising importance of Scarefest reflects its growing popularity, but also that they started closing on selected offpeak days during the season. At Thorpe Park revenue from Fright Nights has grown from 14% to 20% of the yearly total. 20% of revenue doesn't necessarily mean 20% of attendance, as the spend per head might be different during an event. Particularly as some annual pass holders are

---

41   Mickey's not-so-scare Halloween party, Disney Fandom Wiki, https:// disney.fandom.com/wiki/Mickey%27s_Not-So-Scary_Halloween_Party

42   Nick's ERT #55 Liseberg CEO Andreas Anderson, The season pass podcast, http:// seasonpasspodcast.libsyn.com/nicks-ert-55-liseberg-with-ceo-andreas-andersen

43   Merlin benefits from Halloween at Alton Towers and Thorpe Park, Bea Mitchell, Bloo Loop, https://blooloop.com/news/ merlin-announces-revenue-for-halloween-2018-at-alton-towers-thorpe-park/

44   TEA Themed Index 2018, Themed Entertainment Association, https:// www.aecom.com/wp-content/uploads/2019/05/Theme-Index-2018-4.pdf

45   Scarefest 2018 at Alton Towers – tickets and dates as chilling new zombie maze unveiled, David Bentley, Birmingham Live, https://www.birminghammail. co.uk/whats-on/whats-on-news/scarefest-2018-alton-towers-tickets-15095741

excluded. In 2018 Fright Nights ran for 21 nights[46]. If we assume that it did get roughly 20% of the attendance, then that would be about 376,000 people across the 21 nights[47] - an average of 17,905 guests a night. Thorpe Park doesn't officially release their capacity, but I understand it was about 20,000. Fright Nights is consistently bringing Thorpe Park close to its capacity, at what used to be a quiet time of year.

Tim O'Brien is one of the leading journalists for the theme park industry. He has written numerous books about the industry and served as senior editor for Amusement Business Magazine. Before the Internet his coverage was vital for helping people learn about the amusement industry. In 2001 he estimated that the typical seasonal American theme park attracted 70% of its visitors in July and August[48]. At the time there were only a few major Halloween events in the States, such as Universal Orlando and Knott's Berry Farm, although more parks had started introducing smaller scale events. These days, I suspect the figure would be closer to 50%. The percentage of a park's visitors who come over the summer will depend on a range of factors including the climate and the length of the school holiday/vacation.

Events normally start off small and slowly grow in size. Going in too big with an event you haven't done before is a huge financial risk, while overhyping a small event will set you up for poor guest feedback. The event might be a financial success in its first year, but if you over promise and under deliver, people won't come back. California's Great America did their first Halloween event in 2008, which featured 5 mazes. The park's entertainment's manager Clayton Lawrence recalls, "At the time I couldn't pay people to come to Halloween Haunt, but now I get Facebook messages months in advance saying, hi, I'm coming to haunt"[49].

If you look at the major events at theme parks around the world, they generally started off small but high quality. They built up a loyal fanbase that spread ripples through the community. As the event scales up, you need to tread the fine line between diversifying enough to keep it fresh and appealing to a broader audience, whilst simultaneously keeping the brand tight enough to maintain its distinctiveness.

Creating a Halloween Event

A lot of Halloween events include 'scare mazes' (sometimes known as 'haunts'). There are lots of variations on the scare maze concept. The general gist is that a group of people walk through some horror sets where actors attempt to scare them. These scare mazes tend to have low throughputs,

46   2018 Fright Nights calandar, Thorpe Park official website, http://thorpepark.com/fright-nights-2018

47   TEA Themed Index 2018, Themed Entertainment Association, https://www.aecom.com/wp-content/uploads/2019/05/Theme-Index-2018-4.pdf

48   Riding out the slower economy, Karen Farkas, 30/7/2001, The Plain Dealer

49   Clayton Lawrence, California's Great America, episode 335, Season Pass Podcast, http://www.seasonpasspodcast.com/archive/index.html

causing long, slow moving queues to form. I hope to look at ways for improving the throughputs in a future book, but sometimes being overrun by crowds of visitors can feel like a nice problem to have. First of all, you've got to bring the crowds in.

As more attractions use Halloween events to bring people in for the back end of the season, setting your event apart from the others becomes harder. Universals found it easier to build their Halloween Horror Nights event in Florida, where there wasn't much competition, compared to Hollywood, where it was competing with the already successful Knott's Scary Farm. Eventually they found more success in Hollywood by focusing on classic Universals films, rather than on original characters. This helped to differentiate them from what Knott's Berry Farm were doing.

Once you've been to a few Halloween events, they can start to merge into one another. You also want your guests to keep on coming back year after year, and not start thinking, we've already done that. After a few years they came up with the idea of giving each year a signature character. As well as featuring in the event's commercials, the character would normally have their own maze, and also tie some of the other mazes together. Typically, the signature character was a nutter who enjoys killing people. They'd have a backstory about how they ended up the way they are, and a 'signature kill', where they'd kill their victims in some kind of ritualistic way. The implication was that you'd end up being one of their next victims. As we progress through the maze, we'd often see references to this character, such as photos or paintings of them, their reflection in a mirror, their shadow etc. At the climax of the maze, we'd come face to face with them. For big anniversary years Horror Nights brings back the signature characters from previous years.

To establish a successful Halloween event, it's not just a case of seeing what your competitors are doing and trying to do it better, or to undercut them on price. You have to find a unique selling point (USP) that will make yours stand out from the crowd.

Christmas Events

The rise of Christmas events is an interesting proposition, as they take place at a time of year when parks were previously closed. The cost of running these events isn't just all the additional theming and activities, but also the cost of opening a theme parks when it used to be closed. It does also tend to significantly eat into the time the park has to do its winter maintenance. This includes painting, carpentry, fibre glass repairs, building repairs etc, but perhaps most crucially the work the engineers have to do on the rides. On the other hand, it does make their level of employment for the frontline staff a lot less seasonal, which can help with retention. Planning a successful Christmas event isn't easy, and requires coordination between a lot of departments. It's no good if the events team just comes out and says, "Look what we've planned". Making the adjustment from being closed for four-five months to opening in December, is a big step to take, and one that all the departments have to take in sync.

With so many parks doing Halloween and Christmas events now, simply doing something won't be enough to stand out. It's relatively easy to throw down some straw bales and pumpkins or to string up some Christmas lights, but people don't want something that looks generic. An example are the Chinese lanterns many parks are adding around Christmas time. One of the best examples of integrating these in seamlessly is at Phantasialand. It helps that they have a Chinese area where the lanterns find a natural home. In another area of the park, Deep In Africa, they create an animal safari for their Winter Traum (Winter Dream) event. It uses animal themed Chinese lanterns around the Black Mamba B&M inverted coaster.

Phantasialand has also created an original soundscape, rather than just playing generic Christmas music. On Chiapas they play the regular theme, but with the drum beat replaced by jingle bells. In Deep In Africa they play Christmas songs in an African music style. In the Maus au Chocolat station, you can hear the mice singing Christmas songs in their high-pitched squeaky voices. Not every park has the budget to do these things, but since just opening the park for Christmas is a big expense, if you're not able to put on something special, it might not be worth bothering at all.

One of the advantages with doing a Christmas event, is that you have access to a lot intellectual property that's out of copywrite/royalty free. Some parks have bought in intellectual properties to set their event apart from all the other Christmas events, for example the Polar Express at Sea World or The Gruffalo at Chessington World of Adventures. Nonetheless, when parks do a Christmas event, they have access to a whole range of well-known music that can be rearranged and remixed to their hearts content, without incurring any charges. They also have some of the most recognized characters in the world at their fingertips. The most successful Christmas events seem to find the right blend of tradition and innovation. There's enough tradition to give people a sense of comfort and familiarity. But enough innovation to feel like they haven't done a copy and paste event that could have been anywhere.

In marketing they sometimes refer to smashable brands. A smashable brand is one that you could break up into small fragments, and people would still recognise the company from a single part. Coca Cola is often given as an example, because you could tear up a coke label, and just from the shade of red, the white and a bit of the cursive writing, people would know it's Coca Cola. If we apply this theory to Christmas and Halloween, you could take a small aspect of your event, and people would know what the event is and where it's at.

You also want your event to have a sense of warmth. Although Christmas is a Christian event, there's no reference in the bible to Jesus being born on December 25th, and it's not completely clear why this became the date it was celebrated. A popular theory is that people wanted a celebration in the winter to cheer them up at what was a miserable time of year. With electric lighting and modern heating, the winter isn't anywhere near as depressing as it must have been in the past, but the winter can still be a depressing time for people. There's even a name for it; seasonal affective disorder (SAD). We will shortly move onto weather proofing, and discuss how colour can be used to raise people's mood. If your park's in a climate that tends to be cold, wet and grey in the winter, I'd recommend using bright colours, including red, green and gold, rather than having too many blues and silvers. Candles feel a lot warmer than snowmen. This will help to lift the mood when the weather's poor.

Few of the pre-war amusement parks in the northern hemisphere opened in the winter. In the second half of the 20th century there has been a rising number of parks looking to do a Christmas event. In 1983 Walt Disney World introduced their first Mickey's Very Merry Christmas Party[50]. This has helped to inspire more parks to do their own events.

I haven't worked at or visited theme parks celebrating other religions. I therefore don't have the expertise to write about them. However, I'm sure most of the principles would be the same.

Enthusiast Events

These tend to be one day events on a Saturday or Sunday at a relatively quiet time of year, perhaps in the period after the Easter holiday or in September when the parks have a lull between the summer and October. Enthusiasts often know how to time their visits for quiet days anyway, so it's not necessarily about moving visits from busy days to quiet days. It does, however, cause a spike on what would be a moderately busy day, where a park that would normally be at perhaps 40% capacity gets a rise in visitors. It's another tool for raising attendance on a day when the park should be reasonably well equipped to cope with them. A lot of these enthusiasts will share their experience on social media, forums, websites and Youtube, so it's a great way to encourage free publicity, as well building up a loyal fanbase.

Part of running a theme park efficiently is managing your staff so that their time is well utilised. This can be challenging for parks with short seasons or that only open for weekends and school holidays. It's difficult to run a successful business if too many of your managers are seasonal or part time. You end up with high turnover and a 'brain drain' of knowledge, expertise and skills. However, you clearly can't be paying your managers to sit around not doing much. Organising an enthusiast day is a great project for a manager to work on when the park's closed.

Kentucky Kingdom's Key to the Kingdom event includes ERT (exclusive ride time) on coasters before the park opens, behind the scenes tours, the chance to buy a limited edition t-shirt, a panel of theme park Youtubers and an afterhours beach party[51]. Dollywood's Thrills in the Hills event includes a t-shirt, behind the scenes tours and ERT[52]. Holiwood Knights at Holiday

50   The history of Mickey's not so scary Halloween party, Expedition Theme Park, https://www.youtube.com/watch?v=Ci8RTjiirXo

51   Keys to the Kingdom, Kentucky Kingdom, https://shop.kentuckykingdom.com/webstore/shop/viewitems.aspx?CG=specialevents&c=keystokingdom

52   Thrills in the Hills, Dollywood, https://www.dollywood.com/themepark/Festivals/ThrillsintheHills

World was for members of 10 different coaster clubs. It included several sessions of ERT, as well as auctions of memorabilia and experiences (presumably of things like track walks)[53].

Sea World's Inside Look event focuses on those who want to know more about the animals, rather than the rides. Guests can visit areas that are normally closed to the public. This includes the Fish House, where food is prepared for the dolphins, whales and sea lions, and behind the scenes at Shark Encounter, where you can see how they separate the tank for cleaning and the medical pool where sharks go for their annual checkup. There are also extra talks from the animal keepers. People who visit 3 or more of these activities get a free pin badge.

Food and drink festivals

Epcot's Food and Wine festival was born out of the park's desire to bring in more guests for the quiet period between the summer and Thanks Giving. It started in 1996, one year after Mickey's Not so Scary Halloween Party and the same year as Universal's Mardi Gras.

Epcot's festival may or may not have been the first food and drink festival in a theme park, but it was certainly the one that bought it to the global attention of the industry. Let's talk about how and why it started. Epcot stands for Experimental Prototype Community of Tomorrow, and the evolution of the park has an interesting and complex history, that I can't do justice to here. The park they ended up building has two halves to it: Future World - themed to science and technology, and World Showcase - themed to countries of the world. At one point these were going to be two separate attractions and they got pushed together to create one large theme park, in a similar format to a World's Fair.

World Show Case was originally going to have a greater number of small pavilions themed to countries of the world, and each one would be sponsored and put together by that country's government. This idea morphed into a different kind of park with fewer larger pavilions than they originally envisaged, mostly designed by Disney Imagineering rather than the countries themselves. The park ended up only having eleven pavilions themed to; the United States, Canada, France, Germany, Norway, United Kingdom, Italy, Mexico, China, Japan and Morocco. Although Africa isn't significantly represented in the World Showcase, when Animal Kingdom opened in 1998, much of that was themed to Africa. Other pavilions have been planned but not built, including Switzerland and Iran.

Because World Showcase only features 11 of the 195 countries currently in the world, part of the idea behind the Food and Wine festival was to bring people samples of food from countries not represented in the show case. It fits in with the theme of the park perfectly and helps it to tell the story. Guests could even buy a passport to get stamped at the different food units.

---

53   Holiwood Knights, Holiday World, https://www.holi-dayworld.com/shows-events/holiwood-nights/

In the 1980s there had been a small event called the Walt Disney Village Wine Festival at what is now Disney Springs[54]. Producing something bigger in Epcot was also inspired by the Food and Wine Festival in Aspen, Colorado, which had started in 1982 and grown quickly. In its first year, the Food and Wine Festival lasted for 30 days. The schedule has grown over time and in 2002 they added the Eat to the Beat concert series. Because of the success behind the Food and Wine Festival, other parks have been adding their own variants.

Another early food festival was the Garlic Festival at Gilroy Gardens (California). Several of their rides are themed to fruit and vegetables including the Garlic Twirl tea cups, where each cup is a garlic bulb. The festival features a wide range of food from garlic bread to garlic ice cream. The garlic festival often takes place in July, rather than during a quiet season.

Knott's Berry Farm (California) as the name suggests started off as a berry farm. They were the first farm in California to commercially cultivate the boysenberry (a cross between a raspberry, blackberry, dewberry and loganberry). In April they run a boysenberry festival. It features beer and wine infused with boysenberry, boysenberry cheesecake, boysenberry dole whip, boysenberry and cranberry mayonnaise, boysenberry crepes and many other special dishes. There's also an exhibition on the farm's founders (Walter and Cordelia Knott), a kitchen where children can make their own boysenberry pies, a boysenberry pie eating contest where you can't use your hands, and an 80s dance party, because... well why not?

All of the really big food festivals have tied into the themes of the parks they're in. This reinforces the idea that successful parks work with the assets that they've got.

More Events

Knott's Berry Farm are one of the parks that pioneered using events to drive attendance during the quiet seasons. One January in the 1950s the manager of Knott's Ghost Town was having coffee with the newly appointed head of PR (Public Relations – he was the first person to hold the position). He commented on how quiet the park was[55]. He then pointed out that the gold rush in California began on January 24th 1848 at Sutter's Creek. They then created the Prospector's parade to drive attendance in January. The Knott's Berry Farm founders Walter and Cordelia Knott rode in a horse drawn carriage with a sign saying 'Mayor of Ghost Town' and a range of other costumed characters and horse drawn floats were included.

In 1973 they did their first Halloween Haunt, which ran for 3 days[56] and in 1975 it was re-named Knott's Scary Farm. In its opening year both the Friday

54   The history of Epcot international food and wine festival, Expedition Theme Park, https://www.youtube.com/watch?v=rKKp6vYlg9g

55   The season pass podcast, episode 125, Knott's Berry Farm panel

56   The history of Knott's Berry Farm, Knott's Berry Farm, https://www.knotts.com/blog/2020/april/the-history-of-knotts-berry-farm

and Saturday night sold out[57]. Expedition Theme Park summed it up, "It only took a few weeks to assemble Knott's Halloween Haunt. After three nights on unprecedented revelry, the undead dispersed leaving behind a harvest of profits never thought possible in the slow fall season. They were surprised. They were relieved. They were just getting started".

To help market the event it was fronted by Seymour, a sinister character played by actor Larry Vincent, who hosted horror shows on American television. Using an iconic character as a host has become a key part of various Halloween events, including Horror Nights at Universals. Seymour presented a show in the 2,100 seat John Wayne Theatre, which included clips from various horror films. Although other parks around the time were celebrating Halloween with additions like pumpkin carving, Knott's Berry Farm are generally credited with creating the modern-day Halloween event that has been so successful in theme parks around the world. By 1977 the event had become too big for their regular staff, so they began recruiting extra actors just for Knott's Scary Farm, and developed a Monsters College to train them.

Whilst Halloween events and Christmas events are the most common, parks often find other more niche events to bring in extra guests at quieter times of year. American operator Cedar Fair uses the Snoopy and Charlie Brown characters as its mascots and the theme for their Camp Snoopy children's areas. They have added a seasonal Peanuts Celebration event at Knott's Berry Farm, Valley Fair and Carowinds. The Carowinds was their third such event and launched in 2019 in weekends in November, bridging the period between Halloween (Scarowinds) and Christmas (Winter Fest). Around the park there were Peanuts decorations, including yellow bunting, giant comic strips and Peanuts characters and giant speech bubbles floating over paths for guests to stand under for a photo opportunity. As the event is family orientated, they've kept the family rides open with a few thrill coasters closed for maintenance. There was extra entertainment including a costume character show and some 'creative percussionists' who painted patterns on a canvas whilst playing music on a mixture of items normally found in the kitchen. In keeping with Snoopy being a dog, there was also a show from the All Star Dog team. There was a Charles Shultz exhibition (Shultz being the cartoonist who created the Peanuts characters and comic strip), an art class in drawing the Peanuts characters and extra Peanuts merchandise outlets.

In 2006 Alton Towers launched a new event called Chocolate Towers to coincide with the opening of their Charlie and the Chocolate Factory dark ride. Chocolate Towers involved chocolate theming around the entrance and Towers Street area (renamed Cocoa Street for the event). At the end of Towers Street was a chocolate volcano (Mount Chocovuis) that erupted twice a day, shooting chocolate Miniature Heroes[58] into the air for the guests around to catch. You could meet Father Chocolate and get a free Easter egg, get a

57 The history of Knott's Scary Farm: a sinister start, Expedition Theme Park, https://www.youtube.com/watch?v=wvDmgmUBED4

58 Small Cadbury's chocolates themed to their larger bars.

chocolate tattoo, do a park wide Easter egg hunt or for £1 buy a chocolate egg to ice with a message of your choice. Over at the hotels there was a casino where you gambled with chocolate money, and a giant chocolate gunge tank. The park invested in special Chocolate Towers fleeces for their staff.

Having very small pop up events provides something different of interest for regular visitors (such as annual passholders), but it doesn't tend to do enough to encourage people to shift their visits. A question managers should think about is how long would a guest spend on the extra activities? If it's a five second photo opportunity, it probably won't shift a visit. If it's half an hour or more it might do, and if it's an hour or more there's a reasonable chance. Some events extend something a park already does, but that might be confined to a single area or attraction. The Peanuts Celebration and Chocolate Towers are both examples of this. Other events are more generic and could be used interchangeably at any park.

Chocolate Towers didn't last for long, so perhaps it wasn't considered a commercial success by the park's management, but it ticked the box of providing a range of themed entertainment, in keeping with the park's brand (by extending the Charlie and the Chocolate Factory theme). A problem was that Easter was already a busy time for the park, so they didn't need an event to bring more people in, and since the Chocolate Towers concept was family orientated, it wouldn't be appropriate to run it during the week on the quiet school days. They could have moved it to the quieter September, but running a chocolate themed event made more sense around Easter.

Having established Halloween Horror Nights for bringing in guests for the quiet October period, Universals were looking for something to bring in more guests for the quiet period before Easter. In 1995, they introduced Mardi Gras[59].

Mardi Gras is French for 'fat Tuesday' and celebrates the start of Lent. It is what we in the UK call Shrove Tuesday, or Pancake Day. It was originally planned to last from March 6th to April 6th, but it was so successful that in the first year it was extended to April 13th. In its first year it featured 15 floats made by Kern Studios, who made the 'real' Mardi Gras parade flats for New Orleans[60]. There were also over 200 performers. They'd start playing Mardi Gras music at 6pm, at 7pm a parade began and afterwards there was a party with live music, featuring local bands in the week and nationally famous bands at weekends. Pop up stalls sold Louisiana food and beer. By the parade's 25th anniversary they had more than doubled the number of nights to 62.

In 2001 Dollywood wanted their own event to bring in people for the start of the season. They came up with the Festival of Nations. Whilst Dollywood's normal theme is Tennessee culture - its history, its nature and its music - the Festival of Nations celebrates peace between all nations around the world.

59   Try these tempting treats at Universal's Mardi Gras 25th anniversary, Inside the Magic, https://insidethemagic.net/2020/02/universals-mardi-gras-tempting-treats-mg1/

60   The history of Universal Studios Mardi Gras and the 25th anniversary, Expedition Theme Park, https://www.youtube.com/watch?v=-Tk9_EOMSHo

There'd be rows of flags at the entrance, while inside other theming pieces included globes and prayer flags hung like bunting over the pathways. Shows entertained visitors with music from around the world; from African drummers to Bollywood dance music. As time went on, it also developed a Food and Wine festival element, where pop up kiosks sold global cuisine. In 2020 they added another event, the Dollywood Flower and Food Festival. It was scheduled to run from May 8th to June 14th.

Some theme parks hold an Oktoberfest, an event originally started in Munich, Germany. The original Oktoberfest celebrated the marriage between the king and queen of Bavaria on October 12th 1810. People had so much fun it led to an annual event. After a couple of years, the party switched from wine (a drink for celebrating a royal wedding) to beer. At some point the event was moved earlier and started in September, when the weather was typically better.

Quassy amusement park (Connecticut) has made a tradition of celebrating the last day of their season with a one day Oktoberfest featuring German food and music. The park's public relations director Ron Gustafson said, "We don't stay open for Halloween. To do Halloween events, it's so expensive—especially to do it properly. Since we're not open late into October, Oktoberfest fits nicely with the timing. This is a nice way for us to close the year and say goodbye to our customers for the season"[61]. For quite a few years a three-day Oktoberfest was an event featured at Geauga Lake (Ohio). Six Flags Great Adventure ran their first Oktoberfest in 1980[62] and Six Flags Great Escape (New York state) still runs an Oktoberfest. Great Adventure's Oktoberfest was on a lavish scale including a beer cart pulled by the traditional Clydesdale horses, a costumed mascot called Fritz, a parade, the 'world's largest' pretzel, barefoot grape crushing, German crafts (including clock and beer stein making) and an authentic beer hall imported from Germany. In later years a petting zoo was added. Music included oompah bands, bell ringers and yodellers. The event ran between the same dates as the original Oktoberfest in Germany. It's an early example of a theme park extending its summer season beyond the summer. 1992 was the last year of Oktoberfest at Great Adventure, because the park wanted to focus their budget on growing Halloween. In 2020 Gardaland (Italy), Alton Towers (UK) and Thorpe Park (UK) introduced their own Oktoberfests. All three are part of Merlin Entertainments. Thorpe Park's was marketed with the slogan, "Yodel if you want to go faster".

Beer is normally a big part of an Oktoberfest. The Oktoberfest in Munich sometimes calls itself the world's largest beer festival. However, parks need to be careful not to put off families, and also be conscious of the trouble guests can cause if they become intoxicated. In particular there can be safety issues around intoxicated guests and rides.

---

61   Tapping into Oktoberfest, Fun World Magazine, IAAPA, October 2003

62   Oktoberfest, Great Adventure History, http://www.great-adventurehistory.com/OktoberfestNew.htm

One of the quirkiest events is at The Beach water park in Mason, Ohio. The last day of the season is Bring a Dog Day. At the end of the day dogs and their owners can play in the wave pool. Games include seeing which dog can run into the pool and retrieve a tennis ball the fastest. Other contests include a prize for the owner that looks most like its dog.

In 2020 Europa Park opened through November for first time, bridging the gap between Halloween and Christmas. They marketed this period as Hallowinter[63]. (Due to the coronavirus, Hallowinter was cancelled in 2020, but hopefully the concept will get revived in future years.)

Not every theme park has a Universal or a Disney sized budget. However, events like Mardi Gras or Mickey's Not so Scary Halloween Party have grown

over decades. If regional parks want to develop their own iconic events, they have to be willing to give them the time and space to grow. Quite a few regional parks get impatient, or have high turnovers in management who want to make their own mark. Many of these smaller scale events have been killed before they had a fair chance to find success.

Making events pay

Events can be a great way of offering more stable employment, raising attendance and spreading out visitors across more days. They can also become a financial black hole. At least if you build a new ride that doesn't work out, you still have got a ride at the end of it. With events, they can be hugely expensive, and if they don't work out financially, you can end up wondering what you have to show for the venture.

Before introducing an event, you need to think about several things. Firstly, what's it trying to achieve? If the park often has massive queues, opening on extra days can be a sensible option. If the park rarely has a queue, opening on more days might be an expensive mistake. Putting on a big event for a day when the park's quiet might bring more people in. Putting it on for a day when the park's busy anyway probably isn't such a sensible decision.

Does your park have the infrastructure to cope with the event? Opening in the winter when it's likely to be wet and cold isn't a good idea, if few of your rides are undercover and most of them will have to close on some days because of the weather. Will it adversely impact your maintenance programme, and will the event ease your staffing challenges or add to them? If the event involves opening after dark, do you already have a reasonable amount of permanent lighting?

Can an event take advantage of assets and resources you've already got? Do you have carpenters and scenic artists with surplus time that could be used for build theming and sets for an event? Do you have indoor spaces like conference centres, that are busy in the summer with weddings, but rarely used in October? Could they be taken over by an event? Or will you need to hire in marquees and shipping containers? When you're designing an area that's likely to host events, like a central square, have you built in plenty of power points/utility boxes where lighting and sound systems can be plugged in? Is there a head chef who's not already having his time used to capacity, or an entertainments team who are hungry to create something new? Is there a ride operator who's studying music who could do some seasonal mixes of your music? As soon as you start having to take on extra staff, use consultants and outside design agencies, the cost of putting on these events can rise quickly. That might be okay for a large attraction with a lot of potential. It won't be cost effective for somewhere smaller.

Some attractions lend themselves to seasonal variations much more than others. With 4D cinemas, you can replace the film with a seasonal variant at little expense. Fountain shows can be programmed with different music and lighting for a special occasion. Dark rides might be able to have scenes altered for Halloween, Christmas and other events. It is no doubt more special for the guests if the event has completely new attractions, rather than amended versions of what's normally there, but there can also be a significant difference in the cost.

There's an element of luck, but you also make your own luck. If you want to use big events to draw people into quieter times and redistribute your attendance, then you need to make sure you've got the right infrastructure to support the event in a cost effective way: the right level of permanent lighting, weather proofing, attractions that can be adapted for events etc. This is where family businesses can have an advantage over some of the corporate parks. A family business can take long term decisions. If they know they want to start doing more events in five years' time, they can slowly build up the groundwork to support the events before they happen. Corporate parks tend to want quick results and are often reluctant to make that kind of long-term investment. I was a member of junior management at one park that tried to do a lot of events. The vision was to be a permanent festival. But there simply wasn't the infrastructure to support the events they were putting on. Very few of them made any money, and in some cases the loses were huge. It wasn't a surprise when the park went into administration.

Events generally need refreshing each year to keep people coming back. An advantage for chain parks is that theming and props can be moved around between the different parks. For example, Clayton Lawrence is the entertainment manager at California's Great America, a park owned by the Cedar Fair group. Each year he visits the scenery store at Knott's Berry Farm, another park in the chain, to find theming for his event[64]. One year he used the façade from Knott's Berry Farm's Harry Houdini Maze for a maze themed to a wax works. Every March Cedar Fair holds a Scare Convention where managers from across their parks get together to discuss ideas for their Haunts.

Ron Miziker has designed events for Disneyland (California) and Knott's Berry Farm (California) amongst others. He advises, "For those with the responsibility of staging events, I stress the importance of thinking about the project the same as one would a show. For the audience attending, the experience must include a beginning, middle and end. Concentrate on that first impression as well as what will be the guest's final impression. Often these are what they remember most about their visit and what they tell their friends about, but the middle experience cannot be forgotten either. Again, like a show, this middle must provide a sequence of highs and lows"[65].

There are benefits beyond events spreading out attendance. They encourage more repeat visits, because the park isn't always the same. This may help to sell more annual passes. If the event's covered by the media, it helps to promote the park. Compared to a crowd calendar, it might feel like a more positive message. A crowd calendar is saying, don't visit on this day, because it's going to be very busy. An event is saying, come on this day, because you'll get something extra.

Celebrate your birthday

If lots of people visit a theme park to celebrate a big public holiday, then clearly the parks are going to get very busy on those days. What if we could make every day a celebration? Persuading people to time their visit around their birthday is an effective way to do this. Some people's birthdays will fall on big public holidays, but just as many birthdays will fall in the quiet months like September. In fact, September is statistically the busiest month for birthdays, because a lot of pregnancies happen around Christmas. Many parks give out free birthday badges[66] to guests. Make sure a few guests in your adverts are wearing them, to emphasise that this is somewhere people come on their birthday. You can have signs near the entrance saying, "If it's your birthday don't forget to ask for a free birthday badge".

64   Clayton Lawrence, California's Great America, episode 335, Season Pass Podcast, http://www.seasonpasspodcast.com/archive/index.html

65   Make an event of it, Ron Miziker, Park World Magazine, https://www.parkworld-online.com/make-an-event-of-it/

66   Called 'birthday buttons' in the US

In Germany theme parks are normally free if guests show ID proving that it's their birthday. In some countries there might be difficulties with children not having the right ID. Parks might worry about the system getting abused, particularly if there isn't a standard ID that children have.

Using pricing to shift visits

You can encourage guests to visit in a quiet period by putting on an event. But what about dropping your prices? Various parks have peak day and off-peak pricing for tickets. An alternative to changing the gate price, is to run promotions that are only valid at off-peak times. We are going to be looking at various types of tiered pricing, dynamic pricing and promotions. We will also be looking at a history of flexible pricing. I think the history is interesting, because these ideas are older than readers might imagine. There's a good opportunity to learn from the past.

Disneyland has been using promotions to encourage people to visit in the quiet season since the early days. Before Disney introduced a pay one price model, you bought tickets for individual rides you wanted to go on. As well as buying individual tickets, you could buy books of tickets, where each ticket worked out cheaper than buying it individually. Books would include E tickets for the largest rides, as well as tickets for smaller rides. During the quiet season Magic Kingdom Club members could buy books full of only E tickets[67]. These books weren't normally available. The Magic Kingdom Club was started in 1957, and was available for the employees of large companies and the military in Southern California. When Magic Kingdom (Orlando) opened in 1971 it became a national club, and at its peak it had 30,000 members[68]. The Magic Kingdom Club ran for 43 years before being disbanded in 2000. Whilst they ran these special promotions at quiet times, they didn't drop the price of a basic ride ticket. That could have devalued the product.

More recently Disneyland introduced the Californian Residents pass, giving holders cheap entry through most of the winter. Between September – May, with the exception of Christmas, the park was quiet. The Californian Residents pass was available to people living within certain postcodes, and got them a cheap entry to the park during those quiet periods. The feeling was that they didn't need to give a discount to people living further away, because they were less price sensitive[69].

Chessington World of Adventures introduced a parent and toddler annual pass, where a parent and a small child could have unlimited visits during term time for a lower price than the standard annual pass. In the UK indoor soft play centres often do a term time offer, where you get entry and a meal, either for the cost of the normal entry ticket, or for not much more. They

67   Norm Elder on Disney, Universal and state dependent memory, Bloo Loop, https://blooloop.com/features/norm-elder-on-disney-universal-and-state-dependant-memory/

68   Walt Disney's Magic Kingdom Club, Bob Baldin, Yesterland, https://www.yesterland.com/mkc.html

69   In service to the mouse, Jack Lindquist

don't do this combo ticket at weekends and school holidays, when they can reach capacity without doing any discounts. Other parks like Disney and Universals do tiers of annual pass, where cheaper annual passes are blocked out during busy times.

Some parks sell cheaper levels of season tickets/annual passes where the busier days are 'blacked out'. There has also been a growing number of parks offering new season tickets based around quieter periods. In 2019 Cedar Point introduced a new Wild Card that gave you unlimited entry between May 11th (start of the season) and June 30th (when the crowds pick up). To protect the guest satisfaction, you need to convince people that these shorter passes are great value for money. From a business perspective, you don't want to get the same number of visitors, but find that a chunk of them down-graded to a cheaper pass. Often these new passes are going to be combined with raising the cost of a full season pass. You don't want to have too many different passes, because then it becomes confusing for the guests.

The problem with peak and off-peak pricing, is a perception that you're paying more to visit on a busy day, whereas with a targeted promotion, the perception is that you're getting in more cheaply by going on a quiet day. Although they essentially amount to the same thing, do people feel like the 'normal price' is what people are paying on the peak day or the off-peak day? It might seem like an arbitrary distinction, but psychologically it's an import-ant one. It makes a difference to whether or not the guests feel that they're getting good value for money.

Peak and off peak pricing is sometimes referred to as 'surge pricing', because the prices 'surge' when there's heavy demand. This might give us a clue to how most people will perceive it. Another name is 'peak load pricing', again drawing attention to the extra charge at peak times, rather than a saving at offpeak times. You can influence how your guests think, but in the end it's their perception that matters, not yours. You can argue that a peak day ticket is still giving people good value for money, but the customers might not agree with it.

How guests react to a promotion can come down to the kind of language you use. If you advertise peak and off-peak pricing, people are more likely to feel like they're paying extra on a busy day. If you advertise standard pricing and off-peak pricing, they're more likely to feel like they're getting a discount on the quiet days. If you do a standard price, but run a promotion that's only valid for off-peak dates, then the sense of value becomes stronger.

We've already mentioned that Disneyland started using off-peak promo-tions in their early days. However, off-peak pricing goes back further than that. In 1851 the Great Exhibition, also known as Crystal Palace, opened at Hyde Park (London). A big glass pavilion housed displays of scientific and technological innovations. The event ran from 1st May to 15th October and attracted 6,039,722 visitors. The Great Exhibition is generally considered to be the first World's Fair, although there had been other international exposi-tions before that. The Great Exhibition varied their prices depending on how busy they expected to be.

The prices dropped in the summer, when the Parliamentary season drew to an end and the affluent left London[70]. Nowadays, London's attractions are more popular during the summer, but in Victorian times London wasn't a pleasant place in the hotter months. Poor sanitation and overcrowding meant that diseases spread rapidly. Sewers were open with a pungent smell. The Great Exhibition was before London had an underground sewage system. In the 'Great Stink' of 1858 Parliament realised that building an underground sewage system was a matter of urgency, and between 1859-1865 six main sewers totaling 100 miles were created, along with another 450 miles of smaller sewers feeding into them. Using a mixture of gravity and pumping stations, the sewage was released into the River Thames downstream of London. Contaminated water was a serious problem, and The Great Exhibition was only two years after scientist John Snow published his theory about how cholera was being spread. As well as dropping the admission price for the summer, The Great Exhibition also charged extra for Fridays and Saturdays. 170 years later, variable pricing is still a popular method for controlling demand.

We're now going to spend a few pages looking at how the restaurant industry has used promotions to develop an audience at offpeak times. The theme park industry can learn a lot from other areas of hospitality. American restaurants started doing early bird deals in the 1920s. An early bird deal would give diners cheaper meals before a certain time, allowing the restaurants to fill more tables and get a second sitting.

The name comes from the proverb, 'the early bird catches the worm', a phrase going back to at least 1636[71]. The concept arose from prohibition, a period when the US outlawed alcohol. Prohibition of alcohol started on 17th January 1920. Restaurants lost a big chunk of their revenue, and without alcohol, the concept of fine dining changed. Wine had big profit margins, and some customers ate at home, where they could drink illegal moonshine.

At the same time, the 'roaring twenties' had a growing middle class. Early Bird deals became a way of targeting the new middle-class families, bringing them in for a discounted early dinner, and getting two covers on the tables. Prohibition ended in 1933, but by this point the American stock market had crashed and the American economy was in ruins. There couldn't be a move back to how things were before 1920, with one sitting and higher profit margins. The changes to restaurants from the prohibition era stayed in effect, with restaurants looking to keep prices low, broaden their appeal and make up for the smaller profit margins by serving more people.

These days Early Bird offers seem to do particularly well in communities with lots of retired people, who often eat earlier. In America retirees started to become a market for businesses to target after Roosevelt's New Deal in 1935 set up social security. In the 1950s the American economy picked up,

---

70   The Great Exhibition of 1851, Pauline Western Thomas, Fashion Era, https://www.fashion-era.com/the_great_exhibition. htm#Entrance%20Costs%20To%20The%20Great%20Exhibition

71   The extinction of the early bird, Jaya Saxena, Eater, https://www. eater.com/2018/1/29/16929816/early-bird-extinction-florida

and pensioners became increasingly important. Now the baby boomer generation has reached retirement age, retirees can be a business's most affluent customers. They're having to re-think the deal, as giving a cheap deal to your most affluent customers might not be logical. Restaurants are also rebranding early bird deals with names like "Sunset offer" and "Pre-theatre deal", because some customers find the phrase 'early bird' off putting. They associate it with being cheap and old people (and even the elderly don't like to think of themselves as being 'old'). Just as the restaurants in the 1920s gave people a discount for eating at a less popular time of day, theme parks might give people a discount for visiting on a less popular date. And just as restaurants have to be careful about what they call their promotions, so do theme parks.

Children's menus are another invention of the early prohibition period, designed to replace groups of adults with families. This was important, because some adults were eating at home, where they could drink the illegal moonshine. Families also tended to eat earlier in the day. Appealing to families for an early sitting and then to adult groups for a later sitting, was another way of filling the restaurant for longer.

Before the 1920s, restaurants outside of hotels tended to ban children, because they thought it ruined 'the boozy fun'[72]. Early children's menus actually promoted their nutritional value. These days the food on children's menus is mostly deep fried and often less healthy than on the adult's menu. Humes writes, "Children tend to rise to the culinary bar we set for them, and children's menus in America set the bar very low indeed". Although early children's menus were a lot healthier, the presentation was similar to today's. When the Waldorf-Astoria Hotel (New York) introduced their children's menu in 1921, it was illustrated with a drawing of Jack Horner and a dish running away with the spoon. It was after the second world war that cheap processed foods began to replace the healthy options on children's menus. Parisian restaurants had been appealing to families before the American ones, but instead of using separate children's menus, they'd simply do a smaller portion of the adult dishes, for a lower price. Just as the restaurants in the 1920s used children's menu to fill up their tables at quieter times, theme parks might need to consider new audiences if they want to level off their peaks and troughs in attendance. We discuss how theme parks can do this in the chapter called, broadening your demographics.

Happy Hours are a period when people can get cheap drinks (or food). The phrase Happy Hour also goes back to the prohibition era, when people would go pre-drinking for a 'happy hour' in a speak easy, before going to the restaurant. These days Happy Hours (sometimes running for several hours) are used to bring people into bars earlier in the evening when they tend to be quiet. More recently happy hours have become controversial, and are banned in some regions, because they encourage binge drinking. A theme park equivalent of a happy hour would be cheap evening tickets.

---

72   Feeding the kiddie: a brief history of the children's menu, Michele Humes, Slate, https://slate.com/human-interest/2013/08/childrens-menu-history-how-prohibition-and-emmett-holt-gave-rise-to-kid-cuisine.html

It is perhaps ironic that the prohibition of alcohol ended the prohibition of children in restaurants, and that the prohibition era started the concept of Happy Hours and pre-drinking, which are now big factors in binge drinking. Before the 1920s the restaurant industry had been focused on serving smaller numbers of affluent adults. Prohibition disrupted the industry, meaning restaurants that didn't evolve would go out of business. The solution was to broaden their appeal, bring in more diners, and to serve more people they needed to be more efficient. Prohibition fueled efficiency in American restaurants, in the same way that the theme park industry would need to change, when they moved from a 'pay per a ride' to 'pay one price' (POP) model. Early bird deals, children's menus and happy hours were all types of promotion focused on quieter periods. Now most theme parks run a POP model, it's important for them to focus on filling their quiet periods.

Before we come back to theme parks, let us briefly discuss the use of variable and dynamic pricing for transport. In the 1950s the New York subway faced a problem. All fares cost a set price (10 cents). At busy time the system couldn't cope, and building more lines was prohibitively expensive. 17 economists submitted proposals for solving the problem[73]. William Vickey came up with the idea of varying fares based on the time of day and the length of journey. Rather than using an army of clerks and inspectors, which would be expensive, he devised an automated system. "Passengers put a quarter in the entrance turnstile, get a metal check with notches indicating the zone of origin to be inserted in an exit turnstile, which would, through electro-mechanical relays, deliver an appropriate number of nickels according to the origin and time of day,". The machines were considered too complicated and never produced. Vickery worked on a similar proposal for roads called Congestion Pricing, where drivers would pay more to use a road at peak times. Vickery eventually won the Nobel Prize for his work in 1996, just three days before his death.

Surge pricing has become common for public transport, such as airline and rail operators. By 1984 Delta Airlines had 147 staff just to keep on tweaking the prices, with the aim of filling all the seats on a flight at the highest price point possible. Now let's see how the theme park industry mirrors these developments.

Disney World has been running a promotion where guests staying in accommodation at off-peak times of year get Dining Plans, giving them free meals in the parks. The face value of the Dining Plans is more than the cost to deliver them. Dropping the price of rooms could weaken the brand, whereas holding the prices level, but offering guests more for their money, doesn't have the same impact. In the final years before Pleasureland Southport (UK) closed, they tried an 'all-inclusive offer' on off-peak dates. For the price of a normal wristband, you got a free whippie ice cream, a free meal deal, a goody bag with some rock and at Halloween a free pumpkin.

---

73   Is surge pricing a fair way to manage demand, Tim Harford, BBC
News, https://www.bbc.com/news/business-49986191

We can draw another comparison here between the restaurant industry and the theme park industry. Some restaurants found it less cost effective to do an early bird deal where you simply got a discount, than to charge the normal prices, but to give people something extra for free, such as a bowl of soup at the start and a coffee and biscuit at the end. A lot of guests wouldn't have bought the soup or coffee without the deal, particularly as people eating early are less likely to make an occasion of it. Coffee and soup have high margins, meaning the cost to the restaurant is a lot lower than the face value of the product. If customers wouldn't have normally bought these things, you haven't lost any revenue, and the cost of serving them can be low. Disney's Dining Plan and Pleasureland's all inclusive offer, take a similar line of thought. You maintain your price integrity and give people a sense of better value at limited cost to the business.

In 2019 Ferrari World (Abu Dhabi) did a special promotion on Thursday, Friday and Saturday evenings in Ramadan, when the park would be very quiet (because locals had been fasting all day). On these special nights, guests could enter the park for free, and enjoy the attractions on a pay per ride basis.

Europa Park gives their annual pass holders one free ticket for an off-peak weekday in the Christmas season, so that they can bring a friend or family member with them. The winter weekdays are typically Europa Park's quietest time, with coasters like Wodan and Silver Star often running on one train. Now, there is a difference between moving a visit to an off-peak day and trying to attract additional visitors on the quiet days rather than the busy days, but both can be effective in helping the park manage their queues more effectively.

Cynics will be thinking, "Yeah, anyone can bring in new customers if they don't pay anything. What's the point in filling the park up on quiet days with guests who haven't paid anything to be there?" There are various reasons why Europa Park might run this promotion. It's another reason for people to buy an annual pass (The Europa Park Club Card). That doesn't seem to be a major factor though, as the perk isn't even mentioned on the Club Card website. Even if the passholders friend gets in for free, they're likely to spend money on food, drink, merchandise, photography and games. This may well be a factor. Some money is better than no money. They may be hoping that some annual passholders have more than one friend, and end up bringing along a few people and buying some tickets. They may also be hoping that the friend who comes for free is someone who doesn't normally visit the park. If they have a great time they might come back again, or even buy an annual pass themselves.

There is a risk that some of the friends visiting for free are people who would have paid to enter had the offer not been there. Presumably Europa Park are betting on the initiative making more money than it loses.

In 2018 Six Flags Magic Mountain ran a promotion where season pass holders could bring a friend for free on December 30th, the last Sunday of

Holiday in the Park[74]. The park hit capacity. They ran the same promotion in 2019 and the same thing happened[75]. They had to bring in police to close off Magic Mountain Parkway, the road to the park, because the parking lot was full. Even when people got to the entrance it was taking them over an hour to get into the park. Unlike Europa Park they were only allowing the 'bring a friend' on a single day. Inside the park queues were spilling out the lines and advertised at 3 hours for the largest rides.

After the 2018 experience you'd have thought they might have changed the policy in 2019, but they didn't. One can only presume that they wanted to max out their capacity, knowing it'd get them free publicity and maybe even thinking it'd make the park look really popular. It seems like an odd strategy though, and the sort of thing that gets cooked up by the marketing department against the protests of the operations team. It's the any publicity is good publicity mentality. I respectfully disagree. The best form of publicity is positive word of mouth, and your happy guests talking about the good times they had. Not an incredulous news presenter showing miserable guests who've been waiting three hours for a 30 second ride. Despite the huge numbers of people, in an Airtime Thrills vlog from the day it was hard to spot a single person who was smiling. Marketing teams do sometimes think that pushing the park to capacity is a good marketing ploy, and we discuss this in the chapter on opening a new ride.

As well as using promotions to encourage guests to visit at quiet periods, you can also redirect your marketing budget, so that you're pushing the park at times when it's normally quiet, rather than doing an advertising push around the times when you're already busy. Just throwing money on advertising for a quiet period won't do much, but if you can combine an advertising push with a promotion, seasonal event or a new attraction opening, then it helps to drive guests to the park.

I have seen parks running promotions for peak days, for example in the UK Mother's Day and Father's Day are when families often go out and do something together. A number of the smaller parks will say that Mums get in free on Mother's Day and Dads get in free of Father's Day. If you're a really small park that never has queues, it might be a good promotion. But I'm not sure about the logic behind offering a discount on a day when the park's already going to be busy. Although some of these parks do a lot of BOGOFF (buy one get one free) vouchers anyway, so saying that Mums or Dads get in free when they're with someone buying a full price ticket, might not mean that much. Nonetheless, there is a risk that marketing teams do a promotion for a busy day because they like the sound of it, without thinking about how the park will cope with the influx of extra visitors. This is where it's important for the different departments to communicate to make sure they understand each other's needs. If the queues are notoriously

---

74   Magic Mountain's Christmas event

75   Six Flags Magic Mountain hits capacity – again, Airtime Thrills, Youtube, https://www.youtube.com/watch?v=98Ax_iqcu3I

bad on Halloween, then saying that any guest wearing Halloween dress gets in free, might not be a very sensible move. You also tend to get these oddities, when managers are simply judged and rewarded on how many visitors the park gets, rather than on the guest satisfaction. If the visitor numbers are high, but the guest satisfaction is low, then the attendance is likely to decline over time. A successful promotion isn't necessarily one that fills the park up to capacity. It might be one that takes a park from being quiet to being comfortably busy.

The pros and cons of variable pricing

The premise behind variable pricing is a simple one. The more popular days are more expensive. This encourages people to switch their visit to quieter day, and everyone benefits from the shorter queues. It's like a more forceful version of the crowd calendar. But is variable pricing popular with the guests and does it work? This is a complicated question to answer. There's a limited amount of data and plenty of arguments in both directions. Of all the ideas in this book, variable pricing is the most controversial. I can't offer parks a clean solution here. Particularly as it depends on your country's culture, how trusted your park is and how you implement it. What I want to do is run through the different arguments.

Some parks go further than having a peak and off-peak pricing, to other systems where prices can fluctuate a lot more. At the time of writing (2020) a lot of parks offer a great range of prices for events, for instance most people would rather visit a Halloween event closer to October 31st. This can leave the early nights quiet, whilst the park's get inundated with guests for the last few nights. This is particularly a problem for Halloween events, because scare mazes have inherently low throughputs (unless there's a continual stream of guests, which is Universal's approach). By slowly raising the ticket price for Halloween events closer to Halloween itself, you can encourage more people to visit earlier on. John Carter is director of marketing for Silverwood Theme Park (Idaho). He looks back on when they introduced multiple pricing tiers for their Scarywood event, "We found success spreading out the crowds. The Saturdays closest to Halloween are still our busiest times, but we've seen much higher attendance on Thursdays because of the tiered pricing."[76]

At the moment few parks use fully dynamic pricing, where prices rise as more tickets are sold. This is the kind of pricing strategy used by the airline industry. One park that has been doing it is Leolandia (Italy). In 2012 Leolandia switched from a steady price of 24 euros a ticket to prices that fluctuates from 13 euros to 33 euros depending on the date[77]. Leolandia introduced dynamic pricing to help move visits from weekends when they struggled to cope, to the quiet weekdays. What happened if guests booked a date and then found that they couldn't go? Leolandia issued guests with

---

76   Dynamic pricing, Jodi Helmer, Fun World Magazine, June 2019,
https://www.iaapa.org/news/funworld/dynamic-pricing

77   Ibid.

credits for the value of their tickets, that could be used towards another day. We'll come back to Leolandia shortly, but first we'll look at Disney and their use of tiered pricing.

Disney started dividing their one-day tickets into three price bands depending on how busy they expected to be on the date someone was planning to visit. In 2018 they expanded this tiered pricing to include multi-day tickets. Theme Park Insider's Robert Niles wrote, "In Disney's ideal world, attendance would become constant 365 days of the year — balancing at a point each day where the parks are full but do not feel crowded, allowing all attractions to operate at capacity but without having to turn anyone away at the gate or pushing anyone to leave in frustration."[78] Disney's American theme parks reported a lower overall attendance in 2019, despite the Stars Wars Lands opening in Orlando and California. There are too many variables to know whether the variable pricing had any role in putting people off. Tiered pricing as well as a general rise in prices was partly in anticipation of the parks being crammed when Star Wars fans flocked to the resorts. The big crowds never came. Journalist Todd Martens described it, "Little did I know that soon after its May 31 opening, the parks would be a dead zone, with every attraction a walk-on and blissfully bare sidewalks"[79].

Some guests may have been put off by the new pricing strategy, a lack of transparency and a feeling of paying more than they should be. However, there are several other factors. The media predicated massive crowds and unpleasant queues, which do normally accompany the opening of a major new attraction at Disney. Some people may have delayed their visits until the expected crowds settled down. Both Star Wars Lands opened without their headline attractions (Rise of the Resistance), which may have led to delayed visits. This is known as the Osbourne effect, after Osbourne Computers went bankrupt in 1983, partly because people stopped buying their computers after they announced the next model, and then took a year to bring it to market.

Disney World certainly had a lot of construction sites including a Tron motorbike coaster, Ratatouille dark ride, Guardians of the Galaxy roller coaster and Mickey's Runway Adventure, so there was a lot to wait for. The lands omitted the main Stars Wars characters, because they wanted guests to feel like they were the characters in the Star Wars World, rather than passively observing the characters. Disney had done this with some of their early dark rides, but they later added the eponymous characters into the sets following guest feedback. It may be that the Star Wars lands didn't appeal to fans as much as they could have done.

Although My Magic Plus had been around for several years by this point, some guests were already finding planning a Disney vacation more

78   A year later, is Disney World's variable pricing strategy working?, Robert Niles, Theme Park Insider, https://www.themeparkinsider.com/flume/201910/7049/

79   Commentary: what works – what's missing and what needs fixing at Disney's Galaxy's Edge, Todd Martens, Los Angeles Times, https://www.latimes.com/ entertainment-arts/story/2019-10-07/disneyland-star-wars-galaxys-edge-progress-report

of a chore. You're expected to book Fast Pass slots and dining reservations months in advance. Some guests do enjoy planning their Disney holiday, but for others it's a nuisance. There have been books about planning your Disney vacation since I was a child, but you never really needed them. You shouldn't need to study before you can enjoy visiting a theme park. Some guests may have visited Universals instead, if they thought that Hagrid's Magical Creature Motorbike Adventure (launched roller coaster) was a more compelling proposition.

Theme Park Insider reader Russell Meyer writes, "I think the WDW pricing structure adds unneeded complexity to the process, and essentially has become a revenue maximization tool for Disney... in the grand scheme of things, it's [the difference in price between different days] pretty small compared to other considerations like airfare, school schedules, time off allotments, weather, crowds, etc... I just don't think most guests have the ability or flexibility to move their vacations by months to save a few dollars on tickets. Maybe when you combine those lower ticket prices with savings on hotels, airfare, and other promotions, it can provide enough incentive to overcome other factors that influence vacation timing."

Universal Parks and Resorts chairman Tom Williams has cited the relative simplicity of Universal Orlando's ticket pricing as a selling point for Universal Orlando's theme parks[80]. He's not the only commentator who's dubious about overly complex pricing structures. Robbie Baxter worked for Netflix, before becoming a consultant who specialises in helping businesses to develop membership programmes. Her clients have included the theme park industry. She says, "When pricing gets complicated, trust goes down. Because if I have to be an expert on your pricing structure, I'm going to assume that it's possible to make a mistake"[81].

The jury is out on whether dynamic or tiered pricing is an effective way of redistributing attendance, although the author of this book has reservations about it. Technology might allow you to do dynamic pricing, but just because you can do something, doesn't mean that you should. A better strategy might be to publicise when queues are expected to be longer and shorter, and find ways to enhance the guest experience on the quieter days, as well as finding ways to add capacity and improve throughputs to help the park cope with surges in demand.

All of this needs putting into perspective though. Even with a drop in attendance, the American Disney parks are amongst the world's most visited, and Disney World has worked hard to become the world's most visited holiday destination. It might take several years before we get a better idea of whether or not tiered pricing has been a success for Disney. Presumably, these kind of changes weren't entered into lightly. I'd imagine they gave it considerable thought and market research and will continue to monitor its effectiveness.

---

80   Ibid.

81   Episode 145: Robbie Baxter talks about the membership mindset, Attraction Pros, http://attractionpros.com/podcast-details/

We have also ignored an important part of tiered pricing. To judge whether it was successful, we not only have to ask whether it helped to raise or lower Disney World's overall attendance. We also have to ask whether it did help to distribute crowds more evenly through the season. Whilst it can be difficult to draw definite conclusions without data that isn't publicly available, the answer is: possibly. Magic Kingdom used to reach capacity for several days over the Christmas season and Epcot would also reach capacity on New Year's Eve. In 2018, after dynamic pricing, Magic Kingdom hit capacity once on New Year's Eve and Epcot didn't at all. Epcot hitting capacity is connected to Magic Kingdom hitting capacity. Once Magic Kingdom hits capacity a lot of guests hop onto the monorail to Epcot instead. If Magic Kingdom hits capacity later in the day, fewer people will get redirected to Epcot.

Theme Park University wrote, "Why is this happening? Most likely it has to do with price. Since the parks have implemented a dynamic pricing structure to try to drive attendance during lower visited times (and maximize profits), the strategy seems to have worked. Guests are either choosing a cheaper time of year to visit or skipping an Orlando vacation altogether in favour of something with less strain on their wallet."[82]

However, as Theme Park University themselves pointed out, there are other factors and it can be difficult to link cause and effect. The New Fantasy Land expansion would have significantly increased the capacity of Magic Kingdom. It featured a new Storybook Circus area with a second Flying Dumbos ride, a Tangled area with new seating and toilets, the Under the Sea omnimover, Seven Dwarfs Mine Train roller coaster, Be Our Guest restaurant, Gaston's Tavern, Bonjour! Village Gifts and Aerial meet and greet. It nearly doubled the Fantasyland area from 11 acres to 20 acres[83]. Fantasyland had been downsized in 1994 when the 20,000 League Under the Sea submarine ride had closed. 20,000 Leagues under the Sea had a large footprint, was expensive to maintain, and had a relatively low throughput. New Fantasyland was billed as the largest expansion in the park's history and cost $425 million.

It was generally felt that the main purpose of the New Fantasyland was to increase the capacity of the park, rather than to bring in more people. Len Testa from Touring Plans wrote, "Universal made a major statement with Harry Potter that they were going to become a major player, but when you think about the New Fantasyland, it's about increasing the capacity of the park. It's not a response to the gauntlet Universal threw down. It's really about reducing the wait times and providing more things to do in the park."[84] It was pointed out that Magic Kingdom simply couldn't have coped with a

---

82   Why aren't Orlando theme parks filling to capacity in the 2019 holiday season?,
Josh Young, Theme Park University, https://themeparkuniversity.com/theme-parks-101/
why-arent-orlando-theme-parks-filling-to-capacity-during-the-2019-holiday-season/

83   Disney adds to the magic with New Fantasyland, Tampa
Bay Times, https://www.tampabay.com/news/business/tourism/
disney-world-adds-to-the-magic-with-new-fantasyland/1264091/

84   Ibid.

36% increase in attendance like Islands of Adventure had after the Wizarding World of Harry Potter opened. It is however true that Magic Kingdom continued hitting capacity for the first few years after the new area opened, so this doesn't on its own explain the change.

Whilst Magic Kingdom remains the most visited and most iconic of Disney World's four parks, its role was diminished, particularly after the World of Avatar opened at Animal Kingdom. In 2019 the Disney World app seemed to show the Avatar rides having the longest queues of all Disney World's attractions over the Christmas period, with Flight of Passage hitting three hours and Na'vi River Journey 165 minutes.

Trying to work out whether an idea's worked can be difficult, particularly if you don't have access to a business's internal data. Even if you do, there are lots of variables that shape a theme park's attendance and profitability. Having looked at Disney, variable pricing may have put some visitors off, and it may have helped to redistribute visitors more evenly through the season. But we can't have any certainty on either of these points.

Personally, I haven't been keen on dynamic pricing for regular theme park tickets. However, Leolandia has been at the forefront of dynamic pricing and in 2019's Trip Advisor chart of the world's top theme parks, Leolandia was ranked 14th. It was Italy's only theme park to make the list, ahead of larger parks Gardaland and Mirabilandia. It was the 5th highest rated theme park in Europe behind Puy du Fou, Tivoli Gardens, Europa Park and Disneyland Paris. It's difficult to know whether the dynamic pricing has helped Leolandia into its high spot by dissipating queues from the busiest days, but it certainly doesn't seem to have done it any harm. I suspect that some cultures are more receptive to dynamic pricing than others, so it might not be so successful in other countries, but it does seem to be a textbook example of how dynamic pricing can be used to improve the guest experience. After studying Leolandia's example, I've warmed to the idea of dynamic pricing for advanced tickets bought online, and I can see how it can be used to raise guest satisfaction, so long as it's implemented carefully. I still wouldn't be convinced about using dynamic pricing for tickets bought on the gate, where people are unlikely to drive away once they're already there.

Economist David Leonhardt believes that people are more willing to accept varying prices on a luxury item like a theme park ticket, because most people aren't completely sure what a fair price to pay for it is[85]. In 1999 Coca Cola tried introducing vending machines that would have an inbuilt thermometer and vary the cost of drinks depending on the temperature, so a bottle of Coke would cost more on a hot day than a cold day. The plan was cancelled after a big public backlash.

Leonhardt writes, "If anything, people seem more accepting of price changes on expensive items, where such frills are easier to add. On a can of soda - or a copy of Newsweek, which charged as much for the issue after the

85   Why variable pricing fails at the vending machine, David Leonhardt, The New York Times, https://www.nytimes.com/2005/06/27/business/why-variable-pricing-fails-at-the-vending-machine.html

pope's death as last week's issue featuring dinosaurs ("Beyond T Rex: How They Really Lived") - even a few extra cents can seem like an injustice. Part of the issue may be simple recognition: Everybody has an intuitive sense of what a soda or a magazine should cost, but determining the value of an airline ticket is trickier." On the other hand, an airline ticket is slightly different to a theme park ticket. An airplane clearly has a limited capacity. Once all the seats are sold, no one else can buy one. Whilst a theme park does have a capacity, few parks ever reach it, and if they do it's a few days a year. There's still an element of supply and demand, but it isn't exactly the same argument.

Economist Arthur Okin explains opposition to variable pricing (or what he calls do it yourself auctioning) at theme parks, based on a sense of fairness[86]. He argues that it doesn't seem fair for people to pay more for a product, that hasn't cost any more to produce. People might be willing to pay more to eat at a restaurant on Christmas Day, because they know the staff are being paid more. But it seems unfair for a business to exploit a peak in demand by raising their prices, when their cost base has stayed the same and the customer isn't getting anything extra. In the case of a theme park, they're arguably getting less, because the queues are longer. In the report on fairness as a constraint on profit seeking, it's argued that, "The cardinal rules of fairness is surely that one person should not achieve a gain by simply imposing an equivalent lose on another".

Perceptions are important here, and if the perception is that parks are charging more on busy days, just because they can, then they have broken the cardinal rule. The importance of perceptions are referred to in the report as 'naïve economics'. The real arguments around dynamic pricing and operational efficiency are complex and won't be understood by most guests. That's why trust becomes important.

Fairness and trust seem to be at the heart of people's willingness to accept variable pricing. Do people believe that the park's genuinely trying to alleviate waiting, or do they see it as a cynical case of profiteering because they can? There are lots of factors that can affect how trusted a brand is. In this case transparency might play a factor. Do guests know how much the prices can vary by and how they're calculated? Leolandia has certainly been fairly open about what the dynamic pricing is and how it works. The box you click on to buy tickets says, "The earlier you buy, the more you save. Prices may rise every 24 hours". You can then easily compare the price of visiting on different dates. Making prices rise every 24 hours, presumably at night, avoids the frustration of a price suddenly rising while someone's in the process of buying their tickets. At Leolandia the prices can only go up, not down if tickets aren't selling well. Guests don't have the frustration of buying tickets, and then realising they'd have saved money if they'd left it a few weeks.

Whether people see it as a cash grab (maximising profit) or a genuine attempt to reduce waiting times, might well depend on what else the park

---

86   Fairness as a constraint on profit seeking: Entitlements in the market, Daniel Kahneman; Jack L Knetsch; Richard Taler

is doing. If people see it as part of a coordinated attempt to manage queues better, then they're more likely to warm to the idea, compared to if it's the park's only plan of attack.

<	DECEMBER 2019					>
M	T	W	T	F	S	S
						1
2	3	4	5	6	7	8
9	10	11	12	13	14	15
16	17	18	19	20	21	22
23	24	25	26 €31.50	27 €30.50	28 €28.50	29 €27.50
30 €26.50	31 €24.50					

A screenshot of Leolandia's booking calendar.

People are more likely to accept variable pricing if the park can argue that people are getting something extra for their money. If a park normally closes at 5pm, but in the summer they close at 9pm and put their prices up, people might accept the extra cost of tickets, on the basis that the park is open for longer and they can get some rides in the dark. If the cost of tickets isn't anchored to any tangible change in the offering, then people are less likely to tolerate it. People are also more likely to tolerate it if there's an alternative. Let's say a theme park uses dynamic pricing online, but people have the option of buying tickets on the gate for a set price. The set price is at the highest point of the dynamic pricing. This is different to saying that all prices will vary, including those on the gate, so that people don't know how much they're going to have to pay until they get there. Some parks do staggered openings of rides on quiet days. For example, the park opens at 10am, but the back half of the park doesn't open until midday. If the ticket prices are lower on offpeak days, people might be more willing to accept this.

When theme parks are considering dynamic pricing, they need to reflect on how trusted their brand is, communicate clearly, and remember that trust is slow to earn and quick to lose. They also need to remember that if they're pressuring guests to buy their tickets well in advance before they go up in price, people won't be happy if they end up having a miserable time because the weather's bad. In Leolandia's case, if it rains at all in your visit you can come back for free anytime within a month. They also have some indoor attractions, including an aquarium and reptile house. I suspect the dynamic pricing would cause a lot more complaints if they didn't also do the rain check.

Having considered Leolandia's example, it seems to be something for other parks to consider, but not to rush into. Market research can be a part of this consideration. It's also worth talking to your staff. If they don't believe in it, it's unlikely the guests will. When you make a fundamental business change, customers are likely to comment on it. Will you find staff agreeing with disgruntled customers or talking positively about the dynamic pricing and defending the park? Although they shouldn't defend the park to the point of dismissing complaints, not listening and being unempathetic. There's a balance. If you're going to make such a fundamental change to your business model, you need to introduce it to your workforce before you advertise it to the public. You should monitor feedback carefully. If you get emails or comments on social media criticising the move, don't ignore them. You need to engage with your critics.

There hasn't made a mad dash for variable pricing. But it is slowly trickling into the industry. In 2020 Toverland introduced four price bands. These could be bought online with a discount or at the gate. On the gate prices were:

- Bronze: 29.50 euros
- Silver: 33 euros
- Gold: 34 Euros
- Platinum: 36 euros

Offpeak pricing and dynamic pricing are both ways of pricing to control demand. In more general terms, using pricing to control demand can be acceptable on experiences with a limited supply, but there are subtle factors that can change public opinion. The study on fairness as a constraint on profit seeking found that people can react badly to businesses exploiting a monopoly to raise prices.

Let's say a theme park is coping fine with its visitors, and then their main competitor closes. The park becomes a lot busier, and now it can't cope. They decide to raise prices to control demand. On one hand a lot of people are okay with basic supply and demand, and the idea that prices rise when demand outstrips supply. On the other hand, people were probably upset when the other theme park closed, so when the surviving one promptly raises its prices, this could cause a backlash. People don't like to see someone benefit from someone else's misfortune, which is partly why companies tend not to use disasters to increase their costs when supplies are disrupted. Businesses that do are likely to be punished in the long run.

In the study, they found that the extent to which a business raises its prices can be less significant than the perceived motive. Monopolies can be particularly controversial in the theme park industry, because it would be very expensive for a competitor to enter the market. This 'high barrier to entry' means that monopolies are difficult to break. People might be more willing to accept pricing to control demand, if people believe the demand has increased because the park has improved its quality (something they worked for), rather than due to something outside their control (luck). If the park has improved its quality, then the guests are also gaining something. If the quality hasn't increased, but the prices are going up, then the guests aren't sharing in the benefits.

When we analyse guest feedback, it becomes clear that fairness is very important to customers, and when people feel they've been treated unfairly, they can take their money elsewhere. This is why queue jumping can make us feel so angry. When we change our pricing structure, we not only have to show how that it's for the greater good, but also make sure that each individual visitor feels they've paid a fair price for the experience they're getting.

Opening new attractions

When Walt Disney World opened October 1st 1971, they were keen to avoid the overcrowding and chaos that had blighted the opening of Disneyland in 1955. They deliberately opened Disney World in October (the quietest month for tourism in Florida) and on a Friday (rather than a weekend). They also staggered when different representatives from the media visited and had the official dedication three weeks after opening (a kind of soft opening). In 2019 Disney World opened Star Wars Land at the end of August, right at the end of the summer school holiday period. Aside from school holidays and the weather, major new rides are one of the other factors that causes big surges in demand and long queues. A combination of a public holiday, good weather and a new ride could lead to the worst possible queues.

When Star Wars Land opened at Disneyland in California, they ran a system where you had to reserve your entry into the whole area if you wanted to visit between May 31st (when it originally opened) and June 23rd. It was effectively like reserving a Fast Pass to an entire area rather than for an individual attraction, and there was no standby line. According to Theme Park Insider, even on opening day the resort generally felt quiet, there was little waiting to get into the area and queues for the main ride, Smugglers Run, remained at under an hour[87]. This differed to the 7 hours queues for Slinky Dog Dash when it opened at Hollywood Studios a year earlier, five hour queues for the Anna and Elsa meet and greets in the Norway Pavilion,

---

87   Theme park insider, Disney's Star Wars land and the future of queuing, https://www.themeparkinsider.com/flume/201906/6810/

and 7 hours queues for Hogsmeade and Escape from Gringotts when they opened at Universals. The answer to how would Disney handle the demand for Star Wars Land appeared to be very well. Robert Niles commented, "But for now, Disney has made the claim that eight-hour queues are not the sign of a theme park's success"[88].

This strategy of encouraging long queues for new rides perhaps goes back to Disney's original Star Wars themed attraction, Stars Tours at Disneyland, which opened in 1987. After Disneyland first opened (1955) Disney spent a lot of time and money on expanding the park, and this culminated with It's a Small World (1966), Pirates of the Caribbean (1967) and Haunted Mansion (1969). After Haunted Mansion Disneyland spent a lot less on new rides as they focused on their 'Florida Project', which opened in 1971. Disneyland did start to receive more investment with Space Mountain (1977) and Big Thunder Mountain (1979). Investment in Disneyland then subsided again as they focused on Epcot, which opened in 1982. When Michael Eisner became CEO, Disneyland's investment had been limited as they'd focused on expanding Disney World, and all the rides based on Disney films used properties that now seemed quite old. Meanwhile, regional American parks like Six Flags Magic Mountain were offering more thrilling rides. While Disney didn't want to go down the white knuckle route, they did want to compete with parks like Magic Mountain for the teenage audience.

Eisner's solution was to add a package of rides, starting with the 4D cinema Captain EO, which starred Michael Jackson and opened in 1986. It continued with the Star Wars themed simulator Star Tours (1987) and Splash Mountain (1989). All three were designed to appeal to an older audience than the Fantasy Land type attractions.

The lead imaginer Tony Baxter told Theme Park Insider, "He [Disney's CEO Michael Eisner] was a brilliant marketeer. I remember that when we talked about if we should have six cabs or four at Disneyland [on Star Tours] because the space there is so limited — it would have been very, very hard to add two more, he says, 'no, let's open with four. It'll be the first Star Wars, the only one for a while, and I think the idea of a line going all the way out the park and people lined up on Harbor Blvd. is good.' It really says that Disneyland has changed — it's reinventing itself and I've got to see this change. So we did open that way, and that did happen and they were panicked, so they left Disneyland open for three days (laughs), which was pretty cool and everybody was happy. We let the press interview at the exit of the ride and after waiting five hours or whatever it was, and it was incredibly positive"[89].

Massive queues for new rides on their opening day has been a continuing theme. A 6 hour queue was reported for X at Magic Mountain[90], although

88   Ibid.

89   Theme Park Insider interview with Disney Legend and Imagineer Tony Baxter: part one, Robert Niles, Theme Park Insider, https://www.themeparkinsider.com/flume/201311/3760/

90   User JCxHC4Life, What is the longest queue time in theme park history?, Ultimate Roller Coaster, https://www.ultimateroller-coaster.com/forums/roller-coasters-theme-parks/165123

another enthusiast heard it didn't go beyond 3 hours. Someone recalled waiting for 4 hours to ride Top Thrill Dragster at Cedar Point, when it only ran 3 of its 6 trains and went down multiple times due to technical difficulties. Apparently, Millennium Force at Cedar Point opened with just one train and had a queue 4 to 5 hours long. Often reports of horrendously long waits on the opening day of new rides also include the rides running at reduced capacity and with regular down time. User Coaster Fanatic says they waited 8 hours for Flight of Fear, which ran one train on opening day.

Opening day waits, and waits in general, do tend to get disputed. From my own experiences, I've frequently encountered guests adamant that they waited far longer than they could have done. On opening day parks often aren't quite sure how long the wait is, so border on overestimating them. Nonetheless, even if the opening day lines aren't as long as they're sometimes reported, they have built up a certain kind of reputation.

The question for parks is do you encourage these long waits to show how popular your new ride is? Or do you try to keep them as short as possible in the interests of good customer service?

When Sea World Antonio opened Texas Stingray in 2020, it opened on Saturday/Sunday February 22nd/23rd for annual pass holders and the following weekend for regular visitors[91]. This is both a strategy for selling more annual passes, but also for spreading out the surge of guests.

At Merlin's UKs park they do an annual pass holders preview before each season. The weekend before the park opens for the regular guests it opens for annual passholders. The first time they did this it wasn't very successful from a guest experience perspective. The parks were flooded with annual passholders keen to visit the park after the winter when they'd been closed for four months. Many passholders went to the preview expecting the parks to be quiet, because they weren't open to regular visitors. So many people visited expecting the parks to be quiet that they were anything but. This combined with all the inexperienced staff at the start of the season left them struggling to cope. Merlin still does the annual pass holder previews, but quickly learned from their initial problems. Annual pass holders can now attend the previews for free, but they must book a ticket in advance and tickets are strictly limited.

Back in the nineties the major British parks tended to get celebrities to open their new rides. Drayton Manor was famous for it. Splash Canyon was opened by Noel Edmunds, Apocalypse was opened by B*Witched, Maelstrom was opened by Hear Say and G Force was opened by G4. Theme parks have tended to move away from these kinds of celebrity openings for a number of reasons. They're expensive and from a marketing perspective they can overshadow the ride itself. You want the newspaper reports to focus on the new attraction and not on the celebrity opening it. Particularly if the celebrity isn't relevant to the attraction. It's a bit different when it's the cast of

---

91   Opening schedule for Texas Stingray announced, Theme Park Insider, https://www.themeparkinsider.com/flume/202002/7254/

Harry Potter opening the Wizarding World of Harry Potter, or Aerosmith doing a hand print ceremony before taking the first ride on Rock 'N Roller Coaster[92]. But often the celebrity has little relevance to the attraction and an endorsement from someone who's been paid to open the ride doesn't carry much weight, even if you are one of their fans. There is another reason, which is why I'm mentioning it in this book. If a celebrity opens a new ride, you have two groups of fans: the celebrity's and the theme park's. Even without a celebrity the opening day for a major new ride can be busy and chaotic. Why make it more so?

There is still some divided opinion in the industry about whether we want the queue on opening day to be really long to gather headlines, and show how popular the new ride is, or whether we want to control the queue length as much as possible to improve the guest experience and make sure the reviews are positive and not one of anticlimax. Overall, there has been a shift and parks are increasingly trying to avoid a mad queue on opening day as much as they realistically can. It's what Disney might call 'the every guest matters' approach. When we encourage a really long queue to give our marketing team a photo opportunity, we're arguably treating our paying guests like extras in an advert.

Weather Proofing

Pretty much anywhere, a theme park will be quieter when the weather's poor. How big a problem this is, will depend on the climate where the park is, and the culture there. When Disney were planning Disneyland Paris, they based their projections partly on what happened at Tokyo Disney, which had been their first park outside the United States. Tokyo Disneyland opened in 1983 and Disneyland Paris opened in 1992.

The Japanese seemed to be relatively hardy to poor weather, and although Japan has harsher winters than France, Tokyo Disney was relatively busy all year round. When Disneyland Paris opened, the fall in visitors during the wetter, colder periods was bigger than they'd anticipated. This was one of many factors that led to Disneyland Paris's well publicised financial problems.

Not only does weather proofing help you to distribute your visitors more evenly through the season, but assuming you are a seasonal theme park (and not open every day of the year), it also helps to extend the season. Many theme parks on both sides of the Atlantic are now opening for Christmas events of varying scales, and also opening earlier in the year, for example British theme parks are increasingly opening in mid-February for half term (a 9 day long British school holiday). Parks are using events to pull people in at these times of year when the weather is less hospitable. It makes the job easier when the park is naturally weather proofed.

In terms of distributing visitors relatively evenly across your calendar, the optimum situation would be to have a reasonably steady climate and a

---

92   Rock 'N Roller Coaster grand opening, WDW Magic, https://www. wdwmagic.com/attractions/rock-n-roller-coaster-starring-aerosmith/ news/29jul1999-rock-n-roller-coaster-grand-opening-day.htm

culture where people carry on visiting outdoor attractions even when it's cold and wet. The worst case, would be a climate with a lot of bad weather, and a culture of people staying indoors when it's miserable outside. However, a park can attempt to make itself more friendly to guests visiting when the weather's bad. By doing this, over time visitors will learn that even if they visit the park when it's wet and cold, they'll still have a good time.

Weather Proofing by Design

Things to think about when you're looking at weather proofing a theme park:

- How many of the rides are water rides, and how wet do they get you? Some modern water rides can be made wetter of drier depending on the weather that day. Chiapas at Phantasialand does this using electro-magnets under water that determine how quickly the boats slow down after the main drop. Haystack People Driers are coin operated booths guests can stand in, that use a combination of heaters and air to help guests to warm up and dry off quicker.

- It's important to have plenty of nice indoor eating areas, perhaps including a bar. Just because it's raining and people want to escape inside, doesn't mean they've got endless appetites for food. My favourite theme park bars include the Rose and Crown at Epcot, where the Hat Lady entertains guests with her piano playing, singing and audience participation, and the O'Mackay's pub at Europa Park, where drinkers are often entertained by Irish songs and jokes in between.

- Indoor queue lines help, but there can be a trade off. A well themed indoor queue is ideal (Europa Park really excel at these), but not every park has a budget for them. If you end up with lots of indoor switch-back style queues (cattle grids), that aren't themed, then it's not the best experience. They keep people dry when it's raining and shaded when it's hot, and the indoor queueing area may also be heated or air conditioned, but visually they're not appealing places to wait in line. Queue design and 'hygiene factors' such as weather proofing will be an interesting subject for a future book.

- Undercover stations will be appreciated by the guests boarding the ride, as well as the staff.

- An undercover brake run will keep the riders dry if the ride breaks down (which is more likely in the rain), or if it takes a while to load the train in the station.

- Generally having indoor attractions (walk through exhibits, aquariums, museums, live shows, dark rides) helps.

- Some parks have entire indoor areas. These include Wuze Town at Phantasialand, Arthur in the Minimoy's Kingdom at Europa Park and Holiday Indoors at Holiday Park. All three parks are in Germany. Creating an appealing indoor area is difficult. They can feel sterile. If the area has a glass roof and plenty of natural daylight, then you can have plants in the indoor area, although they will need watering. If you have a dark indoor area then water features, rockwork, wood and artificial plants can all be used to create a more natural feel. If there are too many hard surfaces then sound bounces around making it noisy when the area's busy. Soft furnishings and sound absorbent material on the ceiling mitigate this.

Exposed spotlights give the environment an artificial feel. It's best if you can find light sources that naturally fit the area, such as lanterns, festoon lighting and twinkling LEDs embedded into the environment. Although painting the walls of the building is the cheapest option, it also looks cheap. If you can, build a 3D façade in front of the real wall, and have light shining under doors or through frosted windows and sound coming from speakers behind the façade. This creates a powerful illusion that there's life beyond the façade. The cheapest shape for a building tends to be a rectangle, but if an indoor area feels like a box or warehouse, then it doesn't make a great environment. You either want a building with an irregular shape – perhaps centred around a dome – or to break up a rectangular building. Holiday Indoors does this. The area features a Zierer family coaster called Tabaluga's Achterbahn (Tabaluga is a cartoon dragon and 'achterbahn' is German for roller coaster). The building is divided into two halves with the divide being an irregular shape. The main body of the area including the station for Tabaluga's Achterbahn is on one side of the divide and the majority of the roller coaster is on the other side. Therefore, the building itself is a rectangle, but neither half of the building is a neat rectangle. The worst criticism for an indoor area is that it feels like a warehouse/barn/shopping mall.

- Having awnings or some kind of arcade/roof down the side of an area so that guests can move around the park without getting too wet.
- Having good drainage around the park, so that guests don't get wet wading across puddles.
- Choosing rides that aren't affected too quickly by wet weather. Generally, rides that are powered using tyres close very quickly when the weather turns wet, because the rubber loses traction. Colorado Adventure at Phantasialand has six car trains, but when it's wet, they close off the back two cars to make the trains lighter, so they don't slip on the lift hills. Some coasters enclose their tyre driven lift hills, including Incredible Hulk at Islands of Adventure. Good ride availability is really important for reducing queues. We dip into the subject, including how rain and wind can lower ride availability. I hope to cover this more in a future book.

When theme parks have indoor areas, like Wuze Town (Phantasialand) or the Minimoys Kingdom (Europa Park), they understandably tend to end up on the edge of the park. If you put it in a central location you either have to theme the whole exterior (which is expensive) or you have an unsightly warehouse in the middle of your park. In the case of Phantasialand and Europa Park they've also put their indoor areas near housing outside the park, where it'd be harder to get planning permission for outdoor attractions. However, there are advantages to having a central indoor area of attraction, as if it does start raining people don't want to walk too far to get to something indoors. In the case of Europa Park and Phantasialand they do have a lot of indoor attractions around the park, so it isn't really an issue. When you're designing a park, it is worth looking at how far guests in different areas have to go to get to something indoors.

The challenge with tyres

If there's something less fun than going on a ride in the rain, it might be tramping past a load of closed signs. I want to go a little further into the design of rides, and why some attractions are more weather resistant than others. Let's start off with my point about tyres losing traction when they're wet. We're going to discuss the reasons for using tyres and the alternatives. Next, we'll look at the problems caused by high winds and how we can design our way around it. This section might be a little confusing if readers don't already have some knowledge about theme park engineering. I've decided to include it, because it shows how theme parks can face complex challenges with weatherproofing, but that there are solutions. I could have made the issues clearer with diagrams, but I suspect that readers will either already have some understanding of how roller coasters work, or they won't be interested in this next section anyway.

Most roller coasters have chain lifthills. Some coasters have tyre driven lifts, often because the tyres are quieter. They might also use tyre drives to get around bends. Manufacturer Schwarzkopf[93] did develop a curved chain lift which was used on Jetline (Gröna Lund) and Knightmare (Camelot), but chain lifts generally go in a straight line. Tyres are also used on flat rides such as observation wheels, pirate ships and frisbees. For example, on a swinging pirate ship you have a big tyre that spins, and as it rubs against the underside of the hull, it pushes the boat back and forth.

The downside is that when the tyres get wet the trains slip, meaning trains have to be sent with empty cars to lower the weight, and in some case the ride can't run at all. This lowers the throughputs, the ride availability, and makes the park less appealing to visit on a wet day. Let's look at the problem and the solution.

One of the reasons that roller coasters such as Colorado Adventure (Phantasialand) and Thirteen (Alton Towers) use tyre driven lift hills, is to do with the noise. Phantasialand and Alton Towers are parks in sensitive areas with nearby housing. Both parks have found ingenious ways to minimise the disturbance to their neighbours. In the case of Phantasialand, quite a few of their rides are indoors, including Mystery Castle (a 65 metre tall shot tower) and Wuze Town (an entire area with two dueling coasters).

---

93   A German ride manufacturer created by the legendary Anton
Schwarzkopf. They built various rides, but they're best known for
their roller coasters. They were active from 1957-1995.

They have also built massive themed sound berms around the Klugheim and Rookburgh areas. Alton Towers has built Oblivion (a 180ft tall roller coaster, where half the main drop is buried underground in a massive tunnel), and Nemesis (a roller coaster built largely below ground level in a crater, blasted out from the rock). The highest pieces of track on Galactica and Rita are painted a different colour to the rest of the ride, to camouflage in with the surrounding woodland.

Thirteen is a roller coaster with a freefall drop and a backwards section. Alton Towers were able to get planning permission for Thirteen, partly because it replaced the noisy Corkscrew, and Thirteen promised to be a lot quieter. Timothy Cox describes how quiet Thirteen's lift is on his website Roller Coaster Philosophy, "This is possibly the quietest lift I've ever been on, the tire drive mechanisms chosen for that very quality (they even trigger in small 'blocks' as the train approaches and shut off as soon as we pass by so they aren't unnecessarily wasting energy)"[94]. Colorado Adventure uses a tyre driven lift hill for the same reason. Other mine trains built by the same manufacturer (Vekoma) don't. Big Thunder Mountain (Disney), Calamity Mine (Walibi Belgium) and Mammut (Gardaland) all have chain lifthills.

Why are tyre driven lift hills quieter than traditional chain lift hills? Chain lift hills have something called anti-roll backs. This is a 'redundant safety system', but it's also quite noisy. A redundant safety system means it's only needed if another system fails. Anti-roll backs are what make the 'clack, clack' noise as you go up the lifthill, and they catch the train if something goes wrong with the lift mechanism. It could be that the chain breaks, that the train becomes disconnected from the chain, or that the motor goes wrong and starts to run backwards. In all of these situations, the anti-roll backs would catch the train, so that it doesn't run backwards down the hill, potentially crashing into the train behind, or going around a tight bend far too quickly. Tyre driven lift hills don't tend to have anti-roll backs. These lift hills are made up of lots of tyres, each connected to its own motor. If one tyre or motor fails, then the trains can't roll backwards, because there are so many other motors and tyres pushing it.

So, the advantage of a tyre driven lift hill is that it's quieter, and the advantage of a chain driven lift hill is that it isn't affected by wet weather. What if we could find a new design of lift hill that combines the advantages of both designs? Disney Imagineering were perhaps the first company to design a silent anti roll back system to use with a chain lift hill. They used it on Expedition Everest at Animal Kingdom (Disney World, Orlando). This gave them a roller coaster that was very quiet and wasn't affected by wet weather. Why did Disney come up with this?

When Animal Kingdom opened in 1998, they had a massive 110 acres safari called Kilimanjaro Safaris. At the time the whole of Magic Kingdom was only 107 acres. But aside from the safari, the park was small and only

94   Alton Towers (part 2), Roller Coaster Philosophy, https:// www.rollercoasterphilosophy.com/tag/thirteen/

featured one other major ride: Countdown to Extinction. The following year a second 'E ticket' ride opened, Kali River Expedition.

In its early days Animal Kingdom didn't feel like a complete park. Particularly as one of its planned areas, Beastly Kingdom, had been cut from the final design to prevent a cost overrun. It needed another headline attraction, and this eventually came in the form of Expedition Everest (opened 2006). Expedition Everest is notable for its scale and the high quality of its theming, but it also deployed a lot of innovative and state of the art technology. One of these was a silent anti-roll back system, because the Imagineers thought that the 'clack clack' noise would detract from the peaceful atmosphere of going up into the Himalayas.

The system is explained by Stephen Mraz, "Guests first climb aboard a steam-powered train for a trip through a Himalayan mountain pass. But that illusion would be shattered if they heard the familiar sound of a pawl clickety-clacking over anti-rollback teeth as the coaster ascends the first hill. To get rid of that telltale sound, Disney has a special wheel on the underside of the coaster that only touches and turns on a rail on the first uphill section. The wheel generates magnetic eddy currents that lift the pawl and keep it from knocking against the anti-rollback teeth"[95]. I'm not aware of this particular system being used on other rides - perhaps because Disney holds the patent.

Expedition Everest was built by Dutch company Vekoma. Since then at least two other manufacturers have developed silent anti roll back systems that are used with chain lift hills. German manufacturer Gerstlauer used one on The Smiler at Alton Towers (opened in 2013), which even has a vertical chain lift. German manufacturer Mack used one on Can Can Coaster at Europa Park (opened in 2018). Can Can Coaster has a spiral lift rather than a chain lift, where the front of the train has a rod sticking out to the side. It gets pushed up by a big rotating column in the centre, using a similar principle to an Archimedes Screw. Zamperla later used a similar system on their Volare flying coasters. However, Mack's silent anti-roll back system could just as easily be applied to other kinds of lifthill.

All three manufacturers have achieved the same effect using different approaches. Expedition Everest and The Smiler have different systems involving magnets, while Can Can Coaster has a mechanical system involving a little piece of metal gently sliding over a rail. If a train starts to run backwards, the piece of metal gets knocked forward causing the anti-roll back to drop. B&M haven't used a silent anti roll back, but on some of their coasters the anti-roll back dog is made of plastic rather than metal. Whilst steel is harder wearing, plastic creates less noise.

Another downside with tyre driven lift hills is that if the train connects with them too fast, it wears the tyres out quickly. This is mainly a problem for mid-course lift hills where the train can engage with them at some speed.

95   Engineering Expedition Everest, complete with a yeti, Stephen Mraz, Machine Design, https://www.machinedesign.com/markets/recreation/article/21829971/engineering-expedition-everest-complete-with-a-yeti

In the case of Colorado Adventure there's a set of trim brakes[96] before the second and third lift to reduce the speed. Thirteen has a set of magnetic trim brakes on the first drop so that the train doesn't reach the second lift hill too quickly. The downside is that they now have to have a minimum of 18 guests on each train so that the train has enough mass to make it round the circuit. On quiet days they only run one train to make sure they can get the 18 riders, meaning a queue can build up.

As you can tell, creating quiet lifthills that can run in heavy rain has been a technical challenge. There are other engineering obstacles around weatherproofing rides. Often these issues are too complicated to explain to most guests. Your typical visitor isn't going to be thinking about planning restrictions, public relations, redundant safety systems, friction and all the other things that those of us working in the industry have to think about. And to be fair, they shouldn't have to be thinking about those kinds of problem. Our visitors want to immerse themselves in the world's we've created and the stories we're telling.

Other difficult weather conditions

When it comes to weather proofing, attendance can spike significantly when there's a dry forecast. However, there are other types of inclement weather that also cause problems, including high wind speeds. Some rides, particularly taller rides, have to close in strong wind. If people are expecting high wind, and they know that this closes a lot of rides, then people may wait for a calmer day. On top of this, when rides are closed, the queues get longer elsewhere.

The relationship between the number of rides and a park's capacity isn't as strong as you might imagine. Later in this book we will discuss this in relation to Hong Kong Disneyland. In its opening year Hong Kong Disneyland had just 10 rides, but a capacity of 28,000. There are various strategies used by Hong Kong Disneyland to accommodate so many people. It's clear that the park was well weather proofed and designed for strong ride availability. When we look at the most attended parks around the world they don't always have as many rides as we might imagine, but they do have strong scores for ride uptime.

Aside from simply building lower rides that won't be affected so much by wind (and using launched technology, such as magnetic and hydraulic launches, a lower coaster doesn't have to be a slower coaster), you can also build the coaster going into the wind rather than across it. At theme parks next to the sea or a large lake, wind can come in off the water causing ride closures. This is an issue with The Big One (Blackpool Pleasure Beach), Odyssey (Fantasy Island) and several coasters as Cedar Point (Magnum XL, Millennium Force and Top Thrill Dragster).

Often these kinds of theme park build their big coasters running along the water front, which creates impressive visuals both on and off the ride. But it does mean that the wind can catch the whole length of the train as it runs

---

96   Trim brakes *trim* the speed, meaning they slow the train down rather than stopping it.

along parallel to the water. If the coaster is turned around 90 degrees, then the wind coming off the water only catches the front or back of the train, rather than the side, which has a much larger surface area.

Similar to high winds, low temperatures can also cause challenges by making the rides run slower. The trick here is to have excess energy in the train, so that even if it's very cold the train can make it around the track. This can involve having trim brakes so that when it's hot the train doesn't go so fast it becomes unpleasant or damages the ride, but when it's cold the trims have little impact. At Liseberg they designed the B&M dive machine Valkyria to be able to run in up to minus six degree Celsius (twenty-one Fahrenheit). It has a top speed of 65 mph, and heavy trains with more potential energy than lighter trains would have[97]. This means it can run during the winter for their Christmas event, whereas the classic Schwarzkopf Lisebergbanen can't open during the winter. There are several points in the ride where the trains go very slowly, and would stall in the cold winter temperatures.

Mack's launched coaster Blue Fire reportedly closes when the temperature drops below five degrees. Taron at Phantasialand can apparently run in temperatures as low as minus 10 degrees. A key difference is that Blue Fire has moments where the train travels fairly slowly, such as the first turn, where a train could roll back if it's going too slowly. Taron's speed never drops that low, meaning that even if the ride is running a lot slower than normal, the trains will still make it around the track.

Silver Star at Europa Park has a lot of insulation in its maintenance shed where they keep the trains. Wooden boards drop over the track behind the shutters to limit the cold air coming through, and there are several heaters. All of this is designed so that when the trains are bought out in the morning, they are warm. I've seen storage sheds at other parks where they leave the heating on overnight, but there's no insulation, and the trains are still pretty cold when they're bought out.

These are big design decisions that are hard to change once they've been made, and weather proofing can require huge capital investments. But the impact on guest satisfaction is arguably worth it. However, there are smaller operational changes that can be made quickly and cheaply.

How many rides run in wet weather and how much of the park is undercover are clearly important factors in weather proofing your business. Other changes can be subtler. If a park has a dark/grey colour palette and the sky is also dark and grey, then the park can end up with a depressing atmosphere.

I'm not advocating that parks paint everything in bright bilious colours. These tend to be associated with children's areas and when overused they can look tacky and garish. I'm also not adverse to dark, gritty themes. One of my favourite theme parks is Alton Towers, which has done dark and gritty very well on rides like Nemesis, Oblivion, Hex and Thirteen. There's a happy medium, but too many dark colours can be fine on a sunny day when the

---

97   Nick's ERT #55 Liseberg CEO Andreas Anderson, The season pass podcast, http://seasonpasspodcast.libsyn.com/nicks-ert-55-liseberg-with-ceo-andreas-andersen

sky's bright blue, but when the weather's dank and grey, the whole park can feel depressing.

It's not just about painting things in bright colours. Particularly if this ends up looking over the top, or incongruous with the setting you're trying to create. Sometimes something doesn't have to be bright, just a bit brighter. At Disney the rock work tends to have a reddish colour rather than a greyish colour, partly for this reason. Over time the ultra violet light in the sun rays fade paint, making areas duller than the designers intended. Some colours are naturally more resistant to fading, UV resistant varnish and two pack paint, are all part of the defence against fading. Nonetheless, without a continuing maintenance programme, paint becomes faded, and on a grey day the park becomes particularly depressing.

There has been a trend in the theme park industry to move away from real world settings towards fantasy themes. There are all kinds of reasons for this, but it does make it easier for parks to use a brighter colour scheme. If you're creating a real location, then the inclination is to use a realistic colour palette to make it more authentic. If you're creating a fantasy world, then you have much more freedom to pick the colours that will create the best guest experience. If you think that bright colours will create a more cheerful atmosphere, particularly when the weather's bad or in the winter, then you're free to use them.

If bright paints don't feel natural, flowers might. Evergreen shrubs are much cheaper to maintain than flowers, which need a skilled horticultural team. But colourful flowers do create a happy atmosphere. At Disney and Europa Park the flowers are replaced four times a year. In the winter, when the climate simply isn't appropriate for flowers, Europa Park uses dyed heather to add some colour to the flower beds.

Weather Proofing by Operations

We've talked about the design of the park, including undercover areas and rides that are less affected by adverse weather. We're now going to look at how the park's operated and marketed. These aren't alternatives to making those capital investments. However, they do make sure that if you do invest in weatherproofing, you get the most out of it.

Parks often like advance bookings. If you're booking your tickets more than 7 days before your visit, you're less likely to know what the weather's going to be like. More parks are adding accommodation, including hotels, lodges, campsites (traditional and 'glamping[98]'). Some parks give guests a significant discount for booking a specific day more than seven days in advance. However, driving guests towards days with wet weather, without making efforts to weather proof the park and ensure they still have a good time, will lead to unhappy guests, poor reviews and low satisfaction ratings. Ultimately, the goal of efficiency and spreading guests more evenly through the season is

---

98   Glamping is a mixture of 'glamourous' and 'camping'. It's trying to give people a sense of the outdoors, but in an environment that contains the luxuries and home comforts of a hotel.

to improve guest satisfaction. Using advanced booking discounts to guarantee visits on a day when they're going to have a miserable time isn't helpful.

Liseberg has a similar but slightly unusual strategy to encourage guests to book their visit in advance. Rather than offering a discount, if you book your visit in advance, you get four express passes for that date, allowing you to skip the queues on four attractions.

The more rides close during adverse weather, the less likely guests are to visit when the weather might be poor. It also means that when the weather's poor the capacity of the park is significantly reduced. Once you've weather proofed your park, you then need to promote these features. Given the British climate, it's unsurprising that many of the parks in the UK have a put a particular emphasis on their wet weather options. Flambards theme park (Cornwall, UK) has a tab at the top of their home page listing all the undercover attractions[99].

Similarly, Crealy (Devon, UK) divides their rides and attractions into 'outdoor fun and indoor fun'. The Big Sheep (Devon, UK) has the following large logo at the top of their homepage.

---

99   Homepage, Flambards official website, https://www.flambards.co.uk/

If you're going to make a claim like 'All Weather Attraction', you need to have the attractions to back it up. The Big Sheep qualifies their promise with the following explanation: "The BIG Sheep is a great day out whatever the weather! Devon can have unpredictable weather but when you're looking for things to do in Devon, The BIG Sheep should be top of your list.

Almost all of our attractions are either indoors or under cover, meaning you can enjoy our shows, attractions and rides even if it's raining. Our Rampage Rollercoaster cannot run during wet weather for safety reasons and The Twister will not be operated during high winds for your safety. Our reception team will let you know whether there are any unforeseen closures when you arrive."[100]

The Milky Way is another family theme park located just a 7.7 mile drive from The Big Sheep. They make a similar claim on their website, "At The Milky Way we've got attractions to suit all ages, whatever the weather. With over 110,000 sq ft of indoor fun & acres of outdoor activities, The Milky Way theme park is the biggest all weather, family day out in North Devon and it's located near Clovelly, in between Bideford and Bude just 5 miles from the North Cornwall border!". They use the following banner in their advertising[101]:

In 2020, Trip Advisor's algorithm ranked The Milky Way as the 16th best theme park in the world[102].

Toverland in the Netherlands originally opened in 2001 as an almost entirely indoor theme park. The owners realised that there wasn't a lot for families to do in the winter or when the weather was bad, so they spotted a gap in the market for an indoor theme park. Initially small, the centrepiece was a 1,050 ft long custom designed Vekoma roller skater (roller coaster) called Toos Express with a top speed of 37mph.

In 2004, the park invested 15 million euros in a massive expansion with a second indoor hall featuring a Mack log flume (Back Stroke) and a Weigand powered bobsled (Maximus Blitz Bahn). Both of these start off in the hall, but do extend outside. They also added their first completely open-air roller coaster, the world's first Vekoma booster bike, in the same year. Since then Toverland

---

100   The Big Sheep official website, https://www.the-bigsheep.co.uk/plan-your-day/things-to-do/

101   Homepage, The Milky Way Adventure Park, https://www.themilkyway.co.uk/

102   Top 25 amusement parks – world, Trip Advisor, https://www.tripad-visor.co.uk/TravelersChoice-Attractions-cAmusementParks-g1

has substantially expanded into a predominantly outdoor theme park, including the GCI wooden coaster Troy (2007), a Mack spinning coaster and Hafema river rapids (2012) and a B&M wing coaster Fenix and dark ride Merlin's Quest (2018). By 2018 they were getting around 800,000 visitors a year, making them one of the significant European theme parks. Nonetheless, it still helps, that they have two large indoor areas, so guests know that if they visit Toverland and the weather's poor, there are areas where they can still have fun.

I've come across a few small amusement parks offering free hot drinks (tea, coffee and hot chocolate) when the temperature dips below a certain level (for example 5 degrees centigrade). At Disney they offer free hot chocolate at Mickey's Christmas Party, regardless of the temperature. Hot drinks tend to have cheap ingredients with a big mark up on the cost, and if you offer them for free, rather than guests saying, "We won't go out tonight because it's cold", they might say, "Shall we visit the theme park. It's going to be cold, so we'll get free hot drinks".

You just need to make sure you can logistically deliver lots of hot drinks quickly. This could involve a self-service element (like a breakfast buffet at a hotel) and restricting it to simpler drinks (rather than speciality coffees and hot chocolates, which also have more expensive ingredients). Or you could just give everyone one free voucher for a hot drink when they arrive, if they're forecasting it to drop below a certain temperature. If you do this, I'd recommend erring on the side of generosity. For example, if the advert says you get a free hot drink on days where it's expected to go below 5 degrees, I'd hand out the vouchers on any day where the forecast predicts 7 degrees or less. That way you avoid disputes and ill feeling.

Rain checks are another option. For example, you say that if it rains for more than two hours every guest can return later in the season for free. They might need to go to guest services to claim a return ticket, or you could simply post dates on the website for tickets that are valid to return. The downside of posting dates on your website for tickets that can be re-used, is that guests could give their ticket to someone else to use rather than visiting again themselves. However, if the guests have to go to guest services, then it might involve taking photos or linking ID (identification, such as a passport or driving licence) to the ticket. This is time consuming, and if the park is busy you could have massive queues at guest services waiting to do this.

Oakwood (Wales) post on social media when they're re-issuing tickets for another visit. This communicates with the guests who are there that day. It also raises the initiative's profile to other guests who are thinking of making a visit[103].

As with the free hot drinks idea, I'd encourage parks to be generous with a rain check. For example, if the rule is two hours of rain for a free return visit and it rains for 1 hour 50 minutes, if you refuse to re-issue tickets, many guests will feel cheated. You'll get complaints and poor guest feedback.

---

103   Oakwood Theme Park official Facebook page, https://www.facebook.com/oakwoodthemepk

Similarly, you can have block out dates when the free return tickets can't be used (like a major public holiday), but if you put in too much restrictions, you'll also damage your guest relations. Service recovery and promotions can't come with too many strings attached. Customer service is about exceeding people's expectations. It's not about overpromising and underdelivering.

Rain checks work, because they encourage guests to still visit when the forecast's poor. Sometimes the weather isn't as bad as the weather station's predicted, and sometimes the forecast isn't that bad, but people don't want to risk it, if they're spending a lot of money or travelling a long way. A rain check is like an insurance policy for your guests, and encourages them to visit on a day when they might have stayed away.

Part of dealing with poor weather, is having staff with a positive 'can do' mind set. When Disneyland Paris had heavy snow cast members worked quickly and efficiently to clean it up[104]. Some staff shovelled it out the way, some used brushes to get rid of the last bits, and some had squeegees to push the water into the drains. Imagine if all the cast members had sat around in the staffroom saying, "It's snowing, we shouldn't be open". It probably helped that the park's managers were out there helping to shovel the snow.

As a park you can't help the weather, but you can help people to have fun even when the weather's poor. 'The show must go on', as they say. At this point there does seem to be some cultural differences between the United States and the UK, in that at a lot of the regional American parks it's considered acceptable to close because of bad weather, even though it is safe to open. Whereas in the UK the assumption is that even if the weather's terrible and the park's clearly going to lose money, it's bad form to shut the park to save money. Perhaps the difference is partly because a lot more of the regional British parks have accommodation, so you have people staying on site who are expecting to have a park to visit. Having worked at a major UK park that opened for 200 guests, I personally like this every guest counts mentality, and you could argue that

---

104   Towers Street discussion, https://towersstreet.com/talk/
threads/disneyland-paris-general-discussion.2947/page-23

if the park knows they will open whatever the weather, it encourages them to add more indoor areas and attractions to give people things to do when it's wet. However, I do also respect the American tradition. Different countries have different tax rates, wage levels, employment laws and expectations. It's not always fair to have the same expectations in every country.

The service side of weather proofing

When it comes to customer service, it's generally better to proactively prevent problems, than to rely on good 'service recovery'. Service recovery is when you try to turn around a bad experience and win back an unhappy customer. But what happens if the weather's bad and your customers are unhappy? If guests go away and tell people about their miserable visit, then in the long run fewer people will want to visit your park when the weather might be poor. The upshot of this, is that in the long run everyone tries to visit when they think the weather's going to be good, and you end up with these big surges in demand that are hard to cope with. In this chapter I want to talk about how we should respond to customers who are angry because the weather's bad.

I don't want to dwell too much on service recovery, because it's such a big topic and this book's going to be long enough without it. Customer service deserves a book on its own, and several decent books have already been written on the subject. The Wonderful World of Customer Service at Disney by J Jeff Kober is one of the best guides to service recovery in the theme park industry. I will write a little on the specific case of guests who are unhappy because it's raining. If a guest is having a bad time because of the weather, you don't want them venting to everyone about it.

Weather proofing the park, rain checks and free hot drinks are important parts of the arsenal against bad weather, but what do you do when there's an irate guest standing in front of you? I've heard quite a few employees shrug their shoulders and say, "We can't help the weather". It's not very empathetic.

Read any book about customer service and the advice is, "Let them talk uninterrupted. Ask questions to make sure you fully understand the context around the complaint. Ask them if they've had any other issues in their day. Repeat the complaint back to them to check you've understood it. Try to understand not just what's happened, but how it's made them feel. Apologise. Tell them how the company uses guest feedback to improve the attraction for future customers". I've never read a book about customer service that tells you to shrug and say that you can't help the weather.

At Disney they always tell staff to make sure they've really understood the question. The classic example is that when a guest asks, "What time's the 3 O'clock parade?" the right answer isn't to smugly say, "3 O'clock". It's to say, "Well, the parade starts at 3 o'clock, but it'll take about ten minutes to get to this part of the parade route". When guests complain about the weather, that might not actually be the real reasoning behind their complaint.

Here's another example. A theme park has a 'rain check'. The policy is that if you book your tickets in advance and it rains continuously for more than two hours, you get complimentary tickets to come back for free. This benefit is heavily advertised. It rains for 90 minutes. Stops for 10 minutes. Rains for 90 minutes. Stops for 10 minutes... The guest is complaining about how the weather's spoilt their day. The staff member shrugs and says, "Well, we can't help the weather". Clearly the customer is thinking, "Technically you don't have to give me free tickets to come back, but it'd be good customer service to. The rain's affected us a lot more than if it had rained for 2 hours and been fine for the rest of the day". When customers 'complain about the weather', it's unlikely that the weather is actually what they're complaining about. Unless they're really stupid, they do understand that the park didn't make it rain.

When a customer goes to guest services to complain about the weather, making a sarcastic or condescending comment might seem clever. But throwing out the basic guidance about dealing with complaints, won't help you develop repeat custom. You can achieve a lot more when you treat the guest with respect, and genuinely try to understand why they're unhappy.

A lot of parks won't give guests explanations about ride closures. I totally understand why. They're worried about guests mishearing/misunderstanding problems, staff getting messages wrong... etc. Given the nature of social media and journalism, routine ride closures can get blown out of proportion and twisted into something that they're not. On the other side, guests can calm down pretty quickly when they're given a straight answer. When the pirate ship closes as soon as it starts raining and the guest complains, which response do you think is more likely to satisfy them:

Response 1: "All our rides are subject to availability. It's in the small print"

Response 2: "I do apologise. I know it is disappointing when a ride closes as soon as it starts raining. Basically, the ride's powered by a big spinning tyre underneath the boat. When it's wet the tyre becomes slippy and there isn't enough traction for it to grip the boat properly. The engineers have tried different tyres with more tread and different rubber compounds, but unfortunately this kind of ride just can't run in the rain. We'll keep monitoring it, and as soon as the ride's able to run again it'll re-open. I can recommend some undercover attractions if you want...".

At a lot of parks, a ride operator wouldn't be allowed to give the second response, because they're not allowed to give technical information about the rides. If rides close when it starts raining, guests might just think that the staff don't want to get wet or that they can't be bothered. If a customer has lost control of themselves and is shouting and swearing then there's not a lot you can do. But the majority of guests will at least listen when someone tries to give them an honest explanation for what's happening.

On this note, customer service involves service recovery when things have gone wrong, but it also involves managing people expectations. It might seem obvious to the staff and theme park enthusiasts that if the weather deteriorates some of the rides are going to close, but for someone who doesn't visit theme parks very often, it might not be obvious at all.

Guests may find themselves thinking, "If someone had told me that the main roller coaster would close if it got windier, I'd have ridden it in the morning", "If I'd known this ride closed in high winds, I wouldn't have joined the queue... why didn't someone warn me?". This is why when you're dealing with complaints you should ask questions and make sure you've properly understood what it is that they're unhappy about. When staff immediately quip, "We can't stop it raining", it completely dodges the chance to learn from a guest and understand their frustration.

Once a ride has closed because of adverse weather, the guests are thinking, "should I wait for it to re-open or go or should I try something else?". The more you keep guests updated the less frustrated they will get. For example, "Ladies and gentlemen, we closed ten minute ago because it was too windy. Since then the wind speed has carried on increasing, so it looks like we'll be closed for a while". That seems a bit better than not saying anything for twenty minutes and then without warning asking everyone to leave the queue. This can be difficult, because at some parks the staff don't know themselves what's going on. A guest asks an employee when the ride will re-open. The employee responds, "I don't know. I just have to wait for a phone call from the manager".

I was talking to lady who works in customer services at a theme park. It had been raining all day. She said to me, "Neil, you won't believe how many people came in to complain about the weather"

"I bet I can believe it", I said. "What did you say to them?"

"Well, there's not much that we could say. We can't help the weather, I said. We didn't make it rain"

"Oh, right. And what did they say?"

"Well, they huffed and puffed. Told us that they wouldn't come back, and then stormed out the room. It's silly, really."

I was talking to her again a few weeks later. It had been a hot sunny summer day. "Neil, you won't believe how many people came in today to complain about the queues".

"I bet I can believe it", I said. "How long were they?"

"Well, you know how it is. Three hours for the biggest rides"

"That is very long. What did you say to them?"

"Well, there's not much we could say to them. The queues are really long because we're very busy. You've chosen to come on the same day as everyone else. I don't know why people come here when they know the park's going to be really busy."

"What did the customers say?"

"Oh, they weren't happy. They huffed and puffed. Told us that they wouldn't come back, and then stormed out the room. It's silly, really"

A few years later the park closed down. According to the press release, they'd had falling visitor numbers and were no longer a viable business. Hmm, it's silly, really.

The aim is to make visiting your theme park less of a lottery, and to reassure guests that they can have a good experience whatever the weather. The more we consider how different parks deal with poor weather, the more we realise that there are a lot of different approaches to it. And that is partly why some parks have a more uneven spread of visitors than others. The more you weather proof your business, the less you're leaving things down to chance.

Broadening your demographic: appealing to older guests

Earlier, we discussed how American restaurants balanced their books after prohibition and the Wall Street Crash by broadening their audience. Children's menus and Early Bird offers bought in people who hadn't previously visited restaurants. Now restaurants would be busy at lunch time with more working-class adults, pensioners would eat in the afternoon, families would come in the early evening and adult only groups would eat there later in the evening. Theme parks and amusement parks might have thrived off a relatively narrow demographic when people paid separately for individual rides, but it doesn't necessarily work under the pay one price ride all day model. Like the restaurant industry, the theme park industry needs to bring in groups who might not traditionally visit a theme park, but who will come at times when the theme park is otherwise quiet.

A good example of a park that had broadened its demographic is Liseberg (Sweden). Liseberg opened in 1923. It's famously unsentimental about its rides, and has little qualms about replacing older rides with more modern rides. It occupies 42 acres in the city of Gothenburg, and about half the park is on the side of a mountain. Lisberg is well known for its lighting, concerts and world class roller coasters. It consistently attracts over 3 million guests a year. Coasters include the double launched Helix, the wooden pre-fabricated coaster Balder and the Schwarzkopf terrain coaster Lisebergbanen. We're going to look at various changes to Liseberg that tried to even out their peaks in attendance. This included making the park less reliant on the summer holiday, and less dependent on families who were tied to school holidays.

Liseberg wasn't struggling financially when Andreas Anderson took over as CEO in 2011, however their visitor numbers had dipped. According to Anderson, visitor numbers fell by 20% between 2003 and 2013[105]. 2003 was the year that Liseberg opened their Intamin Woodie Balder, so presumably there was an attendance peak during this year. Nonetheless, Anderson was keen to restore attendance to what it had been a decade earlier. Anderson writes about the period when he took over:

"We asked ourselves a lot of questions." The answers, at times, were difficult. "We were seeing declining attendance numbers. We had to stabilize that, and it was clear we had to win back some of our guests," Andersen recalls. "When you have a company like this, that has had more or less the same management for decades, the culture is in the fabric of everything we do—it's in the walls. There was nothing wrong with that culture, but it was in need of a little shakeup."[106]

A key part of Anderson's strategy will be something that any coaster enthusiasts reading this will be already familiar with; they built the world's

---

105   Helix Coaster, August 2014, IAAPA Funworld magazine, http://www.
iaapa.org/news/funworld/funworld-magazine/helix-coaster---august-2014

106   http://www.iaapa.org/news/funworld/
funworld-magazine/cover-story---november-2017

largest Mack launched coaster, Helix. Helix features several inversions and two launches as well as an impressive location on the side of a mountain overlooking the city. The station sits on top of the mountain, and the ride starts off by dropping out of the station and into the first corkscrew, before turning a corner and hitting the first launch. This doesn't have anything to do with operational efficiency, aside from the fact that it added another major coaster alongside Balder and Lisebergbanen, and one that had a high throughput (1,350 guests an hour, according to RCDB[107]). This was achieved by running three trains, the two midcourse magnetic launches counting as block sections, and the fact the trains were quick to load, thanks to Mack's barrier free entry design[108], and the lack of seatbelts. Seatbelts have since been added.

There were three other things that Liseberg did to raise their visitor numbers and to improve their operational efficiency, that have more relevance to this section of the book. In 2015 they introduced their first Halloween event to bring in more guests at the back end of the season. They expected about 80,000 guests over the week, but ended up with over 200,000 visitors in this time[109]. In 2018 this had risen to 380,000[110]. This is a common trend in the industry, where many theme parks are now finding that October has gone from being their quietest month to one of their busiest. Halloween events both encourage people to visit more frequently, but also move visits from the peak summer season to the quiet October days.

Secondly, they expanded their Christmas event, which had been running since 2000[111]. This is another trend in the industry, with visits being moved from the main season to what used to be 'the off season' when the parks were closed. As with Halloween it might also encourage people to visit more frequently, raising their overall attendance.

Thirdly, the park shifted their brand to appeal more to thrill seekers who'd come when the kids were in school. Although the park certainly wasn't turning its back on the family market. Part of this strategy involved a new logo, which might seem like a rather tenuous way to spread out attendance, but it makes an interesting point. A problem a lot of theme parks have, is that most of their attendance base is made up of families with school aged children, and unless they take their children off school to visit the park, the park ends up with a massive divide in how busy the park is between a weekend/holiday and a day in term time when the kids are at school. Some parks simply don't feel it's worth opening during term time, which makes

107   RCDB, Roller Coaster Data Base, https://rcdb.com/11048.htm

108   *Barrier free entry* means that trains don't have sides that people have to climb over. I hope to discuss throughputs further in a future book, including how we can design ride vehicles to make them quicker to load.

109   Meeting the CEO of Liseberg, Theme Park Worldwide Interview, https://www.youtube.com/watch?v=LnyZ8g_Kg9A&t=43s

110   Seasonality, Andreas Anderson's own blog, https://reflections.liseberg.se/seasonality/

111   Christmas at Liseberg in Gothenburg opens tonight – with more lights than ever, Sweden Tips, https://www.swedentips.se/christmas-liseberg-gothenburg-2017/

staffing the park harder, as now they can't offer fulltime jobs. It means they need to rely on a different kind of workforce.

In 2013 Liseberg changed their logo from one depicting the park's mascot (a green rabbit) to one with the park's name simply written in a modern font.

Anderson explains the reasoning behind the change. "A rabbit makes total sense when you want to sell a T-shirt to kids. But it makes absolutely no sense if you want to communicate concerts or a big new roller coaster."

Lisberg re-themed and rebranded their children's area to Rabbit Land, and limited their use of their mascot outside of this area. "We sort of built a fence around that area and said, 'Rabbit, you live there.' That was quite controversial, because we established that green rabbit through 30 years of use. How could we just ditch it?"

Excising the rabbit was part of a "total revamp" of the Liseberg brand. They introduced a sleek new logo, with a more modern font and colours. Marketing efforts shifted to digital platforms as part of "a new take on how we communicate and represent the brand to our guests," Andersen says. The park had a new mission statement, a new business model, new core values, new objectives, an aggressive expansion plan... and some new members of the executive team[112].

---

112   Fun World Magazine, November 2017, IAAPA, http://www.iaapa.org/news/funworld/funworld-magazine/cover-story---november-2017

Theme parks can find themselves broadening their demographic, both because they've saturated a demographic in a particularly area, and because a new demographic will bring in visitors at times when the park is currently quiet. Trying to bring in more of the same demographic simply brings in more people when you're already busy. It is, however, worth noting, that Liseberg is one of Europe's largest theme parks with around 3 million visitors a year. For smaller parks, trying to appeal to too many different audiences and be something to everyone, can mean you end up not really appealing to any group. A small children's park is hardly going to be able to spend the 200 million Swedish Kronor (about £17 million) that Helix cost to build[113].

Nonetheless, for larger parks, as they look to bring in more visitors, it might be helpful to focus on those who won't be at school, either very young pre-school aged kids or groups of adults. Over the next 50 years many parts of Europe and North America are expected to have aging populations, so parks are likely to focus more on how to attract an older clientele.

Of course, it takes more than a new logo to encourage more groups of adults to start visiting, although subtle changes to the branding can shift an attraction's image away from being somewhere you only go to with children. Other changes can include new menus in the restaurants, as older guests often want to eat more 'sophisticated foods', a better focus on live entertainment and cultural exhibits. Older guests are likely to appreciate more places where they can sit down, and gentler attractions.

Although people in the industry tend to talk about older guests wanting 'more sophisticated foods', perhaps this is a slightly loaded choice of words. Certainly, there is a tendency for people to become more health conscious as we get older. Whilst this is a stereotype and there are plenty of teenagers who are very healthy and older guests who don't worry about what they eat, it is the general trend. As we get older our metabolisms slow down and we put on weight more easily. Even if our own health hasn't suffered, we start to know people whose health has declined, so we're less likely to take good health for granted. Providing healthy options can be a challenge, particularly for smaller parks, parks that are only open weekends and school holidays, and parks with big fluctuations in attendance. Fresh ingredients have much shorter shelf lives than frozen and dried foods. Deep fried food cooks very quickly. And it's quite limited what you can offer if you don't have at least one trained chef to lead the operation. Nonetheless, higher quality, healthy foods served in a relaxing environment are important if you want to attract groups of older guests without kids who will come on the school days.

Older guests might experience a park at a slower pace compared to children and teenagers. They like a pleasant environment to wander around with theming and landscaping. There are whole books about themed entertainment and designing spaces. I can't compete with that here. However, I will

---

113   Analysing the cost of rides is problematic, due to inflation and currency conversion rates that can fluctuate significantly. I've tried to limit the number of times I quote prices. The point is that Helix was an expensive ride to build. Almost a quarter of the budget went on rock blasting.

spend a few paragraphs discussing theming at Disney. As we shall discover later in this book, Disney's success partly comes from the fact that their visitors are evenly spaced through the year. They don't have such big swings between school holidays and term time. Disney parks appeal to adults as well as children.

Older guests (perhaps those over 50) tend to be less interested in riding attractions, and more interested in exploring the environment. Although Disney's classic cartoons are generally associated with children and families, Walt wanted Disneyland to be somewhere that the whole family could enjoy. It became known as much for the immersive environments and the presentation as for the rides. New Orleans Square opened in July 1966 and cost $18 million to build[114], which would be $144 million in today's money (2020)[115]. Presumably this included the cost of Pirates of the Caribbean, which opened nine months after the area.

When it originally opened New Orleans Square had no rides. Pirates of the Caribbean and the area's premier restaurant, The Blue Bayou, opened nine months later. Haunted Mansion was the second big ride in the area, and opened about 3 years after the area. New Orleans is generally regarded as being one of the most immersive and best themed areas at any theme park in the world, despite it only being 3 acres, which is a lot smaller than any of the Harry Potter, or Star Wars areas. It shows that smaller parks often do have the space for a richly themed area. Unlike many of the other areas at Disney that focus on a landmark, like a castle or a mountain (what Walt called 'weenies'), New Orleans doesn't have a particularly obvious feature – at least not until Haunted Mansion was built. What's made it such a popular area is the attention to detail and the way that all the architecture works together. Whilst New Orleans Square is beautiful, it certainly doesn't feel like a kids' area. It has quite a few greens and purples, colours associated with New Orleans and Mardi Gras, but the colour palette isn't overly bright.

What we see at many of the regional parks, is they open a new area, but they spend 95% of the budget on rides. Sometimes that's one big ride with a token gesture area/plaza in front of it. Other times, we have a series of themed flat rides. For regional parks looking to bring in more older guests who don't typically visit theme parks, I wonder whether they could spend all their budget one year on creating a really detailed and immersive area that's pleasant to be in and explore. One or two years later they could add a ride. A regional park isn't going to have $144 million to play with, but the same principle could work on a smaller scale. Even Disney had to scale Pirates down a lot when they built it in Florida, as their budget was too limited to build a copy.

There are several challenges for creating nicer themed areas. Firstly, a dark ride like Pirates of the Caribbean doesn't disturb the ambience of the area that

---

114   Disney history: New Orleans Square opens, The Orange County Register, https://www.ocregister.com/2014/07/20/disney-history-new-orleans-square-opens/

115   US Inflation calculator, https://www.usinflationcalculator.com/

it's in. Every attraction benefits from high quality theming, including thrill coasters such as Taron at Phantasialand. But if the objective is to use immersive areas to bring in an older clientele, it might not be so effective if there's a roller coaster dashing around it. Few theme parks still offer a pay per ride model. Now people are paying one price, ride all day, an area with only shops and restaurants can look like a cash grab. The public could take a cynical view on a rideless areas. Enthusiasts' expectations tend to be very high these days. When people have been following the construction online, they might expect a new ride to open at the end of it. We also find that theme park developments are heavily controlled by marketing departments, and that an area that's immersive and fun to explore isn't an easy product to advertise.

There are a lot of reasons why regional parks tend to keep on adding very cheap areas where most of the budget goes on rides. However, if parks have either found that their attendance plateaued a long time ago, or that their visitors are all trying to come on a small number of peak days when they struggle to cope, it is worth them considering other ways to make investments. Investments in themed areas don't tend to deliver the same quick hits. It requires a business to take a longer-term view of things, but perhaps one that will be more fruitful several years down the road.

If a park doesn't have much budget for theming, you can also do a lot with gardens and landscaping. You need to hire at least one horticulturist to manage things, create a backstage landscaping area with some greenhouses, have some basic 'plant' equipment allowing you to water plants efficiently etc You could compost left over food from your restaurants and use it in the gardens and encourage wildlife, for example with bird or bat boxes. You want someone with turf management skills to keep well maintained lawns around the park, as well as knowing how to manage trees and flower beds.

Different parks have different business models, and rightly so. It'd be boring if every theme park was run in the same way. Sometimes the biggest opportunities are in doing the things that your rivals aren't. The parks that tend to appeal most to an older demographic are the more premium parks. Quite a few regional parks have gone down the discount model using cheap season tickets and discount coupons to bring people in. This leads to a low yield per a guest, often meaning they cut back on things like landscaping, theming and live entertainment, which appeal to the older clientele.

Some parks have gone further and introduced an all year dining plan, where every time you visit you get free food. To do an offer like that the quality and choice of food is likely to get pushed down as low as possible, although of course you can have individual items or restaurants excluded from the plan. The discount theme park model can work, and it might be the only viable way to run your business in an area with high unemployment and a weak economy. In these areas lots of people can't afford a premium park. It might also allow you to undercut a more expensive rival that already appeals to the high-end customer. However, these discount parks are generally parks that only open at weekends and school holidays. To open during school term time, you often need to appeal to a broader audience, which the discount parks can struggle to do. In addition, if a lot of your visitors are season passholders, extending your season can increase your costs without having a significant impact on your income.

Some parks no doubt appeal more to adults than others. Some parks also do a better job of marketing to adults than others do. If all the guests in your adverts are families with kids, then these are likely to be the types of people who visit. Europa Park produces a leaflet and video advert specifically for the over 60s and offers them an over 60s discount. If you want guests to visit when the weather's poor, you need to make sure that they still have a good time and then promote this in your advertising. If you want older guests to visit the park during term time, then you need to take the same approach. Make the changes, and then advertise them.

In addition to all of this, there is a cultural element. In some cultures, older people are more likely to embrace going to a theme park than in others. This is the same principle as some cultures being less deterred by poor weather. In the UK theme parks are seen as something for children and teenagers. The mainstream media doesn't treat theme parks as an art form. Newspapers don't have specialist theme park correspondents. If they're reporting on a new roller coaster they often do a 'comedy routine' of sending along someone who at least appears not to like roller coasters. They'll show a clip of them staggering off with a screwed up face and going, That was horrible. We then cut to the chuckling presenters in the studio. Could you imagine sending someone who hates musicals to see the new musical? Or someone who hates Shakespeare being sent to see the RSC's version of Macbeth and they sit there yawning through it? In the UK theme parks aren't seen as a serious piece of artistic expression in the same way that novels, plays, radio, paintings, sculptures and even sport are.

The media in some other countries and regions treats theme parks differently. Part of Disney's success in attracting older guests, is that even though Disney Classics are essentially children's film, Disney have worked hard over the years to get their theme parks taken seriously as an art form. We hear imagineers (Disney designers) talking about the use of colour to evoke emotions. There are discussions about architectural theories; straight lines vs curved lines, forced perspective, the architecture of reassurance. We hear about storytelling, backstory, narrative and character development. They talk about props they've chosen for their symbolism. To be fair, the kinds of ride Disney builds do lend themselves to an artistic discussion more than some of the rides built at regional parks. But even a big roller coaster has interest in terms of the engineering and the way the different elements in the layout flow together. There are many designers in the industry who are interested in artistic expression.

If your theme park is in a country where theme parks are seen as something crass for the kids, then trying to persuade groups of older guests without children to visit can be a hard task. Shifting the image can be a tricky and slow process, but if taken in conjunction with a focus on theming, landscaping, shows, events and food, then slowly you can challenge people's views on who a theme park's for.

Broadening your demographic: Young adults

Families are more likely to visit earlier in the day while young adults are more likely to stay for the evening. Events can help to attract more young adults and we've already discussed Oktoberfests. However, I would advise parks to be cautious about introducing alcohol-based events into a family environment. Some parks have used concerts to bring in a new audience as well as adding repeatability for annual pass holders. Magic Springs and Crystal Falls is an amusement and water park in Arkansas. In the summer they run a concert series every Saturday night at their Timberwood Amphitheatre.

"Aundrea Crary, the park's marketing manager and Timberwood Amphitheater manager, sees the change beginning at 5:30 or 6 p.m. on Saturday nights. The families with children who've been visiting the park since opening begin to filter out; an older crowd, waiting for the concerts to begin, gradually replaces them. It's hard to say if that older crowd would come to the park without the concerts. We have noticed that we are starting to attract an older crowd that only buys its season passes for the concert season. It's a dedicated outing for them 14 days a year"[116].

Magic Springs and Crystal Falls does have several thrill rides anyway, including The Gauntlet (Vekoma SLC) and X Coaster (Maurer Söhne X coaster), so it's not like they're attracting adults to a children's park. There still are the risks of problems if the adult audience disrupts the family audience when they overlap, or if the alcohol leads to trouble. Even during the summer concert series Magic Springs shuts at 8pm, which no doubt curbs how much people drink. Parks often group all their children's rides together in an area that doesn't act as a through path to anywhere, so that younger children haven't got teenagers rushing past them. Any event involving alcohol needs to be planned carefully and monitored to make sure it doesn't cause more problems than it's worth. The type of music, how late you're open, the price of alcohol, how it's promoted, the security presence, the drinking culture in your country and other factors will determine whether people drink in a 'responsible way'.

Broadening your demographic: school groups and pre-schoolers

If you want to grow attendance without growing your queues, you can do it by attracting more adults without kids, but there are two other groups who will also come in term time: school groups and parents with pre-school age toddlers. I haven't got the space to discuss school groups in depth, particularly as parks in different regions of the world tend to deal with schools in different ways. Nonetheless, schools can be an important demographic. I haven't got any figures to show what percentage of a theme park's annual attendance is made up of school groups, but it would be a particularly high number in the UK. They're less significant for many of the parks in North America and elsewhere in Europe.

---

116   Broad appeal, Funworld November 2008, IAAPA

The schools market generally has two functions: pure fun and educational visits. Fun trips happen after kids have sat their exams. For teachers there are three big priorities here. The first is safety. Blackpool Pleasure Beach is a seaside amusement park in the UK. They used to be free to enter. In 2009 they introduced an entry charge which got you entry to the park and included the Chinese Puzzle Maze and the Pleasure Beach Express (miniature railway). You could then buy an unlimited ride wristband or pay per ride. One manager at the Pleasure Beach told me that one of the arguments for introducing the entry charge was that schools felt more secure when it wasn't so easy for anyone to wander in or out. No teacher wants to face the consequences and guilt of something going wrong. Safety is a particular concern for teachers, as groups of school kids can get over excited and not do a great job of following the rules they're given. It's down to the park to make sure that everything's as safe as possible and that his is communicated to the schools.

The second priority is price. Once you factor in the coach to get there, visiting a theme park's an expensive school trip, and teachers don't want it to be prohibitive for too many poorer kids. Schools therefore tend to be very price conscious. The third issue is low hassle. This is problematic at parks where children under a certain height need accompanying on a lot of attractions. Sadly, there is no easy solution to this. To make it less stressful, parks might well include a risk assessment on their website for teachers to use, offer free tickets in advance for teachers to do a reconnaissance trip (a 'reccy') and free tickets for teachers/adult helpers.

The second kind of trip is educational visits. In the US parks are more likely to open for a handful of education days, each with a different theme (e.g. business, marketing, engineering etc). On these days the rides are open and there are several talks/question and answer sessions with senior management. In the UK schools might be able to visit on any day in term time and have a workshop chosen from a list. There could be a dedicated education officer who delivers these. In either case, outside the talk/workshop the children get to go on the rides. Some parks also provide worksheets/booklets for kids to do further learning activities based on the park, either while they're visiting, or back in class.

Building up a schools' base can be a lot of work for relatively little financial return, as the schools' market is so price sensitive. However, aside from the direct income there are couple of benefits to offering a strong schools' package. It means that parks can offer hours to staff when it wouldn't otherwise be worth opening. This can attract a different kind of employee and build a more stable workforce. Secondly, school visits introduced kids to the park who wouldn't otherwise visit. These might well visit again with their family, this time paying full price.

When I worked at Dreamland, I had the opportunity to put together a range of school workshops from scratch, and I found the experience really fun and rewarding. Perhaps I'll write more about it in a future book. The challenge is to make the workshops fun and engaging. It needs to be interactive, but also educational, pitched at the right level for the kids doing it, and possibly tied into the school curriculum for your country. It takes a lot of research and development (R&D) to create a strong schools' program, but it's also a rewarding thing for your staff to get involved with. If you're a seasonal park that's only open at weekends and school holidays, it might give one of your managers something to work on when the park's closed.

The third market is pre-school aged children. Parks might entice these guests to visit with off peak pricing or more targeted promotions. Chessington World of Adventures has sold a 'parent and toddler pass', where in school term time a parent and a toddler get admission for a particularly low price. A few parks organise special events to attract this demographic. Legoland California ran a Model Mom's program. The name was a play on words with Lego models. Clearly the name 'Model Moms' does discriminate against Dads, so 'Model Parents' would have been a better name. Every Thursday in term time they did an activity in the morning for the 'mums' and their toddler[117]. After the activity they could spend the rest of the day enjoying the park. Activities included a stroller walk, playing with Duplo, talks about parenting issues such as teaching a child to swim or sibling rivalries. The Model Moms started in 2002, and by 2003 1,400 care givers were signed up to the program. The program was dropped in 2016.

The Matlock Farm Park (UK) has a program every Wednesday in term time called the Little Explorers Club. It works in a similar way to the Model Mum's club. Activities include making a bird feeder, building a bug hotel, planting flowers and a treasure hunt.

As with the other ideas for broadening your demographic, the design of your park combined with the right marketing and promotions can help to bring in more pre-schoolers during term time. But it can't just be marketing and promotions without the substance to back it up. For a preschooler (under 4/5 in a lot of countries) a theme park can be an intimidating place. Most theme parks now have a dedicated area for younger children. This hasn't always been the case. Towards the end of this book we'll look at Coney Island in the late 1800s and the early 1900s. In the early days of the amusement industry, parks were aimed predominantly at adults, and there were no areas specifically aimed at young children. If you look at photos of early amusement parks, it's hard to spot any children.

It's not clear which park had the first dedicated children's area. Blackpool Pleasure Beach (UK) opened a children's playground in 1924, with swings, slides, a see saw and a paddling pool[118]. In 1927 they opened a mini amusement area called Bingle and Bob with scaled down versions of some of the adult rides. In 1934 the they opened a larger Kiddies Park, which included a creche so that parents could leave their kids while they went off to ride the

117   Joining the club, Frank Elliot, September 2003, Fun World Magazine, IAAPA

118   Bye bye Beaver Creek, Phil Gould, The Magic Eye, https://www.joy-landbooks.com/themagiceye/articles/bye-bye-beaver-creek.htm

adult attractions. Cedar Point opened a Kiddie Land in 1952[119], which was expanded in 1993 and re-named Kiddy Kingdom.

According to Robert Niles from Theme Park Insider, Camp Snoopy at Knott's Berry Farm (California) was the first branded children's area inside a major theme park[120]. It opened in 1983, and has since been rolled out to a number of parks inside the Cedar Fair chain. Their flagship park, Cedar Point (Ohio), now have has two Snoopy areas, called Camp Snoopy and Planet Snoopy. They also have a third kids area called Kiddy Kingdom. After the success of Knott's Camp Snoopy, other parks began branding their

---

119   Cedar Point history, CP America's roller coast, https://www.cpamericasrollercoast.com/park-history.html

120   First time innovations at Disneyland and other California theme parks, Robert Niles, The Orange County Register, https://www.ocregister.com/2015/09/24/first-time-innovations-at-disneyland-and-other-california-theme-parks/

children's areas. In 1985 Six Flags Magic Mountain (California) rebranded their Children's World as Bugs Bunny Land[121]. There is, however, no doubt contention over what counts as a 'branded' children's area.

Even in the 1920s Blackpool Pleasure Beach were thinking of ways to entertain young children. Small children might not have social media accounts, or leave reviews on Trip Advisor, but their needs and opinions are still just as important.

A well-designed children's area has a sense of reassurance. Steps should be avoided where possible. This can be good practice anyway to help with disabled guests, but they can also be awkward for small children and push chairs. Children tend to fall over, so some kid's areas have a soft rubbery surface. Sudden loud noises should be avoided. Kids areas tend to have music with a strong melody that children can hum along to. Bright colours and curved designs create a feeling of comfort.

The area needs to look good when viewed from a small child's height. Walt Disney famously had the windows on Main Street placed lower to the ground than normal shop windows, so that small children could see through them. Pre-school children like familiarity. This can include themes that they're already familiar with, like space travel, castles, dinosaurs and transport. It can also include catch phrases and repeated motifs. Children's areas are generally built around an iconic character, or a family of iconic characters. This might include a mascot who's a baby, like a puppy or a baby guinea pig. The baby character is someone the children can relate to more easily. Alternatively, the adult characters might have a childlike elements to their personality, for example an inventor who likes playing with things or an explorer with a childlike sense of curiosity.

While attractions for older guests might have more complexity in their narratives and settings, very young children enjoy seeing things they're familiar with. Younger children might not understand much language and they won't be able to read, but they often do like sound with a musical quality, like rhymes, alliteration and onomatopoeia. Theme park rides often have very simple storylines, particularly if they're aimed at young children. Shows might have slightly more complex storylines. Often the stories will have pro-social messages. Whilst attractions for an older audience might have a good vs evil type of battle, a children's show could just feature good characters modelling kind behaviour. Modern attractions are likely to represent diversity, perhaps including characters from different ethnic backgrounds, or having a character in a wheelchair. There might be an educational element to the attractions, but they need to be pitched at a basic level, for example helping to teach children colours, shapes, counting etc. For children approaching school age, they could bring in some basic general knowledge.

A children's area needs to have good baby changing facilities and a restaurant selling simple healthy foods as well as some child sized treats. You might

---

121   Bugs Bunny World, Six Flags Wiki, https://sixflags.fandom.com/
wiki/Bugs_Bunny_World_(Six_Flags_Magic_Mountain)

offer free bracelets that parents can write their mobile number on. If the child gets lost, a member of staff can phone the parents. You'll have somewhere that lost children can be taken to, like the first aid centre or guest services. This could have toys for the kids to play with. The staff should be good at dealing with young children, including bending down to their height to talk to them. When you have a well-designed children's area combined with the right promotions, events and advertising, you can start to fill it up on the days when the older children are at school. This consistent flow of guests helps to compensate for the fact that many children's rides have low throughputs and can't cope well with big surges in demand.

There are lots of advantages to having a steadier stream of attendance. It's better for your staff who get more stable employment. If your park's got accommodation, it can give it higher occupancy. As well as a dedicated children's area, some rides can have 'cross over' potential, appealing to young children as well as older guests. These can include transport (railways, cable cars, monorails), family friendly dark rides (like It's a Small World), and walk through attractions (like an aquarium). When your 'cross over' attractions are near the children's area, it works well. If a children's area brings in visitors during term time, it will help to justify opening other attractions and the rest of the park. The more days the park's open, the more opportunities there are for guests to switch their visits. The way a theme park spreads its guests out through the season is based upon a complex eco-system.

There are cultural differences. If parents put their children into daycare soon after they're born and return to work, they might not be able to visit during term time. This puts more pressure on the park at weekends and public holidays. In a culture where parents care for their own children until they start school, their visits can be spread out through the week. A lot of the ideas in this book will work more easily in some countries than in others. This helps to explain why some countries have longer queues than others. It also means that multi-national theme park operators need to be sensitive to cultural differences and listen to local expertise. When we talk about cultural differences, we often think about things like dress codes, religion, language barriers, extraversion and etiquette. We might change the theme or the characters to reflect the local culture. These are all important, but there are also differences that affect attendance patterns and guest flow. When you enter a new market, you might have to change the whole business model.

Disney looks for an older audience

I've tried to make this book less Disney-centric than many other books on theme park management. However, Disney are very good at what they do, and many of my readers will be familiar with the Disney parks. We've looked at lots of ways to re-distribute guests more evenly through the season, and I want to finish this section by looking at some examples from Disney.

Walt Disney World first opened in 1971, with one theme park – Magic Kingdom. Magic Kingdom follows the most famous format for a Disney theme park. A miniature railway runs around the perimeter. Once inside the park, Main Street leads to Cinderella's Castle. The other areas are laid out around it in a hub and spoke layout. Disney now has six resorts around the world, and in each case the first park at the resort has followed this format. It's the one most people would immediately think of if you asked them to imagine a Disney theme park. According to the TEA (Themed Entertainment Association), the three most visited theme parks in the world for 2018 were all Magic Kingdom style parks (Magic Kingdom - Orlando, Disneyland Park – Anaheim and Tokyo Disneyland). Given how successful this format has been, when Disney wanted to build a second park in Florida, it might have made sense to build another park similar to Magic Kingdom. But they didn't. They built something quite different: Epcot Center.

There might have been various reasons for doing this. At the time, Walt's death in 1966 was still fairly recently. Epcot Center opened in 1982, and many of the imagineers who worked on the project had worked with Walt. The management team he left behind were keen to honour his legacy. Walt's plan for his 'Florida Project' had been to build a futuristic city called Epcot. Epcot Center loosely honours his dream. While it isn't a city, it does pay homage to American innovation.

But Epcot Center was also a deliberate attempt to target a completely different demographic to Magic Kingdom. Whilst Magic Kingdom appeals to everyone, it was particularly designed with children in mind. Epcot was designed to appeal more to adults, and originally didn't feature any Disney characters. They say stop while you're winning, and a park similar to Magic Kingdom might have cannibalised Magic Kingdom's attendance. Epcot targeted the growing number of healthy and affluent pensioners, who moved to Florida for the sun and cheap properties. Following America's introduction and expansion of social security (pensions) after Roosevelt's New Deal, and the growing American economy, there was a generation of people with the disposable income to have fun, and no work commitments to limit it. However, appealing to adults without children would also serve the same benefit that Liseberg were trying to achieve when they changed their logo. And in some ways, this would be more important for Disney World than for Liseberg, because Walt Disney World's a 365 day operation, and they have plenty of hotel rooms to fill (35,969 at the time of writing[122]).

Disney World has done a remarkably good job of filling their parks and their hotel rooms all year round. This is down to a combination of weather proofing, using events to drive attendance at quiet times, appealing to adults without children as well as adults with very young pre-school aged children; in fact, Disney World's steady attendance is down to most of the ideas discussed in this section.

Liseberg changing a logo seems rather insignificant, but Disneyland Paris presents us with a rather more dramatic scenario. When Disneyland Paris opened on 12th April 1992 it was a financial disaster, at one point losing over

---

122   Walt Disney World onsite hotels, Touring Plans, https://touringplans.com/walt-disney-world/hotels/number-rooms

a million dollars a day. Clearly it takes a lot of factors to explain such a big loss; but one of the biggest causes of the resort's problems was their struggle to attract groups of adults without children. The park ended up being very busy at peak times, and very quiet at other times. The attendance pattern in Paris was very different to Florida, and although the climate was no doubt a factor, it's more complicated than that.

The problem with Disneyland Paris

On April 12th 1992, Disneyland Paris opened on time and within its \$4.4 billion budget. Despite this, it was soon seen as a financial disaster, losing over \$1 million a day. Within two months of opening, shares in Disneyland Paris had lost 20% of their value[123]. In this time shares in The Walt Disney Company, who owned 49% of Disneyland Paris, also fell in value. Disneyland Paris (then Euro Disney) issued a report saying, "Attendance at the park and guests at Euro Disney's six hotels had fluctuated considerably during the period. Activity on weekends and holidays has significantly exceeded that of midweek periods. It promised new advertising and tight management of costs in response to the situation." They had originally planned to open a second park at the resort in 1996, but it kept on getting pushed back until it eventually opened in 2002[124].

When eventually they did open their second park, it was built as cheaply as possible. They needed to open a second park by 2002, otherwise they'd lose the large bank of land the French government had optioned for them[125]. According to Imagineer Eddie Sotto, when it opened, the entire second park was smaller than just the Fantasyland area of the original park next door[126].

Following the 'financial disaster' of Disneyland Paris other projects had their budgets cut. Disney's Animal Kingdom in Florida (opened in 1998) had just one major 'ride' when it was new (Dinosaur: Countdown to Extinction) and the Beastly Kingdom area of the park was cut from the design. Plans for a Westcot park in California were scrapped and they ended up with the cheaper California Adventure. Several projects planned for the original Disneyland park were also cut, including a Little Mermaid dark ride, a major revamp of Tomorrowland and a Hollywoodland tribute to the 'golden age of movies'. This would have used a piece of backstage land between Main Street and Tomorrowland[127].

Plans were also reportedly shelved at Disney World, including a new pavilion in Epcot's World Showcase, perhaps either themed to Russia or

123   Slow start at Europe's Disneyland, Roger Cohen, The New York Times, https://www.nytimes.com/1992/06/08/business/slow-start-at-europe-s-disneyland.html

124   The bumpy start to Disneyland Paris, Chuck Mirarchi, Walt Disney Info, https://www.wdwinfo.com/disneyland-paris/the-bumpy-start-to-disneyland-paris/

125   The Imagineering Story, Episode 4, Disney Plus

126   The Eddie Sotto interview – part 2, episode 391, The Season Pass Podcast, http://www.seasonpasspodcast.com/

127   26 reasons to regret the existence of Disneyland Paris, Kevin Siruss, Theme Park Tourist, https://www.themeparktourist.com/features/20150821/30494/how-euro-disneyland-derailed-disney-decade

Switzerland, with something similar to the Matterhorn Bobsled. Although they built Muppet 3D in MGM Studios, they had plans for a larger Muppet themed area around it with a dark ride. There were also plans for a Port Disney at Long Beach California, with a cruise ship terminal, five hotels and a theme park similar to the theme they eventually used for Disney Seas in Tokyo. It was estimated to cost around $1 billion. When we look at the scale of the losses, the falling share price and the projects that were cut in the aftermath, it seems fair to say that Disneyland Paris didn't exactly go according to plan.

A lot of problems have been cited for the 'failure' of Disneyland Paris, and almost certainly multiple mistakes and contingencies were to blame. It had been planned when the French economy was doing well, and as is the case for several failed theme parks, it opened at the start of a recession. The name Euro Disney was considered too mundane, with the word 'euro' being associated with financial institutions. The resort ended up being renamed Disneyland Paris. Disneyland Paris was criticised for not serving alcohol, and soon became Disney's first Magic Kingdom style theme park to serve alcohol (Disneyland already served alcohol to members of its Club 55). Phantom Manner had its voice over changed from English to French, as a higher percentage of their guests were French than they'd originally anticipated. The waiting times advertised in lines were wrong, because the Europeans stood closer together than the Americans. As air travel came down in price, higher numbers of Europeans began flying to Orlando for the larger Disney World. Originally, they only sold French sausages, but soon they started selling British and German sausages to help attract more international visitors. Other European theme parks didn't simply rest on their laurels, and formed partnerships, such as allowing season pass holders to have one free visit at each other's parks.

One of the biggest challenges that faced Disneyland Paris, and one of particular interest for this book, was that visitors were bunched up more than they expected, with big peaks and troughs in visitation. They did try to encourage more people to stay in the hotels at offpeak times with higher discounting than Disney normally used. This uneven attendance pattern can be a challenge for any park, but it was a particular issue for Disneyland Paris, where they had six hotels to fill. The Walt Disney Company was used to high occupancy rates at their other resorts. If you have more visitors on peak days and fewer on offpeak days - that's a problem. Once the hotels are full, they're full and it doesn't matter how much surplus demand there is. If few people want to visit on the quiet days, then there's not a lot you can do to fill the hotel rooms. Big peaks in attendance led to low occupancy at the hotels, and the resort's debt load quickly grew.

The other issue for Disneyland Paris, was that they had 12,000 staff[128]. A smaller park might be able to have a more flexible workforce, but you can't find 12,000 staff if a lot of them are going to be seasonal or part time. Part of the reason Disney are able to attract so many applicants, is because they can offer their cast members year-round, reasonably stable employment. This 365 day business model, is also why governments have been willing to invest huge sums of public money into improving the transport around a new Disney resort. Why did Disneyland Paris have such big peaks and troughs in attendance?

To an extent you could say that Disneyland Paris was ahead of its time. As we explain elsewhere in this chapter, it's now not unusual for European theme parks to have Halloween and Christmas events to extend the season. When Disneyland Paris opened in 1992, European theme parks were seen largely as a summer activity, and whilst Disney started to change that perception, cultural outlooks don't change quickly. Disney probably over-estimated the public's willingness to visit outdoor attractions in the colder winter months. A lot of Disney's projections were partly based on the success of Tokyo Disneyland, which had opened in 1983, almost a decade before Disneyland Paris. Tokyo had colder, harsher winters than Paris, but the Japanese seemed to be more willing to go out and visit theme parks when the weather was 'bad'.

Disney were well aware that the weather around Paris wasn't great in the winter, and that their other preferred site near Barcelona (that eventually became Port Aventura) had a better climate for a year-round resort. There were a lot of factors that they took into account, including transport around the two locations (when they were planning a European resort in the eighties, air travel was relatively less important) and the level of government support for the projects, including how much land they could compulsory purchase and at what price, as well as tax breaks. They did feasibility studies for many locations, and concluded that the site near Paris was the best place to build their Euro Disney. We will never know whether it would have been more or less successful had they chosen Barcelona or one of the many other locations they considered.

Well aware of the problems caused by bad weather, 'weather proofing' the park was something they took seriously. At the American parks much of the floor surface was concrete painted red to bring out the green in the foliage. The designers were worried that if they paved the Paris park with concrete, then in the winter water would get into any cracks, freeze, expand and crack the concrete causing a freeze/thaw effect. Instead Disneyland Paris was mainly surfaced with bricks and rock slate paving. There were a lot of undercover arcades, so that guests could stay dry moving around the park in wet weather, and some of the rides such as Phantom Manor were given undercover queuelines, unlike their American counter parts.

Having undercover routes around the park was clearly decided upon early on in the design process. Imagineer Eddie Sotto was responsible for designing the Paris version of Main Street. He was recruited for the project by the lead designer for Disneyland Paris, Tony Baxter. Sotto's first concept was for something completely new, themed to Chicago from the 1920s with a family friendly gangster theme. According to Sotto, the area would have sanitised gangsters in the same way that Pirates of the Caribbean sanitises pirates[129]. For the Chicago concept there'd have been a reproduction of Chicago's CTA elevated railway going down one side, which would have provided shelter underneath it. Eisner chose the more traditional Main Street and the elevated railway was dropped. Instead they put an arcade on either side of Main Street with cultural exhibits. The Liberty Arcade is themed to the friendship between the United States and France. The Discovery Arcade is themed to inventions of the 19th century. Despite a lot of thought going into weather proofing the resort, it wasn't enough to avoid the peaks and troughs in attendance.

Aside from seasonal variations, Disneyland Paris was mostly attracting families. The Magic Kingdom style of Parc Disneyland Paris was always the most family orientated of Disney's different theme park designs. Part of the thinking behind Epcot, the second park in Orlando, was to bring in more adults. Epcot was presented like a World's Fair. Future World displayed developments in science and technology. World Showcase gave visitors a cultural trip around the world. The third park in Orlando, MGM Studios, was aimed more at teenagers with thrill rides like Rock 'N Roll Roller Coaster and Tower of Terror, and brands like Star Wars and Indiana Jones, rather than princes and princesses. Parc Disneyland Paris was always aimed at attracting families, and these were mostly what came.

Nonetheless, there were a couple of problems here. Firstly, they hadn't expected the percentage of families to be as high as it was. In California and to a lesser extent Orlando, there was a generation of adults who'd grown up visiting Disneyland/World. For them, there was nostalgia, and it felt more like a cultural institution. Not to mention that the American parks had more cultural exhibits in between the rides, for example Orlando's Magic Kingdom has Hall of Presidents telling the history of American presidents, Carousel of Progress tells the history of technology in the American home and the Wedway PeopleMover showcases Walt Disney's vision of future transport.

Parc Disneyland Paris was heavily themed and very immersive. At the time it had the longest Main Street, the tallest castle, and the largest most spectacular version of Big Thunder Mountain. The trains were taken to a mountain on an island through two long tunnels. The Paris version of Pirates of the Caribbean was larger than the Florida's version, and closer in size to the original at Disneyland. However, it felt more like a standard theme park, albeit a very well themed one. It didn't have these cultural exhibits. The kinds of things you might call 'edutainment' (a fusion of education and entertainment). This combined with the Disney characters and children's brands like Peter Pan and It's a Small World, meant that unlike the American Disney parks, Paris didn't attract significant numbers of adult groups.

The second issue, was that at the time, in France, there wasn't the culture of taking children out of school to go on 'vacation' like there was in America.

---

129   The Eddie Sotto interview – part 2, episode 391, The Season Pass Podcast, http://www.seasonpasspodcast.com/

The upshot of this, was that most of their visitors were families who wanted to come at weekends and school holidays, and that their attendance was skewed heavily towards the summer season, with guests being more likely to postpone their visit if they thought the weather would be poor. These days it's easier to get people to visit when the weather's poor by giving them a discount if they book more than seven days in advance, when they're less likely to know what the weather will be. But in 1992 few people had the Internet, so getting day trippers to book their visit in advance wasn't really an option.

The success of a Disney theme park comes partly from their sense of quality and ability to command high prices, and the fact large numbers of people are willing to travel a significant distance to visit. It also comes from their ability to attract visitors reasonably evenly year-round and through the week. At least initially, Disneyland's Paris' inability to do this led to significant financial problems. Perhaps over time there would inevitably be an improvement, both as 'off season' events caught on across the European theme park industry, and also as word got around that Disneyland Paris had been designed to offer a more appealing day, even when the weather was poor. Eventually the Internet would also make it easier to attract visitors on wet days. There was still another big problem though. Most of the people visiting were families, and they simply weren't prepared to visit on a school day.

The introduction of alcohol is largely seen as a nod to European culture, but it was also an attempt to attract more adults who'd visit the park in termtime. In the early 90s Europeans had a different attitude to alcohol compared to Americans. America has a higher drinking age than most European countries and some people might still associate it with prohibition, even though prohibition ended in 1933. The debate around Disneyland Paris selling alcohol can be oversimplified. Alcohol was particularly controversial at the original Disneyland (California), as it was the park that Walt had personally designed, and he had been against the sale of alcohol. Disney is a company that's still very conscious of their founder's legacy. At Disney World people could already drink around the world in Epcot. When Disneyland Paris wanted to bring in more adults without children, selling alcohol must have been one of the quickest and easiest ways to get the ball rolling. At least symbolically, it sent out the message that, 'Disneyland Paris isn't just for children'.

There were perhaps three arguments for serving alcohol. Firstly, to emphasise that this wasn't a park just for families. Secondly, because alcohol sales would boost the bottom line. Thirdly, they were trying to attract more international visitors, and having a glass of wine was something people liked to do when they go to France.

Yves Boulanger, a spokesman for Euro Disney, told the New York Times, "It's mainly in response to our non-French European visitors. Visitors from Germany or England want wine because it's part of the French experience."[130] However, he also said it was more about increasing per capita spending rather than boosting visitor numbers.

---

130   New York Times, http://json8.nytimes.com/pages/business/index.jsonp

As well as selling alcohol, they quickly introduced a couple of thrill rides to show that there was more to Disneyland Paris then princes and princesses. Disneyland Paris did open with a clone of Star Tours, a motion simulator through the Star Wars universe, and a slightly faster version of Big Thunder Mountain. According to RCDB (Roller Coaster Data Base) the original in California goes at 28mph, the Florida version goes at 36mph and the Paris version goes at 40mph. But it was still very much perceived as being a park mainly aimed at children. They needed to appeal to a different demographic, who weren't tied down with when they could visit by the school time table. They could have gone for the older guests with cultural exhibits like Great Moments with Mr Lincoln or Carousel of Progress. But this was seen as a difficult and high-risk market to target. They didn't have nostalgia for Disneyland Paris like their equivalent generation in America had for their parks. In America most of their cultural exhibits were about American culture. Exhibits about American culture wouldn't be received so well in France. Disneyland Paris had already been described as an American invasion and a cultural Chernobyl. They could have added cultural exhibits about French or European culture, but Disney was very much an American institution. Did the French want an American company trying to teach them about their own history?

Barely a year after opening, on 30th July 1993, Disneyland Paris opened their first full thrill ride, Indiana Jones et le Temple du Péril. It was also the first Disney ride to go upside. The Paris version of Space Mountain became the second in 1995, and it wasn't until Rock 'N Roller Coaster at MGM Studios in 1999 that another Disney resort got an inverting ride. Indiana Jones was taken from conception to completion far quicker than a normal Disney ride, to help remedy the resort's lacklustre attendance. It received a less than warm reception from the park's fans. Coaster Kingdom gave it one-star, writing, "The ride was incredibly rushed from drawing board to opening, and it shows, blatantly."[131] Disney did later revise the ride to resolve some of the complaints, including replacing the four person cars with six person cars, meaning each train held twelve riders instead of eight. This raised the throughput by around 50%, helping with its notoriously slow-moving line.

Perhaps the feedback from other guests outside the enthusiast community was better. In 2005 they opened a clone of the Indiana Jones layout at Disney Seas (Japan), with similar but different theming, called Raging Spirits. Enthusiast reviews of Raging Spirits are also quite negative, with Disney Tourist Blog writing, "This is the intense thrill ride at Tokyo DisneySea, which has a 360-degree loop. It draws long waits, is incredibly short, and locks you in so tight that the experience really has no sensation. Almost identical in layout to the Indiana Jones coaster in Disneyland Paris, and only slightly better. Theming is good, and the exterior looks really cool at night. Single Rider is available and recommended, but even it moves slowly. The *much* better way to experience this attraction at night is by grabbing a

---

131   Indiana Jones et le Temple du Peril, Marcus Sheen, Coaster Kingdom, http://www.s104638357.websitehome.co.uk/html/indianajones_main.htm

beer and watching the mesmerizing for about 10 minutes. We're not even kidding."[132] To be fair to the Disney Imagineers, Disney Seas is a park that's somewhat restricted in terms of room for development, so they probably didn't have a massive footprint to work with.

Disneyland Paris' second thrill ride, Space Mountain, was much better received. Like Big Thunder Mountain, the ride used a points system to switch the 24 seat trains between two stations. It had one of the highest through-puts on any thrill coaster in the world. The ride was significantly bigger than Indiana Jones and featured a revolutionary uphill launch from a giant smoke-filled canon. For those who saw Disneyland Paris as an American invasion, Space Mountain told the story from the classic French novel From the Earth to the Moon – a novel by Jules Verne originally published in 1865. Slowly Disneyland Paris began the process of raising its attendance on the quieter days, and improving their low hotel occupancy, which had been one of the biggest sources of their financial problems.

The financial problems that plagued Disneyland Paris are essential reading material for anyone planning a new theme park. These days new theme parks in the Western world have advantages that Disneyland Paris didn't have, including more technology to persuade people to come on quieter days, and an established culture of people going to events like Christmas and Halloween at times of year when the weather might be poor. There are still plenty of lessons to learn from Disneyland Paris. To be fair to Disney, a lack of weather proofing was never the main problem. Nonetheless, new projects often emphasise the amount of indoor attractions. In 2014 a Paramount Park was planned for near London, although it later went through quite a few revisions and re-brandings. From early in the process, they pledged that 70% of the attractions would be undercover, and also talked up the less child orientated brands, like Star Trek and Mission Impossible[133].

About the staff

When you're making decisions about your opening hours and operating cal-endar, you need to think about what's good for your guests, and when they want to visit. But you also need to think about how you're going to staff it. We're going to consider the following challenges:

If you have long opening hours to spread out the demand, how can you do this without your staff getting burned out? For example, if your park's open from 9am to 9pm, that's 12 hours. The staff are going to start before the park opens and finish after it closes, so that could be a 14-hour day.

If a park has big peak and troughs in attendance, how can you staff for that? If you need twice as many staff one day as the next, how does this work?

---

132   Best Tokyo Disney Sea attractions and ride guide, Tom Bricker, Disney Tour-ist Blog, https://www.disneytouristblog.com/tokyo-disneysea-best-rides-guide/

133   PY Gerbeau: The London Resort CEO reveals ambitious plans for a word-class theme park, Owen Ralph, Bloo Loop, https://blooloop.com/features/py-gerbeau-london-resort-plans/

The third staffing challenge is one we'll come back to later on in the book, in the section on capacity. Smaller parks might expand quickly, and as they do, they hire more staff. There comes a point where the staff who want to work for you already do. You want to expand the park to increase the capacity, but you start struggling to find the extra staff. The demand for staff outstrips the supply.

We'll start with the first problem. There's a myriad of things that exacerbate or reduce employee burnout. In terms of physical factors, it helps if you give your staff adequate breaks, access to water, shade and sun cream. In terms of mental burnout, you need to promote good teamwork, a supportive relationship between the team members and their managers, and support them in dealing with difficult customers. Nonetheless, even if you get all of these things right, your staff are still going to burn out if they're doing 70-hour weeks.

As you make your days longer, there are two ways to prevent your staff from doing an unreasonable number of hours. The first option is to introduce shifts, where staff aren't working for the whole time that the park's open. An attraction might have optional and compulsory positions. For example, you could have one attendant checking the bars on each side of the train, or you could have two on each side of the train and they check half the bars each. Having one attendant on each side of the train is compulsory. Having two on each side of the train is optional.

You might say that for the first and last hour of the day you will only have one attendant on each side, and then one pair of attendants start an hour after the park opens and the other pair finish an hour before it closes. For a period in the middle of the day you'll have four attendants. This can work at larger parks with more optional positions. There are downsides in having staff with different starting and finishing times. You lose those moments where the whole team gets together has some kind of briefing or motivational activity.

In terms of shifts you could also have two completely different sets of staff, for example when I worked in a restaurant at Disney World, we had one shift who covered the lunch period and a second shift who covered the evening meal. However, logistically it can be difficult having a complete change in staff part way through the day. At Disney the restaurant closed for an hour between lunch and dinner, which made it easier to change the staff.

Having shifts works at Disney World, where they're successful at recruiting huge numbers of staff, and more importantly they're consistently open long enough to justify having two teams. A regional park that occasionally opens for a really long day will struggle. You can't magically find a load of extra staff just for the occasional week.

The alternative option, rather than having shifts, would be to give people more days off. For example, you work long hours, but work four days on and two days off, rather than doing a five-day working week. Again, this needs extra staff. There are pros and cons to each working pattern.

There's no point extending your opening hours, if your staff become burned out, irritable, slow or make mistakes. Alternatively, there's no point in moving back the closing time, if you push up absenteeism and turnover, leaving yourself short staffed.

In a seasonal business most staff will accept that they'll be doing more hours in the busy periods. However, if your staff are doing more than 50 hours a week, then they may burn out. You can't always offer your staff the work schedule they'd ideally like. Most theme parks wouldn't function if they tried to do that. However, it's also difficult to function if your staff are tired out and demoralised. It's important to give your staff a realistic expectation during the recruitment process. If you expect them to work 14 hour shifts during key trading periods, then this should be made clear. You can't hood-wink people into working a lot more hours than they want to. If someone isn't happy about the hours you need them for, then it's better to find out before you've trained them.

If your staff look tired, are complaining about the hours, or there's high turnover and absenteeism, it might mean that the rosters aren't working for them. In this situation, you could consult your staff to find out how many hours they ideally want to work. It needs to be clear that you can't necessarily meet all of their expectations, but that you will factor it into the decision-making process. The bigger the gap between the number of hours your staff want to work and the number of hours they are working, the bigger the problem. If a small minority of your staff aren't happy, then it might just be the wrong job for them. As is always the case though, there's no point in consulting your staff if you aren't willing to make changes. You also need to make sure you're asking the right questions to get the information you need. Simply asking them whether they're happy with the hours they're getting probably won't give you enough information.

Why can't theme parks just 'gear up' for the busy times?

We've looked at the first bullet point in the previous chapter. How can parks cope with long opening hours, without the staff becoming tired and demoralised? Now we move onto the second point. How do parks cope with swings in demand? We'll talk about why it's important to level off those peaks in attendance. We'll discuss the challenges with creating a 'flexible workforce'. This includes the downsides of agency staff, the effect on morale when staff are sent home early because there isn't enough work, and why you shouldn't send out last minute rosters, once the managers have a better idea of how busy the park's going to be. I will be explaining why a 'flexible work force' isn't some kind of cheap alternative to the ideas in this book. Finally, we'll talk about making sure you're adequately staffed at the end of the season. Halloween is often one of the busiest weeks of the year. But seasonal staff are also leaving as their contracts come to an end and they move on to their next opportunity.

If your park always has long opening hours, you can have two shifts or give people more days off. It becomes harder when your park has significant variations in hours through the season. It's also difficult to find staff for extra positions just for occasional days. Let's say you normally need 3 point of sales open, but for a public holiday you could do with 6. This kind of thing is repeated through the park. You need extra cleaners on the busy days etc. The trouble is you can't just suddenly double your employees for a particular day or a short period.

When you analyse the problem it seems straightforward. Having big variations in attendance makes staffing difficult, so we use things like crowd calendars, variable pricing, events, weather proofing and we broaden our demographic to create a more consistent flow of guests. This makes it easier to have the appropriate staffing levels each day. Unfortunately, quite a few parks still get it wrong. The people who are responsible for these big decisions have job titles like CEO, general manager and director. The people who are responsible for writing the rosters and making sure things are staffed properly on a day to day level are supervisors and junior managers. There isn't always the joined-up thinking to make sure the system works smoothly as a whole. When things go wrong, the lines get longer and the guests become disgruntled, as do the cast members serving them.

I visited a theme park on a busy day with a friend. He's an intelligent guy, but he hasn't ever worked in the theme park industry. "They've been saying it would be good weather all week. They knew it was going to be busy, so why didn't they bring in extra staff?". Those of us who've worked in the industry will probably snort at this. I have heard quite a few managers talk about having a flexible workforce, and there clearly is some room for this. But the opportunity is limited.

Here's an example of where flexible staffing does work. Let's say you have an indoor area that gets busy when it's wet and it's relatively quiet on a sunny day. Your water ride is really busy on a sunny day, but it's empty when it rains. Well, it doesn't take an expert to see how you could use flexible staffing to accommodate these shifts in demand.

On a cold day someone might get transferred from the ice cream parlour to the coffee stall, or you might have fewer people working in the takeaway units and more people working at the indoor restaurants. You might not approve staff holiday for key dates. On the few biggest holidays of the year you might deploy managers from the office into frontline positions to help deal with the crowds. Things like training might get deferred to less busy days so that everyone's being used in critical positions at peak times.

However, in my experience, it's somewhat limited how flexible a workforce in a theme park can be, and this is why it's important to level off the crowds on peak days and shift some of these visitors to quieter times. I know one theme park that tried to use agency staff to help with peak times, but generally that isn't a good idea. Agency staff are expensive. They typically get paid a bit more to compensate for the irregularity of their work, plus the agency who supplies them has expenses to cover, not to mention that they want to make a profit. In a lot of regions many of the positions in a theme park require considerable training, particularly due to safety. Having a lot of staff who don't know the park and its culture doesn't help with customer service. People who are dropped into different businesses each day aren't emotionally invested in the company and its success. They talk about 'casual labour', but do you want your staff to be casual? Due to a lack of training and sometimes motivation, agency staff need careful monitoring.

When Disneyland opened in 1955 they used a lot agency staff. Whilst the opening of Disneyland was a commercial and public success, Walt Disney wasn't entirely happy with the level of service. Fairly quickly most of the staffing was bought in house (they did continue using concessions, and still do to this day) and they all went through Disney's own orientation programme. This evolved into Disney University and the Traditions training that the company is now famous for. It included a revolutionary approach to customer service. Visitors would be referred to as guests, and would be welcomed with as much warmth as a guest in your own home. The staff were cast members who put on a show. The Disney sense of show and the way the cast members interact with their guests, is something that theme parks around the world aspire to be like. When you're using agency staff, you don't get the same opportunities to train and develop them.

When some managers talk about a flexible workforce, it means having a lot of staff on their books who get erratic shifts based on demand. Sometimes they roster in far more staff than they need. If people call in sick and it's really busy, they have the staff they want. If everyone turns up and the park's quiet, a load of people are sent home without getting paid. This is a one-sided arrangement. Then the managers complain about unreliable staff when they don't turn up for their shifts or call in sick. There is a noticeable side effect. Managers who are more empathetic are likely to resist sending staff home when they want to work. Companies that use this kind of policy tend to seek out the less empathetic people to be team leaders, supervisors and managers. It leads to bullying and a break down in the relationship between the front-line staff and the management.

How do you decide which staff you're going to forcibly send home? It's very hard to find a method that's fair and is perceived as being fair. Often you end up with favouritism and nepotism. Even if you try to be fair, what is fair? Is it to randomly select people? This might not be practical, for example it could be that not all staff are trained in the same positions, so some people are more useful or can't be sent home. And if you know that one of the older staff members has a mortgage and is already struggling to manage their debt, is it fairer to send home younger staff who live at home with their parents?

There tends to be resistance that often ends with the manager saying, "Well, you can stay, but you won't be getting paid, because I've already signed you out". In the end you get a toxic culture.

You might be able to 'get away with this' if you're in an area with high unemployment and a weak welfare state. In this scenario a poor job is better than no job, and it might be the best that people can get. But your staff won't be loyal. If the economy picks up and a better employer moves into the area, your staff will move on. If your staff don't feel valued, then there will be passive resistance and a lack of motivation. Why would you put more effort in and go the extra mile for an employer that gives so little back?

There is still room to whittle down the staff on a voluntary basis. If you've got a lot of young staff who don't really need the money and the park's quiet because the weather's poor, then there might well be staff who'd happily go home. If the park's that quiet, then staff might be bored. If staff do complain that they're bored, then you can honestly say, "Well, you were given the chance to go home". I think there's a big difference between asking for volunteers, and forcibly sending people home. Forcibly sending people home might allow managers to assert their authority and save money in the short term, but it can cause far greater long-term damage to the fabric of the company.

I've seen businesses that are struggling financially start erratically sending people home to keep costs down. You end up with rampant turnover and low morale. Managers above a certain grade tend to be on salaries and insulated at least in the short term, although they're more likely to be made redundant because their hours can't simply be reduced to save money. The fact that the manager sending people home isn't affected by the cuts can cause more ill feeling. It's one of the factors that will send a struggling theme park in a downward spiral. If anything, it accelerates the park's demise.

An alternative is to have more staff on your books than you often need and roster in extra people for peak times. Managers might use it as an excuse to send out last minute rosters when they know what the weather's going to be like, but this is dreadful for the staff. If they're not going to be working, they want to plan things for their day off. People who work in the theme park industry generally accept that they do need to respond to peaks and troughs in demand. But if staff find themselves with little real idea of how many hours they're going to be working from week to week, then it becomes very unsatisfactory. If a park has double the guests on a busy day as on a quiet day, then they might be able to gear up for it. If they get ten times as many guests, then you can't simply staff up for that.

An added challenge is that the dates when a theme park is likely to be the busiest, can often be periods when there's a natural lull in staffing levels. Halloween events started out as a way of topping up the visitors in October, which was traditionally the quietest month for theme parks. Now Halloween can be the busiest time for a lot of theme parks, although the end of the season is a time when staffing is challenging. People know their contracts are coming to an end and might need time off for job interviews or even leave if they get another job. It's hard to recruit more staff when they know they'll be back unemployed after a few weeks.

More parks are starting to do Christmas events, and this might help with staffing through Halloween, if people know there'll be a job waiting for them in December if they stick around. In the UK theme parks gradually get busier as the summer goes on, but the last two weeks are the most challenging for staffing. Staff might be becoming fatigued and if they're going back to University or school, they might decide they want some time off to relax or to complete any coursework they had to do. Perhaps a lesson here, is that we should aim to keep hours down at the start of the summer, because if everyone starts off doing 50 hours a week, then by the end of the summer people's hours can rise to unmanageable levels.

Waldameer Park (Pennsylvania) runs a bonus system where anyone who's still working for the park at the end of the season gets a bonus based on how many hours they've worked[134].

2020 Pay Rates

Age	Schedule	Wage/Hour	Lifeguard Wage/Hour	Bonus/Hour*
17 & Graduated or Older	There are No Restrictions for Amount of Hours	$10.00	$10.50	$1.00
16 – 17 Year Old	5 Day Week	$9.00	$10.00	$0.50
14 – 15 Year Old	Part-Time 14 Yr Old, works 5 hr. shifts Primarily Weekends	$7.25	$7.50	$0.25

Image taken from the Waldameer website[135].

If someone was 18 and they were still working at the end of the season, they'd get 25 cents for every hour that they'd worked. Cedar Point ran a similar scheme, but dropped it in 2009 to partially absorb the cost of the minimum wage going up.[136] At the time of writing Adventureland in Iowa also offers an end of season bonus for anyone who's been working there since the start of the season.

Knott's Berry Farm found that their Halloween scare actors were often quitting part way through the event. To encourage them to stay until the end, anyone who completed the event was given a t-shirt saying, "I met the challenge and it kicked my ass!", with a drawing of a tired looking employee[137]. Since Halloween events get busier closer to October 31st, it's a problem if towards the end of the run a lot of the actors have quit.

Being 'an employer of choice' is a phrase that gets bandied around in HR circles. In theory, being an employer of choice means applicants choose to come and work for you when they've got other options, rather than because it's the only job they've been offered. Even if they get offered similar roles in similar lines of work, they'll choose your company, because you're the employer of choice. Being an employer of choice tends to get thrown around

---

134   Official website, https://waldameer.com/about/summer-jobs/

135   Summer jobs, official Waldameer website, https://waldameer.com/about/summer-jobs/

136   Reviews, Glassdoor

137   The history of Knott's Scary Farm: a sinister start, Expedition Theme Park, https://www.youtube.com/watch?v=wvDmgmUBED4

as a meaningless, self-proclaimed slogan, but if you genuinely are an employer of choice it gives you a big competitive advantage. You shouldn't need to worry about not filling vacancies and should be able to cream off the strongest candidates leaving the weaker ones for your competitors. Your staff will take pride in knowing that what they do is highly sought after. Unfortunately, I see quite a few companies pushing zero-hour contracts to the limit, offering unfavourable working contracts, few perks and little meaningful staff development, and yet they refer to themselves as being an employer of choice. Even as they struggle to fill positions, they continue to throw around these meaningless words.

What is the solution to all of this? Using some flexible staffing techniques in a limited form will help, particularly if it's done fairly and transparently. Having strong recruitment techniques and being an all-round good company to work for will also help. But even taking these things into account, you can't allow guest levels to swing too wildly from day to day. This creates a need for the staffing levels to also swing wildly to match, and this is very difficult to manage. You need to have incentives for staff to stick around until the end of the season or the end of the summer. Your staff will work harder and for more hours in the busiest periods, but this needs to be controlled. Otherwise they'll burn out. Using the ideas in this chapter, you can flatten off your attendance between days, making it much easier to adequately staff your attraction in a sustainable way.

Making the numbers work

Theme parks want to make their queues shorter, but they need to do it in a sustainable, cost effective way.

Some of the ideas I've given can quickly become hugely expensive. You want to flatten off the peaks in attendance, but not with it coming at a big cost your park can't afford. Weather proofing often requires big capital expenditure and has a long term, uncertain benefit. However, if your park is in an area with poor weather, it often turns out to be one of the more effective ways at redistributing crowds, reducing complaints and raising guest satisfaction.

Broadening the demographic of the park is a fairly long-term project, perhaps a decade or longer. You don't want to oversell and underdeliver. There's no point in trying to market you park to people with pre-school aged children or to groups of adults without children, if the product doesn't have the scope, breadth and quality to satisfy them. The ideal is to slightly broaden the market of the park, so that people who are on the margins of whether they'd want to visit feel it's worth coming. Trying to market yourself to people who firmly don't like theme parks is a losing game.

There can be advantages to extending the season and opening the park on days when it was previously closed. It helps with retaining staff and giving people hours. But opening a theme park is expensive, so it's often more economical to bring in extra visitors on a quiet day rather than on a day when the park was previously closed. Aiming to open for more days is a worthwhile thing, and opens up other doors like the option of guest accommodation (hotels etc) which might not be viable if you're only open at weekends and school holidays. However, if you're going to extend the operating calendar, you probably need to raise your attendance rather than simply moving existing visits to the extra operating days.

Events can be effective at moving visits to less busy days. You're treading a fine balance between doing enough for people to feel it's worth shifting their visit, but not wanting to spend so much on an event that the cost outweighs the benefit. There is a temptation to do a cheap event on a quiet day and market it heavily. However, you can disappoint people once, but they might not let you do it twice.

Discounting to bring people in at quiet times can be effective when it's carefully targeted, for example doing a student deal at local universities encouraging them to visit on offpeak days, or a parent/toddler deal for quiet times. However, with discounting you want to be careful not to damage the brand and its pricing integrity. You also don't want to end up with a situation where you get the same number of visitors, but with some guests getting discounts they hadn't previously had. The other alternative is to hold your pricing on quiet days, but offer something extra free. Disney do this with their free dining plans when you stay in a hotel at a quiet time of year. Alton Towers have done this where people can visit in September (which is usually quiet) and they get a free t-shirt if they ride on the five biggest coasters. I'd avoid dynamic pricing for regular tickets and use it only for accommodation and seasonal events like Halloween. Over using dynamic pricing confuses guests, is off putting and can leave a lot of your visitors feeling like they've paid too much.

Redistributing Guests within the Park

Redistributing crowds within the park

We've talked about how a theme park can redistribute guests through the season, encouraging some of the people who visit on the busiest days to visit on a quieter day. You can also find that guests aren't distributed evenly around a park, and that one area can be relatively busy, while another part of the park is a lot quieter. How can we move guests from the busier areas to the quieter areas?

In this section we're going to look at the layouts of different parks. A well-designed layout will help to disperse the guests evenly through the park. I've started with the layout first, because this is one of the first things you need to think about when you're planning a new park.

We then look at other ways to distribute guests more evenly through the park. These are things that can be done retrospectively with an existing park. With modern technology, such as mobile apps and waiting time boards, it is easier to communicate where the shortest waiting times are. For this reason, having a layout that naturally helps with guest flow is less important than it was in the past. Nonetheless, it's still useful for designers to think about the layout. We consider virtual queuing and some lower tech ideas, such as wayfinding and encouraging guests to plan their day. Before we get onto that though, we're going to talk about ring shaped parks and parks with a hub and spoke layout. How do these layouts improve the guest flow?

Ring shaped parks

Coaster Kingdom gives the following description of Port Aventura's layout, "The path is designed as a large circle meaning rides' queues are normally quite short and don't suffer from early morning and late evening rushes as people work their way across the park"[138]. A lot of parks are designed as a loop, where guests can scatter in either direction. This is sometimes called 'a ring layout' or a 'Duell Loop'. The layout is designed to be easy to navigate and disperse guests fairly evenly around the park, although not as effectively as the hub and spoke layout, which we discuss later. Epcot's World Showcase (Disney World, Orlando) and Islands of Adventure (Universal, Orlando) are two other examples of a loop shaped layout. Both of these have a lake in the centre, which makes it more obvious. But you can have a main path going around in a big ring, with rides and theatres in the centre, rather than a lake. Compared to a grid shaped park, it's less confusing for new visitors. If they keep on following the loop, they'll eventually get to where they want to.

The architect Randall Duell founded a company called Duell Associates, which designed over 40 theme parks. This includes Six Flags Over Texas (1961), Astro World (1968), Magic Mountain (1971) and Opryland (1972) as well as some international parks including Everland (South Korea), Parc Astérix (France) and Bellewaerde (Belgium). He also designed the UK and France pavilions for Epcot[139], presumably because Disney Imagineering were too stretched to design everything in house. Everland and Parc Astérix were both originally based around the Duell Loop, as were most of the others, including his first park, Six Flags Over Texas[140]. This is why the ring-shaped parks are sometimes called a Duell Loop. Six Flags St Louis (1971), originally known as Six Flags Over Mid-America, used a Duell Loop centred around the Palace Theater. It was the third Six Flags park and the final one they built from ground up. Other historians have argued that St Louis deviated a bit from the classic Duell Loop[141].

Magic Mountain (California) was originally going to be built as a loop with a tunnel dug through the mountain, but this was cut due to budgetary constraints. This is partly why Magic Mountain ended up with some of its early

---

138   Tutuki Splash, Coaster Kingdom, http://www.s104638357. websitehome.co.uk/html/tutukisplash_main.htm

139   Randall A Duell, Harry Michelson, Amusement Parkives, https:// amusementparkives.com/2017/07/31/randall-a-duell/

140   Book review and giveaway: Imagineering an American Dream-scape, Coaster 101, https://www.coaster101.com/2020/08/05/ book-review-giveaway-imagineering-american-dreamscape/

141   Six Flags Over Mid-America: last of the original, Barry R Hill, River Shore Creative, https://www.rivershorecreative.com/ blog/2020/7/23/six-flags-over-mid-america-last-of-the-originals

major coasters near the front of the park. Magic Mountain's designer Randall Duell said, "This turned the park literally into two cul-de-sacs. People were tending to pile up in the rear of the park and management felt that a big magnet was needed to pull them back to the front. The marketing department also had a great deal to say about it. They felt that a coaster would be visible from the highway generating more business from passing traffic. The loop has recently been completed making the park far more flexible".

The hub and spoke layout

The most famous theme park layout is no doubt the hub and spoke system used by Disney for their Magic Kingdom style parks. The parks are arranged like a wagon wheel. Main Street takes you down to a central hub in front of the castle, and from there you can choose to visit any area in the park. It was used for the original Disneyland in 1955, and it's served them so well, that they still used it for Shanghai, which opened in 2016 - 61 years later.

In a moment I will describe the main features of the hub and spoke layout, and afterwards I will provide a basic diagram.

What are the main features of the hub and spoke layout?

Main Street takes you directly from the entrance to the centre of the park. Or at least, what was the centre of the park when it was originally built. Main Street has various shops and eateries, but it doesn't have any rides, aside from the railway station. This is important, because having rides would defeat the point. The rides in Main Street would get clogged at the times when everyone enters and leaves the park. There is the Mickey Mouse meet and greet at the Town Hall Theatre, and this can get long queues.

Main Street has to be wide enough, and free of obstacles, to cope with the rush of guests at the end of the day when everyone leaves. This is particularly true when there's a big rush, either because the fireworks have finished, or because the park's closing early for Mickey's Not So Scary Halloween Party or Mickey's Very Merry Christmas Party. Given that Main Street has to be wide anyway, it makes it a good location for the parade.

There aren't any rides at the centre of the park in the hub, because these would also get clogged when people arrive early in the day, as everyone gets funnelled towards the hub.

A lot of people will pass through the hub getting to other areas, so like Main Street it has to be spacious and reasonably free of obstacles.

You can pass between the areas further out from the centre, without going into the hub. This eases congestion in the hub. For example, you can walk between Tomorrowland and Fantasyland without having to go back into the centre of the park.

The hub is where people make a lot of their decisions about where to go. There has to be clear signage for wayfinding, and ideally information about the queues. This can be relatively straightforward now with computer screens, and used to be done with a big blackboard.

Most of the E ticket rides (major rides) are around the edge of the park. This hasn't always stayed the case as the parks have expanded. For example, at the original Disneyland, The Matterhorn Bobsled became landlocked early on in the park's development. To ease congestion, the entrance to the Matterhorn Bobsled is on the far side of the ride to the castle, putting distance between it and the hub. Big Thunder Mountain has become largely landlocked by Galaxy's Edge. Nonetheless, the space between the central hub and the big E ticket rides is roughly equidistant.

By having the E ticket rides around the edge, you can have an access road around the outside of the park, which helps with deliveries, maintenance and emergency vehicles.

Around the edge of the park is a steam railway, which can help those with reduced mobility get around the park easily.

At Magic Kingdom, the world's most visited theme park, there is a system of 'Utilidors' under the park. Utilidor is a contraction of 'utility corridor'. This helps staff get around the park quickly and without being seen. The staff canteen is under the castle, where staff from around the park can get to it quickly.

The hub and spoke pattern lends itself to a circular shaped park. Disneyland was built on a square plot of land. The park itself is roughly circular, and then the space around the edge is the backstage area, for example workshops, storage facilities for parade floats, storage for merchandise and food, costuming, staff smoking areas, training rooms, rehearsal space for entertainers, offices etc.

From the bottom to the centre we have the long Main Street. In the middle we have the circular hub and the spokes coming off it. The white circle is the park itself and the grey areas are the backstage spaces.

The hub and spoke design does put pressure on Main Street, which is the only way to and from the entrance. The centre of the park does get particularly congested. When they designed Magic Kingdom (opened 1971), they made Main Street wider than the original at Disneyland, and the hub was almost double the size[142]. This served the park well most of the time, although on particularly peak days such as New Year, they would open a path through the backstage area so that guests could bypass Main Street. By the 2010s the park was struggling to cope more often. In 2008 Magic Kingdom got an estimated 17,063,000 guests[143]. By 2018 this had risen to 20,859,000[144]. In addition, the centre of the park was becoming increasingly congested in the evenings with the Main Street Electrical Parade, Celebrate the Magic (projection mapping show) and Wishes (fireworks). In 2014 they expanded the hub's pathways by removing some of the grassy areas, and putting in bigger shrubs and trees around the edge to create a new berm between the hub and the lands around it. In 2019 they made the moats around the castle smaller to allow for further expansion of the pathways[145].

For Disneyland Paris (1992) they tweaked the design. At Magic Kingdom and Tokyo Disney they have to close the path through the castle when shows are on in front of it. At Disneyland Paris they put a little outdoor theatre to the side of the castle, so that they can do costume character shows without congesting the area[146].

In Disney's Magic Kingdom style parks there aren't normally any rides in the hub at the centre, because this is where most of the guests are funnelled towards, so any rides in the centre could become very busy. It's like putting a ride next to the park's entrance. The Future World section of Epcot does have Spaceship Earth in its hub. Because Epcot has two entrances, not all the guests will pass through the hub on their way into the park, although most of them do. Spaceship Earth is significantly busier in the morning than it is later on in the day. However, being an 'omnimover' type ride, it does have a very high throughput and compared to Soarin' or Test Track, it's not a ride that so many guests want to start off their day with. Typically, Spaceship Earth will have a twenty-minute queue near the beginning of the day, but it will be walk on later on. If Spaceship Earth had a lower throughput, or a stronger appeal, then its location in the hub could be a problem.

The hub and spoke design has been used for many cities through the ages. Walt was probably inspired by Washington DC, which was designed with this radial pattern by architect Pierre L'Enfant. Many airports are now also designed with this structure. Walt believed that the hub and spoke pattern would make his park easy to navigate, spread people out and limit

---

142   Why Disney's Magic Kingdom hub needed expansion, Theme Park University, https://themeparkuniversity.com/disney/disneys-magic-kingdom-hub-needed-expansion/

143   2008 Attraction Attendance Report, Themed Entertainment Association, http://www.teaconnect.org/images/files/TEA_23_503031_140617.pdf

144   2018 Themed Index, Themed Entertainment Association, https://aecom.com/content/wp-content/uploads/2019/05/Theme-Index-2018-5-1.pdf

145   Sidewalk expansion behind Cinderella Castle in Disney's Magic Kingdom, Ziggy Knows Disney, https://ziggyknowsdisney.com/cinderella-castle-pathway-construction-update/

146   Disneyland Paris – The hub and Sleeping Beauty Castle, Jack Spence, All Ears, https://allears.net/2009/02/09/disneyland-paris-the-hub-and-sleeping-beauty-castle/

the amount of walking people had to do. According to Disney historian Jim Korkis, "Years later, the Disney company bought expensive time on a massive computer to determine the optimum design for an entertainment venue that would handle "x" number of customers, have "y" number of areas for them to visit, etc. The results were that the computer recommended the exact same design that Walt had come up with, which included a single entrance and a centralized hub"[147].

In 2018 the three most visited theme parks in the world were the Magic Kingdom style parks in Orlando, California and Tokyo, all using the same hub and spoke system. The hub and spoke system seems obvious, but it wasn't something they came up with overnight, and the plans for Disneyland evolved from a much smaller Mickey Mouse Park attached to the Walt Disney Studio in Burbank. At the time the thought was that a small theme park could be linked to a tour of the studio next door, perhaps inspired by the studio tour Universal were already doing nearby. The Mickey Mouse Park could double up as a tourist attraction and film locations, part offsetting the cost. Thematically Mickey Mouse Park was going to fuse together Disney icons and American history. There'd be a recreation of the cottage from Snow White and the Seven Dwarfs and a canal that floated through the whale from Pinocchio. Areas would be themed to traditional Americana, including a small-town square, perhaps partly inspired by Walt's hometown of Marceline and a Wild West town.

The planning that went into guest flow shows that Walt was aware that his bigger Disneyland park would need to have the capacity to handle large crowds of people. Once Walt had the investment, Disneyland went from the drawing board to opening astonishingly quickly, but by this stage a lot of thought had already gone into developing the idea. Walt Disney famously said, "I never could convince the financiers that Disneyland was feasible, because dreams offer too little collateral". But he wasn't just showing them some 'dreams'. He was showing them detailed plans for a new concept. The railway around the outside was actually one of the things that stayed more or less constant in all of Walt's plans. He had a lifelong love of trains, and had built a miniature railway around his garden in 1950. Most of the illustrations of the park were aerial drawings that clearly showed the spacing between attractions. However, the concept drawing most people will think of are the 3D drawings used to woo investors, including a drawing by John Hench and another by Peter Ellenshaw.

After opening Disneyland, Walt turned his mind to another even bigger project. He wanted to design an entire city. Walt didn't want his city to be congested, and he wanted people to be able to get around on foot as much as possible. The hub and spoke layout would have kept the distance between housing, schools, shops and work as small as possible. It was going to be a very different kind of city to Los Angeles, where everything is very spread

---

147   Walt Disney World Chronicles: history of the hub, Jim Korkis, All Ears, https://allears.net/walt-disney-world-chronicles-history-of-the-hub/

out and reliant on the car. Sadly, Walt died in 1966 and the city was never built. The field of urban planning looks at the design of cities and how they evolve, and some its theories can be applied to theme parks, and vice versa. What made Disneyland so successful, was that it combined functionality with feeling and emotion.

Urban planner Stephen Rowley describes Disneyland, "Generally Disney's original scheme holds up incredibly well, coping with visitor numbers the original designers could never have envisaged. The park is easy to navigate, with its radial layout and highly visible landmarks assisting orientation and allowing visitors to move from one part of the park to another with little fatigue or frustration"[148].

Keeping a coherent layout when you expand

Realistically most parks aren't going to be able to follow a perfect hub and spoke pattern, and even Disneyland hasn't as its expanded. The idea was that originally, you'd go down Main Street to the hub at the centre of the park, where you could access all the areas. Mickey's Toon Town was added in 1993 and sits out on a limb at the back of the park behind It's a Small World. Normally you put a big ride at the back of the park to draw people to it. When it first opened Mickey's Toon Town didn't have any significant rides, unless you count the small Vekoma Gadget's Go Coaster. A year later they opened Roger Rabbit's Cartoon Spin. It's a decent dark ride, but not an E ticket (headline) ride. Eventually they planned to add a copy of Mickey's Runaway Adventure to the area in 2022. At the time of writing it looks like this is still going ahead, despite the current coronavirus pandemic.

The other big area tacked on to the back of the park is Galaxy's Edge, which you can access from Fantasyland or Frontierland. It's only really going to be possible for a maximum of about 5 areas to join up with the central hub, and the bigger the park gets, the harder it is for the Main Street to actually take you to the centre of the park, not to mention that you can't very easily move the castle back once it's built. Magic Kingdom style parks tend to have fewer areas than some other parks. For example, Europa Park currently has 18 areas. Imagine trying to link all of those up to a central hub.

There is a risk that a park that starts off with a coherent structure becomes increasingly chaotic through piecemeal developments. Parks can mitigate this in a couple of ways. Firstly, they can look to expand without significantly altering the layout of the park's pathways and areas. A famous example of this is the Indiana Jones Adventure at Disneyland. The park sits inside a berm (mound of soil) with the Disneyland Railroad running inside it. The Indiana Jones dark ride is set outside the berm, but rather than building paths out to it and creating a new area, the entrance and exit to the ride is in the original Adventureland, and a really long queue and exit ramp take guests to and from the ride. The advantage to doing this is that the pathways and areas within the park aren't altered, preserving the hub and spoke principle.

---

148   Walt Disney: Urban planner, Sterow, http://www.sterow.com/?p=2368#.XsDcx8BS-Un

The downside is that if the park expands, but the pathways and areas don't, then they can become increasingly crowded. Although not as extreme, Magic Kingdom's Space Mountain uses a long queue and exit ramp that go down under the Disneyland Railroad to the ride, which sits outside the main area of the park.

Disneyland does get particularly huge numbers of visitors, and considerably more now than it did when it first opened. Originally Adventureland was just home to The Jungle Cruise and the Swiss Family Robinson Treehouse (rethemed to Tarzan's Treehouse in 1999). In 1967 Pirates of the Caribbean opened. Technically it's in New Orleans Square, but it sits at the conjuncture between the two areas. Then in 1995 they added the Indiana Jones Adventure ride. As mentioned, the ride's show building itself sits outside the berm, but the entrance to the queue is inside Adventureland between The Jungle Cruise and Pirates. Since then Adventureland has tended to get very crowded.

Park capacity is an issue that deserves its own chapter, but easing congestion in Adventureland has been a challenge since Indiana Jones Adventure opened. In 2017 they had their first attempt at tackling this. They closed two giftshops: the Indiana Jones Adventure Outpost and South Seas Traders. The Bengal Barbecue moved seating into these shops and removed outdoor seating, making the path wider. The Tropical Imports fruit stand was moved, freeing up space for a new stroller parking area, as these were blocking up the pathway. In 2019 more changes came. Disneyland went completely smoke free, meaning smoking areas could be eliminated. They put in new restrictions on the sizes of strollers that guests could bring into the park[149]. As part of the Project Stardust initiative to raise the park's capacity, the entrance into Adventureland was widened to remove the bottleneck. There is a balance between having enough paths, shops, eateries and toilets to handle the crowds, but not wanting to have so many areas it makes the layout unnecessarily complicated and expensive to run and maintain.

In April 2020 Nick Sim from Coasters 101 ran a feature looking at rides that use long queues, where the entrance to the ride is some distance from the ride itself[150]. He identified The Bat at Kings Island, American Eagle at Six Flags Great America, The Boss at Six Flags St Louis and Mind Eraser at Darien Lake. American Eagle sits the other side of an access road and the railway. The Boss is the other side of the Go Karts. Mind Eraser is the other side of a lake.

It's not common for a long queue and exit path to separate the entrance to the ride from the ride itself, but there are situations where it can work. If your paths are congested, then it makes sense to build a new area to spread the guests out more. If they're not overly busy, then it can be useful to keep the existing infrastructure in place. It avoids having too many cul-de-sacs, dead ends and it helps to keep the park's layout simple. It also means that

149   To handle Star Wars crowds – Disney nixes smoking areas – bans wide strollers, Hugo Martin, Los Angeles Times, https://www.latimes.com/business/la-fi-disneyland-crowds-star-wars-20190328-story.html

150   Longest walks to ride a roller coaster, Nick Sim, Coaster 101, https://www.coaster101.com/2020/04/24/longest-walks-to-ride-a-roller-coaster/

you can add new rides without the cost of building a new area to go with it, including toilets, theming and whatever else you decide an area needs.

If the entrance to a roller coaster is some distance from the ride itself, it might cause confusion. Guests can be trying to find a path that takes them to the roller coaster, rather than an entrance some way away. In these situations, it's important to make the entrance very big and obvious, and to have clear signage directing guests to it. Bear in mind that some guests won't know the names of the rides. They'll just be thinking, I want to get to that big wooden roller coaster. It can be useful to have a picture of the ride on the signage. In the case of a dark ride like Indiana Jones Adventure, this isn't an issue, because the ride's in a show building that the guests can't see.

A second option is to build a park with plans for development built into it. Disneyland Hong Kong was built with an expansion ring around it, so that the park had the potential to grow in all directions[151]. It allows for what Imagineerland calls "controlled expansion". Like most of the other Magic Kingdom style parks, Hong Kong Disneyland has a steam railway in a big loop. The expansion ring takes place outside the railway tracks. Magic Kingdom (Orlando) and Parc Disneyland Paris are almost entirely within the railway tracks. Disneyland (California) was also almost entirely within the railway until they added Mickey's Toontown in 1993 – 38 years after the park opened. This means that the railroad at Hong Kong Disneyland is shorter than the ones in California, Orlando and Paris. Instead of creating a berm around the outside of the park, it creates a berm within the park between the different themed areas.

It's not been possible to include maps or aerial photos for most of the parks I've written about. But if you search for these online, you'll be able to see more clearly how the different parks are put together, layout wise.

The World Showcase at Epcot (Orlando) has empty plots for more pavilions. It's more obvious from the access road behind the Showcase that the staff buses run on, than from the guest areas. Despite the possibility for more pavilions, so far they've only added one pavilion since the park opened. This was the Morocco Pavilion in 1984 – two years after the park opened. Originally Disney had hoped that the different areas in the World Showcase would be sponsored by the governments of their countries. Morocco was the only government that agreed to sponsor a pavilion. I think there are various reasons why they haven't added more areas, which I will explain in a moment. Nonetheless, the basic principle of leaving room for expansion is still there, regardless of whether or not it was used.

It's partly because Epcot cost roughly double the original budget. After Epcot was completed there was limited appetite to spend more on it, and initially funding was prioritised for the original Disneyland in California. Disneyland's investment had dried up as money went into Epcot Center. Once Disney began pressing ahead with Hollywood Studios (Disney World's

---

151   The theme park environment: the urban plan, Imagineerland, http://imagi-neerland.blogspot.com/2016/02/theme-park-environmentals-urban-plan.html

third park), there wasn't much money left over for new pavilions in Epcot. Each pavilion costs a lot to run, in terms of sourcing staff, merchandise and authentic foods from that country. The Future World half of the park arguably dated quicker than World Showcase, and that's where the upgrades have tended to go, such as Mission Space and Test Track. When they did get to expanding World Showcase, the feeling was that it needed rides more than areas, so the money that could have gone into a new pavilion instead went on the Ratatouille trackless ride. So it is, that despite leaving space for more areas, the World Showcase hasn't actually added any. Nonetheless, the foresight is something that other parks can learn from.

At Disneyland Shanghai there's a much larger 11 acre hub compared to at the other Magic Kingdom style parks. This means that there's a bigger ring for the different areas to join up with. This has created quite a bit of space that can be fleshed out with future rides in empty areas between the different lands. For example, rides like Space Mountain or It's a Small World can be added within the park's existing footprint. Given the population of China and the rising middle class, it is possible that this could one day be the world's most visited theme park, even though it'd need several more rides to stand any chance of that. The 'Shanghai Metropolitan Area' currently has a population of 34 million.

Above is the park's opening map. Toy Story Land has already been added on the outer ring between Tomorrowland and Fantasyland.

What lessons can we borrow from the hub and spoke layout?

It isn't going to be possible for every park to follow a hub and spoke design. In fact, most won't. Disney are able to build relatively large parks from scratch, making it easier to plan. Most parks grow slower and more organically. Disney parks are always built on flat pieces of land that provide a blank canvas. Other parks have to work with the topography of the land, existing structures, as well as more rigorous planning rules which can dictate where things have to go. A hub and spoke pattern works best with a circular shaped park. Many parks have more rectangular shaped plots of land. Luckily most parks won't get over 20 million visitors a year, like Magic Kingdom did in 2018.

Even Disney hasn't used a perfect hub and spoke layout for their non-Magic Kingdom parks. Disney designer Tony Baxter says, "The Disneyland layout is the finest one we've ever done. Everything else has been trying to work around it and avoid the cliché of using it again, so you've got a lake in Epcot, you've got kind of a randomness about the Studio Tour, and maybe even Animal Kingdom, that I don't think is as clear to the public"[152].

The hub and spoke system relies on guests being taken to a point close to the centre of the park. In Magic Kingdom's case, it's down Main Street. It seems to work for Disney, but Disney have no shortage of shops to fit into Main Street. Not only are the parks themselves popular, but Disney own so many iconic brands and characters, that the shops are practically a licence to print money. Main Street at Disneyland currently has 16 shops and there are a staggering 38 shops that have come and gone. Magic Kingdom's Main Street has 10 shops. Tokyo Disney's has 14. Disneyland Paris has 14 and Hong Kong Disney has 12.

A lot of parks do have equivalents to Main Street. For example, Alton Towers has Towers Street. Europa Park has Deutsche Alley. Parc Astérix has the Via Antiqua street, that merges architecture from the different themed areas within the park (Roman, ancient Greek, ancient Egyptian, Viking). But most parks don't have the number of shops and restaurants that would be needed to take the area far enough to reach the centre of the park. Also, Disney use their Main Streets for the parades and as viewing areas for the nightly firework shows. Without these, those areas could feel very much like a cash in/dead space. It also must be noted that Disney parks cost vastly more than regional parks to build. Your typical regional park isn't going to want to waste lots of money with a long-themed corridor going into the centre of the park. An advantage of the loop shaped parks, like Islands of Adventure and Port Aventura, is that the entrance can feed straight onto the loop where the attractions are.

Some parks fuse together the hub and spoke and the loop. For example, Epcot uses a spoke system for Future World and a loop for the World Showcase.

The hub and spoke layout won't be practical for most attractions. However, there are still lessons they can take away from Disney's design. The entrance is going to get busy at the beginning and end of the day, so it needs wide paths even if they won't be needed for much of the time. The same is true for the toilets. The entrance will need a generously sized toilet facility, even though this might be underused for much of the time.

---

152   Theme Park Insider interview with Disney Legend and Imagineer Tony Baxter: part one, Robert Niles, Theme Park Insider, https://www.themeparkinsider.com/flume/201311/3760/

A lot of theme parks do have an access road that runs around the outside, although this can be a challenge for very compact parks like seaside amusement parks. Junctions in paths are where people make decisions, so clear wayfinding is important. Ideally you should avoid having most of your big rides in one half of the park. This might not always be possible, for example if one half of the park is nearer housing and has tougher planning restrictions, but even then you can look at dark rides and enclosed areas.

Large parks often will benefit from a transport system joining up points around the edge. Efteling opened in 1952, three years before Disneyland. One of the early attractions was the narrow-gauge railway in 1969. The railway originally ran a there and back route, but was extended to make a loop in 1984. The line has four steam engines, plus a diesel for maintenance. When Six Flags Great Adventure opened in 1974 the two biggest rides were the log flume and the cable car. In 1953 Alton Towers opened one of their first attractions, the miniature railway. It carried guests between what is now Mutiny Bay near the front of the park, to the Chinese Temple near the back. In 1963 they added their first cable car, which now resides at Flamingo Land.

Whilst most parks won't lead guests straight from the entrance to a hub in the middle, most parks do avoid putting their entrance in a corner.

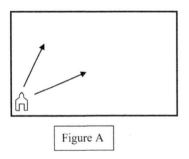

Figure A

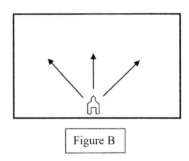

Figure B

In figure B the guests are fanned out around the park more effectively than in figure A. In Europe and the United States we might not see that many new theme parks in the future, as it's a mature industry where most markets are already served. Building a park from scratch is very expensive due to land prices, planning processes and the cost of putting in the infrastructure. However, even if we're not designing an entire park, these principles would apply to an individual area within a park, where it disperses guests better when they enter from the centre of the area, rather than from a corner.

We've just focussed on the layout of an individual park, but we might also want to think about the guest flow around a resort. As well as a theme park there might well be car parks, a water park, other second gate attractions (such as an aquarium, mini golf) hotels, restaurants etc.

Other design considerations

When a large show empties out, it can cause an influx to the queues on the attractions near it. This is a particular problem if a large show empties out and the rides nearby have low throughputs. If a large theatre is on the edge of the park the guests tend to all empty out into one location. If a theatre's landlocked in the middle of the park, you can have multiple exits emptying into different areas. At Europa Park their ice show is in a circular theatre. The doors on one side empty into the Greek area. The doors on the other side empty into the England area.

Some research has suggested that when people are choosing directions, they tend to follow their dominant hand[153]. Since roughly nine out of ten guests are right-handed, most guests are inclined to go right. If we get people heading for a specific attraction rather than blindly following paths and hoping to stumble across attractions, it makes this bias less relevant. It might also be something we can compensate for when we're designing a park. For example, if a lot more guests are taking the right-hand path, we can do something to draw more attention to the left-hand path, like using a brighter coloured sign. It's going to take some experimenting to get the balance right, and to avoid overcompensating.

Tony Baxter is a Disney legend whose designs include Big Thunder Mountain, Star Tours and Splash Mountain. He was also the lead designer for Disneyland Paris. In an interview with the Season Pass Podcast, he talked about the decision-making process for choosing new rides[154]. There are plenty of factors parks take into account including planning regulations, the height restriction (demographic who can ride it) and the throughput. He also tells us that they tend to place new attractions in areas of the park that currently have lower footfall. His example is Splash Mountain.

At the time Critter Country (originally Indian Village, renamed Bear Country in 1972 and finally Critter Country in 1988) was relatively quiet. The Country Bear Jamboree animatronic show had two theatres offering the same show. By this point they were only using one theatre to keep the costs down, and over the course of a day it was still using less than 50% of its capacity. "There were many fans of the Country Bear Jamboree, but they weren't going in the ride. The turnstile tells the tale". Baxter explains that the executives wanted to get 3-4% more of the park's guests into Critter Country to relieve pressure on the busier areas. "So, we put in Splash [Mountain] and that did it. It delivered 2000 guests every hour. You can do the maths on that. If you had 50,000 people in the park and you had 2,000 of them going on that ride. And we thought that families with little kids will go on the Country Bear Jamboree, but they didn't". Eventually in 2001 they closed Country Bear Jamboree and replaced it with the Many Adventures of Winnie the Pooh tracked dark ride.

In Disneyland's case, Splash Mountain failed to boost the popularity of Country Bear's Jamboree. However, it is a general principle that a lower key ride will be more popular when its entrance is near a more popular ride. The

153   How to avoid the slowest line at a theme park, John, Coaster101, https://www. coaster101.com/2020/01/31/how-to-avoid-the-slowest-line-at-a-theme-park/

154   The Tony Baxter interview part 9, episode 383, The Season Pass Podcast, http://www.seasonpasspodcast.com/index.html

Oriental Scenic Railway at Luna Park (Coney Island, New York) was built in 1901 or 1902 and lasted until 1954. In 1924 the Mile Sky Chaser opened next door. At the time it was Coney Island's tallest and longest roller coaster. You might imagine that having a bigger roller coaster opening next door would have nicked the Oriental Scenic Railway's custom. It actually had the opposite effect[155]. It bought more guests over to that area of the Coney Island district and the Oriental Scenic Railway benefitted from that.

When Rita opened at Alton Towers in 2005 the queues seemed to get a bit shorter for Corkscrew, the other big coaster in the area. This is the opposite of what happened at Coney Island. This might be because you had to walk past the Rita entrance to get to Corkscrew. If it had been the other way around it could have been better for the guest flow.

Hershey Park (Pennsylvania) is perhaps most famous for two things: its relationship with the iconic American chocolate and its roller coasters. At the time of writing (2020), it has 14 roller coasters. Only six parks in the world have more. Hershey Park is one of America's more compact theme parks, so fitting in a new coaster can be a challenge. However, they don't want to just squeeze in a new coaster wherever there's room. They also want to distribute the major coasters evenly around the park to spread out the crowds. When they were planning Skyrush, a 200ft tall Intamin wing coaster that opened in 2012, they identified two areas of the park with older rides where the crowds were thinner: The Kissing Tower (named after Hershey's Kisses) and Comet Hollow (named after their Comet wooden coaster built in 1946)[156]. In the end they chose Comet Hollow. Some locations are harder for building new rides, based on issues such as the topography of the land (how hilly it is) and how close it is to nearby housing (causing noise restrictions). Building a ride in the easiest locations won't necessarily create the best guest flow.

When Great Adventure opened in 1974 the headline ride was its Log Flume, then the world's longest and with a rotating turntable to give a high throughput. It was so popular and with such long queues, that the following year they added Hydro Flume, another log flume type attraction. They deliberately built the Hydro Flume on the opposite side of the park to the Log Flume to help spread the guests apart[157]. A common design for a theme park is to have a hub in the centre with shops, restaurants, a guest service and potentially games (sideshows). The main rides are placed around the edge of the park. If the biggest rides are clustered together in the centre it isn't ideal, but each park has its challenges and you have to work around what you've got.

Some parks are more spread out than others. At one end of the spectrum we have compact amusement parks like Gröna Lund (Sweden) and Blackpool Pleasure Beach (UK). At the other end we have spread out parks with lots of

155   Coney Island, independent rides, Jeffrey Stanton, https://www.westland.net/coneyisland/articles/independentrides.htm

156   On thrill rides like Hershey Park's Skyrush, math and physics rule, Nick Malawskey, Penn Live.com

157   Hydro Flume, Six Flags Great Adventure History, http://www.greatadventurehistory.com/HydroFlume.htm

woodland and gardens like Alton Towers (UK) and Efteling (Netherlands). In some ways spread out theme parks have an advantage in that guests are physically spaced out over more acreage and the time guests spend walking between the attractions is time when they're not queuing. However, I wouldn't encourage parks to deliberately make their park unnecessarily spread out or make their paths unnecessarily winding and indirect. Personally, I like walking, but some guests have small children, pushchairs, disabilities and other mobility issues. For spread out parks it's useful to have a transport system, like Alton Tower's cable car or Efteling's steam railway. If there are long paths it's good to have things for people to look at, whether it's models/ tableaus, well landscaped gardens, a model village or animal enclosures. The point is though that you want each area/land to have a similar density of guests in it. If you walk into one area and it feels packed whilst another area is like a ghost town, then that's a poorly designed park. With mobile apps they can track where guests are and create heat maps showing how well distributed your visitors are.

The need to spread guests out is different at an international resort like Disneyland, compared to a regional park. At Disneyland the paths can become unpleasantly busy, particularly when guests are taking photos, or sticking together as a group. When paths become overly crowded, guests are more likely to get jostled and small children can get lost in the crowd. If there are too many guests concentrated in a particular area and something causes them to panic, such as a fire, or a terrorist attack, then there's a real risk of guests getting crushed at bottle necks and pinch pints. This can cause serious injury. Congested paths make it difficult to get emergency vehicles through. We discuss this risk and how to manage it in the section on park capacities. This could also be an issue at seaside and urban amusement parks where everything's packed together very tightly.

For most regional parks, dispersing guests isn't as safety critical. It can still be beneficial though. Imagine that there's one third of the park, where the restaurants have big queues at lunchtime, and the toilets are hard to keep clean because of the amount of traffic they get. In another area of the park, the toilets are barely used, and the restaurants tend to have empty seats and surplus capacity. You can imagine which area of the park you might want to build the next big roller coaster in.

Timed ticketing (virtual queues)

Virtual queuing means that instead of guests standing in a traditional line, they reserve a spot on a ride and can experience other attractions while they're waiting. We're going to look at different kinds of virtual queuing, how they can be used to move crowds around and what the guests can do while they're waiting for their slot on a ride.

In 2017 Efteling introduced timed ticketing for their Vekoma Python roller coaster. Karin Koppelmans is a communication and PR advisor at Efteling. At the time of writing she has worked there for around 28 years - since 1991. She told the BBC news, "You can do other fun things while you are virtually waiting, a bit of organising and a bit of wandering and being enchanted"[158]. Efteling has a beautiful setting and a lot of animatronic tableau themed around traditional fairy tales, myths and legends. Guests can wander around soaking up the atmosphere of the park, rather than slowly moving along a line. Ride reservation systems with timed tickets might well work better in parks where there is plenty to do between the rides. The companies who produce reservation systems push increased revenue from retail as a key advantage. When guests are waiting for their time slot, they might spend time in the gift shops. But if there's an hour's queue guests aren't going to spend an hour in the gift shops. Zoo areas, aquariums, museums, animatronic tableau and streetmosphere all give guests something to do while they're waiting for their timeslot.

In 2017 Europa Park opened their flying theatre Voletarium. Let's talk about why Voletarium needed a virtual queue and why it works so well. It's in their German Alley area at the entrance to the park. Having a major ride right by the entrance can cause a problem, as it gets very busy early on in the day, and then in the afternoon it can become quiet once a lot of visitors have moved through the park towards the back. Voletarium became the first, and currently only, ride at Europa Park to deploy a free reservation system. The idea was to encourage visitors to grab a ticket and delay riding until later in the day when the initial rush would have died down. There is a second rush at the end of the day when guests pass Voletarium on their way to the exit.

Walt Disney got around the problem of the ride nearest the entrance getting swamped, by using his hub and spoke layout. We've already discussed this. From the end of Main Street guests can get to several big rides in roughly the same distance. This is arguably the most successful layout for a park. Although Disney's Main Street has no 'rides', there is the Main Street railway station just inside the entrance, which takes guests on a steam train trip, stopping off at station in the other lands. At Disneyland Paris, the Main Street station has an average waiting time of 43 minutes, the second longest wait for any ride in the park after Big Thunder Mountain[159]. Although the railway has four trains, it is very popular and all the stations are quite busy.

At Voletarium they don't issue tickets for roughly the first and last 90 minutes of the day, when the ride gets a surge of visitors. Time slots are half an hour. Less than half an hour and a lot of guests would miss their slot. Longer and you can find that guests can join the reserved ticket line in waves. The idea is that people join the time ticket line at a steady rate. Otherwise you either have a queue building up in the reservation line, or the main queue freezes for a while. It's not advertised (except for in this book), but guests can arrive 15 minutes early for their time slot. If people are late staff tend to let

158   Roller coaster queues: theme park tries to cue waiting times,
BBC news, https://www.bbc.com/news/av/world-europe-41285046/
rollercoaster-queues-theme-park-tries-to-cue-waiting-times

159   Disneyland Park Paris Queue Time Statistics, Queue-
Times, https://queue-times.com/parks/4/stats

them ride regardless of how late they are, rather than having an argument with them. It's unusual for guests to be significantly late.

The time slots move in five-minute intervals, i.e.

10:00-10:30
10:05-10:35
10:10-10:40
10:15:10:45

The theory is that although people are given a thirty-minute window, a disproportionate number of people come near the beginning of their time slot. If the windows shifted by 15 minutes each time, then every 15 minutes you'd have a surge of guests coming with their time tickets. It also means that if there's a group of people and some of them are given tickets for one slot and some are given tickets for the next one, there will be an overlap of 25 minutes.

In 2020 Liseberg (Sweden) opened their first 'major' dark ride - Underland. Why did Liseberg think that this new ride needed a virtual queue when none of the others had one? It comes down to the ride's potential popularity and its throughput.

Liseberg previously had a suspended dark ride called Sagoslottet, which used a ride system similar to Peter Pan's Flight at Disneyland. It opened in 1968 and was removed in 2017 to free up space for Valkyria, a B&M dive machine which opened a year later. This meant that Underland would be Liseberg's only dark ride. The last couple of major attractions: Helix (2014) and Valkyria (2018), had been aimed at thrill seekers. In contrast, Underland was primarily a children's' ride in their Rabbit Land area. They therefore expected Underland to at least initially be very popular. It had a theoretical throughput of 850 guests an hour and would use 18 vehicles carrying 4 riders each (72 seats) on a ride lasting 3 minutes and 20 seconds[160]. Following the examples set by Efteling and Europa Park, Liseberg decided to add a virtual queue. Liseberg's system was custom designed by Creuna, a local web agency[161]. Guests could reserve a free time slot on the Liseberg mobile app and enjoy the rest of the park. Shortly before their slot, the guests will get a reminder on their phone.

One problem with fast track schemes, whether it's something you pay extra for or is included in the entry price, is that people with the ticket sometimes expect to get on the ride instantaneously. This might not always be possible, for instance if the ride goes down due to a technical issue and then there's a backlog of tickets, or if the ride is running at a reduced capacity because a car has a problem, but the tickets are allocated on the assumption that the ride is running at its normal capacity. It isn't always possible for everyone with a reservation to ride straight away.

With time ticket schemes there can be some users who act with a sense of great self-entitlement, waving their tickets in the staff member's face and

160   Liseberg reveals details of new family dark ride Underland, Bloo Loop, https://blooloop.com/news/liseberg-family-dark-ride-underland/

161   Liseberg introduced virtual queuing system for new dark ride, Park World, https://www.parkworld-online.com/liseberg-introduces-virtual-queueing-system-for-new-dark-ride/

demanding that they get let on immediately - even when the main queue is long and the staff member's clearly trying to deal with a lot of things. Some theme parks put a lot of effort into managing their queues, but unfortunately some guests are too ignorant and self-centred to appreciate it. Although I don't believe in covering yourself with too much small print, it is important to do what you can to manage the guest's expectations.

If you tell guests they can "come back and skip the queue", or "fast track the queue", then some people will interpret that as instant access, which can be difficult to deliver at busy times. If you tell guests that they can return "for a shorter queue" or "a reduced waiting time", then that plants the idea that there will still be some waiting.

How does Fast Pass work?

Fast Pass is the brand name for Disney's virtual queuing system. While Europa Park, Efteling and Liseberg have all introduced time ticketing for one individual ride, Disney's reservation system was available on most of their larger rides. The purpose seems to be a little different to the parks that use it on a single attraction. Rather than trying to level off a peak on a single ride that gets particularly busy, they're encouraging people to spend less time waiting for rides, and use that time for eating, shopping, watching shows and exploring the park. People can also ride attractions with shorter queues while they're waiting for a more popular one. As with the reservation systems for individual rides, you reserve a time slot at a ride, visit in the time window and ride with a shorter wait. This is traditionally done by collecting a ticket from the ride's entrance, although more recently hotel guests have been able to reserve slots on a website before their visit, or during their visit using a phone app.

We're going to look at Disney's Fast Pass, how it works and why they introduced it. We'll then look at how easily it can be copied by other parks, and what they can learn from it. Should more parks be introducing a Fast Pass type system? If not, are there smaller aspects that they can replicate?

Disney described the introduction of Fast Pass in their 1999 annual report, "Response to FASTPASS was so overwhelmingly positive that the system was implemented at several attractions at Walt Disney World and Disneyland last year and will be expanded to Disneyland Paris this year"[162].

Not many parks have introduced a Fast Pass system on a range of larger attractions. Aside from Disney, the Tussauds Group briefly ran a reservation system called Virtual Queue in the early 2000s. It operated at Alton Towers, Thorpe Park and Chessington World of Adventures. The canopies for some of the ticket machines are still there and now house things like lockers. Virtual Queue was eventually replaced with a paid for system called Fast Track. Lotte World in South Korea run a free reservation system similar to Fast Pass. Lotte World's is called Magic Pass and gives 30-minute windows

---

162   1999 annual report, The Walt Disney Company, https://thewaltdis-neycompany.com/app/uploads/2015/10/1999-Annual-Report.pdf

rather than 60-minute windows like Fast Pass[163]. You can now use Magic Pass either by collecting physical tickets at the entrance of the ride by scanning your park ticket, or by making a reservation on the Magic Pass app. The Magic Pass app can only be used inside the park, and is activated by keying in your ticket number[164]. At Lotte World you can also pay extra for Magic Pass Premium, where you use the Magic Pass lines but you don't need to make a reservation[165].

Everland in South Korea has a free reservation system on T Express (Intamin prefabricated wooden coaster) and the Flume Ride. I'm not sure if it's available on other rides. The system works a bit differently to the reservation systems at most other parks. Guests visit a staffed booth outside the attraction where a staff member checks the tickets and then gives them a ticket with a time to return[166]. The system hasn't been automated.

With a Fast Pass system that's used on lots of rides, you need activities for the guests to do while they're waiting for their next time slot. The Thinkwell Group estimate that in a Disney style park, the average guest spends 15% of their day shopping[167]. If a guest spends 10 hours in the park, then on average they're spending 90 minutes shopping. This means the shops are taking them away from the rides for 15% of the day, lowering waiting times. It also gives Disney a huge opportunity for making money on 'secondary spend'. Most theme parks don't have the brand power and iconic characters that Disney has, so they have less opportunity for enticing guests into their shops. What this means is that instead of guests standing in a queue, they're browsing the park's shops while they're waiting for their time slot to come up.

Epcot (Disney World, Orlando) shows us how a combination of shops, street theatre and Fast Pass combine to deliver an extraordinarily high capacity. Epcot can hold around 90,000 guests, making it one of the highest capacity parks in the world. At the time of writing Epcot has 53 shops[168], but it only has 15 'rides', about half of which are film experiences of one kind or another, including 3D and 'circle-visions'. In fact, there are currently only 8 actual 'rides' where you sit in a moving vehicle, although that will imminently increase when they open Remy's Ratatouille Adventure Ride and Guardian's of the Galaxy Cosmic Rewind. Disney did announce their first Mary Poppins

163   Lotte World: What to do at the world's biggest indoor theme park, Bryan Wawzenek, Theme Park Insider

164   Lotte World Magic Pass, Google Play, https://play.google.com/store/apps/details?id=com.lotteworld.android.lottemagicpass&hl=en

165   Magic Pass Premium, Lotte World, https://adventure.lotteworld.com/eng/price/premium-magic-pass/contentsid/472/index.do

166   Garet's Everland/Lotte World TR's 2014/2015, Theme Park Review, https://www.themeparkreview.com/forum/viewtopic.php?p=1473106

167   Designing a physically distanced theme park, Thinkwell, https://thinkwellgroup.com/2020/07/22/what-if-we-designed-a-theme-park-with-physical-distancing-and-health-safety-as-a-guiding-principle/

168   Shops at Epcot, Disney World, https://www.disneyworld.co.uk/shops/epcot/#/sort=location/

ride for the UK Pavilion. Sadly, this might have been axed in the cutbacks following the coronavirus crisis. Epcot attracts extraordinary numbers of people for a park with such a low ride count. According to the TEA (Themed Entertainment Association), in 2019 Epcot was the 7th most visited theme park in the world[169].

Presumably Disney do feel that Epcot could be a better and more successful park with a few more rides. Disney were prioritising the Mary Poppins ride over a new pavilion themed to another country, like Brazil. They felt that the World Showcase needed extra rides more than it needed extra shops and restaurants. In the early plans for Epcot there had been a Switzerland pavilion with a copy of the Matterhorn Bobsled, but that was cut due to budgetary constraints. Nonetheless, it's astonishing that Epcot can have a 90,000 capacity and become the 7th most visited park in the world, with just 8 actual rides and 15 attractions. Whilst more rides will no doubt be welcome, Epcot's ability to handle such large crowds hinges partly on its ability to keep people away from the rides. Fast Pass is one of their strategies for doing this. You visit the ride, collect a ticket with a time to come back, and then you do other activities while you're waiting for your reservation slot. There are various activities you could be doing, including eating, drinking, meeting Disney characters, watching street theatre and shopping. We're going to focus on this last point in a little more detail. How does shopping expand a park's capacity and draw people away from the queues?

Shopping at Disney (and other parks)

A lot of Epcot's guests must spend quite a bit of time browsing the many shops, which sell Disney branded merchandise, and in the World Showcase authentic products from the countries being represented. I looked up my local shopping mall, Westwood Cross (Thanet) and it currently has 46 shops. That's 7 fewer than Epcot! It's no exaggeration to say that Epcot has as many shops as a mid-sized shopping mall.

When I first heard the estimation that Disney guests spend 15% of their day shopping, it seemed too high. When I go to a park, I spend most of my time riding the attractions, although I do collect theme park 'merch'. However, for Epcot to sustain 53 shops it's clear that the average guest must spend quite a bit of time shopping. I'm not the typical visitor. The statistic still sounds high to me, so I'd be interested in knowing more about how the figure was arrived at. For Epcot and perhaps Tokyo Disneyland, I can see that guests might spend 15% of their day shopping, but it does sound high for some of the other Disney parks. Presumably the figure would vary depending on how long the queues are, and the mix of guests in the park. Are they mostly regular annual pass holders? Or more international visitors on vacation? However, even if a guest spent 10% of their day shopping, that's still a big chunk of their time.

169   Theme Index 2019, TEA, http://www.teaconnect.org/ images/files/TEA_369_936023_200716.pdf

According to a Bloo Loop article from 2011, Universal typically got 15% of their revenue from merchandise sales, while at Tokyo Disney it's 20%[170]. Another article said that in 2002 Gardaland (Italy) made 14.2% of its revenue from merchandise. Gardaland developed its own mascots including the Prezzemolo character[171]. In the early 2000s, Gardaland's Prezzemolo comic was available outside the park with sales of 30,000 a month. These statistics support the idea that guests can spend a big chunk of time shopping. Tokyo Disneyland park has more shops (40) than any other Disney park except for Epcot, also implying that the Japanese are particularly keen on merchandise. Norm Elder explains, "The Japanese, because of their culture, are huge buyers of merchandise so when people go away they usually come back and bring gifts for their friends and that encourages a lot of additional incremental buying, plus they love the Disney characters".

A few of these shops are at the exit to rides, for example Journey into the Imagination passes through a small gift shop, mainly selling merchandise themed to the ride's character Figment. However, most of the shops stand alone. People aren't just traipsing through these shops on the way out and making the occasional impulse buy. People are actively choosing to spend their time browsing Epcot's shops. Shops that people choose to go in, rather than being funnelled through, are sometimes called 'destination shops'.

There does seem to be a big difference between shops based around impulse buys and shops based around browsing, where they're an attraction in their own right. Shops based around impulse buys do a harder sell. Guests are funnelled through them at the exit to attractions. The shop windows are full of the merchandise you can buy. They do a lot of promotions, like BOGOFFs (Buy One Get One Free), 3 for 2s, lots of signs reminding you that you can get a discount with your annual pass, piles of cheap sweets around the tills, the staff are trained to upsell... these are legitimate and potentially successful sales strategies. 'Exit through the giftshop' has become a cliché, because it's proven to work.

Parks don't need to have the same kind of destination shops that Disney has. Lots of parks have failed when they've followed 'the Disney way'. Some parks cater to a less affluent demographic. Some parks cater more to regular annual pass holders. Different parks appeal to different age groups. If your park gets fewer than 500,000 visitors a year, it's difficult to provide an interesting range of shops, because there isn't the footfall to support them. What works at one park might not work at another. If your retail offering is primarily based around impulse buys and promotions, then people tend to spend less time browsing the shops. If you make your retail into more of an experience, then it's likely to provide a longer diversion.

We're going to be looking at how parks can shift their guests from queues to shops. It is worth stressing that there are ethical considerations here.

170   Norm Elder on Disney, Universal and state dependent memory, Bloo Loop, https://blooloop.com/features/norm-elder-on-disney-universal-and-state-dependant-memory/

171   Gardaland, Juliana Koranteng, All Business

Sweets are poor for people's health, whilst many souvenirs are made from single use plastics that can quickly end up in landfills. A lot of merchandise is made in countries with low wages, low safety standards and few environmental regulations. On the flip side, 'brick and mortar' retail (compared to online retail) tends to pay more tax, provide more jobs and arguably more fulfilling jobs. I'd like to encourage parks to develop their retail in a responsible way. Generally, retail based around impulse buys is likely to be at the lower end of the ethical spectrum.

When Disney set up the Disney Stores in 1987 CEO Michael Eisner took advice from retail experts. They told him that the shop window should be full of Disney merchandise. Eisner didn't think this would be very special, and instead filled the windows with models of Disney characters. If you wanted to see what the shops were actually selling you had to go inside. Disney often use the same principle in their parks, where shop windows have models, theming and animatronics rather than merchandise. Disney talk about 'merchantainment'. This is a fusion of 'merchandise' and 'entertainment'. This can include cast members playing with toys you can buy, handing out free samples of sweets, glass blowing, craft making and fudge making. Regardless of whether you're aiming more for impulse buys or experience shopping, basic merchandising practices apply. These include clear pricing and placing items for children nearer the floor and items for adults higher up[172].

Disney doesn't publish official capacities for their US parks, but it's generally estimated that Epcot's capacity is around 90,000. If the park was at capacity and 15% of the guests were shopping, that would mean that 13,500 guests were in the shops. With 53 shops, that's an average of 255 guests per a shop. To give a couple of capacities, Legoland Florida currently (2020) has a capacity of 12,000 guests. When I worked at Chessington World of Adventures (UK) the capacity was about 17,000 guests. The combined capacity of Epcot's shops, is similar to the entire capacity of a medium sized theme park.

In many ways Epcot is the model example of how the Fast Pass system is supposed to work. If the park had 90,000 guests and half of them were at the 15 attractions, then each attraction would have 3,000 people either on it or waiting for it. Only five of Epcot's attractions could be described as major rides: Soarin', Test Track, Journey in the Imagination, Spaceship Earth and Mission Space. Frozen Ever After is perhaps close, due to the power of the Frozen brand and the quality of the animatronics. Epcot's able to 'get away' with a fairly small number of rides, because a lot of the guests are eating, drinking, shopping, meeting Disney characters, watching street theatre and looking at the non-ride attractions, such as the Living with the Sea aquarium with its dolphins and manatees – or the Stave Church, German model village or the Terracotta Warriors in the World Showcase. Often guests do these things whilst waiting for their Fast Pass slots to come up.

---

172   Making the most of retail, Gabrielle, Inter Park, https:// interpark.co.uk/making-the-most-of-retail/

NEIL WILSON   137

It is worth noting that while Fast Pass might have encouraged guests to spend more time shopping, shops had always been a big part of Disneyland, long before Fast Pass came along. The prospectus used by Disney in the early 1950s to attract investors, made a big feature of the shops the park would have[173]. In a moment we will compare the number of shops at different parks. Whilst Disney parks all have fairly high numbers, other parks without Fast Pass also score highly, including Europa Park, Silver Dollar City, Universal Studios Orlando and Cedar Point. Fast Pass isn't a prerequisite to having a big retail offering, although it might help.

Here's a table showing the number of shops (2020) at different parks. The data is taken from the official park websites and doesn't include pop up shops for special events. I've included sweet shops, but I haven't counted onride photo booths, unless they sell merchandise as well. I haven't counted face painting/caricatures/costume photo studios – although these are sometimes counted as 'shops' on the official websites and maps:

Epcot	53
Europa Park	45
Silver Dollar City	44
Tokyo Disneyland	40
Universal Studios Florida	35
Magic Kingdom	34
Cedar Point	34
Hollywood Studios	30
Animal Kingdom	30
Disney Seas	30
Disneyland (California)	28
Islands of Adventure	28
Parc Disneyland Paris	25
Shanghai Disneyland	24
Everland	22
Dollywood	20
Universal Studios Hollywood	19
Ocean Park Hong Kong	18
Six Flags Great America	18
Six Flags Over Georgia	18
Disneyland Hong Kong	17
Six Flags Magic Mountain	17
Port Aventura	17
Sea World Orlando	16
California Adventure	14
Disney Studios Paris	14
Carowinds	14
Six Flags Great Adventure	14

---

173   Disneyland's original prospectus revealed, Boing Boing

Tivoli Gardens	13
Six Flags New England	12
Knott's Berry Farm	11
Hershey Park	11
Sea World San Diego	11
Legoland Florida	9
Alton Towers	8
Efteling	8
Kings Island	8
Dorney Park	8
Thorpe Park	7
Chessington World of Adventures	7
Phantasialand	5
Kennywood	5
Legoland Windsor	4
Holiday World	4

Quite a few of the locations at Animal Kingdom and Shanghai Disney are relatively small, so it has less space allocated to shopping than the number of locations implies. It'd be interesting to compare the surface area given to retail at the different parks, but this information is harder to come by. The Californian Disney resort generally has fewer shopping options than the Floridian parks. This might be because guests pass through the Downtown shopping area on their way in and out of the parks, or because the Californian resort has a higher proportion of locals who visit regularly, and have lower spends per head.

Universal Studios Florida has more shops than all but two of the Disney parks. Twelve of these are in the Diagon Alley area themed to Harry Potter. The fact that over a third of the shops at Universal Studios Florida are in the Harry Potter area shows how powerful the Harry Potter brand is. Particularly when you consider that there are more Harry Potter shops in Islands of Adventure. At Universal Studios Hollywood 9 of the 19 shops are based around Harry Potter. Universal Studios Florida opened the Diagon Alley area in 2014. In its first year the park's merchandise sales doubled to $48.7 million[174].

Legoland Windsor has surprisingly few shops, partly because they've got one very large shop near the entrance ('The Big Shop'), which they can open when the park's closed, particularly in the run up to Christmas. As well as the 11 shops inside Knott's Berry Farm, there's an additional 5 shops just outside their main gate in the California Marketplace. Magic Mountain has four sweet shops, including one dedicated to Jelly Belly jellybeans and two specialising in homemade fudge and caramel apples. Another five shops specialise in DC comics merchandise.

The idea that Disney's guests spend a significant portion of their time

---

174   Theme parks expect new rides to send merchandise sales soaring, Hugo Martín, Los Angeles Times

exploring shops while they wait for their Fast Pass slots, isn't just wishful thinking. It's part of what helps the Disney parks to cope with such large volumes of people. For people to spend an average 15% of their visit shopping, these clearly aren't people just buying essentials, like a rain coat or sun cream, or impulse buys like grab bags of sweets. These are people taking their time browsing and exploring the different retail offerings.

Disney shops are nicely themed and presented. They want to make the retail space a fun environment. General gift shops don't tend to be as appealing for browsing, although most parks have a general gift shop just inside the entrance. A trick used by some parks is to break a large shop down into several smaller shops, but where you can walk between them and perhaps only have a till point in the middle one. From the outside each shop has its own name and a distinct façade. Inside each shop is clearly different, with its own colour scheme and flooring. However, there are big arches that let you walk from one shop into the next so that they don't all need to be staffed separately. It also means that if the weather's poor guests can walk from one shop into the next without going outside. Most parks have much smaller budgets than Disney and Universals, but money spent on theming the shops can be well spent. Without theming, the shops make the park feel more commercialised and if they feel like something out of a regular shopping mall, you lose the sense of escapism.

Common things for theme park shops to sell include:

- Ride merchandise, including 'cheap mementos' (such as keyrings/ magnets) and more expensive memorabilia (such as models of coaster trains and board games), as well as branded clothing (such as t-shirts and baseball caps).
- General gifts (such as candles, magic tricks, practical jokes)
- Merchandise themed to the park's characters and intellectual properties.
- Merchandise themed to the park's different areas (for example pirate toys in a pirate themed area)
- Merchandise themed to the park's food, including recipe books and take-home sauces.
- Park media, such as CDs, DVDs and books.
- Take home food (such as sweets, biscuits, jams)
- Arts and crafts (often made on site)
- Personalised goods (for example with the guest's name on it), as well as things the guests might help to make, such as Build a Bear, build your own jewellery, build your own lightsaber.

According to Europa Park's director of shopping, Ralf Stumpf, in 2010 roughly a third of their merchandise sales were sweets, a third was branded goods and a third was non-branded[175]. At the time of writing they have about

---

175   Retail – it's in the detail, 9th March 2010, Park World Magazine

500 people working in their retail department[176]. It's not clear whether this includes the shops at their hotels. In total Europa Park's shops sell about 13,000 different lines. This means you could buy a different item from Europa Park every day for 35 years without running out of things to buy.

Although Europa Park is themed to different countries, authentic goods from these countries doesn't fill the shops like it does at Epcot. Europa Park has a strong portfolio of merchandise branded to the attractions. It sells some merchandise themed to external intellectual properties including (at the time of writing), Paddington Bear, Jim Knopf and Arthur and the Minimoys, as well as merchandise themed to their own mascots. Some shops are themed to external brands including Lindt Lindor (Swiss Chocolate), Coca Cola, Mustang (fashion), Camp David (fashion) and Adidas (fashion). Based on my own observations, the fashion shops are generally the quietest. There aren't a lot of people who go to a theme park to buy a high street clothing brand. Europa Park did recently open a new Camp David shop in their rebuilt Scandinavian area, so presumably it's been reasonably successful for them. As well as the general Camp David range, it includes a Camp David line that's customised for Europa Park. Camp David is a popular German fashion brand, that has now spread to Austria and Switzerland.

Getting high quality bespoke merchandise made often takes time, particularly if it's going to be imported from another region. If parks want to sell high quality merchandise, they need to plan well in advance. When new attractions are being planned, they need to start thinking about the merchandise early on in the attraction's development.

In this book I haven't talked about project management. You can deliver projects more quickly with strong teamwork, motivation and the right focus. However, if you try to rush the creative process, you often end up with half-baked ideas and unintended side effects. The original Disneyland was famously built in around a year, which was fast even for the 1950s. However, Walt Disney had spent several years mulling over ideas before pushing ahead with his plan for Disneyland. The Disney archive is full of unused patents and planned concepts that never got built. There are even several whole theme parks that Disney planned and never built, including Disney's America (35 miles from Washington DC) and Westcot, which we'll be discussing in the next section. Disney is famous for their efficiency, but one thing that tends to move very slowly is their creative development process. This is why it's important that things like merchandise aren't treated as an afterthought.

If you want your guests to spend more time browsing the shops, it's not just about having more shops. Quality is important as well as quantity. You might be able to bring in some more interesting shops using concessions. In this case you need to find concessions you trust and believe in, so that you can give them a long enough tenure. This means they can invest in their shop and make sure it's themed. You don't want to have concessions on short-term

---

176   Shopping and games, Business Divisions, Europa Park official, https://corporate.europapark.com/en/business-divisions/shopping-games/

leases running pop up shops, as these will look cheap. The concessions should feel integrated into the park, for example wearing the same uniform/costumes and potentially doing the same customer service trainings, being invited to the park's parties etc. Concessions work well for something that involves specialist knowledge, such as craft demonstrations, a magic shop where you might be demonstrating the tricks, a sweet shop where the sweets are made on the premises etc. Some parks can be tempted to use concessions either to mitigate risk, or as a cost cutting measure. However, these are poor reasons for using them. Remember, you've chosen to bring concessions into your park, so you shouldn't be seeing them as competition to your own shops. It's your job to give them the right support and a fair chance of being successful.

Whilst there are things that other parks can learn from Disney, Disney does have a lot of advantages when it comes to developing a wide choice of retail outlets. Mickey Mouse first appeared in 1928. After almost a century of developing their characters and stories, Disney has the most extensive intellectual property portfolio in existence. They have a wide range of properties that appeal to boys and girls as well as adults. Besides the theme park enthusiasts, there is a massive Disney fanbase including a lot of adult Disney fans. Many Disney films generate more revenue from the merchandise than they do at the box office, although much of this is sold outside the theme parks.

The Force Awakens grossed $2 billion at the box office, but they forecast $5-6 billion of *Star Wars* merchandise sales in the first year after it came out[177]. *Toy Story 3* generated over $1 billion at the box office and over $10 billion in merchandise sales[178]. The first two *Cars* films took less than $1 billion between them at the box office. However, between 2006-2011 the first *Cars* film sold over $10 billion worth of merchandise[179]. In the early 2000s Disney's animation department struggled to find box office hits. This was partly what led to their CEO being ousted (in 2005) and Disney buying Pixar, whose films were being more successful. *Frozen* (released in 2013) is the film credited with pushing Disney's traditional animation studio back to the top. The original *Frozen* film took $1.27 billion at the box office, but in 2014 they sold over $5 billion worth of *Frozen* merchandise[180]. At Disney it's their characters rather than the rides that sell the most merchandise. The demand for merchandise branded with the Disney characters makes it relatively easy for Disney to push shopping as a core part of their theme park experience.

177   A breakdown of Star Wars merchandise sales this year, Paul Bond, The Hollywood Reporter, https://www.hollywoodreporter.com/news/a-breakdown-star-wars-merchandise-849861

178   Pixar sequels draw bigger roles in company's future, Marc Graser, Variety, https://variety.com/2014/film/news/toy-story-the-incredibles-cars-pixar-future-sequel-plans-1201350707/

179   Movies that made more money on merchandising than at the box office, Jacob Shelton, Ranker, https://www.ranker.com/list/movies-that-made-money-merchandising/jacob-shelton

180   Ibid.

The Six Flags parks have a surprising number of giftshops when you consider their attendance and the fact that they often attract a lot of regular guests who buy the season tickets. Many of these shops sell merchandise themed to DC comics and Looney Tunes. A lot of theme parks have been making deals to buy in more IPs (intellectual properties), for example Thorpe Park have used *Angry Birds*, *Derren Brown*, *Saw*, *The Walking Dead*, *I'm a Celebrity* and *Black Mirror*. Other UK parks have also jumped on the intellectual property wagon, including Thomas and Cartoon Network (Drayton Manor), Nickelodeon and Wallace and Gromit (Blackpool Pleasure Beach), C Beebies and David Walliams (Alton Towers) and Beano and Julia Donaldson books (Chessington World of Adventures). The upside for Disney is that they own most of their IPs, so they're not having to license them. Many other parks pay a royalty to use outside brands, so they have to decide whether the benefits justify the costs. But that's a debate for another day.

Intellectual properties and their well-known characters generally spawn gift shops at theme parks. There are notable exceptions to this. Cedar Point has an astonishingly high number of shops – 34. Aside from Snoopy, Cedar Point doesn't have any intellectual property and many of its shops are based around ride merchandise. It may be that because Cedar Point has become internationally known for its roller coaster, more so than any other park, that they are able to shift significant quantities of ride merch.

Silver Dollar City is another anomaly, with 44 shops. Out of the parks I've researched it is only surpassed by Epcot and Europa Park. It has no well-known intellectual properties. In 2018 Silver Dollar City broke its attendance record with 2,184,000 visitors[181]. This means it has roughly one shop for every 50,000 visitors. That's a very high ratio of shops to visitors. In comparison Magic Kingdom has about 617,000 visitors for every shop and Epcot has 235,000 visitors for every shop. The comparison's not completely fair, because Silver Dollar City's seasonal, whereas the Disney parks are open 365 days a year. However, it does show how exceptional Silver Dollar City is.

Silver Dollar City is run by Herschend Entertainment (who also run Dollywood) and located in Branson, Missouri. It is themed to the history and culture of the local area. Many of their shops sell local crafts, sometimes with demonstrations of them being made. Shops includes one selling food products made from 'apple butter', a shop selling honey, a candlemaker (who makes and sells the candles in the shop), a Dulcimer shop selling traditional folk instruments, Casey's Dugout (baseball shop), Granny Lye Soap (where soap is made on the premises) and Christmas Hollow.

Disney currently has six resorts around the world. Often more than one resort will have a copy of an attraction such as Tower of Terror, Space Mountain, Pirates of the Caribbean or Big Thunder Mountain. This means they can develop a range of merchandise themed to a specific ride, but sell it in multiple giftshops around the world. Disney parks also get astonishing

---

181   Record coaster drives record attendance at Silver Dollar City, Robert Niles, Theme Park Insider, https://www.themeparkinsider.com/flume/201901/6514/

volumes of visitors. They can order product lines in much larger bulk than a typical theme park, giving them high profit margins.

Epcot is an anomaly in the theme park world, even by Disney standards. It might well have more shops than any other theme park, although I've never seen this being quoted. Disney in general stands out as being exceptional. I don't think the visitors at many parks would spend an average 15% of their time shopping. This helps explain why most other parks aren't interested in their own versions of Fast Pass. They don't think the gains are worth the cost. Even if a park isn't interested in doing something like Fast Pass, parks can use shops to mop up some of the crowds and divert them away from the rides. Advantages include the fact that shops can make money, whereas things like street theatre, streetmosphere and animals are always a cost. Shops can be closed on quiet days without disappointing guests too much, although it helps if you theme the doors/shutters so that the shops don't look too sad when they're closed. Shops can be easily integrated amongst the rides, whereas animal areas tend to be clumped together away from the rides, which can be noisy.

"Hey Amigo's, we are currently closed. Bandits have raided us..." – an example of a themed shutter in the Mexicana area at Chessington World of Adventures. Compared to the rides, guests are less bothered if the shops and restaurants are closed on quiet days. Themed shutters have a better sense of 'show' than if they aren't themed.

In this section I've focused on retail, partly because it's less obvious how retail can add to a park's capacity. Whereas I think most people can see how shows, meet and greets, museums, aquariums and animal areas can add to the park's capacity and draw people away from the rides. We will consider the capacity of different parks in the final section of this book, including a look at Hong Kong Disneyland. Disney parks typically have remarkably high capacities and attendance relative to how many rides they've got. The amount of time guests spend shopping is clearly just one of many factors.

One of the advantages with encouraging guests to spend more time shopping, is that shops aren't costing the park money. They can be cost neutral or even make a profit. There are other activities that take guests away from the rides that make a profit. Whilst pretty much every park has an F&B (food and beverage) offering, time guests spend eating and drinking is time when they're not adding to the queues. The key here isn't to have long queues at your food outlets, as that just shifts the problem. It's about encouraging guests to switch from fast food to table service, where it naturally takes longer. Or encouraging people to stop for a drink. You might also encourage guests to stop and play games, like throwing a basketball into a hoop, or knocking down some tin cans. A food operation, retail department or games division should make a profit. A viable theme park normally depends on it. However, if your only goal is to squeeze as much money as you can from these things, and to rely on short-term hits, then in the long run they won't create the fuller experience that leads to longer dwell times.

From studying operations, it's striking that at the rides the general goal is to get people on and off the rides as quickly as possible. In other areas, you might want to encourage guests to slow down and take their time over an experience. You're not trying to slow things down by creating unnecessary hassles, poor wayfinding, disorganised shops and queues elsewhere. But if your park is getting complaints about the queues for the rides, it can be beneficial to move a chunk of guests over to these other activities.

In a theme park you've got people spending time at the attractions; the rides, shows, looking at animals etc. Then you've got all of these incidental activities. Walking between attractions, stopping to take a photo, stopping to put sun cream on, going to the toilet, changing the baby's nappy, looking at your onride photo, buying your onride photo, browsing around the shops, playing in the arcade, watching someone play a game, having a drink in a bar or a coffee shop. Encouraging people to spend more time on these incidental activities doesn't help the average guest to get on more rides, but it does make the queues for the rides shorter.

Dwell times aren't the main criteria that retail's measured by, and I don't think it should be, particularly as it's hard to calculate. Spend per guest or spend per square foot are more likely to be the measurements. However, if the only yardstick for measuring the success of your shops is revenue and profit, you can miss out on the broader benefits that they bring. Parks that are successful in managing their queues, tend to make it everyone's responsibility to reduce the waiting times. Parks that have long, slow moving queues, are often ones where most of responsibility gets placed on one or two departments, or an individual manager. On the surface the retail department doesn't have any bearing on the queues for rides, but as we have seen, even retail can have a knock-on effect. If the average guest at a regional park spends 3% of their time shopping and you can double that to 6%, then that will ease congestion elsewhere. An extra 3% of their time in the shops might not sound like a lot, but these things are cumulative. Maybe they also spend a bit longer watching street theatre, or having a drink whilst listening to a musician. Maybe you improve your ride availability by 2% and your throughputs on the rides by another 3%. Slowly, the queues can start to seem more reasonable.

In this section we're looking at ways to redistribute guests from busier areas of a park to quieter areas. We consider many ways for doing this: park layouts that promote good guest flow, display boards with queue times, mobile apps, My Magic Plus, promoting good guest planning, amongst others. Some of these we've covered already. Others we will move onto shortly. The point is, that you can only shift guests to quieter area of the park if there are quieter areas with surplus capacity. If every area and every aspect of your park is jam packed with people and struggling to cope, then there is no opportunity for re-distributing guests. That doesn't mean you shouldn't still have queue time boards or a mobile app. They help to manage expectations and allow your guests to make better informed choices. But the more unevenly your guests are distributed, the more these other ideas will help you.

Theme parks only have a finite amount of money and resources. If you're trying to reduce the queues, you have to work out where to prioritise. There might be lots of things that would reduce the queues, but you need to work out what's going to be the most cost effective. If the whole park's rammed with people, you're more likely to look at ways to shift visitors onto the quieter days. If there are quieter areas within the park with surplus capacity, particularly at certain times of day, you're more likely to look at ways to redistribute the crowds around the site. You would also look at whether there are activities away from the rides you can shift guests onto, whether you can make the queues pleasanter/more entertaining and whether you can improve the throughputs on the rides to make the queues move faster.

Benchmarking against Disney

This is going to be a different kind of chapter to the others in this section. Rather than focusing on one particular area of operational efficiency, we're going to bring some of the ideas together to look at how park capacities work. We're then going to talk about the Hard Rock Park (Myrtle Beach, South Carolina). We'll compare it to some Disney parks, and for a bit of fun do some armchair Imagineering. I'll ask readers to consider whether or not they think Hard Rock Park's capacity was realistic. The idea behind this is to go through the process that feasibility studies and investors go through when they're trying to decide whether or not a project's realistic.

I have found that new parks, or inexperienced managers, sometimes look at how many visitors the Disney parks hold, and end up with unrealistic expectations about their own parks. There are a lot of nuances in why some parks are able to handle crowds better than others. Fast Pass, My Magic Plus, the appeal of Disney's parades, the level of weather proofing and the success of their retail are just a few of them. It's worth considering Disney and Universal to get an idea of what's possible. But if you want to accurately assess a project's potential, you're better off comparing yourself to other projects with a similar budget, acreage and other metrics.

When new theme parks are being planned, it's not unusual for managers to use Disney parks, to make predictions about the potential of their own park. They might look at how many rides the parks have, and roughly what type of rides they are. They miss the subtle factors that give Disney parks their high capacities. I was part of the management team that re-opened the Dreamland amusement park in the United Kingdom. Several of the managers had been to Disney parks or knew people who had. Since we had more rides than some Disney parks, they struggled to understand why our capacity would be so much lower. Our entire site was about 16 acres, including the amusement area which was about 11 acres. The total budget was about £25 million ($32 million). If you've been reading this book from the start, I'm sure you can already suggest some reasons.

In this chapter, we're going to look at why the Disney parks cost so much to build, and whether it's realistic to achieve comparable capacities on much smaller budgets. We'll focus on Epcot, and try to understand why it's such an anomaly, being a park with 8 proper rides and a 90,000 capacity. We'll then look at Hard Rock Park, which opened in 2008. I'll ask my readers to apply the lessons we've learned in this book so far, and try to decide for themselves how realistic they think the projections were, and what were the potential challenges. If you were planning a new park, or a major expansion, what lessons would you learn from it?

There can be misunderstandings about why the Disney parks cost so much to build. People might put it down to how much the Disney directors get paid, Imagineering being inefficient and planning a lot of attractions that never get built, the amount of exclusive technology, the level of detail in the theming or figures simply being inflated for marketing purposes. At least some of these things do contribute to the costs of building a Disney park. Disney can no doubt justify a high investment relative to their park's capacities, partly because Disney parks charge more than regional parks, and partly because they're open year-round - so the capacity gets more use. It certainly is possible for parks to achieve much higher ratios of investment to capacity than Disney does. A really strong example of this is Holiday World (Indiana), a park we shall come back to later.

It's not unusual for managers to think that they can match Disney's capacities on a much smaller budget. There are some opportunities to do this, particularly if their park has less theming. The question is though, how much further can a park realistically stretch their budget? It's easy to underestimate how hard it is for a park to manage such large crowds. Disney parks cost a lot to build partly because they've been designed to handle vast numbers of people. A lot has been written about Disney's leadership, how they train and motivate their staff. Disney's training is highly regarded, but this mainly affects how staff approach customer service and to an extent safety. Motivated staff will work harder and strong teamwork can promote efficiency, but Disney's capacities aren't primarily to do with their training. It's to do with the way the parks are designed.

The whole last section of this book is looking at capacities, so bringing them in here too might be jumping the gun. But I'm going to do it, because it puts the last few chapters into perspective. Things like Fast Pass and a park's retail offering work together, shifting guests around the park, as well as increasing the overall capacity. How much of this is transferable to a regional park?

In the previous section I mentioned that Epcot (Disney World, Orlando) achieved a 90,000 capacity with 15 'attractions' including 8 rides. This does show that you can achieve remarkable capacities with low numbers of rides. But other parks shouldn't overlook that fact that Epcot is 300 acres, has 53 shops, at least 15 different meet and greet locations[182], 10 different street shows and 22 table service restaurants, where dwell times are longer than in a fast-food outlet. If we were to study Epcot's capacity only looking at the rides, we'd get a rather lopsided view of what a park's capable of. It takes a lot of money to build an Epcot.

On the surface Epcot seems like a license to print money – a theme park where guests spend a lot of their time eating, drinking and shopping. It might feel like guests are paying to spend money. It must be remembered that no one, including Disney, has built another Epcot. That might be partly because tastes have changed, and indeed Epcot's morphed over the years. Epcot now leans a lot more heavily on Disney's branded characters.

It's also because Epcot's 300 acres. There were plans in the early nineties for a Westcot at the Californian resort. Westcot would have been a similar kind of park to Epcot, like a permanent world's fair themed to science, technology and the cultures of the world. Eventually the Westcot plan was dropped and in 2001 the original Disneyland finally got its second park – California Adventure. This was more of a traditional theme park, themed to California's history and culture. Why did Disney drop Westcot and build California Adventure instead?

Disney's original resort, Disneyland, is a lot smaller than their second one in Orlando. It's about 510 acres[183], including two theme parks, which between them occupy 171 acres. That means the theme parks themselves occupy around a third of the entire Disneyland Resort. The other 339 acres includes 3 hotels, the Downtown Disney shopping and dining area, parking garages and backstage areas. By contrast, Disney World (Orlando) is about 27,000 acres, or 47 square miles. This means that Disney World is about 53 times the size of Disneyland. Disney World's about double the size of San Francisco or 80 times the size of Monaco. About 7,100 acres

---

182   Live Epcot character meet and greet times, Laughing Place, https://www.laughingplace.com/w/p/epcot-character-meet-and-greet-times/

183   Disneyland and how it all began, Visit Anaheim, https://visitanaheim.org/blog/disneyland-and-how-it-all-began

of Disney World is developed[184]. Epcot is over half the size of the whole Californian resort.

There are various reasons why Disneyland is a lot smaller than Disney World. The Walt Disney Company itself was smaller when it planned Disneyland, land prices were higher near Los Angeles than in Florida at the time, the theme park concept was a proven formula when they planned Disney World, and they became aware that if they didn't acquire the land initially – it'd be hard to later. The upshot of all this is that Westcot was going to be a similar kind of park to Epcot, but condensed into about one fifth of the space.

Epcot would have been reduced from around 300 acres into about 70 acres. Even after losing the 40 acre World Showcase Lagoon, they had to lose another 190 acres. Not only would it involve losing a lot of surface area, but they also wanted to incorporate two or more hotels into the park[185]. Disney's CEO Eisner had originally wanted to do this in Hollywood Studios, where the Hollywood Tower Hotel (housing Tower of Terror) would have also functioned as a real hotel. A park that has successfully incorporated hotels into its themed environments is Phantasialand (Germany). Disney hotels tend to be much larger than the ones at regional parks, so incorporating multiple hotels into the 70 acre park would have taken away more real estate. This poses two questions: could a much smaller version of Epcot still be appealing, and would a much smaller version still have the kind of capacity that Disney expected of its parks? Or would a different kind of park get a higher capacity from the space?

There were lots of different ideas for Westcot. One set of ideas would have included pavilions or attractions based on cities rather than countries, including New York, London and Tokyo. To fit it into less space countries might have got fused together with pavilions representing continents rather than countries. For example, each side of a square could be a different country or city. It may well be though, that an Epcot style park doesn't suit such a compact site.

They also dropped Westcot, because Epcot was a very expensive theme park to build. A lot of authentic theming was imported from the World Showcase's countries. When Disney built Epcot, their mission wasn't to build as many shops and restaurants as cheaply as possible. The World Showcase is staffed by 'cultural representatives' from each pavilion's country (I was one myself!) and this is also expensive to set up. For instance, you need to build staff housing for the cultural representatives to stay in. Epcot has a very big and expensive infrastructure. To understand the capacity of a park and how it manages a certain volume of visitors, it's no good just focusing on one or two statistics. You have to look at the bigger picture. Disney might have a sense of magic, but even Disney can't distort the rules of basic maths.

---

184   Walt Disney World history 101: how to buy 27,000 acres of land and have no one notice, WDW Radio, http://www.wdwradio.com/2005/02/ wdw-history-101-how-to-buy-27000-acres-of-land-and-no-one-noticeq/

185   Tony Baxter.... On Westcot, Ross Plesset, http://savehorizons.tripod.com/westcot1.htm

Disney parks like Epcot and Animal Kingdom aren't typical theme parks. This can make them tricky to benchmark against. If you're planning a new park and you want to get a realistic idea of its potential capacity, it's better to compare yourselves to other parks with a similar design and budget to the one you're planning, rather than parks that are completely different.

It's not often now that a new park gets built in Europe or the United States, as both are mature markets. One of the most recent examples of a major new theme park was the Hard Rock at Myrtle Beach. It opened in 2008, went bankrupt before the end of the first season, opened in 2009 under new ownership, before closing for good. Myrtle Beach in South Carolina is a fairly small beach resort with about 35,000 residents. The nearest big city was Charlotte, which was about 175 miles away and served by its own theme park, Carowinds. However, Myrtle Beach and other nearby resorts attracted a lot of vacationers, and that's who Hard Rock Park wanted to attract when it opened in 2008. Compared to most major theme parks it served a very small resident population, and that turned out to be its biggest downfall.

I want to look at Hard Rock Park in a bit of detail. This isn't to be judgmental. The fact that they were able to open a major new theme park in North America was a massive achievement, and the fact it opened in the wake of the 2008 financial crisis was bad luck. The leadership behind Hard Rock Park have been unusually candid about the park's problems, which has given the industry and an important opportunity to learn from their mistakes. The reason I want to discuss Hard Rock Park, is because it's a good platform both for discussing how you plan a park, and for seeing how the ideas we've discussed so far fit together. We can admire the creativity and attention to detail in the Hard Rock project, but also use it as a cautionary tale about being realistic when you're setting your figures. The question we are most interested in, is did Hard Rock park over predict its capacity?

I suspect that most people reading this book will be familiar with the story. The Hard Rock Park was going to use the famous rock brand, known best for its Hard Rock Cafes, but also for its Hard Rock Hotels and Hard Rock Casinos. It would be the first theme park to use the Hard Rock brand, although the Hard Rock company wouldn't be involved in running or designing it. A completely separate company owned and operated the park, and paid Hard Rock a royalty for using their brand. It was a novel theme, and made a refreshing change from the many other parks themed to films. The park included a mixture of rides and shows, and would end each day with a Queen themed Bohemian Rhapsody show on a lake with fireworks and lazars. Key rides included a Led Zeppelin the Ride looping coaster, and a Moody Blues inspired Nights in White Satin dark ride.

To understand the boldness of Hard Rock Park, I want to compare it to Disney's most recent park. The Disneyland Shanghai Resort, which cost $5.5 billion[186] and opened in 2016. Hard Rock theme park (Myrtle Beach)

---

186   Just how big is Disney's new Shanghai Disney resort?, Jethro Mullen, CNN, https://money.cnn.com/2016/06/15/media/shanghai-disney-china-by-the-numbers/index.html

opened in 2008 and officially cost $400 million[187], although that included interest on the money they'd borrowed. The real cost was more like $225 million. They expected 3 million visitors in their first year, and more after that. That was very ambitious for a park that cost $225 million to build. Admittedly, Disneyland Shanghai's budget included buying up surplus land for expansion, two hotels (with 1,220 rooms) and the Downtown Shopping Area, complete with the 'Art Deco' Broadway style theatre. We don't know how much Disney spent just on the theme park, but it was probably at least ten times the cost of Hard Rock Park, but Hard Rock Park were hoping for a quarter of Disneyland Shanghai's attendance and half of their capacity. To give another comparison, it's generally estimated that Radiator Springs Racers (opened 2012) at California Adventure cost around $200 million[188] – more than four fifths the cost of the entire Hard Rock Park. Radiator Springs was a particularly expensive ride even by Disney's standards, with a lot of artificial rockwork, a very expensive ride system and highly sophisticated animatronics. However, by 2008 it wasn't unusual for Disney to be spending $100 million plus on a single ride.

Clearly Silver Springs Racer didn't cost $200 million just to give it a high capacity. It cost a lot because it's a cool ride. The question is though, is it realistic to expect a park to have half the capacity to a Disney park built on ten times the budget? This isn't a question I can answer definitively. What I'm going to do is compare Hard Rock Park to some Disney parks and Alton Towers, to show the complexity in estimating a park's capacity. I will show how parks can draw misleading comparisons with Disney and cherry pick statistics.

When you're looking at a failed project, you're looking at it with the benefit of hindsight. I would ask readers to consider the facts in a critical, but balanced way. How plausible were Hard Rock Park's projections? If you were an investor, would you have been convinced by their figures? What questions would you have wanted to ask them?

Hard Rock Park's capacity was advertised as 30,000[189], although it was sometimes mis-quoted that they hoped to attract an average of 30,000 guests a day[190]. By comparison, Disneyland Shanghai's initial capacity was around 55,000. Hong Kong Disneyland's capacity was initially 28,000, and that struggled to cope when full. We will talk about Hong Kong Disneyland's capacity in more detail later on, but its overcrowding in the first season led to a simplified Autopia being fast tracked into the park.

187   Hard Rock Park rocks hard, CBS, https://www.cbsnews.com/news/hard-rock-park-rocks-hard/

188   Can Cars Land revive California Adventure?, Brad Morris, CNN, https://edition.cnn.com/travel/article/disney-cars-land/index.html

189   Hard Rock Park comparison, Melissa Haneline, The Post and Courier, http://www.charleston.net/news/2008/aug/31/hard_times_at_hard_rock52654/

190   Ibid.

Alton Tower's (UK) capacity is also believed to be around 28,000 now[191]. It's hard to see how the park would have coped with more visitors than Alton Towers does now or Hong Kong Disneyland did when it was new. I haven't seen Hard Rock Park's workings and there were some talented people involved with the project, but it is possible that they got carried away when they calculated their capacity. It's hard to think of another park that has such a high capacity for such a small investment. They certainly overestimated their attendance.

Hard Rock Park had 5 roller coasters compared to Disneyland Hong Kong's 1 (Space Mountain). But it wasn't a vast number compared to many other regional parks in the US. One of these coasters, Maximum RPM, barely operated in the first season due to technical issues, although they wouldn't have known that when they were making their calculations. When it did work it had a unique 'Ferris Wheel' lift which was slow to line up with the track, lowering the ride's throughput. Slippery When Wet had individual cars with fours guests in a car, giving a low throughput here, too. The Vekoma Mine Train, 'Eagles Life in the Fast Lane', had relatively short 4 car trains, compared to 5 cars on Big Thunder Mountain (Disney) or 6 cars on Colorado Adventure (Phantasialand). It also had just two trains. Hard Rock Park had 11 rides in total, including 1 dark ride, 5 'flat rides' (roundabouts) and 5 coasters. Most regional parks with a capacity of 30,000 have triple that. For reference, Alton Towers currently has 10 roller coasters, 3 dark rides, 2 water rides, a cable car and numerous other smaller rides. Even taking into consideration that Hard Rock Park had more shows, it seemed poorly equipped for 30,000 people. When they had special concerts on, their indoor Hard Rock Live concert venue had 1,500 seats.

Hard Rock Park has a similar number of rides to some of the Disney parks, and they expected a similar capacity, but they had the same kinds of rides as a typical regional park and it was built on the kind of budget you'd associate with a mid-sized regional park. They didn't have Fast Pass, a parade, and I doubt many guests spent as long shopping or meeting characters as they would in a Disney park. They had left a route with particularly wide pathways to give them the option of adding a parade in a future season, but it was never needed.

They had thought about how they could manage the crowds. They created pre-shows and queue line entertainment, including a unique live karaoke in the queue for Maximum RPM. All the queues were undercover and some were air conditioned. Compared to a typical regional park, they were expecting guests to spend less time at the rides. There were curiosities around the park to occupy small pockets of time, like a Whac a Boy Band game (a version of Whac a Mole) and Roto, the interactive cow fountain. There was also the Whammy Bar where each guest could listen to live music.

---

191   When I worked at Alton Towers in 2008 28,000 was cited in the staff magazine, *The Source*. In 2020 Channel 4 ran a documentary called Alton Towers: A Roller Coaster Year. This suggested that the park's capacity was still 28,000 – Ride Rater article - https://riderater.co.uk/8582/review-alton-towers-a-rollercoaster-year/

Kerry Graves, the vice president of marketing and sales, said, "It's not your traditional theme park. If you're coming for a ride park, to ride all the cool rides, the biggest, the tallest and the fastest, that's not us. We are probably the coolest park. But Hard Rock's all about the experience". Hard Rock's statistics seemed to rely on an average guest spending less than a quarter of their time at the rides. Whilst they did provide plenty of options for spending your time, it's hard to know whether this was realistic.

They had also planned a string of events, which would help to attract visitors outside of the peak summer, including a Rocktoberfest as well as Halloween[192]. It was a problem though that a lot of Myrtle Beach's visitors came in the summer for the beaches, and that there wasn't the local population to support the park outside the big vacation peaks. They clearly had some exceptionally talented creatives working on the project, but did they know what they were letting themselves in for operationally? There have been a few failed theme parks over the years led by talented creatives and marketing people, but that struggled from an operational perspective.

Another question is, could a $225 million, 55-acre park (including an 8 acre lake) and 11 standard amusement park rides have a 30,000 capacity? If it could, that sounds like a strong return on the investment. It is hard for a new theme park to get the kinds of figures that would excite most investors. There can be a temptation to over-project the figures, including the capacity, although this doesn't necessarily mean that Hard Rock Park did that.

Very broadly speaking, a park's capacity is determined by its design and the way it's operated. If you want to reach a particular capacity then there's going to be a tradeoff between the two. The more you spend on building it, the less you'll need to spend on operating it. You might be able to squeeze more out of a park by hiring lots of staff. You can have a large entertainments team with lots of street theatre, shows and meet and greets, and have rides with lots of team members working on them. If you do this, the park might cost less to build, but more to operate. When you're looking at your budgets, you're either going to have to push up your build cost or your operating cost. There can be a tendency for parks to want to get the most capacity they can with their capital investment. The advantage is that they don't need to borrow as much money. The downside is that they end up with a park that's expensive to operate.

In this book we've considered how events and entertainments can be an important part of a successful park. At the time, Hard Rock Park's founder and CCO (Chief Creative Officer) Jon Binkowski's main experience was in entertainments. He worked his way up through Sea World's entertainment department to become vice president of entertainment, an important role at a large operator known for its shows. It wasn't surprising that shows and events would be a big part of the park. Shows would help to distinguish them from Six Flag and Cedar Fair type parks, and it used expertise that the design

---

192   Led Zeppelin – Moody Blues rides at new Hard Rock Park in SC, Bruce Smith, Pittsburgh Post Gazette, https://www.post-gazette.com/life/travel/2008/05/17/ Led-Zeppelin-Moody-Blues-rides-at-new-Hard-Rock-Park-in-SC/stories/200805170167

team already had. It makes sense to play to your strengths.

With new parks there can be a tendency to use shows and events to make up for a lack of rides and infrastructure. Certainly, Dreamland (UK) tried to do that. Whilst shows and events can be an important part of a theme park, and perhaps particularly for one themed to rock music, the jury is still out on whether Hard Rock Park had the infrastructure to cope with 30,000 guests.

Shows and events can be relatively cheap to set up, but expensive to operate on a day to day basis. This means you need a high critical mass of visitors to make them viable. There is a minority of parks around the world that derive a large chunk of their capacity from shows, including the Sea World parks, other marine parks and some anomalies such as Hollywood Studios and Le Puy Du Fou (France). The final one is almost entirely shows, with no rides. Other parks where shows contribute significantly to the park's capacity, but no more than the rides, include Europa Park (Germany) and Port Aventura (Spain). Shows were a big part of Gardaland (Italy) before Merlin took them over. However, there aren't many parks around the world where the park's capacity was based so little on what the rides could cope with. Hard Rock Park never claimed to be a typical theme park, but were their projections realistic?

The capacity of a park isn't directly proportionate to the cost of building it, but a theme park is only going to be able to punch so far above its weight. In the end Hard Rock Park's real problem wasn't that it couldn't cope with the crowds, but that the crowds didn't come, and it went bankrupt at the end of its first season. New parks often do relatively well in their first season due to pent up demand. Hard Rock Park only averaged 2,000 guests a day[193], so the 30,000 capacity was never properly tested.

We don't know how Hard Rock Park arrived at this 30,000 figure and whether it would have coped if they had attracted the attendance they'd forecast. It does raise several questions for those developing a new park:

Are your projections overly reliant on comparisons with Disney and Universal?

If they are, can those comparisons be justified?

If you're using figures from Disney, how reliant are they on the Disney brand? For example, would your shops, character meets and greets or parade have the same draw?

If it doesn't sound plausible, is that because you've been very clever in how you've designed the park? Or have you been unrealistic?

Based on the acreage, level of investment, and the number of staff, does the projected capacity sound plausible?

At different points in the day, what percentage of your guests are doing different activities? For example, eating food, queuing for rides, etc?

At peak times, how long would the queues for the rides be?

Would the queues be able to hold that many people?

---

193   The extremely hard lessons that the themed entertainment industry learned from Hard Rock Park, Jim Hill, Huff Post

How long would a typical person be willing to wait for that kind of ride?

If your numbers are high, is that through design? Or have you been tempted to inflate the numbers to appeal to investors?

Are your capacities calculated through honest logic or wishful thinking?

Where are the capacities distributed through the park, and do they match what the guests are expecting/wanting? For example, if your park has rides and animals and most of the capacity is in the animal side, are the guests expecting to spend most of their time looking at the animals?

Is the marketing team selling guests an accurate picture of how the park's expecting them to spend their time?

How reliant is the park's capacity on a specific attraction? What happens if a particular attraction has to close for some reason?

If you're a new park, have you built in any margin for error?

Despite the lackluster attendance and huge losses, Hard Rock Park did have its achievements. It was delivered on time and in budget. It had a strong and unique brand, resisting the temptation to ape Disney or Universals too closely. Those who visited generally had a good time, perhaps helped by the short queues. They also enjoyed the humour and the musical quality of the park. Not many people have achieved what the team behind Hard Rock Park achieved.

Although Hard Rock Park's failure came from them not attracting enough visitors, it's a good opportunity for designers to think realistically about how well a new park will be able to cope with certain sized crowds. Disney parks are abnormal in many ways, including the use of Fast Pass, and the way the Disney brand helps to drive people towards shopping, meeting characters and watching parades. This can make it tricky for independent parks to benchmark against them.

Disney are so good at what they do, that they can make handling large crowds look easier than it is. Their parks don't always have many rides, but the rides they do have tend to cost a lot to build and use a high number of staff. Disney are very talented at managing crowds. But we shouldn't under-estimate how much money it takes to make the Disney dream a reality. We'll come back to park capacities in the final section of this book. We'll discuss the safety factors and the guest experience factors we need to consider when we're setting a park's capacity. We will look at some regional parks that have been very successful at managing their queues, including Holiday World (Indiana) and Dollywood (Tennessee). Having zoomed out to look at the bigger picture, we're now going to go back to some more specific things that parks can do to spread their guests out around the site.

Adjusting the demand for rides with pricing and advertised waiting times

If you can advertise accurate waiting times for attractions (and this isn't as simple as it might sound), then guests can be encouraged to move from rides with longer waiting times to those with shorter waiting times. The same principle applies to parks where you pay per ride, but in this case, you can tweak the popularity of an attraction by adjusting the price. If a ride often has long queues you can nudge the price up, or adjust it down for a ride that tends to have empty seats. If it's a ride with an undetermined ride time, such as a flat ride, then ride cycles might be lengthened at quiet times and shortened at busy times.

Simply having prices relative to the size and quality of an attraction doesn't tend to do a perfect job of redistributing guests. Parks with a pay per ride model that are also popular enough to have queues, might look at additional tricks to drives attendance to the less popular attractions.

When the original Disneyland opened on July 18th 1955 an entry ticket cost $1 (including tax) and then you bought tickets for the rides you wanted to go on. The bigger the ride, the more expensive the ticket. This wasn't an entirely satisfactory way of distributing visitors around the park. Even though the bigger rides were more expensive, they still ended up with considerably longer queues than the smaller rides.

The public relations director for Disneyland, Ed Ettinger, had a plan[194]. On October 11th 1955, less than two months after the park opened, they introduced ticket books. Rather than buying individual tickets for the rides you wanted to go on, you bought books of tickets including A, B and C tickets. The ticket each attraction required depended on how big and popular it was. 'A' ticket attractions were the biggest and 'C' ticket were the smallest. In 1956 they added a package of smaller rides; *Storybook Land Canal Boats* (which offered a significant enhancement to the former *Canal Boats of the World*), *Tom Sawyer Island Rafts*, *Indian War Canoes*, and the *Rainbow Caverns Mine Train*. A new 'D' ticket was introduced for these smaller attractions. In 1959 the park had a major expansion when they added the Matterhorn Bobsled, Submarine Voyage and Monorail. To coincide with this, they launched a new fifth ticket level, the 'E' ticket. But whereas before the closer to the start of the alphabet, the bigger the ride, the E 'tickets' were for Disneyland's largest rides.

The advantage of the ticket books is that people would pay more for the book than if they were just buying a ticket for one big ride, but they still only got one go on the big ride that had the queue. Guests felt they were getting value for money with the ticket books, but the additional rides they were getting were on smaller rides with surplus capacity. In other words, there were two advantages of Disney's ticketing system. People could buy more or fewer tickets depending on how much money they had and how keen they were, but also by adjusting the tickets in a book you could push the demand up or down for different groups of attractions. The aim was to fill the seats on a ride and use its capacity without long queues forming.

Other attractions copied Disney's ticket book idea. For example, before Blackpool Pleasure Beach introduced wristbands, they had ticket books similar to Disney. Once wristbands came in, they wanted to encourage people to buy the wristbands, so they replaced the ticket books with a new system

---

194   E ticket memories: Five favourite facts about ticket books, Steven Vagnini,
D23, https://d23.com/e-ticket-memories-five-favorite-facts-about-ticket-books/

where each ride was a set number of tokens. Towers Street member Jon81uk explains how it worked. "You paid £15 or whatever and got one AA ride, two A, two B, three C and three D (or something like that)."[195]

After they stopped doing the ticket books Blackpool Pleasure Beach used another trick to push demand for the second-tier attractions. They gave away vouchers for free goes on a 'random' ride when you bought a meal or drink. It was a bit like the Monopoly promotion McDonald's later did. Presumably a promotion like this can be skewed to give away more free rides on the less popular attractions than on the headline rides with the long queues, like The Big One and Valhalla. When we visited as kids my brother and myself had wristbands. When my parents came to pick us up, they used the free ride vouchers we got with our lunch.

For POP (pay one price) parks they can't control demand for rides by charging a higher price or giving fewer tickets in a book, but they can advertise the waiting times, so people can decide to go for a better ride with a longer wait or a lesser ride with a shorter wait. Just as charging more for the bigger rides didn't stop long queues forming for the bigger rides at Disneyland, advertising a longer queue length for a bigger ride won't necessarily stop the queue forming. However, it can have an impact and it helps people to make informed decisions about which ride they want to wait for.

There are various ways you can advertise the waiting times:

- TV screens dotted around the park
- Screens at the entrance to queue lines
- A member of staff at the entrance to the queue line telling people the waiting time
- Announcements to the queue, probably using a PA (public address) system, telling people the waiting time
- A mobile phone app with wait times

If you're placing centralised screens with the waiting times for various rides, then there are two considerations: where are the points with high foot traffic - so lots of people will see the screens, and where are they going to have the biggest impact on influencing people's decisions. We know that rides near the entrance tend to get long queues at the beginning and end of the day when people pass them in and out of the park, so it makes sense to have a screen near the entrance. Hubs with paths leading off in multiple directions tend to have high traffic, and are also points where guests make decisions about which attraction they will head to next.

This is another reason why parks with circular patterns of paths and lands flow better than ones with dead ends. It means there are more decision points where guests can be persuaded to head off in a different direction to a less busy area. If guests know there's another coaster with half the waiting time, they may well choose to ride that one instead, but not if it's going to be a long

---

195   Jon81uk, Blackpool Pleasure Beach general discussion, Towers Street Forum, https://towersstreet.com/talk/threads/blackpool-pleasure-beach-general-discussion.147/page-392

walk. Having a spread-out park is a double-edged sword. On one hand, a park with a large area physically spreads the guests out, and all the guests who are walking between attractions aren't waiting in a queue. On the other hand, if there are other attractions with shorter waits close at hand, they are more likely to head to them.

Some parks have colour coded waiting times. A waiting time of 15 minutes or less might be green. An hour or less might be amber. Over an hour is red. The idea is that people make quick decisions about which attraction they're going to visit next, and that a colour system helps with this process. It's the same principle as traffic light systems for food. In some countries colours are used to show health factors in food, such as salt, sugar, fat and saturated fat. The argument is that simply giving a quantity is difficult for shoppers to compute quickly, and giving a percentage of a person's GDA (guideline daily amount) is problematic because different people need different amounts depending on their gender, body mass and other factors. Although all systems for labelling food have some degree of controversy, in Britain the traffic light system has been endorsed by the British Medical Association and the Food Standards Agency. Studies have shown it to be an effective way of helping to guide shoppers towards healthier options, because the information is quick and easy to digest and to compare products with.

In 2003 the PEGI (pan European game information) system was introduced for rating video games. It standardised the different approaches in different countries for giving guidelines for how old someone should be to play a game. In 2009 the logos used were changed from all being black, to a traffic light system. Green is for games suitable for children aged 7 and under, amber for 16 and under, and red for over 18s only. As with the food labelling, the traffic light system was to help shoppers quickly spot which games were suitable for their child's age group.

Most people won't stop for long to compare waiting times on a screen. They want to get to the next ride. A traffic light system allows guests to analyse the data efficiently. Once people have chosen to head to a ride with a shorter waiting time, they need to know how to get there. Near a screen with waiting times, you want to have a park map (with something to show guests their current location, ideally with an arrow pointing in the direction they're facing to help them orientate themselves), and direction signage pointing to rides.

You can theme the screens, so they blend them into the environment. The wait time board at the entrance to Outlaw Run at Silver Dollar City (Missouri) is done in a rustic metal style. It says, "Your stagecoach heads west in [wait time] minutes".

On the Disney mobile app, you can choose whether you want the map to be labelled with the attractions, entertainment, dining, shops, restrooms, photopass, events, tours, guest services, hotels or recreation. 'Photopass' are points where you can have your photo taken. 'Tours' are guided tours of the park that you pay extra for. 'Recreation' are leisure offerings at the hotels, such as play centres, gyms and swimming pools. You chose what you want the map to be labelled with so that it doesn't get too crowded. If you select 'attractions' the labels change as you zoom in. If you're zoomed out you just get the waiting times. If you zoom in you get the waiting times and the attractions names. Here's a map taken from Hollywood Studios (Disney World, Orlando):

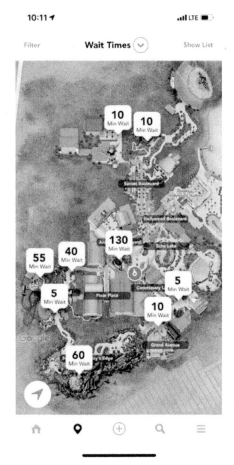

Screenshot taken from Mice Chat[196].

Giving just the waiting times when you're zoomed out, prevents the map from becoming overly cluttered with information. It helps guest to locate a short queue near where they are, rather than them trekking across the park to find a short queue. In the above screenshot, guests are clearly bunched up around the new developments, while the older rides in Sunset Boulevard (Rock 'N Roller Coaster and Tower of Terror) only have a 10-minute wait. This screenshot was taken early in the day, and later on the guests began to filter out more evenly through the park.

---

196   Walt Disney World Update: Loopholes, Cancellations, & a Day at Hollywood Studios, Chloé Ferreira, Mice Chat, https://www.micechat. com/264567-disney-world-update-delays-changes-hollywood-studios/

Estimating the queue times

Communicating the waiting times to guests is important in busier parks, but it's only helpful if these estimates are accurate. I've been to parks where their estimations are wildly out, and while the screens and apps look good in theory, they cause more annoyance than benefit. How can it be so difficult for parks to estimate their waiting times and how can we make them more accurate?

There are several factors that determine how easy it is to work out the waiting times for an attraction. These include:

Is the capacity of the attraction consistent? If a ride regularly has seats/ cars not in use due to maintenance issues, then this makes it harder to calculate the waiting times. If for any other reason you often don't fill all the seats, it makes estimating the queues harder. If there are irregular numbers of people in each vehicle/train, then the queue will move forward at a less reliable pace.

If it's a ride that doesn't load continuously, are the intervals between loading regular? For example, on flat rides (roundabouts), the ride times might vary and be at the discretion of the operator. On other flat rides the ride might run on a timer and have an exact ride time (e.g. four minutes).

How consistent are the loading times? Rides with simpler loading processes and restraint systems tend to have more regular loading times. More complicated restraints systems, such as on flying coasters and stand up coasters, have less predictable loading times. Similarly, if height checking happens on the platform, this can also slow things down.

Does the ride draw a regular number of riders from the main (standby) line? Or are there other queues including Fast Track guests (who've paid to skip the queues), disabled riders and people who've been given line jump tickets as a form of service recovery? At Disney Fast Pass tickets for skipping the lines is theoretically based on a percentage of the ride's hourly capacity, so while it will slow down the standby line, the number of ticket holders is reasonably predictable. At other parks, it might be very difficult to predict when guests with tickets to skip the queue will turn up.

All this assumes that the staff are genuinely trying to accurately calculate the waiting times. It might be that a park sends staff home to save money if the queue drops below a certain time. Whether or not the staff want to go home early, will help to determine their 'estimation'. At one park I worked in, if queues for a ride hit two hours, they stopped selling Fast Track tickets for that attraction. Operating the ride with such a long queue would become stressful before it reached that point. As the queue got longer, there was more queue jumping, more people legitimately needing to go to the toilet, guests became irritable, things flared up if a child got to the front and was too short, and if the ride had any downtime things would kick off quickly. If the queue reached ninety minutes, the operator might call through a two-hour waiting time, so they'd stop selling Fast Track tickets. In one topic on the Towers Street Forum members felt that staff were deliberately over-estimating the wait times at the end of the day so that fewer people joined the queue, meaning they could go home quicker[197]. Member Tom described an employee at the entrance to one ride advising guests that the waiting time was far longer than it was, "A number of people did turn around after receiving the advice, which was delivered in a very polite way but it still used language designed to repel people in my view". The general view was that managers turned a blind eye to the practice, either because they too wanted to get home early, because they were trying to save on staffing budget, or because they couldn't be bothered to have an argument with their team.

In books about customer service they often talk about staff engagement. The definitions of staff engagement can vary, but a general definition is that engaged staff are behind the aims and objects of their company. When it comes to queue line management you can have a lot of politics. Operators deliberately post inaccurate waiting times. People record inaccurate figures for how many guests have been on their ride each hour. Managers are more concerned with being seen to put pressure on their teams to work quicker, than on actually supporting them and looking for practical ways to improve throughputs. In these kind of workplaces, queues become politicised and 'efficiency' is treated as a game, rather than something that's important to give the guests a positive experience. People lose sight of why they're there - which is to serve and entertain the public. Politics becomes normalised.

It's harder to keep waiting times accurate on rides with low throughputs, because relatively small fluctuations of guests can cause a significant difference in waiting times.

Let me illustrate this point. In June and July, the British theme parks get a lot of school groups. It used to be that primary school classes (children aged eleven and under) would get put into small groups and sent off with a teacher, parent or other school employee. More recently there has been growing concern in the UK about 'safe guarding' children against abuse. A lot of schools won't send one adult off with a group of children, even though theme parks are public spaces with a lot of other people around, CCTV etc. Because adults can't be on their own with children, it tends to mean a class of thirty children will go around the park together. Sometimes two classes will stick together, meaning sixty people join a queue all at once. If a ride has a throughput of 1,000 guests an hour and 60 people suddenly join it, this only affects the waiting time by about 3.5 minutes. If it has a throughput of 200 guests an hour, then the waiting time suddenly rises by over 15 minutes.

When queue times do suddenly change like this, it's much easier for ride operators to keep on top of it when they change the waiting time themselves, rather than having to phone or radio a control room and rely on them to manually change the waiting times in different programmes. When a park has a lot of inaccurate waiting times, it tends to be due to a combination of these factors.

In some cases, the technology is all synchronised. The operator of a ride adjusts their queue time from the control box, and this updates the mobile app, the screen at the ride's entrance, the centralised screens around the

---

197   Being warned of a 'long queue' when entering just before ride close, Towers Street Forum

park. In other parks someone will have to input the data into the different systems separately.

Parks with older technology that's been added piecemeal might end up with disconnected systems. Moving to an integrated system costs money, but it saves on labour costs further down the line, and is likely to be more accurate. When the data has to be manually added into multiple systems, there is more room for mistakes or for the person doing it do get distracted.

At Europa Park each ride has a touch screen computer interface. As well as telling the operator useful information, such as the park's closing time (normally finalised around 12:30 each day) they also use it to set the queue time, and this updates all the systems automatically.

I've worked at other parks where the operator phones or radios a central unit to tell them the queue times and they update the different systems. The central control room are getting lots of calls about queue times, as well information about ride closures and other incidents in the park such as first aid requests, security call outs etc. At busy times they get overwhelmed and can't keep up. Coordinating first aids and ride break downs take priority and the waiting times become less accurate. Ironically, it's the busiest times when the waiting times become most important, and these are the times when they don't get updated properly.

Parks often work on the assumption that it's better to manage expectations by overestimating queue times than to underestimate them. It's better to say that a 60 minute wait is 70 minutes than to advertise that it's 50. However, if waiting times aren't fairly accurate, they can still quickly lose their meaning. In the past people paid per a ride and you'd pay more for the bigger rides than for the smaller rides. People decided which rides to go on based on a combination of how good they looked and how much a ride cost. Nowadays most static attractions offer a pay once ride all day system. A small ride is free, and a major ride is also free. Now the currency that helps people decide what to go on isn't the cost of a ride – it's the waiting times. If people know that the small ride has a ten minute queue and the big ride has a thirty minute queue, they can decide whether the bigger ride is worth the longer wait (triple the waiting time). If the waiting times aren't accurate, then guests can't make an informed decision. Now this economic theory of waiting times doesn't work out. Going around a theme park not know how long the waiting times are, is like going around a shop trying to decide what to buy when you don't know what the prices are.

If guests don't know how long a wait will be, it makes it harder for them to plan their day. There might be a show they want to see at a particular time, a VIP experience (like a meet and greet with an animal) or if a park has a time ticket/reservation system, they might have a slot to go on an attraction at a particular time. If people don't know how long a queue is, they might pass on a ride they could have been on, miss out on an experience because they're stuck in a queue, or end up leaving a queue half way through.

Of the parks I've visited Europa Park has some of the most reliable waiting times. Various things work in the park's favour. It helps that the operators can set the queue times themselves rather than needing to phone a central control room. Staffing levels aren't normally changed on the day because of waiting times. The rides tend to have simple restraints (no seat belts etc) making loading times fairly regular. Height checking is done at the entrance to the queue line preventing unpredictable hold ups to the dispatches. It's rare for seats/cars to be out of order. Whilst studying operational efficiency, one of the things that jumps out is that things tend to have unplanned consequences. We could call this the butterfly effect. Simpler loading processes not only speed up the throughputs, but make predicting the waiting times more accurate.

If you're going to advertise the wait time, you need to make sure it's accurate. How can you do this? Here are four different methods for estimating queue times. Each one has its pros and cons:

The ride operator can look at the queue and judge it. An experienced operator might be able to do this fairly well. It relies on the operator being able to see the whole queue line, either directly or with CCTV. At a lot of larger regional parks this isn't possible. There needs to be a system for the operator to update the queue board, either directly or via a control room. Some parks have a map of the queue in the control box with waiting times marked on it, to show how long the wait would be from certain points in the line.

You can give guests a token when they join a queue. When they get to the front of the queue, they hand it to a member of staff. This can be used to work out the wait time. For years Disney used this. If the wait time changes between them joining the queue and getting to the front, it won't factor this in. This system tells you how long the wait time was when they joined the queue, so if they wait an hour, it tells you what the wait time was an hour ago.

You can have people counting cameras that count people in and out of queue lines. These can accurately record queue times and throughputs, but it's expensive technology.

Using Bluetooth beacons, you can track people using the park's phone app. These can report back information on queue times. This system works if there are quite a few people using the park's phone app.

For a small park, having the operator look at the queue and then do an announcement every 15 minutes, is the most cost-effective way of doing it. You can also have signs in the queue, for example '10 minutes from this point'. This used to be the standard practice for advertising waiting times before more sophisticated electronic solutions came in. For larger parks, there are other ways of measuring and communicating wait times that are more expensive, but also more effective.

In 2013 Disney introduced My Magic Plus. This had numerous advantages for the company, including allowing them to nudge guests towards quieter areas of the park and helping them to estimate queues more accurately. Guests were encouraged to wear wristbands with an RFID (Radio Frequency Identification) chip that could communicate with short range sensors (to pay for stuff) and long-range sensors for other uses (for example an animatronic in a ride could greet them by their name). These long-range sensors could track where guests were in the park. They could track individual guests moving along a queue line to get a very accurate estimation of queue times[198]. If one area of the park was getting particularly congested, they could decrease Fast Pass slots in that area of the park and increase them for another area to try to move guests around the park. By allowing guests to book Fast Pass slots on their mobiles it's easier to encourage guests to book a timeslot in a different area of the park. They could also send extra cast members (for example cleaners) to parts of the park that are busier. We will come back to My Magic Plus in more detail shortly.

As I mentioned previously, estimating queue times becomes a lot more complex when the throughputs on a ride are inconsistent and there are riders coming from alternative queues (Fast Track, disabled, etc). If the queue moves at a consistent pace, then you can simply look at where the end of the queue is and know how long the waiting time is. There was an unexpected issue when Disneyland Paris opened, that shows the subtle process of adapting a business model to another culture. They had signs telling you the waiting time from that particular point, for example, '45 minutes to the front of the queue'. It turned out that European's often stand closer together than Americans do (or at least they did in 1992), so queue times were substantially longer than the signs suggested. Once the park opened, they had to recalculate the estimated wait times and adjust the signage accordingly[199]. To work out the waiting time for a new ride you need to estimate how many people each section of line can hold and the throughput. You can then know how big a distance of line each five minutes of waiting time looks like.

I've noticed that when a queue moves forward slowly, or not at all for a period, it tends to bunch up like traffic in a jam. People shuffle forward closer to the person in front. When the queue moves steadily, there's more space between each guest. A lot of people will use how quickly the queue moves forward to judge how efficient it is, so the effects of high or low throughputs become magnified.

A lesson from Anaheim

So far, we've had a few history lessons. We looked at variable pricing for the Great Exhibition (1851) and about Disneyland's early use of ride tickets and ticket books (1955). We're now going to take a trip back to 1960 to see how attitudes to queues have changed. It's now assumed that we should try to communicate how long the queues are. It helps guests to make informed decisions. As we shall see, this view hasn't always been the case. In this book I haven't had the time and space to write in detail about queue design, and the theming, entertainment and storytelling found in queues. However, in

---

198   The messy business of reinventing happiness, Austin Carr, Fast Company, https://www.fastcompany.com/3044283/the-messy-business-of-reinventing-happiness

199   From the earth to the moon, launching Disney-land Paris' legendary Space Mountain, Brian Krosnik, Theme Park Tourist, http://www.themeparktourist.com/features/20170325/32580/earth-moon-disneyland-paris-legendary-lost-space-mountain?page=2

this chapter we are going to learn a little about how theme parks approach designing queues.

Like a lot of enthusiasts, I love reading stories about Walt Disney. Disneyland isn't the only theme park in Anaheim (California) and Knott's Berry Farm is about 7 miles up the Santa Ana Freeway. Knott's Berry Farm opened on December 29th 1920, 35 years before Disneyland opened on July 17th 1955. Walt Disney and his imagineers visited Knott's Berry Farm for ideas, and perhaps most famously, Tony Baxter took inspiration for Splash Mountain (opened in 1989) from the Timber Mountain Log Ride at Knott's Berry Farm (opened in 1969).

One of the most widely printed stories about Walt Disney is recalled in the O.C. [Orange County] History Roundup blog. It describes the time when Walt Disney visited Knott's Berry Farm to ride the new Calico Mine, which opened in November 1960[200]. It took riders on a train trip through the caverns inside the Calico Mountain, complete with scenes of animatronic miners. Both the Timber Mountain Log Ride and Calico Mine were designed by Bud Hurlbut.

"Walt Disney knew Bud and would come over to see his progress on various projects. When Walt came to see the new Calico Mine Ride, he had no idea that the apparent entrance to the ride was only the beginning of a hidden, winding, and attractively themed queue area. Even with a *long* line, it would appear to passers-by that the line was *short*. And once in line, the guests were appeased by the colorful and dynamic surroundings. "You sneaky S.O.B.!" Walt exclaimed to Bud, upon discovering about a hundred people were already ahead of them in line."[201]

I think the story appeals to us partly because of Walt Disney's alleged colourful language. Walt (sometimes referred to as Uncle Walt), was the biggest icon of family entertainment. We don't imagine him calling someone a son of a bitch. At the time Disneyland and Knott's Berry Farm operated a pay per ride model, so people were paying to queue for a ride without knowing how long the wait would be, and that's what made him "a sneaky S.O.B."

Back in 1960 theme parks hadn't started using signs with wait times. According to Josh Young from Theme Park University, signs with wait times were first used for attractions at the New York World Fair in 1964[202]. Disneyland began advertising the wait times soon after. When Calico Mine opened you had no way of knowing how long the wait would be when you joined it.

These days theme parks still tend to hide their queues away, because they think it's 'bad show' (poor presentation) to have visible queues around the park. Theme parks are often trying to create a particular environment, like

200   Calico Mine Ride, Knott's Berry Farm, https://www.knotts.com/play/rides/calico-mine-ride

201   Bud Hurlbut (1918-2011), O.C. History Round Up, http://och-istorical.blogspot.com/2011/01/bud-hurlbut.html

202   Disney legends remember 1964 World's Fair at IAAPA, John Young, Theme Park University, https://themeparkuniversity.com/disney/disney-legends-remember-1964-worlds-fair-iaapa/

a Wild West main street, or a futuristic space port. None of these things would have queue lines everywhere. It also makes the park feel stressful and crowded when you're walking around and seeing queues everywhere. Even if the park is crowded, you don't want it to feel crowded.

There's something really interesting about how people's behaviour changes when they feel like they're part of a crowd. You hear about mob mentality and crowd psychology, where people do things they wouldn't normally do when they're in a crowd, because they lose their sense of individuality. People in crowds are often less willing to help someone in need, perhaps because there's a 'diffusion of responsibility', where everyone assumes that someone else will help. For various reasons crowds can make us feel uncomfortable, which is why theme parks are often designed to break them up.

At Disney they talk about the architecture of reassurance, and breaking up crowds is a part of that. The architecture of reassurance is about making people feel like they're big in a small world, rather than feeling small in a big world. Disney even has a ride called It's a Small World. The most famous aspect of Disney's architecture of reassurance is their use of forced perspective, where building and structures aren't built to full scale. Often the part closest to us is full scale (for example, the ground floor of a building), and then those parts further away (for example the turrets at the top of Sleeping Beauty's Castle) are built smaller than they should be. This helps to save money, as structures like castles and mountains don't need to be full size, but it also makes the guests feel bigger, because they are bigger relative to the buildings around them.

The effect that forced perspective has on us is an interesting, and slightly paradoxical one. On one hand it allows a structure to look bigger than it actually is, for example Expedition Everest (Disney's Animal Kingdom) is a lot smaller than the real Mount Everest. But on the other hand, although our brain is partly fooled into thinking a structure is bigger than it is when it uses forced perspective, we also feel relatively large compared to the structure. Particularly when we're standing close to it. Part of our brain thinks we're standing next to a real mountain, and part of our brain feels large compared to that 'real mountain'. If we were standing next to the real Mount Everest, we'd feel a lot smaller compared to when we stand next to Disney's fake one.

In customer service they stress the importance of making people feel like an individual rather than a number. Being in a big indistinguishable mass of people doesn't help with that. Finding ways to break up masses of people gives us that sense of reassurance and makes us feel more comfortable. Having the queue in a separate space to the main paths around the park, does that. Knott's Berry Farm were pioneers in separating their queues from the main pathways. However, parks now do more to advise people about the queue length. This is easier to do with modern technology than it was in 1960.

It's considered good practice to inform guests how long the wait is before they join the line. Not only is it courteous, but it manages their expectations, and from a psychological perspective we find uncertainty stressful. None of us want to be waiting in a line, with no idea whether we'll be there for 10 minutes or 2 hours. It also helps us to plan our day. Nowadays few large parks use a pay per ride model, so it's a different dynamic compared to when each ride was run by an individual concession competing for a guest's money. In fact, so many parks charge people to skip the queues, cynics would argue that parks have a vested interest in making sure the guests know full well if the lines are long, so they're more likely to buy a ticket to jump it.

I think a good strategy is to hide the queues away, but to use electronic boards, apps, signs, announcements and staff members, to advertise the waiting time before people join the line. Most of what has been written about efficiency and queue line management (and not a lot has been) is about Disney and the major theme park resorts. That's partly because most of what's been written about theme park management, generally, is about Disney. But also, because when we think about managing queues, we often think about expensive technology and having lots of staff everywhere. I believe that every theme park can benefit from some efficiency and queue line management techniques.

A smaller park might not have the budget for a themed queue or to hide the queue away completely. But just separating the queue from the main paths around the park makes a big difference to the general ambience of the midway. If you haven't got the money for themed queues, just put a border between the main area and the queueline. It could be a thin flower bed or a narrow pond/water feature, perhaps with some little fountains, or how about some jumping fountains? It could just be a thin border with some basic theming like barrels and wagon wheels. If you're worried about guests walking on the flower beds, go for some raised planters. People are less likely to trample on these. It's a small investment compared to even the cheapest rides, and it breaks up the two masses of people: those walking around the park and those queuing for a ride. This makes it a pleasanter experience for everyone.

My Magic Plus

In the chapter on 'estimating' queues were briefly mentioned My Magic Plus. It's helped Disney make their waiting times more accurate. We're now going to look at the system in more detail. My Magic Plus is exclusive to Disney. However, other parks and businesses are coming up with their own alternatives. Just as Fast Pass paved the way for other kinds of virtual queuing, we're likely to see more systems like My Magic Plus. We will look at how My Magic Plus nudges guests towards quieter areas, but we will also take a broader look at how it makes the park more efficient.

My Magic Plus is a computer system that Disney began developing in 2008 for managing the flow of guests around their parks, and other functions. After about 5 years in development, in January 2013 Walt Disney World began rolling out the My Magic Plus system. From a guest's end they used the system with a Magic Band (a bracelet on their wrist) or their smart phone. Their Magic Band/smart phone could be used to pay for things, record onride photos, open lockers or their hotel room. Their band/phone could also be read by sensors nearby. This could be used for gimmicky interactions (for example an animatronic that knows the guest's name, or that it's their birthday), but it could also be used to track how quickly guests are moving through queues, hotspots in the park with high densities of guests, and other information. For years shops have been using loyalty cards to track customer behaviour, and now My Magic Plus gave Disney unprecedented information about how their guests spend their time and make decisions.

My Magic Plus combined some of the advantages of a loyalty card, next generation Fast Pass, and merging various other cards (such as a park ticket, photo pass, and hotel room key) into one. From a psychological perspective, guests are less conscious that they're spending money when they're swiping a bracelet on their wrist. In a swimming pool or water park there are advantages to being able to buy things with a waterproof wristband, rather than having to pop back to a locker for your wallet.

Some of these advantages are primarily for Disney, for example if people lose track of how much they're spending. Some of them are win/wins, for example making it easier to spend money in the water parks. Some of them might be more a convenience for the guests, such as merging tickets and cards together. As this is a book about efficiency, we will pay particular attention to efficiency, and how My Magic Plus helped to manage crowd flow around the parks and increase their capacities. It also speeded up payments, encouraged people to order food from their phones, provided new queue line entertainment and streamlined customer service.

According to Tom Staggs (formerly chairman of Walt Disney Parks and Resorts) My Magic Plus increased the capacity of Magic Kingdom by 5,000[203], although many fans were skeptical of this claim. To put this into perspective, in 2020 Legoland Florida cited that their capacity was 12,000. 5,000 was therefore 40% of Legoland Florida's total capacity. To put it another way, My Magic Plus increased the capacity of Magic Kingdom by around 5.6%.

Stagg's theory was primarily because guests could use a mobile phone app to book Fast Passes for attractions at the other side of the park rather than having to visit the entrance to an attraction to pick up a Fast Pass. Using the phone app Disney could offer shorter wait times to attractions a distance away, encouraging guests to move over to quieter areas of the park. They could also track the location of guests in the park a lot more accurately using their Magic Bands, potentially sending more staff (such as cleaners, security and entertainers) to more congested areas. By using sensors to monitor people's movement in a queue, they can advertise more accurate waiting times, at least letting people make better informed decisions about where to spend their time when the parks are at their busiest. It would also speed up transactions at tills (cash registers) where guests would tap a magic band on their wrist to pay, rather than having to delve into their wallet to retrieve a card or money.

203   The messy business of reinventing happiness, Austin Carr, https://www. fastcompany.com/3044283/the-messy-business-of-reinventing-happiness

Disney's theme park operation is on a different scale to any other. According to the TEA (Themed Entertainment Association) in 2019 Magic Kingdom was the world's only theme park to get over 20 million visitors[204]. In 2019 their parks collectively attracted 155,991,000 visitors. That's more than double their next biggest competitor, Merlin Entertainments, and many of Merlin's visitors come from their midway attractions (Dungeons, Sea Life Centre, Madame Tussauds wax works, Eye branded observation attractions etc) rather than their theme parks. Because their theme park portfolio is so big, even a small improvement can have a big impact. For example, if data collected from My Magic Plus allowed them to tweak their operations and increase their attendance by 0.5%, that's equal to an extra 800,000 visitors. Disney's scale makes it economical to apply a kind of science to their operations that wouldn't be worthwhile for many smaller companies.

The potential to track crowds using this system and move entertainers around accordingly reminds me of a story I read on Theme Park Insider by user E Ticket[205]:

"One of the hottest summers on record at Universal Studios Hollywood, probably 1988 or 1989. Trams were backed up all over the backlot, so the tram loading area was really, really backed up (the old one, up top behind the ticket booths, sort of where the Universal Store is now at CityWalk). Boarding passes were out well into the evening, and the actual wait in line, even after you brought your boarding pass, was at least two hours (these are the days before any "rides", kids... just the stunt shows and the tram tour). One manager was convinced that all the situation needed was some entertainment, a costumed character to placate the near-rioting guests. He got on the radio and broadcast to everyone within earshot, We've got a bad situation here, send in the wolfman. To this day, me and many of my friends and ex-co-workers (and, from what I hear, even some folks who still work at the tour) use the term send in the wolfman when things are at their most ridiculously dire."

When I worked at Dreamland, we could radio for our entertainments team The Fun Fairers to send a flash mob to a ride with a long queue or that had broken down. They'd turn up with a battery powered speaker and do a dance.

Another big development with My Magic Plus, was that you could book three timeslots in advance, if you were staying at a resort hotel. This feature is sometimes called 'Fast Pass Plus', and was another step towards getting guests to plan their day, rather than moving around the park in a more spontaneous way. This gave people an extra incentive to stay on site. You could also reserve Fast Pass spots on the day using the My Magic Plus app, rather than visiting a machine at the entrance an attraction and collecting a physical ticket. This encouraged people to download the My Magic Plus app. There are some guests who use theme park apps anyway, but plenty of others that need a little nudging.

204   2019 Theme Index, Themed Entertainment Association, http://www.teaconnect.org/images/files/TEA_369_611616_200731.pdf

205   Theme park cast member stories, Theme Park Insider, https://www.themeparkinsider.com/flume/200905/1196/

Letting hotel guests book three rides in advance was also one of the more controversial aspects of My Magic Plus. Annual pass holders and day visitors could feel disadvantaged, as could visitors who didn't know the parks so well. Some people found planning their vacation months in advance exciting, while for others it became a chore. I do think that letting people book their Fast Passes in advance had much more to do with encouraging people to stay at Disney's own hotels and download the Disney app, than it did with directly improving the guest flow.

In order to use Fast Pass Plus, guests needed to download the app onto their phone. By getting lots of guests to download the app to book their Fast Passes, it meant that flow could be tracked around the park and lots of guests had access to all the waiting time in the palm of their hands. Encouraging people to book Fast Passes on their phones rather than using paper tickets, would make people more likely to use mobile ordering for food, as they were booking stuff on their phones anyway. This speeded up service at the fast food outlets, as well as reducing staffing numbers.

My Magic Plus also paved the way for new types of interactive queue. In the queue for Test Track[206] you go to a computer terminal, tap your wristband and design a car. At the station you tap your wristband again before boarding. At points in the ride screens show a picture of each car designed by the people riding in the vehicle and give a score for how each person's car did in that function test (the premise of Test Track is we're performing a series of function tests that a car manufacturer might perform on a new car design. The ride ends in the speed test where we break out of the building for a high-speed sequence). I personally find the design a car feature on the new Test Track (opened 2012) too obtrusive. However, I'm more impressed with the interactive feature they added to Rock 'N Roller Coaster in 2016[207]. Guests' Magic Bands have the guest's name and their hometown. Giant screens in the queue have movie posters, which are personalised with the names and hometowns of guests waiting nearby.

Bands could also be used as pagers, where a guest in a queue explores a themed area and their band buzzes when their wait is over and they can go to the loading area. An example of this is Dumbo the Flying Elephant ride at Magic Kingdom, which was remodeled as part of the New Fantasyland expansion. On the new ride children could play on an indoor play area while they waited for their time slot. One challenge is that a lot of guests don't currently wear Magic Bands, and if the park becomes reliant on them then those without will end up having a poor experience.

In this book we haven't looked too much into the relationship between customer service and efficiency. It's generally acknowledged that there's a compromise between service and efficiency, where the longer a cast member

---

206   A thrill ride in Epcot, where you ride around in motorised six seat cars that accelerate quickly. It's like a giant 'slot car'/Scaletrix.

207   Photos: Rock 'N Roller Coaster debuts new interactive element, Tom Corless, WDW New Today, https://wdwnt.com/2016/04/photos-rock-n-roller-coaster-debuts-new-interactive-element/

spends interacting with a guest, the slower the queue moves. This is a challenge for Disney. Customer service has always been part of the 'Disney difference' that keeps people coming back to their parks. However, they also get vast numbers of customers. Technology like My Magic Plus and the Disney parks app reduces the amount of interactions that guests have with the cast members, for example instead of ordering their dinner from an employee, they order it using their phone. The number of people visiting the Disney parks has tended to keep on going up and up, putting them under pressure to keep on being more efficient. Otherwise the queues could slowly grow in length. Finding that sweet spot between service and efficiency is critical, as queues tend to be the biggest source of complaints, while outstanding customer service tends to be the biggest source of positive guest feedback.

Customer service is also something that's difficult to scale. You might be able to create a 'magic moment' for a family by letting them ride on a float in the Disney parade, but you can only do that for one family each day (or two if the parade runs twice). If there are 80,000 guests in the park, you can only provide these kinds of experiences for a small percentage of them. Over the years Disney has had to look for ways to streamline their guest service. My Magic Plus was one attempt at doing this. Everyone agrees that customer service is important, but not everyone has quite the same opinion on what great customer service looks like. When people are asked to describe great service, they often say that it should feel personal. How do you personalise the experience when attractions are having to process 2,000 guests an hour? Using technology to insert people's name into attractions is an attempt to do this. In Disney's documentary The Imagineering Story (episode 6) they said that a key priority for the Smugglers Run ride was that it could process 1,800 guests an hour, but offer each one a personal experience. A combination of technologies, including AI (artificial intelligence), attempt to replace some of the personal interactions that are hard to have in such busy theme parks. Of course, Disney realises that while technology can create a more personal experience, machines can't experience empathy, sympathy or take a genuine interest in someone. However busy the parks get, it's important to make sure that the cast members still have time to stop and talk to the guests.

Although My Magic Plus is a bespoke system developed by Disney, other companies are offering theme parks the chance to buy similar technology, for example the Connect and Go system. Connect and Go are very open on their website that this is an equivalent to My Magic Plus. Current clients include Canobie Lake (independently owned theme park, New Hampshire), Six Flags and Winter Wonderland (London) where they provide the RFID technology for the Coaster Pass. At Six Flags guests can buy a season ticket that includes one meal on each visit. The RFID technology allowed guests to redeem their free meal quickly by having their annual pass scanned. It replaced a slower process where staff had to manually check the person hadn't already claimed a free meal that day using paper coupons[208].

---

208   Six Flags La Ronde, Connect and Go, https://connectngo.com/project/la-ronde/

In 2017 Efteling (Netherlands) hit their goal of attracting over 5 million visitors. They launched Vision 2030, a project to push their attendance up to 7 million by 2030. In 2017 they had introduced a virtual queue for Python with timed tickets. According to Efteling's CEO Fons Jurgens, this was a trial and that they hoped to introduce more virtual queues[209]. Their eventual aim was to introduce a scheme similar to My Magic Plus, but where all guests would plan their day in advance and arrive with an itinerary. Clearly there would be challenges with this, including unforeseen ride closures and the fact that the last guests to book their tickets could end up with a poor day where they can't go on much. It's an intriguing vision of the future and it's good that Efteling are thinking so far ahead, because not many parks do.

Guest planning

If we had to sum up Disney's strategy for managing the crowds around their parks, it's to get people to plan ahead. If Disney parks were designed differently, a guest's day could look like this. People could enter the park, and then wander around it semi-randomly. When they pass a ride that looks appealing, they could join the queue. When they get to a junction in the paths, they could make an arbitrary decision about which way to go. One direction might look nicer. They might decide to go the busiest route, assuming that most people know where the best rides are. We could call this a wisdom of crowds – a kind of social conformity. Most people will naturally follow the majority. There's a good reason for this. Historically, we've been more likely to survive if we stick together as a herd. It's like the saying, 'There's safety in numbers'. The issue here, is that if we follow the big crowd of people, they're probably going to lead us straight into the longest queue. They might be inclined to take the right-hand path, if that's their dominant hand. These arbitrary thought processes lead the majority of guests to the same destination.

A problem with this kind of decision making, is that the brain's thought process isn't really random. If we leave people to spontaneously move around the park, a lot of guests will end up in the same place, and we end up with some rides having disproportionately long queues while others are relatively quiet. What we're trying to do, is get people to plan their day around avoiding the worst queues, by giving them the information they need to make informed decisions. It's not just Disney who are doing this. It's what most parks do. It's just that some are better at it than others.

There are various things we can do to promote good decision making. Parks with a clear layout that's easy to navigate with good signage lend themselves to wayfinding, rather than guests just hoping they find something fun. People don't like walking too far to reach the next attraction, so designing a park that gives people options that are a similar distance helps. Most parks give us a map at the entrance and also feature larger maps around the park with 'You are here' markers. There might be a screen with the wait time at the entrance

209   My conversation with the CEO of the Efteling about the future of customer experience, Steven Van Belleghem, https://www.youtube.com/watch?v=cwcZSRHezsw

to lines, or screens with the waiting times for all the larger attractions at key decision making points. There could be a phone app that gives people the waiting times for the rides around the park. The park map might have tips for avoiding the queues printed on it. They might give us a ticket reservation to come back to an attraction at a particular time and skip the queue.

The Disney experience is based around helping us to avoid the queues. To do this, they encourage us to plan ahead and make informed decisions. Some of their methods are slightly subtle. When we enter the park, we pass posters for the main rides, done in the style of the classic hand drawn film posters you used to see outside cinemas. There are a couple of reasons for this. The first, is that walking into Disneyland is a bit like walking into a film. The ground outside Magic Kingdom is coloured red, like a red carpet at a film premier. We then pass the posters, and just inside the park is a popcorn cart, as much for the smell as for the sales. The second reason, is to help visitors less familiar with the park decide which rides they want to head to first. You can see signs pointing to different rides, but if you don't know what the names mean, it's difficult to make a decision. The posters try to capture the essence of each ride.

With wayfinding, you're not helping people who visit regularly and already know the park well. Wayfinding is there to help the first time or infrequent visitor. Posters at the entrance to the park can help people familiarise themselves with what the rides are. Inside the park, guests might need reminding. Regular guests might know that Shockwave's a roller coaster and Tidal Wave's the big water chute, but that might not be obvious to every guest. A guest might think, "I want to ride the big stand up coaster", but they might not know what it's called. I find it works best if the signage has a simple illustration of each ride, next to its name. You might also colour code each area. For example, all the rides in the Africa area could have a red sign, and all the rides in the Wild Woods area could have a green sign. If guests get lost looking for the ride they want, they'll become frustrated. They might also give up looking for it and join a queue for something else nearby. A lot of the ideas in this section only work if guests are able to make informed choices and plan their days around avoiding the worst queues.

Discounted evening tickets

We've looked at ways to spread guests out geographically around the park. These have included the park layout, virtual queuing, screens with waiting times and better wayfinding. We're now going to look at how to spread guests out through the hours of the day. If a park's open for 10 hours and the average guest stays for 7 hours, you don't want most of your guests coming for the middle period with much quieter periods at the beginning and end. We'll look at how we can use a promotion to bring in more guests for the evening, and events that can encourage guests to come for the beginning and the end of each day.

The idea of a discounted evening only ticket, is that as guests start to leave, more people come in with reduced entry for the last few hours of the day. There is another secondary advantage. For larger parks you find that the rides near the entrance get very busy in the morning, because people see the first big ride and gravitate to it. Then later in the day the rides around the entrance are relatively quiet, because people have worked their way deeper into the park. How big an issue this is depends on how large the site is (acreage), whether there's one or multiple entrances, and the shape of the park (we've already established that Magic Kingdom's hub and spoke layout is designed to distribute guests more evenly around the park). If the attractions near the entrance are quiet later in the day, it can be useful to have a second hit of guests. At Europa Park, Voletarium's queue would be long in the morning, as it was right by the entrance. The queue would die down, and then during the winter there'd be another influx of guests at 4pm when the evening tickets came in. As this second swell subsided, it would get busy again as people passed it on the way out.

A number of factors decide whether or not this will work:

You need to have an accurate idea of when people leave the park and the queues start to come down. If you let people in too early, then you end up flooding the park with extra visitors when it's already busy and the queues can't cope. This is an argument for tracking waiting times, something we consider in more depth elsewhere.

The capacity of the park can't drop significantly in the evenings. For example, in Europe the working time directive means under 18s can't work for more than eight hours a day. If a theme park has to send a load of their staff home at 4pm because they've worked their hours, then it might not be possible to flood the park with extra guests at this time.

The park needs to be open late enough for it to be worth coming in for the cheap tickets. I suspect that less than three hours isn't worth it for most people. If the park only begins emptying out an hour before closing, then discounted evening tickets aren't going to work.

You have to be able to get the guest in without the queues getting too long. If most of your admissions team start early and go home early afternoon, then you need to have enough staff on the entrance to cope with a late surge when the cheap tickets start.

The point of a reduced rate evening ticket is to bring extra visitors in at a time when the park is emptying out. If you end up with the park being quiet in the day and busier in the evening, then the balance isn't quite right. You also don't want to find you've got the same number of visitors, but a big chunk of them have bought half price evening tickets, meaning your attendance stays flat and your revenue goes down.

Evening tickets tend to appeal more to locals, or to people who are already in the area. They might work better for an urban park or a park near a big conurbation, than for a park in a very rural area where most of the visitors have travelled a long way to visit.

A number of parks have used reduced rate evening tickets very successfully. It might be more effective to lengthen your opening hours and bring in extra visitors for the evening, than to extend the season and open on more days. But you also have to look at it holistically. How easy will it be to staff your park for longer hours? Is your park geared up for evening openings, with decent lighting and the capacity for evening meals? I've seen parks with poor attendance throw in some kind of cheap evening deal to beef up their attendance. That's unlikely to work as a strategy.

As well as their discounted evening winter tickets, Europa Park has another plan for adding some extra guests in the evenings. If you stay at their hotels, then on the day of your arrival you can enter the park for free from 6pm. In the summer the park typically shuts at 20:00 or 20:30. Accommodation has become a big source of revenue for a lot of theme parks. However, it's often difficult for them to compete on price with other nearby hotels. Rival hotels are likely to be part of chains that benefit from huge economies of scale, and may be in a better location for attracting non-park visitors. Theme parks need to offer perks to differentiate themselves and to justify a higher price point. If the park has surplus capacity towards the end of the day, this can be a good way to use it.

With these kinds of decisions, you have to consider what counts as surplus capacity. At what point do you decide that the park's quiet enough to justify adding more guests into the park, and how many extra guests can you reasonably add? This in itself begs the question, "What is an acceptable waiting time?". Theme parks with long queues often argue that they don't decide how busy they are or when people want to come, but in situations like this, they do get a say.

Evening entertainment

The alternative to bringing in a second wave of guests with discounted evening tickets, is extra evening events. Parades, fireworks and atmospheric lighting all give people another reason to visit for the evening.

Disneyland debuted their first night time parade, The Main Street Electrical Parade, in 1972. It's successor, the Paint the Night parade, has over one million lights covering the floats[210]. The Paint the Night Parade debuted at Hong Kong Disneyland in 2014. The invention of LED lighting has helped to take the concept to the next level. The introduction of computerised technology allowed them to divide the parade route into 23 audio zones, rather than the original 5. Now floats can trigger the nearest speakers to play the music associated with their particular float, so that a wave of music can flow through the park along with the parade. These are all things that are only possible for a permanent parade, and the cost would be completely prohibitive for a short-term carnival. They also require a significant production cost. At big parks like Disney and Universals, a new parade might not be quite comparable with a new E ticket ride, but they're certainly seen in the same category as the slightly smaller rides. These are major investments, not minor fillers.

---

210   The secrets behind the sparkle of Disney's parades, Christian Sylt, Forbes, https://www.forbes.com/sites/csylt/2018/05/26/the-secrets-behind-the-sparkle-of-disneys-parades/#3ca3e7e16792

Don Dorsey is one of the leading designers and innovators for Disney's parades and night time shows. He says, "Along the parade route we have to control hundreds of individual speakers, lights, video projectors and effects machines along the wayside. We have to track where each float and group of performers are down to an accuracy of about one foot. We can bring the show above, behind and around the guests to match each traveling scene as it passes by, wherever they may be in the park."[211]

Most parks don't have parades, and when you start looking at the costs associated with them it isn't difficult to see why. It's not just the cost of creating all the floats, the costumes and the sound system to go with it, but you also need a big warehouse to store all the floats in when they're not being used. Then there's the issue of finding and paying all the performers to go in it. In the past British parks Alton Towers and Pleasurewood Hills had their own day time parades. Alton Tower's ran from 1988-1993, and featured floats themed to the rides, shows and areas in the park[212]. As the parades at Disney, Universals and other major resorts have grown in complexity, it's hard for a smaller park to keep up.

Night time shows can also be expensive, particularly if they involve fireworks. In the final section on capacities we will discuss the phenomenon of Disneyland Paris and Hong Kong Disneyland. On the one hand, they attracted remarkable numbers of visitors with very few rides in the early days. On the other hand, both resorts still managed to lose a lot of money. The costs of putting on a nightly firework show 365 days a year, was one of the many reasons for this.

Shows with lower running costs can be produced using projection mapping, lasers and fountains. These shows might have a high set up cost, but relatively low running costs after that. Aquanura at Efteling cost 17 million euros[213]. This is almost the same as the cost of building their Baron 1898 roller coaster, which cost 18 million euros and opened three years later[214]. Aquanura takes place on a lake at the entrance to the park, and according to Efteling's press release can be enjoyed by up to 6,500 visitors at a time. On peak days they run the show more than once. An advantage of having guests watching a night show spread out around a big lake, is that it helps with crowd control, rather than having 6,500 guests crammed together in a tight location, which creates its own challenges. We talk about the importance of good crowd control in the section on park capacities.

211   Ibid.

212   Henry's Parade, Towers Times, The secrets behind the sparkle of Disney's parades, Christian Sylt, Forbes, https://www.forbes.com/sites/csylt/2018/05/26/the-secrets-behind-the-sparkle-of-disneys-parades/#3ca3e7e16792

213   Efteling theme park opens Europe's biggest fountain spectacle, official Efteling press release, https://www.efteling.com/en/press/efteling-theme-park-opens-europes-biggest-fountain-spectacle/

214   New Efteling dive coaster Baron 1898 opens to the public, official Efteling press release, https://www.efteling.com/en/press/new-efteling-dive-coaster-baron-1898-opens-to-the-public/

Why are parks willing to make these large investments on bringing in people for the evening, and improving dwell times? Longer dwell times can help to justify raising ticket prices. People might be willing to wait in queues for longer, if they know the park's open for more hours, so they will still get on plenty of attractions. They're likely to spend more, particularly if they buy an evening meal. At Disney the table service restaurants have different, more expensive evening menus compared to what they serve at lunchtime, because a lot of people have a higher pricing point for what they're willing to spend on an evening meal. They're also more likely to stay in the park's own accommodation, if they won't be leaving until late.

There do seem to be two tactics used for filling parks up in the evening. One involves discounted tickets to bring in extra visitors as the day time visitors leave and the other involves additional entertainment to persuade the day time visitors to stick around for longer. Both of these tactics can work, partly because they're helping the park to use their resources more efficiently. A theme park has a lot of fixed costs, regardless of their opening hours. The cost of maintaining the rides, landscaping and infrastructure is similar regardless of how many hours a year the park's open for. There are of course additional costs in opening for more hours in terms of hourly staff, electricity and wear and tear, but opening for more hours when the park's going to be busy is generally profitable, even if the same visitors are staying for longer. Because it costs a similar amount to maintain our assets regardless of opening hours, we could call this process, 'sweating our assets', or to use a slightly seemlier phrase, 'maximising the use of our assets'.

Sometimes it's more effective and efficient to get your current guests spending more, than to focus on trying to bring in additional visitors. If you can't get your visitors on more rides by making the queues shorter, you might be able to get them on more rides by extending your opening hours and giving them more time to enjoy the park in, and the additional spending may well cover the investment. Particularly as increasing dwell times doesn't necessarily need any more advertising, compared to increasing visitor numbers, which often does. Making money from longer dwell times might certainly be better than trying to bring in extra visitors to a park that's struggling to cope with the crowds it's already getting. What you don't want to do, is extend your opening hours if most visitors are still going to leave at 5pm, and in the evening a lot of the rides are going to have a surplus capacity.

In operations, a basic set of questions we often ask, is:

- How can we justify raising our ticket prices/discounting less?
- How can we persuade our visitors to spend more?
- How can we bring in more visitors?
- How much is this all going to cost us?
- Will the gains outweigh the expense?

Theme parks don't normally release figures to show the rate at which guests enter and leave their park. We don't know what percentage of guests in a Disney park at the end of the day are the same ones who were there in the morning, and if they're different whether that's just because people park hopped, or whether new guests entered/left the resort/returned to their hotels. What we can say, is that the world's most visited theme parks tend to be the ones with regular evening hours and longer openings. That doesn't just apply to Disney and Universals, but also to the most visited regional parks, such as Efteling, Europa Park, Tivoli Gardens, Liseberg and Port Aventura.

Morning entertainment

Parks have fewer tactics for encouraging guests to arrive earlier in the morning compared to staying for the evening. However, there might be advantages to trying to influence when guests arrive. We're going to look at a few parks that do have opening ceremonies and why they do it.

If you can space out when your guests arrive for the day, there are advantages. If a park opens at 10am and 15,000 guests all aim to arrive at 9:40, then there's a risk of the roads becoming gridlocked, particularly for parks in more rural locations. You've got the logistics of getting these people into the parks, which might involve selling tickets, explaining discounts and promotions, checking tickets, doing bag checks and height checking kids. There are ways to streamline these processes. Selling tickets in advance helps, so guests arrive with a bar/QR code that can be scanned at the entrance. Nonetheless, if you can space out the arrival of your guests, you can get them into the park more quickly. Opening earlier than 10am might well assist with this, even if you only have a limited number of rides open before 10am, or the area at the back of the parks opens later on in the day. Parks like Universals, Disney and Europa Park typically open at 9am.

You're never going to get two neat sittings of guests, and if you did the entrance would become incredibly congested as they change over. Nonetheless, if the park's open 9am – 9pm, it isn't helpful if the first two hours of the day the park's dead, because no one wants an early start. Even if your park shuts at 6pm, opening at 9am rather than 10am allows guests to get on more rides. It helps them to feel a sense of value for money even if the queues are long.

We can help ease congestion in our parks if we extend the opening hours, but only if we can spread out when people visit us. There's no point in being open for 12 hours if everyone still tries to visit us for the middle chunk of the day.

A few parks have done opening ceremonies. A lot of guests won't be bothered about getting to a park for 9am, because they'd rather sleep in and most people won't be planning to spend all day in a park if it's open for 10 hours or longer. As a park we want to persuade more of them to come for 9am. They'll benefit from the park still being quieter than it will be later in the day, and if we get them into the park earlier, they might well leave earlier, meaning there's less cross over with the guests who arrive for the evening. Either way it means they'll get on more rides.

Magic Kingdom's opening used to involve a horde of Disney characters arriving at the park's entrance on the Disney World Railroad. It started off with them playing an opening song, "Step inside our storybook and imagine what's in store…" Then the chief of the volunteer fire brigade stepped up onto the platform to welcome us all to the Magic Kingdom. Some dancers appear and dance while singing a "Good morning, good morning" song. They got everyone in the crowd to count down from 10 to the park opening. Some outdoor fireworks created smoke, sparks and flashes and the park was open. This was changed due to the number of people turning up for the event. There wasn't always enough space between the turnstile and the gateway into the park under the railroad tracks for everyone who wanted to see it. It has now been replaced with a higher capacity alternative.

In 2017 they launched 'Let the Magic Begin'. An hour before the advertised opening guests could enter Main Street where selected shops are open, including the Main Street Bakery. The show takes place in front of Cinderella's Castle. It starts with a fanfare and one of the 'royal majesty makers' comes out of the castle, looks up at the clock on its front and says, 'Oh my goodness, is that the time?', in a posh English accent. Cinderella is a traditional story passed down orally. There's no reason to believe it's set in England, but the English Royal Family is perhaps the most famous in the world, so presumably the English accents feel regal. They pull out a scroll and read, "It is hereby decreed that all are welcome in this happy place. Where the young and young at heart can explore and laugh and play together." Mickey Mouse walks in wearing a sequin tuxedo. He asks the crowd, "Are you all excited to be here today?". Everyone shouts yes. "I thought so". Incidentally the Disney character costumes have got more advanced over the years. This one can blink and open and close its mouth along with the sound. He then tells us that folks from around the Kingdom wanted to come and give us a great big welcome. Zip-a-dee-do-dah plays while the characters come on stage. The curtains on the Castle's balcony opens and the Fairy God Mother appears with a wand to spread magic around the Kingdom. Lights flash around the castle. She gets the crowd to say the magic words with her, "Bibbidi bobbidi boo".

Not many other parks do an opening ceremony, although Europa Park does one for the opening of their Horror Nights involving quite a few fire balls. Warner Bros World (Abu Dhabi) does one that's described by Jordan Middleton from the Cups and Coasters blog, "The opening show to that park is the best thing they've [her parents] ever seen. They said they were just stood there. There was a crowd of about twenty people waiting to go into the park. They just stood there and this incredible show happened… everything's a fanfare. Everything's an extravaganza"[215]. It's perhaps ironic that Warner Bros World apparently has a really impressive opening ceremony, but apparently they don't get enough visitors for it to really be needed, although it does clearly create a strong first impression.

215   Nick's ERT #64, From Europa to Dubai, Nick Hutson and Jordan Middleton, Seasonpass Podcast, http://www.seasonpasspodcast.com/index.html

Park capacities

Park Capacities

The park capacity is the number of people you can fit in a park before it's full.

When I hear people complaining about the queues in theme parks, one of the most frequent comments is, 'They let in too many people'. Most parks do at least have a theoretical capacity, although it might be so high, they rarely reach it. Many parks won't ever reach their capacity. I've known Thorpe Park (UK) close its door during Fright Nights close to Halloween. Alton Towers (UK) has hit capacity when they do their end of season fireworks. And Disney World (Orlando) often does a phased shutdown of its parks on New Year's Eve. In recent years Magic Kingdom followed by Epcot have been the parks that hit capacity, but that might change as new attractions open and events change.

Whilst each country has its own laws, capacities are generally set by the parks themselves, rather than by governments and public law enforcement. Factors can include the size of the park, guest comfort, parking availability and the guidelines set down by their insurance companies[216]. A series of risk assessments focussing on different areas of the park and different scenarios can help to reach a sensible figure.

We will look at the issues that affect a park's capacity, starting with safety factors and then moving onto issues around the guest experience. We zoom in on some specific parks. We will consider why Six Flags ran into financial problems when they poured money into new rides, with a particular look at Geauga Lake. We will go back in time to Coney Island in the younger years of the industry and find out how early parks managed their crowds. We will visit Holiday World (Indiana) to find out how you build a park with a high capacity and high guest satisfaction, on a limited budget. We will move onto how and why Dollywood (Tennessee) expanded their capacity with the Wildwood Grove children's area. Dollywood is one of the world's best regarded regional theme parks. We will explore the development of Hong Kong Disneyland, tracing its development alongside a rising capacity. We will then consider how typical the development of Hong Kong Disneyland is compared to other Disney parks.

What is a reasonable capacity for a theme park? Parks don't normally release their capacity figures. However, during 2020 the coronavirus pandemic forced parks to run at a reduced capacity to help with 'social distancing'. This meant that guests had less close contact, so that the virus couldn't spread so easily. When parks released plans about re-opening, we got some interesting insights into their normal capacities.

- Gulliver's Valley (Rotherham, UK): 4,000[217]

---

216   Big Disneyland crowds raising safety concerns, Marla Dickerson, Los Angeles Times, https://www.latimes.com/archives/la-xpm-1996-10-03-fi-49823-story.html

217   Rides – slide and virus risk traffic lights: inside the new £37m theme park opening in pandemic, Colin Drury, The Independent, https://www.independent.co.uk/news/uk/home-news/gullivers-valley-theme-park-opens-coronavirus-covid-19-rotherham-a9614221.html

- Legoland Florida: 12,000[218]
- Parc Astérix (France): 30,000[219]
- Cedar Point: Around 54,000[220]
- Europa Park, 60,000 (various sources)

Legoland is one of the biggest theme park brands. The original Legoland opened near the Lego factory at Billund, Denmark, in 1968. There are currently 8 Legolands, a Lego water park in Italy, and 27 smaller Lego Discovery Centres. Several more Lego attractions are currently under construction. Legoland Florida seems to be reasonably typical of a Legoland park.

Cedar Point is sometimes known as the roller coaster capital of the world. At the time of writing, it has 17 coasters. It has built up a reputation for building the biggest. They have a roller coaster over 200ft (Magnum XL), over 300ft (Millennium Force) and over 400ft (Top Thrill Dragster). When they were built, Raptor was the tallest, fastest and longest inverted coaster, Mantis was the tallest, fastest and longest stand up coaster and Gate Keeper was the tallest, fastest and longest wing coaster.

Europa Park in Germany is the world's most visited seasonal theme park, with 18 areas, mostly themed to different European countries. Parc Astérix is themed to a popular French comic about French warriors fighting the Roman republic. Parc Astérix opened in 1989, three years before Disneyland Paris. Parc Astérix features a lot of water rides including a log flume, rapids, water chute and dingy slide. There is also a Madhouse, several shows as well as 8 roller coasters (soon to be 9).

Gulliver's Valley was a new children's theme park in the UK that had just opened (opened 2020). It was perhaps the first theme park to open during a pandemic. It was the fourth park in the Gulliver's chain, all of which were in the UK and focused predominantly on the 8s and under. Its capacity was based on 23 rides, plus several small play areas, an indoor theatre, an area with digger activities and mini golf, although a couple of rides were delayed by the pandemic. This gave them about 174 guests for each ride in the park. The style of children's roundabouts they have at Gulliver's have low throughputs. At the same time, 23 rides is a decent number for a park that's just opened. Children's rides are typically cheap to build, maintain and operate, but they have low throughputs.

In different sectors there are key metrics that give you a rough idea of how likely a venture is to be successful. In hotels we talk about room occupancy, meaning what percentage of the year is an average room occupied for. In retail we talk about sales per square foot. In food and beverage there tends to be a focus on what percentage of a sale the ingredients account for. When

---

218   Legoland Florida re-opens to guests, Theme Park Insider, Robert Niles, Theme Park Insider, https://www.themeparkinsider.com/flume/202006/7496/

219   Based on research by Sazzle from Towers Street. Various media outlets reported that Parc Astérix had capped their capacity at 15,000. According to the park's official Twitter account this was 50% of their normal capacity.

220   Can theme parks make money at reduced capacity, Brady Macdonald, Bloo Loop, https://blooloop.com/features/theme-parks-reduced-capacity/

we're assessing the viability of a park, knowing its capacity, its typical occupancy as a percentage of that and the annual attendance are all key statistics. If a park's not making a healthy profit, is that because the park's poorly designed, poorly operated, has insufficient demand...? Before you make a big investment, you want to make sure you're spending it on the right things. To work this out, you need to know the capacities.

There is no specific formula for working out a park's capacity. However, when businesses are doing feasibility studies[221] for new parks, they have to estimate the capacity based on the acreage and budget without seeing specific designs. The Thinkwell Group believes that a major theme park can handle around 500-650 guests per a square acre[222]. This is roughly the figure used by Harrison Buzz Price, who did feasibility studies for Disney and Universal. This figure only includes the park itself and no other areas of the resort, such as the parking lots, backstage areas and accommodation. In fact, assuming the parking lot is on a single story, the parking lot might end up being over half the size of the park. It also only includes developed space. For example, at some parks like Efteling (Netherlands) or Alton Towers (UK) there are pockets of attractions interspersed amongst woodland.

The Park Database suggests that in an indoor park you might be able to get away with as little as 3-4 square metres per guest[223]. In an outdoor park you might look for something closer to 10 square metres per a guest. 10 square metres per guest works out at about 405 guests per acre.

If you're using a park's area to gauge its potential capacity, it's important not to include the car park (parking lot). For a rural park, where most of the guests come by car, a single-story car park might cover between half and two thirds the surface area of the actual park. Disneyland (California) illustrates this point really well.

Disneyland opened in 1955, but they didn't open their second park, California Adventure, until 2001. Between opening their first park in California and their second, they built four parks in Orlando. Why didn't they build a second park in California sooner? There were a couple of reasons. Firstly, Orlando had space for a lot more hotel accommodation, meaning that additional parks in Orlando could help to fill hotel rooms more than a second park in California. Secondly, they were pressed to find the space for a second park on the Californian site. In the end they did it largely by replacing the single-story parking lots with multi-story parking garages, which provided the same number of spaces over a much smaller area. Building these parking garages was very expensive, but it freed up

221   A feasibility study is literally asking, *is this theme park feasible?* If we open a theme park of this size, in this location, will it be viable and will it give us a return on our investment?

222   Designing a physically distanced theme park, Brad Kissling, Thinkwell, https://thinkwellgroup.com/2020/07/22/what-if-we-designed-a-theme-park-with-physical-distancing-and-health-safety-as-a-guiding-principle/

223   How to size an attraction (of any kind), The Park Database, http://www.theparkdb.com/blog/how-to-size-an-attraction-of-any-kind/

the space for a second park largely using what had been parking spaces. The fact that Disney were able to build a theme park largely using what had been parking lot, shows how much space the parking lots can take up. If you include the car parks in your calculations for capacity, it will significantly distort the numbers.

Some parks, such as Epcot (Orlando) or Islands of Adventure (Orlando), have big lakes. Epcot is often cited as being 300 acres. Using the Thinkwell/Buzz Price formula it would have a capacity of 150,000 – 195,000, but the World Show Case Lagoon (lake) is about 40 acres[224], and Epcot also features several areas that are largely shuttered. At the time of writing the Wonders of Life Pavilion that used to house Body Wars (simulator) is only used for events. The upstairs area of the Imagination Pavilion is now a lounge for the DVC (Disney Vacation Club) rather than an attraction, while the current Journey into the Imagination ride only uses part of the building to fit in a new smaller Image Works on the ground floor. Parts of the Food Rocks animatronics show sits abandoned in The Land Pavilion while the Odyssey building and World Showplace are further event spaces that aren't always open. Even taking these points into account, Epcot's capacity is still a little lower than the Price formula predicts. Disney haven't officially released the capacities for the American parks, but it's generally believed that Epcot has a capacity in the 90,000 – 95,000 range. Using the Buzz Price formula Epcot should need 180 acres or less. In Epcot a lot of the buildings are single story, meaning the park is less compact than some other major parks.

Here's a table for different Disney parks showing their acreage, their believed capacity, and the number of guests per an acre. Some of these capacities, such as Shanghai Disneyland and Hong Kong Disneyland, have been released in official statements. Some capacities are based on rumours on the Internet, taking into account how common the rumour is and how reliable the sources appear to be. For the purposes of this chart, we're not going to break the acreage down into 'highly developed space' (like rides and shops), 'less developed space' (like gardens) and very undeveloped space (lakes, woodland etc). It will give us a flavour of how many guests per acre the Disney parks have. The statistics are the most recent I can find (2020), but over time they will grow out of date as the parks expand.

Park	Acreage	Capacity	Guests per acre
Hong Kong Disneyland	68	48,000	706
Disneyland Shanghai	100	80,000	800
Parc Disneyland Paris	126	80,000	635
Magic Kingdom	105	90,000	857
Disneyland Park California	99	85,000	859
Tokyo Disneyland	114	85,000	746
Epcot	300	90,000	300

---

224   How big is Epcot, Magic Insiders, https://magicinsiders.com/how-big-is-epcot/

All the Magic Kingdom style parks have more guests per acre than the Thinkwell/Buzz Price estimations suggest. This might be partly because Buzz Price was working before the age of Fast Pass, phone apps, single rider queues, and other technology or techniques used to maximise efficiency. It might also show how untypical the Magic Kingdom style parks are.

I looked at Epcot in some details in the section on Shopping at Disney and Benchmarking against Disney. Even if we ignore the 40 acre World Showcase Lagoon, it still only has 346 guests per acre.

What gives the Magic Kingdom parks their high capacities and could you go higher? When you look at aerial photos, they're densely developed, although the Rivers of America sections are the least 'developed'. If you have a park divided into themed areas, you have to have some kind of 'berm'/border dividing each area up. This can include a themed berm made up of buildings/fake rock, or woodland and gardens. The Magic Kingdom style parks have limited woodland and gardens (Shanghai is something of an exception to this) and typically use theming and buildings to divide the areas up. It's easier to 'get away' with thinner berms between areas when a lot of the rides are dark rides, because the berms aren't trying to absorb noise from outdoor thrill rides, and dark rides don't typically go high in the air, where it's harder to obscure their visual impact. In the Magic Kingdom parks, the different areas are physically close to each other.

Disney use a lot of large family rides, including dark rides. These either have no restraints or simple restraints, making them quick to load, and you can take bags on with you. Fast Pass, single rider queues and height checking at the entrance to rides rather than on the platform, all speed up the loading processes. The rides generally are designed for high throughputs, including rides with large boats, omnimovers (continuous chains of cars) and roller coasters with dual stations side by side.

On the other hand, Disney doesn't typically integrate their queues into the ride areas like a lot of regional parks would. Disney's dark rides generally only use a single story, rather than using a couple of stories like the dark rides at many other parks. Although some of the theming structures, particularly the castles, are tall, Disney doesn't add more attractions to their parks by building higher into the air, or digging underground. For instance, at Phantasialand the Geister Rikscha dark ride extends under a chunk of the Chinese area. The Magic Kingdom parks look more compact when you see them from an aerial photo, than they might feel to many of the guests inside the park. Arguably this is a sign of their clever design.

To understand why the Disney and Universal parks are able to have such a high density of guests, it might be worth comparing their budgets:

Park	Area	Year opened	Cost to build	Acreage	Cost per acre
Universal Hollywood	Wizarding World of Harry Potter	2016	$265 million[225]	6	$44 million
Animal Kingdom	Pandora – the world of Avatar	2017	$500 million[226]	12	$42 million
California Adventure	Cars Land	2012	$230 million[227]	12	$19 million
Disneyland	Star Wars: Galaxy's Edge	2019	$1 billion[228]	14	$71 million
Dollywood	Wildwood Grove	2019	$37 million	6	$6 million
Paultons Park	Peppa Pig World	2011	$8 million[229]	3	$2.6 million

These budgets may well be contested, particularly as Disney parks buy their attractions from Disney Imagineering, which is another division of the same company. Disney Imagineering manage the project and do some of the work themselves, but they also subcontract a lot of work out to third parties. Budgets for new attractions can include a range of things, such as the ride itself, developing intellectual property/research and development, and marketing the attraction. Some figures may be theoretical, such as loss of business caused by the disruption of a construction project. If an area replaces an existing one, it might be able to use some of the previous infrastructure. There will have been some inflation between the earliest area listed and the most recent, and different regions pay different taxes. For all of these reasons it's problematic when you compared budgets between different parks. You're not always comparing like with like. Nonetheless, these figures do give us a rough idea about the budgets between different levels of park. Even allowing for a margin of error, it wouldn't be reasonable to expect a regional park and a Disney park to squeeze the same capacity out of each acre.

---

225   Some sources have quoted $500 million including *facility and infrastructure upgrades at the adjacent television and move studio,* I've taken a figure that just seems to include the area, 10 questions about Wizarding World at Universal Studios Hollywood, Brady Macdonald, LA Times, https://www.latimes.com/travel/la-xpm-2013-apr-25-la-trb-wizarding-world-harry-potter-universal-studios-04201325-story.html

226   Disney to license rights to Avatar for theme park attractions, Dawn C Chmielewski and Rebecca Keegan, Los Angeles Times, https://www.latimes.com/business/la-xpm-2011-sep-21-la-fi-ct-disney-avatar-20110921-story.html

227   It's widely reported that the area's main ride Radiator Springs Racer cost $200 million. A figure isn't given for the rest of the area, but it seems fair to assume that Radiator Springs made up the bulk of the cost

228   Galaxy's Edge has generally been referred to as a billion dollar area, although some fans have questioned whether this price tag is exaggerated. It certainly is a very high cost per acre. If it's accurate, then the two Star Wars lands cost more than the valuation of some major regional theme park operators.

229   Peppa Pig Land originally occupied 3 acres, although it has since been expanded by a further acre. It reportedly cost about £6 million to build the first phase.

Acreage, budget, the number of rides, the number of shops and restaurants, the number of 'major rides'; these are all features that help us to
estimate a park's capacity. However, there is no perfect formula. It is an art
as well as a science.

If feasibility studies are trying to estimate the capacity and demand for
a project, then the capacity should in theory be the easy part. The capacity
is almost entirely within your control. Whereas demand is based on a whole
range of variables such as the strength of the economy, what competing parks
are doing and trying to put a value on your brand and creativity. The basic
process for calculating a park's capacity also works fairly well in any country
or region. There might be some differences in terms of safety codes, how
much people value their personal space etc, but if you can predict the capacity of a park in one country, you can pretty much do it anywhere. It's much
harder to estimate the demand for a park without knowing the local culture.

Nonetheless, it's remarkable how much some feasibility studies do
over-estimate their capacities. They make hugely optimistic assumptions,
and comparisons with other parks that have too many differences that they
haven't accounted for.

Earlier in the book we mentioned Hard Rock Park (Myrtle Beach, South
Carolina). Hard Rock Park was 55 acres[230] and had a capacity of 30,000.
According to the Thinkwell/Buzz Price formula a 55 acre major park could
potentially have a capacity between 27,500 – 35,750 guests. However, the
lake was over 8 acres, reducing the park's area to 47 acres. This would give
the park a capacity between 23,500 – 30,550. Hard Rock Park's overall capacity was 545 people per acre, or 638 when you ignore the lake. Based on the
formula of guests per acre, Hard Rock's capacity was achievable and lower
than most of the Magic Kingdom style parks. However, it was high relative to
the number of rides they had and the type of rides. The jury is out on whether
30,000 was a plausible figure.

It does become difficult to safely hold more than a certain number of guests
in a given area, although building a park on multiple levels, like a multistory
carpark/garage will increase the capacity per an acre. Chopping out gardens
and theming features will also increase the capacity, but doing so lowers the
appeal of the park. You might end up with a situation where you've increased
the capacity, but the extra capacity is no longer needed. We will talk about the
safety side first. It must be remembered that parks aren't pleasant places to be
when they're at capacity. The park's capacity isn't the number of guests we're
aiming to attract each day. It's the maximum we'll let in.

Safety first

There are two grounds for limiting the capacity of a park: safety reasons and
to improve the guest experience. I think the second one is fairly straight
forward, so let's focus on the first. Each country has its own laws about crowd

230   Gates open to Myrtle Beach's latest attraction, Park World,
https://www.parkworld-online.com/hard-rock-park/

control and managing densely populated spaces. I'm not a legal expert, and laws will vary between countries. In the UK specific laws seem to be minimal, although reputable events do tend to follow 'The Purple Guide', a guide produced by the events industry and endorsed by the UK HSE (Health and Safety Executive). Events not following their guidance, are likely to be prosecuted under the Safety at Work Act if something does go wrong.

Some of the points in The Purple Guide are quite specific, for example they recommend having at least 1 toilet for every 100 women, 1 toilet for every 500 men, 1 urinal for every 150 men and 1 washbasin for every 5 toilets (presumably counting urinals as 'toilets'). You also need to think about disabled toilets and baby changing facilities. It's not difficult to see hazards if you don't meet these levels, for example people not washing their hands if there's a queue at the basins, or people urinating behind trees etc. To offer a high quality experience, and to allow for cleaning, you're going to want to go above and beyond the minimum recommended by safety bodies. At the same time, I can also see how these things can get cut back. Some parks are tight on space, and taking up more space for toilets might take away room for something that generates money, like a gift shop or a food outlet. Parks have finite budgets, and money spent on an impressive new toilet block eats into another budget. But when parks are designing their facilities, they need to be mindful that these 'little things' can often be the ones that determine a park's capacity. For a teenager benches might be little more than décor, but for someone elderly, disabled, ill or needing to breast feed, a bench could be vital.

Other factors to consider include the ratio of first aiders to guests, the number of first aid rooms in the first aid centre, the number of security guards and the ability to serve water and other cold drinks in a timely manner. These are all basic parts of running a theme park. When a park's putting on a big event, they start looking at P&L (profit and loss) sheets. They consider hiring in toilets, extra security, extra first aiders. What initially looked like a guaranteed cash cow starts to shift. When one looks back through the major accidents caused by crowd control, not specifically in the theme park industry, but in general, then a common root cause is cost cutting. Someone in charge of the finances couldn't see beyond the costs and figures on a spreadsheet. Dealing with big influxes of people is costly, which is another reason to look at flattening off peaks in attendance and trying to distribute guests more evenly through the season. We had a whole section looking at this in detail.

One park hired in extra security and first aiders for a big event, but they didn't have any extra radios. They ended up with calls for security and first aiders being unanswered. Another park had enough drinks in their storeroom, but they weren't able to get them to units that sold them when they ran out half way through the day. About half an hour before they ran out, managers were shouting down radios that people needed to work faster, because they were running out. They didn't seem to shoulder any blame for poor management. Having free drinking fountains with water helps to solve the issue of guests becoming dehydrated, if the queues for drink get too long.

Indeed, dispensing water is generally fast if you're not taking money, even if there's someone serving it. Other hazards can include a risk of assault to staff and other guests when queues become too long and poorly managed - and the general stress of working at an attraction that clearly isn't coping with the volume of people. Queue line management, queue jumping and work-related stress, are all pertinent topics that I hope to cover in a future book. They are all indirectly caused by the park, making it easier to shift responsibility. However, these things can be accounted for in a decent safety strategy.

Some countries have fire safety codes limiting how many people can be in a building. The International Building Code (IBC) recommends 0.3 inches of fire exit for every person in a building for fire escapes that go down stairs and 0.2 inches for all other fire exits[231]. In the United States the National Fire Prevention Association (NFPA) doesn't allow fire exits to lead people through kitchen or storage areas on their way out of the building. The ratio of fire exits to guests is something that needs to be considered when designing indoor queues.

In some countries the building's maximum capacity has to be displayed on a sign near the building's entrance. Whilst most theme parks are primarily outdoors, there will be buildings like shops and restaurants. When you're designing buildings, you need to think carefully about evacuation and how quickly you can get people out. People will go slower down a set of stairs, and if a fire exit opens out into a confined backstage area or a bottleneck this will slow down the process of getting people out. Regardless of whether your country has specific building codes, it's useful to build up a relationship with the local fire service. You can offer them the chance to review your park's capacity as well as the evacuation process for getting people off the rides if they get stuck at heights.

You need to have an evacuation plan that not only considers how to evacuate individual rides, but potentially how to evacuate multiple rides at the same time. In the event of a power cut to the whole site, you could have multiple rides stuck at heights. There is a balance between using more experienced or better qualified staff to evacuate rides, but not letting this pool of staff get so small that rides are sitting there for ages waiting for a team to get to them. Parks can have to limit the number of vehicles on a ride if they don't have enough engineers to evacuate them all safely. Whether rides should be evacuated by engineers, managers or the operators/attendants is a debate that most parks have had. Decisions need to be based on informed risk assessments that consider a range of factors from staff turnover, age/maturity, frequency and level of training etc. What works at one park won't necessarily be suitable for another.

In the past theme parks have worked out their capacities through a process of trial and error. The Mark Twain river boat at Disneyland takes guests on a trip around the circular Rivers of America in the Frontierland area of the park.

---

231   How the maximum occupancy of a building is calculated, Sarah
Stone, Today I found out, http://www.todayifoundout.com/index.
php/2014/08/maximum-occupancy-building-calculated/

A captain controls the speed, and uses a horn and bell for communication, but they don't steer the boat, because it follows an underwater 'I' shaped rail.

A well-known story is that on Disneyland's opening day the boat was overloaded. It came off the track, because there were too many people on board. After half an hour they got it back on, but then as it was coming back to the station all the guests rushed to the exit causing it to sink again. Review Tyme tells the story, "Guests now had to wade through water to exit the attraction, which made some of them understandably a bit upset. His boss [Terry O'Brien's boss, a cast member working on the ride] came over and asked how many people he let on, to which Terry mentioned that it was around 250. His boss said that he'd better keep it to 200 and left. But afterwards he remembered that he had a clicker in his pocket. He pulled it out and was shocked to notice that he'd actually let on 508 people. He never told anybody, and it never happened again"[232]. It's generally reported that the boat's capacity was soon set at 300 and has remained so ever since. A lot has changed since the 1950s. Parks are now expected to take a more strategic approach to managing their capacities, rather than just hoping for the best.

Crowds can also pose their own challenges. You can get crushings if a large volume of people suddenly move to escape a hazard, including a fire, an escaped animal if there's a zoo, an accident or a terrorist attack. On 4th November 2018 a wall display of menus fell to the floor at the Blue Water Shopping Centre in the UK[233]. It created a loud bang, causing people to run shouting 'bomb, bomb'. Luckily one person didn't run and helpfully filmed it on their phone. We hear one guy in the background say, "We should call the police". A woman replies "What's happened?". The guy says, "I don't know". Meanwhile lots of people are running past. The Sun writes, "Many shoppers had no idea that a falling display board was behind the melee, instead being swept up by the public hysteria. Eleanor Perkins, who was there during the alarm, told KentOnline, It was just a feeling of sheer panic. So, so terrifying." As the event at Blue Water shows, a stampede of people can happen unexpectedly and escalate quickly.

As well as people fleeing from something, crowds might also block access to an area, for example if you need to get an ambulance or fire engine to an area of the park. You can reduce the odds of these things happening, for example with good fire prevention. If you do have a crowded amusement park, then fires can spread quickly. Using fire resistant building materials and sprinkler systems can help. But any park could need to get an emergency vehicle through, or have a situation where people run away from something.

As with other areas of efficiency, planning is the key, rather than relying on individual heroics. Having well trained managers and a competent incident manager are important, but you can't just assume that one person can work their magic when a situation suddenly presents itself out of nowhere. In

232   The $1,100,000,000 mistake of Disney's California Adventure Park, Review Tyme, https://www.youtube.com/watch?v=8qmg25yeaeM

233   Shoppers stampede, Dan Hall, The Sun, https://www.thesun.co.uk/ news/7657094/bluewater-bomb-scare-shoppers-flee-in-terror/

a theme park, people aren't typically as densely crowded together as they are in something like a concert or a sporting event. However, crowds might come together for something like a firework show. You might also get a big crowd gathering at the entrance, who suddenly surge through the park together. I've heard this referred to as 'the running of the bulls'. These stress points need particular consideration.

Managers might big up their credentials and talk with a lot of confidence, but you mustn't let their bluster convince you that they can cope with anything, because they can't. No one can. Even the most experienced or confident person can't make up for an overcrowded park that's exceeded its safe capacity. I'm not encouraging parks to waste large sums of money on excessive capacity, which isn't cost effective and might divert resources away from other areas of health and safety. However, a bit of humility is important when it comes to safety. An if you dream it, you can do it attitude sounds good on a motivational poster, but it's not a defense in court when you fail to handle a crisis properly.

Controlling crowds can be difficult. There's no collective brain. Crowd mentality isn't the easiest thing to reason with, particularly when people start reacting quickly to something. Nonetheless, if crowds do gather somewhere, such as at the entrance, or for a show, it can be important to have a PA (public address system), so that you can issue safety instruction if there is a crowd surge or a stampede. You can also preempt some situations, for example the early morning rush when the gates open. At Europa Park the rides were very reliable, but a few times Silver Star did go down. Once we started running test trains, a crowd would gather in front of the entrance. When the ride re-opened, a couple of staff members would walk down the queue in front of the line, so that everyone didn't run, pushing and shoving. It's sometimes easier to prevent a stampede from happening, than to slow it down once it's already started

It's useful to mind map the potential causes of people running, so that they can be mitigated. If there's a torrential rain storm, there could be a sudden dash for cover. We touch upon the issue of weather proofing in the section on distributing guests through the season. The more undercover spaces there are, the less likely there is to be a suddenly concentration of people in a particular, potentially small, building.

To prevent crowd crushings, we might try to limit the number of people congregating, for example Disney sometimes puts on two performances of its firework shows. This is also a matter of customer service and making sure everyone can enjoy it properly, something we come onto later. We can use various techniques to distribute guests more evenly through the park, for example Disney's Magic Plus system. This is discussed in its own chapter. Crushings are most likely to happen when a large volume of people gets funneled through a bottle neck or into a dead end. A bottle neck becomes like a clogged artery, where people end up joining the back of a crowd quicker than they can leave it at the front. Having circular routes around the park and emergency gates that can be opened up is important. A competent, well trained incident manager knows when to deploy certain systems, but they can only do that if they have the right systems to use. When you have good crowd control measures, your guests might well not even realise that there was a problem. Hazards get resolved before they become a problem.

In the UK, we sometimes call routes for emergency vehicles blue routes, because of the blue flashing lights these vehicles have. Theme parks are often designed with access routes around the outside of the park, so that emergency vehicles can get close to an incident before they actually have to enter the park where the guests are. They might well be given an escort vehicle, such as a golf buggy, to follow. For compact amusement parks in urban areas, there might not be any access roads causing an additional challenge. In this case, the regular roads around the park might be able to act as the access route, if there are big gates around the edge of the site leading into the park that something like a fire engine or an ambulance could get through. Designers need to bear in mind that emergency vehicles are taller than some standard vehicles and won't fit under low structures.

Project Star Dust

At the time of writing Disneyland is the second most visited theme park in the world, but only 60% the size (acres) of Orlando's similar Magic Kingdom (it does have more rides though!). The TEA (Themed Entertainment Association) estimates that 18.3 million people visited the park in 2017. Ahead of Galaxy's Edge (Star Wars Land) opening, Disneyland ran an initiative called Project Stardust to improve guest flow and capacity in the park. The name Stardust being a mixture of 'Star' from Star Wars and 'Dust' from pixie dust[234].

This included making planters and flower beds smaller to enlarge the pathways between them. They also planted trees straight into small gaps in the walkways, rather than in planters/flower beds which takes up more room. They removed seats from walkways and added additional seating areas and stroller parking in buildings that had previously been shops, reducing the amount of retail space around Disneyland. They looked to remove pinch points, such as where the entrance structure for an area narrows the width of the pathway.

18.3 million visitors a year works out as 39,315 visitors on an average day, although it wouldn't be distributed evenly through the year like that. Also, Disneyland has long opening hours, so not every visitor on a day would be in the park at the same time. Disney don't release official park capacities, but a Google search suggests the park's capacity is around 80,000 – 85,000. With such large volumes of people, it's not just about guest comfort and experience. It's also a safety issue. What would happen if there was a major incident in the park and suddenly there was a rapid surge of guests heading in one direction? If there are pinch points, would there be a crush? What would happen if there was an incident like the one at Blue Water, where the sign fell down creating a big bang? If this happens you wouldn't want people to get injured at the bottle necks. In these situations, people at the back of the crowd can keep on

234   What you need to know about Disneyland's Project Stardust, Dusty Sage,
Mice Age, https://www.micechat.com/215336-disneyland-project-stardust/

pushing forward unaware of the crushing and potential fatalities at the front of the crowd. In Belarus in 1999 52 people died when a sudden stormed caused large numbers of people to rush into a nearby underground station[235]. As a theme park you need to reduce the risk of there being a sudden crowd surge, and make sure that if there is there are ways for people to get out. John Fruin, a retired research engineer, wrote a paper in 1993 called 'The cause and prevention of crowd disasters'. He estimated that around 7 people per a square metre was the density at which crowds can become fatal. If people fall over they get crushed under the weight of people, while people can even die of asphyxia (death through lack of oxygen) while standing up. According to Seabrook's article in the New Yorker investigators have found 'steel guardrails' capable of withstanding a thousand pounds of pressure bent by the force of people pushing against it. This is why in indoor spaces it's important to have sufficient fire exits. If there is a fire, people can panic and move towards the escape route very quickly, causing a crush at the bottleneck.

Around the world there have been numerous incidents where crushings by crowds have led to large scale fatalities. Following these events there have been changes to the way that crowds are handled, for example since the Hilsborough disaster in the UK where 96 people died, football stadiums above a certain size have no longer been allowed to have standing areas. Everyone must be seated. Crowds are monitored through raised viewing areas and CCTV. Tanoys (public address systems) are used to communicate with people at the back of the crowd.

Whilst it might seem disappointing to lose some flower beds and midway seating to improve guest flow, Disney's priorities have long been safety, courtesy, efficiency and show (in that order). Using this decision-making tool, compromising on some show elements to improve safety and efficiency is an easy decision to make.

As well as making the flower beds smaller, they reworked some of the queue lines to make waiting more pleasant. The Flying Dumbos' queue was enclosed in a themed circus tent environment while Space Mountain had an additional indoor queuing area in the disused Starcade amusement arcade that had closed in 2015.

The guest experience

The guest experience is likely to dip to an 'unacceptable' level before it becomes a genuine safety hazard. Particularly in a modern theme park with more space, compared to a much more compact amusement park where the safety challenges become tougher. Knott's Berry Farm executive Don Troudy says, "It basically comes down to guest service. Theoretically, we could cram 50,000 people in here, but we'd never do it. That's just too many people"[236].

---

235   Crush Point, When large crowds assemble, is there a way to keep them safe?, John Seabrook, Newyorker.com, https://www.newyorker.com/magazine/2011/02/07/crush-point

236   Big Disneyland crowds raising safety concerns, Marla Dickerson, Los Angeles Times, https://www.latimes.com/archives/la-xpm-1996-10-03-fi-49823-story.html

Project Star Dust document taken from Mice Chat article by Dusty Sage[237].

So why don't parks put greater limits on the number of guests to improve the guest experience? There are a couple of issues here. Firstly, when people complain about too many guests, they always assume that they'd have been one of the ones who'd have been let in. Imagine driving two hours, or spending a significant amount on public transport, and then being told that the park's full. Or imagine being the employee who has to tell them that it's full.

Secondly, theme parks often aren't the cash cows the public think they are. Running a theme park is hugely expensive. There's electricity, insurance,

---

237   What you need to know about Disneyland's Project Stardust, Dusty Sage, Mice Age, https://www.micechat.com/215336-disneyland-project-stardust/

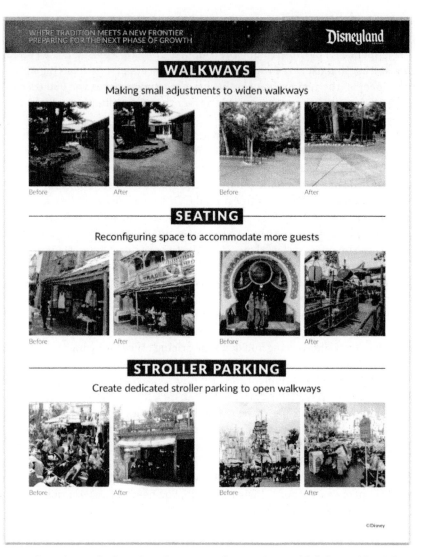

WHERE TRADITION MEETS A NEW FRONTIER
PREPARING FOR THE NEXT PHASE OF GROWTH

Disneyland

WALKWAYS
Making small adjustments to widen walkways

Before   After   Before   After

SEATING
Reconfiguring space to accommodate more guests

Before   After   Before   After

STROLLER PARKING
Create dedicated stroller parking to open walkways

Before   After   Before   After

©Disney

parts for rides and a lot of staff. Most parks simply wouldn't be viable if they started turning away large numbers of visitors to improve the guest experience. Many parks did go down the reservations only route during the corona virus pandemic, so it is technically possible, but limiting capacities too much doesn't make for a viable business. When theme parks did limit tickets, one of the side effects was tickets for a sold-out date being resold for more than its original value[238]. Tickets for concerts and sporting events often get re-sold on websites like Stub Hub. Touts buy up tickets for that very purpose. I don't think this would ever happen to the same extent with theme park tickets, where people can always pick another date. However, parks don't want to

---

238   AT86, Thorpe Park: General discussion, Towers Street Forum, https://towersstreet. com/talk/threads/thorpe-park-general-discussion.8/page-398#post-308411

encourage people to buy and re-sell tickets. There's always the risk that guests will unwittingly buy counterfeit tickets.

I've spent a lot of time reading the comments on Trip Advisor. It does seem that at least in most cases where people complain about a park letting in too many people, the real problem is the way the park manages the queues and efficiencies once the guests are inside, rather than them simply letting in too many people through the gates.

In recent years quite a lot has been written about nudge theory, although nudge theory is arguably a new name for an old idea. Nudge theory finds ways to subtly influence behaviour, rather than giving people direct orders. Let's say you want to make people eat more healthily. The government could ban some of the unhealthiest foods. Or they could introduce a tax on sugar and salt, and ban advertising certain foods near schools. A café could nudge people towards healthier options, by putting them before you get to the unhealthy ones, rather than after. Most parks don't lower their capacities to make them pleasanter, but they do try to nudge guests towards the quieter days, using all the ideas we discussed in the first chapter of this book. According to behavioural economists Richard Thaler and Cass Suntein, "To count as a mere nudge, the intervention must be cheap and easy to avoid"[239]. Most of the ideas we looked at for 'redistributing guests' fit that description. Although if variable pricing and dynamic pricing cause big swings in the cost of entry, we might argue that they go beyond a simple nudge.

You won't read any comments on Trip Advisor saying, "They need to nudge people towards the quieter days". But when people complain that the park's letting in too many people, often this will be a factor.

Although I don't know of a park that regularly closes its gates to improve the guest experience, Disney has done something not completely dissimilar with the opening of its Star Wars areas. They didn't turn guests away from the park to keep crowding down. But to visit Galaxy's Edge at Disneyland or ride Rise of the Resistance at Disney World, you needed a reservation, which all went very quickly after the park opened. If you didn't log onto a website quickly enough, or turn up to the park early enough, you could visit, but you wouldn't be able to experience the new attraction. The benefit was that they avoided the long waits that new attractions at Disney and Universals often have. The downside was that people who didn't book a long time in advance/turn up very early simply weren't able to experience the attraction. They didn't have the choice of waiting in a very long line.

It's not clear exactly how long the queues can get for the new attractions at Disney and Universals. Seven-hour queues have been advertised on opening days, although this initial surge subsides somewhat fairly quickly. Also, a park advertising a seven hour wait for a new ride doesn't mean it actually is a seven hour wait. They're probably being very cautious with the waiting time, to manage expectations and because they're not completely sure what kind

---

239   Nudge: improving decisions about health, wealth and happiness, Richard Thaler and Cass Suntein

of throughput a new attraction will achieve. They might also over inflate the waiting time for a new attraction to get people talking and to reinforce the idea that their new ride must be very special and exciting. Nonetheless, even a four hour queue would be unpleasant.

Taking away the option to stand in line for a new ride is an interesting development. Even when you inform people about what they're waiting for, there's a risk of 'buyer's remorse'. People might think they're happy to wait four hours to ride the hotly anticipated new ride, but three hours down the line they might have changed their mind. Preventing guests from waiting in such a line removes a source of complaints. Another problem with allowing such a long queue to develop, is by the time people get to the front their expectations have become very high. People expect a ride of an incredibly high standard to justify the wait. You end up with guests coming off disappointed, being critical of the new attraction, and that can hurt the business in the longer term.

I've ridden a couple of rides on opening day. Both times I queued up far longer than such a ride would normally justify, often in a temporary overspill queue with little visual stimulation. Both times I came off underwhelmed. This contrasts with press nights, where the reviews are generally glowing because people can ride a major attraction without any waiting, there are often extra entertainers to jazz the event up, free food and merchandise. Part of the reason parks do press nights, is because they know the experience on opening day can leave people disappointed and they want to make sure they get strong reviews from the main influencers. The other reason parks tend to do press previews now, is because the media tends to stop operations while they take photos and do their filming. If the ride has a massive queue on opening day, you don't want the ride to stop for ten minutes whilst a presenter interviews someone in front of the train. With larger parks, including international resorts, but also the bigger regional attractions, by the time it gets to opening day it's just the regular public riding. The operations can go relatively uninterrupted.

Historically when Disney or Universals opened a new ride there was no reservation system, partly because new rides are often unreliable (have more downtime). If the ride goes down and guest have booked slots for a particular time, then they keep on turning up and then when the ride re-opens it gets swamped with the backlog of guests with reservations. It's also because Disney and Universals know that theoretical throughputs/hourly capacities aren't always entirely accurate. It takes time for them to get an accurate picture of the ride's capabilities so that they can allocate a specific percentage to guests with a reservation.

When Disney did reservations only for Galaxy's Edge and Rise of the Resistance, it used a different kind of reservation system. Instead of being given a timeslot to return, you would simply get given a broad time of day (morning, afternoon, evening). When it was time for your slot, you'd get a message on your phone. This avoided the problem with guests turning up at their designated time and finding they'll still need to wait 60 minutes because the ride had broken down for an hour earlier in the day. This kind of virtual queue only became possible as new technology developed.

Looking at the comments online, people were fairly divided on whether this new form of virtual queue was a good idea or not. Jeremygary wrote on Theme Park Insider, "Nothing like the joy of visiting a theme park ... only to find out that the virtual queue is filled for the day and you have no chance of even entering a regular line if you wanted to."[240] Mikew argued the other way, "It is interesting as I still see some folks old-school enough to wait hours on end to ride when chances of it breaking down are clear. But each to their own as this is much easier in many ways for those who'd rather visit the rest of the park than spend half the day for one ride."

As far as the guest experience is concerned, you can get an idea of whether a park can cope with its capacity just by wandering around it on a busy day. Imagine there are cars driving around the car park looking for a space. A lot of the bins are overflowing. An elderly couple are struggling to find a bench. The boxes of park maps are all empty. There's a big queue for the toilets and inside the soap and toilet roll dispensers are empty. The shops are asking everyone to pay with card or exact change, because they've used up all the float in their till. The queues for rides are spilling out the lines and some of them have a three hour wait. The catering units have run out of half the items. In this scenario the park's absolutely not coping. I don't think many parks get that bad, but these are the kinds of warning sign you'll be looking for.

When you're designing a park, an area or an attraction, the capacity's important. Once you know the budget for a development, the next two questions are likely to be:

- How many visitors will it attract?
- How many people can it cope with?

Both of these figures are critically important if the investment's going to be viable. However, the goal when you're designing a theme park certainly isn't to make the highest capacity you can. If it was, you'd end up with a boring park that not many people want to visit. Areas of theming, garden and landscaping add limited amounts to the capacity, but they make it a more appealing park to spend time in. Switchback queues are a very efficient use of space, but themed queues are much pleasanter. Bruce Vaughn, chief creative executive at WDI (Walt Disney Imagineering) said, "Queue lines are a very efficient use of space, they're just a really bad guest experience"[241]. A high-speed roller coaster might only have 48 riders on it, but it takes up a lot of space. A roller coaster could have a low ratio of guests relative to the space it takes up. A park with little theming, wide expanses of asphalt, switchback queues and high capacity dark rides like omnimovers would have a high capacity, but it wouldn't be an appealing park to spend time in. The key thing is that the capacity and the density of guests has to be appropriate.

---

240   Jeremygary, why virtual queues need to become a theme park standard, Theme Park Insider, https://www.themeparkinsider.com/flume/201912/7148/

241   Episode 5, The Imagineering Story, Disney Plus

Throughout the book we've considered a lot of ideas and theories about how parks can reduce their waiting times and manage their crowds. We will now look at some case studies of different parks, to see how these strategies can work in practice. Our focus is still on operational efficiency. However, I'll also be talking a bit more broadly about the parks I've chosen to put things into context. I don't want to give the impression that operational efficiency is the only factor that makes or breaks a business. Other areas like marketing, branding, customer service and the quality of the rides also makes a difference.

The sad tale of Geauga Lake

What happens when your attendance grows and the capacity doesn't keep up?

In this section we're going to look at what happens when a park's attendance increases and why some parks sustain those increases, while others don't. We'll consider Geauga Lake (Ohio) and Alton Towers (UK), where visitor numbers rose, before dropping back down. We'll look at Great Adventure (New Jersey), and why their $40 war on lines struggled, despite adding 27 new rides in a single season. We'll also consider how Peppa Pig World at Paultons Park (UK) and Wizarding World of Harry Potter at Islands of Adventure (Florida) bought in a big rise in attendance that held up.

How crowded a theme park gets can be a classic example of supply and demand. The park's capacity is the supply. The number of guests is the demand. If the supply gets too big compared to the demand, the park isn't profitable. If the demand gets too big, then the guest satisfaction goes down. We're going to discuss how Six Flags created a lot of demand for Geauga Lake, but failed to increase the capacity enough to cope with it.

The downfall of Geagua Lake, which closed in 2007, has been much discussed. We'll take a ride through the park's history and then look at where things went wrong. In recent times, only a few major US parks have closed. Those that have like AstroWorld (Houston, Texas), Hard Rock Park (Myrtle Beach, South Carolina) and Geauga Lake have attracted a fair amount of interest. Geauga Lake's origins as an amusement park began in 1889 when a steam powered carousel was added beside a lake. This was part of a modest amusement area that was expanded into a full amusement park in 1925, when the Big Dipper was added. In 1969 Geauga Lake was purchased by a group of ex-Cedar Point managers and the following year Sea World opened a marine park on the other side of the lake, although Sea World's park didn't include any rides. They had animal attractions including dolphin and orca shows. In 1995 Geauga Lake was purchased by Premier Parks, who in 1998 bought Six Flags. This is where things really picked up pace.

At the time there were three large theme parks in Ohio: Cedar Point (owned by Cedar Fair), Kings Island (owned by Paramount) and Geauga Lake (owned by Six Flags). Six Flags started pumping vast amounts of money into Geauga Lake, planning to turn it into Ohio's premier theme park. In 2000 they invested $40 million into the park, which included 20 new rides and 4 new roller coasters. One of these was Batman Knight Flight, a B&M floorless coaster that was 157ft tall and 4,210ft long. This is the biggest B&M floorless ever built – slightly taller and longer than Kraken at Sea World Orlando. Another coaster was Steel Venom, a 180ft tall, 70mph Intamin Impulse Coaster. Other attractions included a shoot the chute water ride, a new wave pool in the water park and an expanded children's area.

In 2000 Six Flags purchased Sea World Ohio for $110 million in cash. They merged the two parks together, creating one 700 acre mega park, which they called Six Flags World of Adventure. By acreage it was the largest theme park in the world. In 2001 the resort continued expanding with a Vekoma flying coaster. When Premier Parks took Geauga Lake over in 1995 there were four roller coasters, the most recent of which had been added in 1988. Between 1995-2001 Six Flags added 7 roller coasters – a rate of one a year. Whilst Six Flags didn't have exactly the same policy for all their parks, around this time many of the parks were going through a similar pattern of development and struggled with the same problems.

In 1999 the park had only attracted about 1.2 million visitors, so they were making huge investments for the size of business[242]. By 2001 the attendance had more than doubled to 2.7 million, before falling to 2 million in 2003[243]. Despite the huge investments, in 2004 attendance declined to about 700,000 - less than the park was getting before they ploughed roughly $160 million into it[244]. By 2004 the whole Six Flags chain were facing major financial difficulties. The reasons for this are too complex to discuss here in any depth, but Six Flags had expanded incredibly quickly in the 90s, reaching around 38 parks in total, but taking on considerable debt in the process. A couple of months before the 2004 season they sold Geauga Lake to rival Cedar Fair, who closed down the marine side, which had originally been the Sea World. In 2007 Cedar Fair closed Geauga Lake down for good, and that was 118 years of amusement history destroyed in a few years.

There are various reasons why the story of Geauga Lake has captured so much attention. The story involved three of the world's biggest theme park companies: Six Flags, Cedar Fair and Sea World. It marked something of a turning point for all three companies. Over the years a great number of theme parks and amusement parks have closed, but few were on such a large scale, and even fewer recently enough to be captured by a large number of vloggers. Whilst Six Flags did take a loss on the property, they managed to restore a sizeable chunk of their investment when they sold the park to Cedar Fair. Nonetheless, Geauga Lake's demise has become symbolic of why Six Flags went wrong and ended up filing for bankruptcy in 2009. It seems astonishing that you can invest about $160 million into a park and after a few years leave it with 200,000 fewer visitors than you found it. For anyone studying theme park management, it feels like there must be

242   The Vindicator newspaper, December 8th 1999

243   Plain Dealer report, December 22nd 2003

244   Park closing down doesn't thrill fans, Sean D Hamill, Chicago Tribune, https://www.chicagotribune.com/news/ct-xpm-2007-10-23-0710220585-story.html

lessons to learn. Plenty of commentators have had a go at explaining the park's demise.

Airtime Thrills (Youtube channel) argues that a combination of bold marketing, discounts and new roller coasters bought in huge crowds that the park wasn't able to cope with. This led to low guest satisfaction, that quickly pushed attendance back down.

According to Airtime Thrills, "Combining two small regional parks does not automatically prepare the property to become a destination park. Destination parks also require a certain amount of infrastructure in the surrounding area. Most notably, roads and hotels"[245]. Youtuber Forgotten Places says that the park was 15 minutes from the nearby highway, and that "Traffic was bad"[246]. Airtime Thrills continues, "Six Flags needed to see a jump in attendance to justify these investments and they got what they wanted, but it turns out that they were woefully unprepared for the results of their success. The two year investment was certainly drawing in bigger crowds and neither park was meant to handle that many people, causing uncomfortable congestion and crowds. So people came to see the park, had a bad experience and didn't come back".

Brandon Elliot wrote in his account of visiting Geauga Lake in 2003, "Clearing my way through the now staggering density of park guests, I tried desperately to get through. I was forced to go around the main path, and I stepped in some disgusting mud-filled mildew as I banked to the left of a pylon where it was less crowded, by a restroom"[247]. Even if this was a particularly 'bad' day for crowds, this was in 2003 when the annual attendance had already dropped significantly from the peak in 2001. As someone who never visited Geauga Lake, I can't comment on the proficiency of individual employees and managers. However, when a park's so busy people are struggling to fit on the pathways, even the hardest working, most disciplined staff are going to struggle. Reviews of straining parks would often be accompanied with comments about grumpy stuff. I don't think the long queues though were primarily caused by grumpy staff not making an effort. The grumpy staff were demoralised, because they were constantly under stress and dealing with one angry customer after another.

It's very difficult for a park to manage a rapid expansion in guests, unless there is already a significant amount of surplus capacity. It comes down to everything from the size of guest services, the size and number of toilets, to the back of house areas. A bigger park needs more staff, which means bigger lockers areas, bigger canteens, a bigger staff car park, more training rooms, more offices for managers, more engineering workshops etc. If you expand

245   How Six Flags built and destroyed the world's largest theme park, Airtime Thrills, Youtube, https://www.youtube.com/watch?v=_TURwEOZyTo

246   Geauga Lake: why it closed..., Forgotten Places, Youtube, https://www.youtube.com/watch?v=42tuWvoYpfI

247   Geauga Lake vs Six Flags Worlds of Adventure, Brandon Elliot, RC Pro, file:///D:/Theme%20parks/Theme%20parks/Operators/Cedar%20Fair/ GEAUGA%20LAKE/Six%20Flags%20era/Criticising%20operations.htm

too quickly and the infrastructure doesn't keep up, you end up with poor cleanliness, unreliable attractions, demoralised staff etc. Geauga Lake is often seen as a powerful reminder that the capacity of a park is about far more than just its rides, and that even if you can build the rides quickly, scaling up the operations and staffing poses additional challenges.

I don't think this entirely explains why Geauga Lake had such a big fall in attendance. When Sea World sold their property to Six Flags, they took the dolphins and orcas with them. Six Flags only managed to acquire one Orca, which lived on its own. The dolphins and orcas had been costly and controversial, particularly as they couldn't be kept through Ohio's harsh winters, so every winter they'd been transported to Sea World Orlando[248]. Likewise, Six Flags had to relocate their orca and dolphins during the winter. Six Flags World of Adventure may have found themselves on the wrong side of evolving attitudes towards animal welfare.

They also lost Sea World's Shamu brand and their expertise in marine shows. At the time the Sea World group was owned by the brewing company Anheuser Busch, who made Budweiser. They used to give out free beer samples at their parks, which were lost in Ohio when Six Flags took over. Six Flags presumably hoped that losing the free beer samples could be seen as a positive, by making the park more family friendly. It may have had a worse impact than they realised. Six Flags clearly thought there was an advantage in merging the Sea World and Geauga Lake park together, perhaps partly because they could lay off 40 salaried staff by having one person doing functions that were duplicated between the two parks[249]. It also meant there weren't two parks using advertising to build up brand awareness separately. But when the two parks got merged together, the Sea World side lost a certain amount of its appeal.

Geauga Lake was 90 minutes' drive from Cedar Point, with Cleveland being in between them. Cleveland had a population of almost 400,000 people, making it a key market for both parks. In 2003 Cedar Point added Top Thrill Dragster. At 420ft it was the world's tallest roller coaster. Kings Island added Delirium, the world's largest 'frisbee' ride (a spinning disk on the end of a giant pendulum), which swung guests at 76mph. Ohio was a competitive market and attention could move on just as quickly as it came.

The attendance boost from Geauga Lake's flying coaster (X Flight) in 2001 was short lived. The feeling of flying is an appealing concept, which might explain why so many people visited that year. Vekoma had developed a very innovative product and those who rode it generally found it fun and exciting, however it suffered from quite a lot of downtime[250]. Competition from Top Thrill Dragster and Delirium along with X Flight's reliability issues and a two

248   Sea World in Cleveland Ohio, Love 2 Know Theme Parks, Michele Wanke

249   Nearly 40 Six Flags World of Adventure full-tim-
ers go, The Plain Dealer, December 15th 2001

250   Coaster tech: an insiders look at flying coasters, Russell Meyer, Theme
Park Insider, https://www.themeparkinsider.com/flume/201407/4145/

year pause on new rides, helps to explain why Geauga Lake's attendance fell by 700,000 over two seasons.

In 2001 Six Flags trialled a system where guests at their parks could pay extra to skip some of the queues. In 2002 this Fast Lane system was added to Geauga Lake. Whilst this would have bought in additional revenue to help with Six Flags' debt load, it also exacerbated the problems where attendance had outstripped the capacity. Removing the remaining marine life in 2004 had a devastating impact, as the park had lost the attraction that made it unique in Ohio and appealed to more of the families. When Cedar Fair took over there was also a controversy around the park not honouring free tickets given out as a social responsibility initiative with DARE (Drug Abuse Resistance Education)[251]. Geauga Lake was losing its touch with the local community. Between all the changes in ownership and the changes in name: Geauga Lake, Six Flags Ohio, Six Flags World of Adventure and then Geauga Lake again, there was quite a bit of brand confusion. The rebrands were also expensive in terms of replacing merchandise, signage, etc.

Whilst there are multiple reasons why Geauga Lake's attendance crashed, the general consensus is that their attendance rose faster than their capacity. This led to long queues and disappointing guest feedback, which demoralised staff. Once the attendance melted away the park's capacity and running costs were now too high for the volume of people. Once a park has expanded beyond its means, it's tough to then downsize it back into something reasonable. As a park expands, every aspect of the business needs to work together.

It might be that Geauga Lake expanded beyond what the local market could support. Between them Ohio and Pennsylvania had a population of around 24.5 million people. Major parks included Cedar Point, Kings Island, Geauga Lake, Waldameer, Kennywood, Dorney Park, Hershey Park, Knoebels and Seasame Place. The demand for theme parks is driven by several factors: the size of the population within certain distances of the park, the quality of transport and how quickly those guests can get there, the average age of the population, the amount of disposable income they have, the amount of leisure time that they have and how strong the competition is from other forms of entertainment. A feasibility study has to assess all of these variables, as well as estimating the park's capacity and its appeal. No wonder feasibility studies often get their predictions wrong.

There is also a lesson that parks need to be realistic about marketing and promotions, if they're likely to drive more guests to a park than it can comfortably cope with. These kinds of attendance increases are unsustainable, while the cost of the additional advertising and promotions significantly curb even the short-term rise in profits. For example, Six Flags did a partnership with AOL (American Online) where everyone in the Cleveland area who used AOL got a free Six Flags ticket and 25% off additional tickets[252]. Although it is also worth noting that while Six Flags did heavy discounting and cheap

---

251   DARE kids upset by Cedar Fair, Maverick Mark, Thrill Network

252   Six Flags killed Geauga Lake, Chelie, August 7th 2000, Epinions.com

season tickets, they also raised entry prices from $28.99 for an adult in 1999 to $39.99 in 2002.

It'd be very simplistic to say that Geauga Lake failed just because it became too crowded and that it expanded its rides without expanding its infrastructure. But this was a factor in the park's demise.

Alton Towers has a similar, although substantially less dramatic, story. In 2002 they added a B&M flying coaster called Air[253]. I'd argue that Air is one of the UK's best coasters. The technology behind the flying system is still incredibly impressive almost two decades later. As is usual with B&M the ride is very smooth and comfortable. Designer John Wardley did a fantastic job with moulding the layout around the hill it's on, and capturing the flying sensation.

You might imagine that with a fantastic new roller coaster Alton Towers' guest feedback would have gone up. At the time Alton Towers was part of the Tussaud's Group, and Bruce McKendrick was the group's director for theme parks. He told Attractions Management Magazine, "Last year [2003] was more difficult than planned for the parks. Also, in 2002 we launched a new ride at Alton Towers called Air. It led to big queues and customers' expectations went down. Because we hadn't delivered as well as we should have, it may have put some people off"[254]. He implies that lots of visitors came in 2002 to experience Air, and that Air and perhaps some of the other rides struggled to cope with the demand. 2002 was also the year that Alton Towers introduced Terror of the Towers, their first major scare maze. There are always lots of factors that can affect guest feedback and attendance, but presumably their director of theme parks was well placed to make an informed analysis.

His interview seems refreshingly candid. Social media has made many parks more guarded about their reputation. These days managers avoid saying anything that can be construed as negative about their attraction. This minimises the risk of controversies and scandals, but it also makes the interviews bland and corporate.

At the time Tussaud's and Alton Towers were very conscious of queuing and the impact it had on the guest experience. Air was part of a series of roller coasters that Alton Towers added called Secret Weapons, which were built every four years: Nemesis (1994), Oblivion (1998) and Air (2002). Each one added another high throughput thrill coaster. They slowly replaced the park's older coasters from the 80s, which had substantially lower throughputs. B&M coasters are generally able to shift large volumes of people, because each train has four people in a row, giving them a high capacity. In 1998 Alton Towers had trialled a free Virtual Queue reservation system,

---

253   In 2016 Alton Towers added virtual reality to Air and a small amount of extra theming, including a smoking portal you fly through near the beginning. It was re-named Galactica.

254   Attractions Management Magazine, 3/4/2004

like Disney's Fast Pass. It was rolled out further in 1999[255]. In 2002 Terror of the Towers had been introduced as part of a growing initiative to move visits to October, when parks have traditionally been quiet. Alton Towers had teams of engineers working overnight trying to resolve the issues Air had, and it also opened before the rest of the park for ERT (exclusive ride time), to maximise the number of people who could ride it each day. Any problems Alton Towers had around that time weren't for lack of trying. All this shows that even when a park is doing its best to be efficient, it can be hard to raise the park's capacity quickly enough to cope with a big influx of extra guests.

Because Air was such a revolutionary ride it did have a reasonable amount of downtime in its opening year. Impressive new rides may well bring an influx of extra visitors into a park, but whether they come back for more the following year often depends on how much they enjoyed themselves. Some theme parks consider themselves to be marketing led businesses. Whilst strong marketing campaigns and appealing new rides can bring in a rush of extra visitors, the attendance boost quickly subsides if there isn't strong guest feedback. Maintaining strong guest feedback relies on having the infra-structure and operational capacity to cope with the extra visitors. I don't think Alton Towers did anything particularly wrong with Air. This just goes to show that the amount of people who visit a theme park isn't just about the demand, but also about the supply. Stories like this highlight the care that needs to be taken around opening a major new attraction.

Let's go back to Six Flags, a chain that deserves to have its own book. In the 1960s Six Flags pretty much invented the American regional theme park. They chose locations near highways, popularised the pay one price (POP) model, created highly themed environments and were the first parks to feature a log flume, a river rapids and a mine train. The history of Six Flags is complicated because it involves numerous takeovers and mergers, and it's easy to attribute things to Six Flags that their parks did before they became part of Six Flags. It's not completely unfair to do so either, as when Six Flags took over parks, they often acquired their managers and their innovators pooling that expertise together. If we look at the Six Flags of today their parks are responsible for the first B&M (Bolliger and Mabillard) inverted coaster and the first RMC (Rocky Mountain Construction) hybrid coaster. Their early parks were well themed and featured dark rides. Premier Parks, who later bought Six Flags, bought intellectual properties (Looney Tunes and DC Comics) to regional theme parks when intellectual properties were less common in the industry. For several decades Six Flags were extraordinarily innovative, ambitious, built up a strong brand and were incredibly successful.

Then they started expanding beyond their means. According to Six Flags' own reports for shareholders, they lost money every year between 1999 to 2009[256]. In some years they were spending over $200 million a year on

---

255   Virtual queuing in 2021, Kraken27, Towers Street Forum, https://tow-ersstreet.com/talk/threads/virtual-queuing-in-2021.5679/page-2

256   Six Flags – The rise and fall... and rise again, Company Man, https://www.youtube.com/watch?v=MiME7Lr1MtY

interest for their debt. After bankruptcy they were able to emerge without much of their debt, which has at least in the short-term made them profitable. However, they now use a discount model, which has led to an aging base of large attractions and new rides have been generally low budget. Six Flags has become the go to story for how to build up a successful theme park company, and then how it can go wrong.

From the mid-90s onwards, their model for acquiring parks was often based on a build and they will come mentality. They'd take over a park, re-theme a kid's area to Looney Tunes, add in a big package of rides and rebrand it as a Six Flags park. For example, when they took over Walibi Belgium they added 25 new rides[257], including a Vekoma wooden coaster (Loup Garou), a Vekoma Boomerang and a Vekoma SLC (suspended looping coaster). In 2003 they added the Challenge of Tutankhamun, a shooting style dark ride by The Sally Corporation. When it opened the Challenge of Tutankhamun received rave reviews from the enthusiast community. This is a different strategy to Dollywood, which we shall discuss shortly, where they've tended to expand their capacity more in response to visitor growth than to encourage it. Based on anecdotal evidence from enthusiast forums, Six Flags tried to free up as much investment for new rides as possible, partly by minimising their expenditure on infrastructure as well as operations. This meant that they were making these big investments in new rides, but ride availability was falling and throughputs were falling, so that the park's ability to handle the crowds wasn't shifting.

Whilst more attractions often do help a park to handle bigger crowds, growth needs to be carefully managed. Adding more rides can also be an expensive way of reducing queues. Other Six Flags' parks conformed to Geauga Lake's pattern of a big investment followed by a shortly lived attendance spike, although Geauga Lake's was particularly severe. Six Flags Holland's attendance rose from 680,000 in 1999 to 1.5 million in 2000[258]. Visitors seemed to subside quickly, with most visitors returning to Efteling. It was reported on various Internet forums that by 2005 attendance had dropped back to around 700,000 a year. In 2018 the park attracted 855,000 visitors[259]. Clearly a question parks need to ask themselves, is not just how do they attract more visitors, but how do they do it in a sustainable way.

Geauga Lake is one example of where Six Flags borrowed heavily to invest in new rides, but where the park wasn't able to cope with influx of visitors. A slightly different example would be Six Flags Great Adventure (New Jersey), where in 1999 Six Flags invested heavily in a 'war on lines'. In a single season

257   Six Flags expands in Europe as company marks 40th anniversary year, Hospitality Net, https://www.hospitalitynet.org/news/4007174.html

258   Six Flags Inc, Reference for Business, https://www.referenceforbusiness.com/history2/80/Six-Flags-Inc.html

259   Number of visitors to theme park Walibi Holland, Statistica, https://www.statista.com/statistics/670941/visitor-numbers-to-theme-park-walibi-holland-in-the-netherlands/

27 rides were added to the park, including three roller coasters[260]. A press release from the park said it represented a $42 million investment. That's roughly the same as their investment in Geauga Lake around the same time. They wrote, "We declare war on lines. Our guests will have more rides to ride and, with the increased capacity, they will be able to more fully enjoy the park's extensive entertainment presentation... The park will be bigger and better than ever in 1999. In fact, the expansion and additions are so extensive that it will be like experiencing a whole new park".

In 1999 Great Adventure had 67 rides, which according to Six Flags was more than any other park in the world[261]. In essence, with the rides that Six Flags bought for Great Adventure for one season, they could have built an entire new theme park. Despite the huge investment, the park didn't increase their prices in 1999.

Rides included a large B&M floorless coaster called Medusa, a Vekoma Mad House called Houdini's Great Escape, a Zierer family coaster called Blackbeard's Lost Treasure Train, and several flat rides (roundabouts) including a Chance Chaos, an Evolution, a Zamperla Regatta called Jolly Roger, a Huss Jump called Jumpin' Jack Flash, a Huss Frisbee called Pendulum, a Huss Break Dance called Rodeo Stampede, a Polyp called Spinnaker, a Chance double inverter called Time Warp, a Huss Top Spin called Twister. The rest of the number was mainly made up of children's rides. Not only did they add a lot of rides, but they also went for the high throughput options. Houdini's Great Escape was the larger model of Mad House with 78 seats. The Chance inverter was the twin model giving it 38 seats in total. The B&M floorless coaster had 3 trains with 32 seats on each. Whilst there was always going to be a compromise between the quantity of rides and the quality of them, this wasn't a case of Six Flags buying as many rides as they could at the lowest possible prices. This was a valiant effort to get rid of the lines. What went wrong?

According to the Great Adventure History website there were a couple of problems. Firstly, they struggled to recruit enough staff to run the extra rides, and although they did add some more staff accommodation in 2000, they also opened a new $40 million Hurricane Bay water park[262] which required even more staff. It wasn't unusual for the new flat rides to end up being left closed because the park was too short staffed to run them. Adding so many rides at once meant that the engineering department had a lot of new rides to get to grips with all at once, and at least a couple of the flat rides turned out to have significant inherent problems that couldn't be resolved. Even though flat rides are fairly small, they also need quite a lot of attention from the engineers. There can be a lot of moving parts that are baring considerable loads and pressure, and the restraint system that holds people in takes a disproportionate

260   The war on lines, Great Adventure History, http://www. greatadventurehistory.com/WarOnLines.htm

261   1999 Year Book, Great Adventure History, http://www. greatadventurehistory.com/1999_Yearbook.htm

262   2000 Year Book, Great Adventure History, http://www. greatadventurehistory.com/2000_Yearbook.htm

amount of inspection and care relative to the size of the parts. Several of the flat rides didn't last long before they were either relocated to other Six Flags parks, or scrapped. However, the lost rides have largely been made up for with impressive new additions including El Toro (prefabricated wooden coaster) and Kingda Ka (currently the world's tallest roller coaster).

We don't have any data to show how successful the War on Lines actually was at reducing the waiting times. Geauga Lake and Great Adventure both expanded quickly, and in both cases, there were negative reviews about dirty paths and closed rides. If the people involved with running these parks were to read this book, they might feel hard done by. They'd no doubt say that they worked hard and that the problems were out of their control. That's the point I'm making though. When a park expands very quickly, even if the staff work hard, there are likely to be negative side effects.

Because we now know that Six Flags went through a major financial crisis that took them into bankruptcy, it's easy to look back with hindsight and assume that all their decisions were bad. To be fair to Six Flags, ever since they bought Great Adventure it has been one of their largest and most successful properties, less than two hours' drive from New York city and barely an hour from Philadelphia. Disney themselves looked at building a park for the New York market. They dropped the idea because New York has harsh winters, and Disney didn't want to build a seasonal park. Their investment in the park and their commitment to reducing waiting times is admirable. But like Geauga Lake, there were challenges around adding so many rides so quickly. At the very least, when a park is looking to expand quickly, all the departments need to work together to make sure their infrastructure and operations are prepared.

While it was Six Flag's policy to put large packages of rides into parks, they generally went for tried and tested technology like Boomerangs and SLCs (suspended looping coasters), and bought from manufacturers with a proven track record like Vekoma and B&M. There were exceptions, like X Flight and Jumpin' Jack Flash, but for the most part they went for the 'safe options'. This wasn't enough to stop their ride availabilities falling, although we don't have specific statistics. Six Flags' strategy was no doubt based partly on assumptions about economies of scale. This is another area of efficiency that we don't have time to cover in this book. By building a massive chain they expected cost saving through increased buying power, branding power and centralised management. It's likely that Six Flags overestimated the efficiency savings they could make, particularly as redundancies lower morale and damage the fabric of an organisation, and a local management are more in tune with their guests and the catchment area.

In the case of both Geauga Lake and Great Adventure they made significant investments whilst holding down prices or introducing new promotions. Often a successful drive to reduce queuing will be a linked with a move to re-position the park as a more premium product, with either a higher pricing or smaller discounts. In the case of both parks, there seemed to be a significant investment in attractions, but it didn't raise the park's capacity as much as you'd expect. I don't think the case of Six Flags should put parks off parks expanding quickly, or adding multiple rides in a season. It isn't always going to make sense for a regional park to be managed like a Disney park where they tend to have a low ratio of rides to guests and focus their investment on fewer bigger rides rather than more smaller rides. However, parks mustn't be complacent about the challenges of expanding and how quickly things can unravel if you don't get it right.

One of the questions that sometimes comes up, is will a new ride increase a park's attendance? There are several factors here. The quality of the ride and how appealing it looks is no doubt one of them, but it is certainly not the only one. What is the ride adding to the park, and how is it enhancing the guest's day? Other factors include whether the park is increasing its ticket prices, what competing parks are doing, the potential of the park's market, but also how much surplus capacity the park has. Occasionally we hear about a new ride or area significantly adding to a park's attendance. Other times a new ride adds nothing. Enthusiasts often take this to be a sign of the ride's quality or how well it was marketed. They don't consider the role that the park's capacity plays in the increase. When a park's attendance suddenly jumps up, it's often partly because they've done the ground work over the previous years.

If a park adds a high-quality new ride, but the park's capacity is already stretched, then there's limited scope for a big increase in attendance, unless the new ride or area significantly increases the park's overall capacity. On the other hand, if a park has some surplus capacity and the queues are typically reasonable, then there's more scope for the attendance to rise. For example, when Paultons Park added Peppa Pig World visitors doubled from 500,000 a year to over a million. This is partly a reflection of the strength behind the Peppa Pig intellectual property and the high quality of the new area. However, before the expansion the park rarely had queues and the new area was able to hold quite a few extra people.

A difference between Paultons Park's expansion and Six Flags', is that Six Flags' budget went almost entirely on rides, whereas Paultons Park spent a significant chunk of the Peppa Pig World budget on infrastructure such as toilets, eateries and a shop. Following Peppa Pig World the park invested heavily in improving its infrastructure, including a new engineering work-shop, a new learning centre for schools (Professor Blast's Laboratory), and a new entrance area featuring a new bigger gift shop (The Big Toy Shop) and a new restaurant (Wild Wood). Corporate theme parks can feel under pressure to beef up next quarter's results. CEOs frequently have short tenures and managers jump around between positions, or get moved around in the next restructure. Bonuses can depend on hitting short term targets. However, while focussing most of your investment on new rides can bring in more guests in the short term, it can lead to the whole park feeling overcrowded, which causes harm in the longer term. Particularly as rides generally cost more to maintain than infrastructure, since parts wear out, need daily inspections by engineers and annual strip downs.

Paultons Park quickly increased their attendance using a combination of a big brand (Peppa Pig), a high quality new area and filling surplus capacity the park already had. Islands of Adventure (Universal Orlando) was able to do something similar when they added the Wizarding World of Harry Potter.

In 2009, the year before Wizarding World of Harry Potter opened, Islands of Adventure attracted 4,627,000 visitors[263]. The year after it attracted 7,674,000 visitors[264]. That's an increase of around 40%. 2009 had been a particularly poor year for Islands of Adventure with a 600,000 dip in attendance, perhaps partly because people were delaying their visits until Wizarding World opened, and because 2009 was at the height of the financial crash. In 2009 all four of Disney World's parks had increases in attendance, while both of Universal's, Sea World and Busch Gardens saw significant falls, so I'm not completely sure what we should make of that. For the whole of 2009 part of Lost Continent was closed while Wizarding World was constructed. This include The Flying Unicorn roller coaster, which was renamed Flight of the Hippogriff. Duelling Dragons stayed open until the start of 2010. When parks have a big jump in attendance, you do sometimes find that it follows a year with an attendance drop.

Whilst there might have been some uptick in 2010 regardless of new attractions, it seems fair to say that most of the 3 million extra visitors to Islands of Adventure came because of Wizarding World. This includes the strength of the Harry Potter brand and the quality of the area itself. The whole area was highly themed, including bespoke merchandise and menus (did someone say Butter Beer?), as well as what was arguably the greatest dark ride in the world – Forbidden Journey. However, visitors also increased from a low point. Whilst 4,627,000 visitors would be a dream for most park, this was at a park that's open 365 days a year, so that's an average of about 12,700 guests a day. Islands of Adventure was typically open about 12 hours each day, so longer than most regional parks. Most people don't stay for all 12 hours, so the park would often have under 10,000 visitors in it.

At the time Islands of Adventures only had 13 rides, although there were non-ride attractions including the Camp Jurassic play area, the Jurassic Park Discovery Centre, various meet and greets and the Eighth Voyage of Sinbad stunt show. Many of the rides at Islands of Adventure had very high throughputs. For example, Jurassic Park River Adventure ran 16, 25 seat vessels carrying almost 3,000 guests an hour. That's almost a quarter of the park's attendance for an average day. Duelling Dragons could also do close to 3,000 guests an hour, as each train carried 32 rides in 8 rows of 4. There were separate offloading and loading platforms. Guests left all their loose articles and bags in lockers outside the ride, meaning the trains could be loaded very quickly. Due to a combination of a single rider queue and batching, height checking at the entrance to the ride rather than in the station,

263   2009 Theme Index, Themed Entertainment Association, http://www.themeit.com/etea/2009report.pdf

264   2011 Theme Index, Themed Entertainment Association, http://www.aecom.com/deployedfiles/Internet/Capabilities/Economics/_documents/Theme Index 2011.pdf

and free lockers outside the entrance, Incredible Hulk could do around 1,700 guests an hour.

In both the case of Paultons Park and Islands of Adventure, there was scope for them to significantly increase their attendance without queues having a major impact on the guest experience. Both parks have consistently featured in Trip Advisor's chart of the world's top 25 theme parks. In 2019 Islands of Adventure came out first and Paultons Park was 24th. If there had been the demand for Peppa Pig World or Wizarding World, but the parks hadn't had the capacity to cope with the crowds, then guest satisfaction would have plummeted and any upswing in visitors would have been short lived. In the long run, if a park wants to boost visitor numbers and sustain them, you can't rely on marketing power, or even on the quality of one or two headline rides. You have to be able to offer a fun day out, and that means keeping queues reasonable, relative to the quality of the attractions that people are waiting for. In its opening year Wizarding World often was crowded and Forbidden Journey tended to have long queues. However, guests knew that if they left Wizarding World, there were plenty of other high-quality rides where the waits would be a lot shorter.

This also helps to explain why Phantasialand in Germany hasn't managed to increase its visitor numbers, despite heavy investments. From 2005 onwards, the TEA (Themed Entertainment Association) provides us with estimated visitor figures for Phantasialand. Before 2005 it's harder to obtain figures. They show that in this time visitor numbers to the park have been static, despite them adding world class rides such as the inverted coaster Black Mamba, a floorless Top Spin with fire - Talacon, Mouse of Chocolate interactive dark ride and Chiapas flume with extraordinary theming and some truly impressive technology. It is possible that Phantasialand had saturated much of the market in that area, and that they weren't able to draw significantly more people from further away who were tending to visit Europa Park or Efteling.

Few people will deny that Phantasialand is a park of astronomical quality. These rides use state of the art technology, original concepts and detailed theming. Unfortunately, Phantasialand has a small footprint, meaning they've not been able to increase their capacity significantly, despite having one of the highest quality parks in the world. That's not to say that their high quality and impressive rides are pointless. They have good price integrity and strong guest loyalty. By demolishing older rides to build new rides, it also means that they haven't ended up with lots of older less popular rides that need maintaining and operating.

When a park increases its attendance there can be one individual attraction that sweeps up most of the credit, but behind the scenes it takes a team effort and multiple additions to lift attendance in the long term. Since Peppa Pig World opened in 2011 Paultons Park has resisted the temptation to build any really big rides, and has continued to invest money on improving theming and infrastructure across the board, for example in 2020 adding screens in the park with waiting times. Two stand out rides are the Vekoma suspended family coaster Flight of the Pterosaur (2016) and the Mack family spinning coaster Storm Chaser (2021). However, Paultons Park is a prime example of fairly standard rides being combined with good operations, good infrastructure and great aesthetics to make a strong all-round package.

There are two sides to the equation. One side is that it's difficult to keep on increasing your attendance when the park feels crowded and the queues are long. The second is that if your capacity becomes too big in relation to your attendance, then it becomes difficult to remain viable. You're paying to run and maintain attractions you don't need and the ratio of staff to guests becomes too high. The aim certainly isn't for your park to feel dead. There's a healthy point where you're coping well enough with the crowds to give them a pleasant day and a sense of value, as well as allowing room for growth, but you're also not haemorrhaging money running an empty park either. If you reach a point where your park has to be over crowded in order to make money, then something's gone wrong. Perhaps you don't own some of your assets, for example if you're leasing the land, some of the rides or you're spending a lot on licencing intellectual properties. Perhaps you've got too much debt. Perhaps your attendance is too clustered around a small number of days or a particular area of your park. Perhaps your rides are being operated inefficiently, or you've over invested in rides at the expense of infrastructure. Good guest satisfaction and profitability shouldn't be mutually exclusive.

We've considered expanding the capacity and attendance of an existing park, but how do you know whether a new park will be successful? You're relying on your projections, which is why it's critically important that they're accurate. We have already discussed feasibility studies near the start of the book. Remember, when new parks fail, it's mostly because they've either over estimated the number of people wanting to visit, or because they've overestimated the park's capacity. You mustn't let your creatives and marketing team design something that looks cool and then expect your operations people to bend the numbers to make it work.

In some ways the safety side is more problematic than the guest experience aspect. Everything might seem okay, until suddenly it's not okay. Most of the time your park might function. It's only when there's a fire, something causes a stampede, a guest is taken urgently ill and you need to get an ambulance through, there's a fight... that things go horribly wrong and suddenly you realise that the park was overcrowded. Emergency drills can help, but these tend to be done with small groups of staff. They don't simulate what happens when a park is packed with tens of thousands of people. Experienced incident managers and a strong crisis plan can help to coordinate things, but things can escalate very quickly in a crowded theme park. It's important to set capacities and design parks to move the odds in your favour.

Park under the spotlight: Coney Island

Throughout this book I've tried to add a bit of historical context. We looked at the Great Exhibition in 1851 and how they used variable pricing to shift demand. We discussed American restaurants in the 1920s, and how they pioneered techniques for getting multiple sittings out of their tables. We looked at Disneyland's original design in 1955, and their approach to managing guest flow around the park. We shall now step back in time to the very early days of the amusement industry. These days Coney Island's (Brooklyn, New York) heyday seems like a very long time ago. When we think about Coney Island, we might imagine fires, crime and the cruelty of a freak show or a human zoo. For the purposes of this section we're not looking at the morality of Coney Island in the late 1800s and early 1900s, nor are we focussing on why it declined. In its heyday Coney Island was phenomenally popular and developed a lot of the ideas that modern theme parks use for managing their crowds. This is what I want to focus on.

We might think that Disney were the first people to think about capacities, but in the early 1900s the Coney Island collection of amusement parks were entertaining vast crowds. Coney Island was a series of amusements located along the boardwalk (promenade) behind the beach. The most notable parks from Coney Island's heyday were Sea Lion Park, Luna Park, Dreamland[265] and Steeplechase Park. There were also various standalone, independently run rides and attractions in between the enclosed parks. According to historian Jeffrey Stanton, the enclosed amusement parks never occupied more than about 20%-25% of the amusement area[266].

By the early 1900s Coney Island was remarkably modern. There were big lighting displays, large night time shows featuring fireworks and special effects, staff wore costumes - including being dressed as Eskimos at the 20,00 Leagues Under the Sea ride and as jockeys at Steeplechase Park, there were parades, there was a ride that exited through a gift shop, there was themed food including Moon Cheese (green cheese) at the Trip to The Moon, there were simulators and special effects shows and there was a fully enclosed 'scenic railway' wooden coaster.

Coney Island was a shaped by several social changes. Cities had formed after the industrial revolution, when large populations formed in concentrated places. New York was one of these places. The railroad had significantly speeded up travel, meaning that ideas and attractions could move around relatively easily. For example, attractions from the Exposition in Chicago could then be moved to Coney Island. Technology had been rapidly developing, and by the early 1900s things were possible that might not have been a short time earlier. While lightbulbs had been around for many decades, they burned out quickly and soot from the filament blackened the bulb. They also needed to work at an appropriate current. One of the secrets was to put the filament inside a glass bulb with a vacuum inside, so that the filament wouldn't oxidise. Electricity and motors were progressing and LA Marcus Thompson's invention of the Switch Back Railway was a vital step in the evolution of the roller coaster. Immigrants from around the world visited New York, and so ideas and technologies were bought together. New York was a

---

265   The author of this book worked at an amusement park called Dreamland in the UK. It was named after the 'original' Dreamland at Coney Island

266   Coney Island, independent rides, Jeffrey Stanton, https://www.westland.net/coneyisland/articles/independentrides.htm

financial hub, including various railroad magnates who were happy to invest in the area's amusements. Changing labour laws started giving workers more time off, and Coney Island was allowed to run on Sundays, when most people had their time off. There were also some extraordinarily talented artists, designers, inventors, engineers and entrepreneurs working on the Coney Island projects.

The Coney Island area provided pretty much all the types of entertainment you could have at the time: exotic animals, horse racing (there were three different racing grounds), theatre, ballrooms, historic re-enactments, scientific demonstrations (including a pavilion with premature babies in incubators), casinos, brothels (one brothel was inside a giant elephant), bathing pools, cultural exhibits, human zoos and vast numbers of rides and amusements.

It wasn't unusual for 250,000 postcards to be sent from the Coney Island post office in a single weekend and on one record breaking day over 200,000 post cards were sent[267]. We don't know how many visitors this represents, but it must have been a tremendous amount. One of these parks was Luna Park, which charged for admission, as well as for each ride. In 1909 they attracted about 20 million visitors, which is similar to what Magic Kingdom gets today[268]. Stanton says that, "Two hundred thousand people came to Coney on weekends in 1905; 600,000 by 1915, and over a million after the subway arrived in 1920"[269].

Early amusement parks often claim to have attracted vast numbers of visitors, which is quite plausible, given the pay per ride structure, the more limited alternatives for people seeking entertainment, and the more casual attitude to safety, which allowed attractions to handle incredible volumes of people. However, Coney Island's visitor numbers were extraordinary even for the time. Perhaps the closest comparison I can find is with temporary exhibitions. The 1893 Chicago Exposition is said to have attracted 27,300,000 visitors in the six months it ran for[270]. On Chicago Day, October 9th, the Fair attracted 751,027 visitors. The centre piece of the fair was the world's first ferris wheel, which stood at 264ft high. It had 36 cars each carrying 40 people, giving it a capacity of 1,440 people. Plans to move the Ferris Wheel to Coney Island fell through, however some of the pavilions from the Chicago Exposition did find their way to Coney Island.

When the 22 acre Luna Park opened in 1903, its layout was designed with the major rides spread out around the park with smaller attractions in between, to help disperse people around the site[271]. Each of the parks at Coney Island were set up and managed by a single company, which potentially

267   The Coney Island album, Coney Island the People's Playground, Michael Immerso

268   Coney Island the People's Playground, Michael Immerso, p. 81.

269   Coney Island, independent rides, Jeffrey Stanton, https://www. westland.net/coneyisland/articles/independentrides.htm

270   History – World's Fairs, Libbey House Foundation, http://libbeyhouse.org/worlds-fairs/

271   Coney Island – Luna Park, Jeffrey Stanton, West Land, https:// www.westland.net/coneyisland/articles/lunapark.htm

had various investors. They'd allow concessions to run rides within the park, in exchange for giving the park a cut of any takings. Luna Park's standard cut was 20%. This cut along with an entrance fee to the park gave them a significant budget for theming, infrastructure, lighting and other entertainment between the rides. Ride plots in these parks were sought after, so the parks could be quite picky about which rides they allowed and how they were presented.

On its opening day 60,000 people entered the park. Shortly after the opening night, Luna Park had a power failure, and some guests got trampled, when around 60,000 people surged towards the entrance all at once[272]. This is the kind of scenario that modern day crisis planning attempts to avoid. 60,000 people crammed into a 22 acre amusement park represents 2,727 guest per acre. That's over triple the density of guests that I believe any modern theme park has. Luna Park was incredibly successful in its opening year, and on 4th July 1903 they sold 142,332 admission tickets. This was slightly more than the 135,000 who visited Dreamland on its opening day a year later in 1904[273].

For the second season they added an arcade down either side of the main plaza with a rooftop garden. According to historian Jeffrey Stanton, "It was a clever solution of both widening the Court of Honor for Luna's increasingly larger crowds, and for providing the visitor with two options for strolling; along the sunny green roof garden decorated with Oriental plants, or beneath through the shaded arcaded walkway that provided shelter if it rained". In 1905 the entrance to Luna Park was widened to accommodate more people. By 1906 the park was packed with attractions, but they expanded the capacity by building another large rooftop Garden of Babylon. At Dreamland there were two piers into the sea for steam ships to moor at. They were almost half a mile long and on two levels, which maximised the surface area for the guests to walk along.

Many of the attractions at Coney Island were indoors. There could have been for various reasons. It allowed them to use lighting effects and take guests away from the noisy atmosphere outside. At the time engineering was more temperamental, so it protected the ride mechanics from the weather. It also helped to weather proof the parks for the guests. Coney Island's first enclosed park, Sea Lion Park, closed at the end of 1902. This was partly because it was struggling to compete with newer attractions in the area, but also because the 1902 season was particularly wet. After that, the other Coney Island parks often featured undercover arcades, enclosed areas - such as the 5 acre Pavilion of Fun at Steeplechase Park, and undercover rides and shows. To give a comparison, the world's largest show building today is the original Pirates of the Caribbean at Disneyland (California). In total it's

---

272   Ibid.

273   Coney Island – Dreamland, Jeffrey Stanton, West Land, https://www.westland.net/coneyisland/articles/dreamland.htm

112,000 square foot, which is roughly 2.6 acres[274]. The world's largest indoor water parks (including Rulantica and the Dreamworks Water Park) are about 8 acres. This puts into perspective how big the Pavilion of Fun was.

The Pavilion of Fun was sometimes likened to the UK's Crystal Palace, and featured various funhouse attractions and a big model elephant. Judging by the building's size, it probably housed various attractions that have been forgotten about. The parks would have what would now be called large 'show buildings'. The buildings themselves could be kept while the rides inside them would be changed, for example at Dreamland the submarine attraction was replaced by Hell Gate, a boat ride where guests travelled down a whirlpool and beneath the earth's surface. Luna Park replaced their indoor submarine ride with Dragon's Gorge, the indoor themed Scenic Railway. Universal now does something similar, where show buildings are kept, but gutted with new rides, like Kongfrontation being replaced with The Mummy or Twister being replaced with Race Through New York.

While Luna Park was set back from the sea front, Dreamland was built directly onto it with a water inlet into the park and two piers for steamships to moor at. You could get a steamship to the park including entry for 35 cents at weekends and 30 cents on weekdays[275]. In 1908 Dreamland was struggling to attract enough visitors in the week to be viable, so they ran a promotion where on weekdays outside of public holidays the entry charge was dropped. Once inside you still had to pay for the rides you wanted to go on. Dreamland certainly didn't invent variable pricing, for example it was being used at the Great Exhibition in London in 1851. But it's clear that like many modern parks, the Dreamland of 1904 was looking for ways to level off their peaks and troughs in attendance.

We might associate night time entertainment most readily with Disney and the firework shows and their illuminated parades, but the parks of Coney Island were also designed to be popular through the day and into the evening. Since these parks ran a pay per ride model, the typical dwell time might have been relatively short, with guests perhaps visiting a few attractions at the parks alongside time on the beach and Board Walk. To bring guests in after dark, they had spectacular lighting displays. Luna Park was famous for its lighting displays, starting out with 250,000 lights. The park was named after one of the co-owner's sister, Luna[276], however it also makes us think of Lunar and the night. When it opened in 1904 Dreamland had over one million incandescent lamps[277]. Given the flammable building materials and the Edwardian lighting technology, this was a massive fire hazard.

---

274   From big to GARGANTUAN – these are the enormous showbuildings you never see, Brian Pacifico, Theme Park Tourist, https://www.themeparktourist.com/features/20181011/34473/largest-theme-park-showbuildings-disney-and-universal-parks?page=3

275   Ibid.

276   Coney Island the People's Playground, Michael Immerso, p. 62.

277   Ibid, p. 71.

Coney Island's amusement parks also featured large scale night time shows. James Pain ran an English firework manufacturer and presented his displays at London's Crystal Palace and Alexandra Palace. He realised that he could make his displays more entertaining by adding storylines and action on the ground. In 1877 James and his son Henry moved to New York and began putting on firework displays at Coney Island, which could be viewed from a big amphitheatre. The amphitheatre contained seating and standing areas, a manmade lagoon and behind it a big stage for large sets and actors. In 1879 they were ready to start putting on shows – five years before LA Marcus Thompson introduced the first roller coaster to the area. Themes for shows included big naval battles, The Last Days of Pompeii, Bombardment of Alexandria, Storming of Pekin, Burning of Moscow and The Great Fire of London[278]. Often the historical re-enactment would play out, before finishing with the fireworks. In the early days of Coney Island film was very basic and museums were mainly cases of artefacts. For those wishing to see historical or current events bought to life in a colourful way, Coney Island was the best place to go.

At Luna Park, each evening a show called Fire and Flame saw a cast of 1,000 people fight a recreated city block that had been set on fire[279]. Dreamland topped it with their own nightly show featuring a cast of 2,000. Dreamland's Fighting the Flames show only lasted for the 1904-1905 season. It must have cost an incredible amount to stage, and meant that a large plot of land was only being used for one show a day at a park that was open for perhaps 12 hours. By 1907 Luna Park had 1.3 million lights[280]. From 1907 there were nightly firework shows at Brighton Park, with themes such as, "The destruction of Jerusalem" and "Battle in the Clouds", which featured balloons and airships. One shudders to think about the safety of combining fireworks and airships.

The rides coped with the crowds using a combination of quantity and scale. It is believed that by 1899 there were 15 carousels operating at Coney Island and that in 1938 there were still 13[281], despite America's economic problems in the 1930s. Over time the carousels tended to get bigger and more elaborate. For example, the El Dorado carousel, added in 1910, was on three tiers and could seat 140 people. Tiered carousels were popular in mainland Europe, but not in the UK where showman felt they could get people on and off quicker on a single-story carousel, where guests didn't have to go up and down stairs. In the UK larger carousels were four abreast rather than three abreast, but they weren't on multiple stories.

At least some of the rides used a system where you bought a ticket from kiosks in front of the ride, and handed them over when you boarded[282].

278   The story of Pain's Manhattan Beach Firework Shows, Heart of Coney Island, https://www.heartofconeyisland.com/pains-fireworks-manhattan-beach-coney-island.html

279   Coney Island the People's Playground, Michael Immerso, p. 73.

280   Ibid, p. 74.

281   Coney Island – historic carousel list, Jeffrey Stanton, Westland, https://www.westland.net/coneyisland/articles/carousellist.htm

282   Ben Hur Racers Roller Coaster, Heart of Coney Island, https://www.heartofconeyisland.com/ben-hur-racers-roller-coaster.html

This meant that the people operating the ride were only having to collect tickets, rather than handle money where people might have needed change. This system is still used on the rides at major fairs and festivals. This ticket system combined with no need to check heights, store loose articles, or check restraints, meant that guests could be loaded onto the rides very quickly.

We might presume that early roller coasters would have had low throughputs. Although the origins of the roller coaster probably go back to Russian Mountains in the 16th or 17th century, La Marcus Thompson's Switchback Railway at Coney Island (New York) in 1884 was certainly one of the earliest 'proper' coasters. It cost 5 cents to ride and took an average of $600 a day[283]. This meant that around 12,000 people a day were riding it, and that it was a huge money-making machine. For the sake of argument, we'll assume it carried 1,000 guests an hour. Guest rode in individual cars with sideways facing seats. Let's imagine that each car carried 10 guests. A car would have needed to be released every 36 seconds to achieve such a throughput. On the busiest days the ride took $700 and people queued for up to three hours[284].

At the time there were no 'block sections' and brakes and there wasn't a powered lift hill. Some cars would have gone faster than others depending on the weight of guests. Perhaps partly due to the lack of brakes and the risk of collisions, cars never travelled at more than about 6mph. Guests would climb stairs to a platform and staff would push the cars to the top. It must have been incredibly hard physical work for the staff working on the ride. In 1885 Philip Hinkle invented a roller coaster with a powered lift, which must have been a huge relief for ride operators at the time, and paved the way for roller coasters becoming much larger and more elaborate. If we look at the coasters from the 1880s, their throughputs were comparable to many major coasters in modern theme parks today.

According to various sources the water chute at Dreamland could carry over 7,000 riders an hour, making it perhaps the highest throughput ride ever built. Guests reached the top of the structure probably using a kind of funicular, before boarding the boats at the top. These went down one of two slides, where they splashed into a big pool at the bottom. Gondoliers on each boat would guide them to the side where guests climbed out, before the boats were steered over to a lift hill to take them back up to the top. It's not clear why guests didn't ride in the boats to the top. This was before anti-roll backs were invented, which caught cars if the chain broke or they became disconnected. It might have been a safety measure. It might also be because the system couldn't cope with the weight of full boats. Each boat carried up to 20 passengers[285], so the 7,000 figure represented 350 full boats an hour, or 175 down each chute. This would entail a boat going down each chute at least

---

283   Coney Island, independent rides, Jeffrey Stanton, https://www.westland.net/coneyisland/articles/independentrides.htm

284   Coney Island the People's Playground, Michael Immerso, p. 39.

285   Ibid, p. 68.

NEIL WILSON   217

once every 20 seconds. Archive film footage of the water chute at Luna Park suggests that this was achieved[286].

In 1895 or earlier 'Merrill's Toboggan' opened. It's not clear whether it was built with two twin tracks that raced each other, or whether a second track was added afterwards. Certainly by 1903 it was a racing coaster[287]. The racing element added to the thrill, as well as providing the throughput of two coasters using the footprint of one. It's astonishing that such a ride could have opened so soon after LA Thompson's Switchback Railway. Thompson's Switchback wasn't capable of going around bends. Guests had to get off for the cars to change direction. There was no mechanical lift hill. Guests climbed stairs and boarded cars at the highest point, which had been pushed to the top. Clearly the roller coaster evolved very quickly. The three hour queues for the Switchback show how popular it was, and this enthusiasm for roller coasters didn't fade. Inventors were presumably looking for ways to carry more passengers on their rides, and providing a twin track racing element was one way to do this. Other racing coasters at Coney Island included The Loop the Loop (1901-1910). This was replaced by another racing coaster – The Giant Racing Coaster (1910-1926). The Giant Racing Coaster was replaced by perhaps Coney Island's most famous roller coaster, the Cyclone which still runs today, and is the only historic roller coaster now at the site.

Today's coasters can be considerably safer, faster and do things that the Victorian inventors might not have even dreamt of, but throughputs haven't really increased, and the Scenic Railways that were built from the early 1900s through to the 1930s, have throughputs far higher than most modern coasters. When we look at the evolution of ideas around efficiency, it's not so much been about raising throughputs, so much as preventing them from falling, as safety becomes more rigorous and attraction designs become more ambitious.

We could imagine that queues would be a fairly modern thing. One account from 1908 wrote, "A million rides a day at 10 cents per ride is the average record on the mechanical riding devices of Coney Island, when the season is good. People stand in line an hour for a ride that is over in two minutes"[288]. We don't tend to see picture of rides with massive cattle grid queues in front of them. It is possible that they hid the queues away like Knott's Berry Farm ended up doing. If they did, then this was one of many things that were highly progressive. Although there are a few aerial photos and you can't see any queuelines hidden away.

Dreamland was one of three main amusement parks at Coney Island and when it opened in 1904 it had been designed for huge crowds. Coney Island was often called the People's Playground. Blackpool Pleasure Beach in the UK has a similar nickname. These businesses were based around low margins and

---

286   Shooting the chutes - Luna Park – Coney Island, Library of Congress, https://www.youtube.com/watch?v=EYa2EGs6BnM

287   Merrill's Star Double Toboggan Racer Roller Coaster, Heart of Coney Island, https://www.heartofconeyisland.com/star-double-toboggan-racer-roller-coaster.html

288   Coney Island the People's Playground, Michael Immerso, p. 97.

high volume. This wasn't expensive entertainment for the wealthy. This was cheap entertainment for the masses, and making money was based on being able to get a high volume of people into the parks and through the rides.

It's clear from Coney Island that most of the practices for handling large crowds were thought of early on in the industry. Coney Island had it all. Undercover rides and shows, indoor pavilions and undercover arcades, so that people would still visit when the weather's bad. Variable pricing for peak and off-peak days. Big lighting displays, night time shows and firework displays to attract people in the evening as well as the day. Wide midways around the parks, with major rides spaced out as much as possible. Large entrances into the gated parks to handle the bottleneck. Attractions with low throughputs were quickly removed or enhanced. The parks looked for ways to expand their capacities, including with rooftop gardens. It might sound like they're following the Disney script almost 50 years before Disneyland opened. Whilst originality and innovation are important, there are basic principles that never die.

Park under the spotlight: Holiday World

We mentioned Holiday World (Santa Clause, Indiana) near the beginning of this book, in a chapter called, what is an acceptable waiting time? Holiday World is an interesting park to look at, because it's a different kind of attraction to many of the ones we've analysed. There are some basic principles of efficiency that most successful parks use. However, there is also quite a lot of variation. Disney and Universal are the market leaders, but not every location supports that kind of park. Holiday World shows us how to run a successful park in a much more sparsely populated and seasonal location.

Holiday World has four areas, each one themed to a different celebration (Christmas, Halloween, Independence Day and Thanks Giving). Today they are best known amongst enthusiasts for their three wooden coasters: Raven, Legend and Voyage. They also have a B&M launched wing coaster, called Thunderbird. Holiday World has built up a strong relationship with the enthusiast community. As well as the normal social media channels, they have a vlog and a podcast. They have an enthusiast event each year. It was originally called Stark Raven Mad, and now it's called HoliWood Nights. Because of the relationship they have with their fans, and the quality of their coasters, a lot has been written about Holiday World. But most of the interest has been in their coasters. There are lots of reviews discussing how they use the topography of the land, and how the coasters balance positive gs, airtime and lateral gs. Needless to say, that I'm not here to review their coasters. We're going to be looking at how Holiday World functions as a business.

Holiday World opened in 1946 and it was originally called Santa Claus Land. It made sense in a place called Santa Claus, and the whole park was themed to Christmas. It was renamed Holiday World in 1984, and more areas were added themed to other 'holidays'. Like a lot of theme parks, their early growth was relatively slow. In 1990 they added a river rapids, which was a massive investment for such a small park. Following the rapids, Holiday World's growth accelerated very quickly. They opened their water park in

1993 and Raven (wooden coaster) in 1995. It was so successful that in 2000 they opened a bigger wooden coaster called Legend. In the next period they expanded the water park. In 2006 they added the Thanksgiving area, featuring The Voyage (wooden coaster) and Gobbler Getaway (dark ride).

Here are a few figures from Holiday World's growth:

- 1975: 100,000 visitors[289]
- 1995: 400,000 visitors
- 1999: 564,373 visitors[290]
- 2002: 760,000 visitors
- 2003: 782,800 visitors[291]
- 2004: 883,000 visitors[292]
- 2006: 1,004,788[293]

Most of the parks in this book have fairly long seasons, and we spent the first big section of this book looking at ways to extend the season and redistribute guests more evenly through it. By contrast, Holiday World is only open for about 115 days a year. It's very weather dependent, because it places a lot of emphasis on their outdoor water park (Splashin' Safari) and it doesn't feature many undercover attractions.

Holiday World has extended their season by doing Happy Halloween Weekends in October, and they do have clear advisories on their website encouraging guests to avoid Independence Day and Labor Day. These are the busiest days of the year. Nonetheless, Holiday World are dependent on a very short season with massive spikes in attendance. Based on the lessons we've learned in this book, this shouldn't make a successful park. But Holiday World's reviews and awards speak for themselves, as does the steady growth in their attendance. Let's take a look at how they did it.

In 2002 Holiday World's busiest day attracted 16,222 visitors[294]. In 2003 it went even higher with 20,000 guests[295] on a single day. These were spread across their theme park and water park (Splashin' Safari), which are both included in the same entry price. In fact, one of Holiday World's biggest selling points is that their admission is all inclusive. At the time of writing the admission price includes the theme park and water park, free parking, free wifi, free sun cream and free fizzy drinks.

---

289   Cover story: Applause Award to honour one of three parks, James Zoltak, All Business

290   Free soft drinks, 6th February 2007, Park World

291   Paula Werne interview, January 15th 2004, On Ride Central

292   "This awards is a reflection of the spirit of our staff" – Will Koch, Paula Werne, Holiday World blog, https://www.holidayworld.com/holiblog/2004/11/17/holiday-world-wins-international-applause-award/

293   Free soft drinks, 6th February 2007, Park World

294   More attendance records toppled – Holiday World plans expansion, Raven Maven, Coaster Buzz, https://coasterbuzz.com/Forums/Topic/more-attendance-records-toppled-holiday-world-plans-expansion

295   Cover story: Applause Award to honour one of three parks, James Zoltak, All Business

16,222 visitors in one day was a remarkable number, considering how small the park was at the time. It must have taken them very close to their capacity. In 2002 Holiday World attracted around 760,000 visitors. This means that their busiest day accounted for over 2% of their annual attendance. In total Holiday World was open for 113 days in the 2002 season, giving them an average of 6,726 guests per day. In 2019 Holiday World was open for 118 days. Holiday World currently gets around 1.1 million visitors a year, giving them an average of around 9,322 guests per day. Let's compare Holiday World to some other parks to see how dramatic these statistics are.

In 2002 Holiday World and Chessington World of Adventures (UK) had roughly the same capacity, but Chessington got about 1.6 million visitors a year. Chessington and Holiday World had roughly the same capacity, but Chessington had over double the annual attendance. Clearly some parks have longer seasons, more operating days and their visitors are better spread out. Here's a table showing a few parks, and what percentage of their annual attendance they could accommodate on a single day if they hit their capacity.

Park	Attendance 2019[296]	Park capacity	Park capacity as a percentage of their annual attendance
Europa Park	5,750,000	60,000	1.04
Cedar Point	3,731,000	54,000	1.45
Shanghai Disneyland	11,210,000	60,000	0.54
Magic Kingdom	20,963,000	90,000	0.44
Chessington World of Adventures	1,690,000	17,000	1.01
Holiday World	760,000 (2002 attendance)	17,000 (2002 capacity)	2.24

This table shows us how concentrated Holiday World's attendance was over a short season, with its big peaks. There aren't many parks that get over 2% of their annual attendance on a single day. Most physically couldn't. In contrast, when it hits capacity Magic Kingdom can only hold 0.44% of its annual attendance. If you filled Holiday World to capacity 45 times, you'd get their annual attendance. You'd have to fill Magic Kingdom to capacity 228 times to get their annual attendance. If you wanted Magic Kingdom to hold 2.24% of its yearly attendance, the capacity would need to be 469,571 people.

These are significant statistics for several reasons. The closer a park comes to its capacity, the more crowded it feels. It shows that while Disney parks have big capacities, this alone doesn't explain how they're able to attract such vast numbers of people each year. It also shows us that successful theme parks can have radically different business models. Holiday World and Disney have both been commercially successful and gone through periods of rapid growth. Different styles of business work better in different locations.

There are similarities between Disney and Holiday World. Both companies now use single rider queues to fill in the empty seats on their rides and both

---

296   Figures taken from the Themed Entertainment Association 2019 index, https://www.teaconnect.org/images/files/TEA_369_611616_200731.pdf

have Halloween events to shift more visits into October. Beyond efficiency they're both known for their service and cleanliness, their innovation and they both have charismatic figures who developed the parks and big fan-bases. But when we start analysing the key statistics behind their businesses, we can see how different they are. Disney fans often share Walt Disney's quote, "It's fun to do the impossible". Of course, neither Disney nor Holiday World are actually doing the impossible. Neither business got to where they are through positive thinking and bravado. Both parks became successful through hard work, a constant determination to get better, re-investing in their businesses, and a long-term approach to problem solving.

What did Holiday World look like in 2002? They had one kids coaster and two wooden coasters. One of these, Raven, had a single train. The second train wasn't added until 2005. There was the Frightful Falls log flume and the Intamin Raging Rapids as well as various classic flat rides, mainly aimed at young children and families. The water park featured a wave pool, water play structure (Monsoon Lagoon), lazy river (Congo River) and various slides. The most recent addition was the 887ft long raft ride ZOOMbabwe, which was marketed as the world's largest enclosed water slide[297].

Holiday World's high capacity shows us that outdoor water parks can accommodate large numbers of people when they're using a wave pool, lazy river and sunbeds, as well as the slides. In many climates indoor water parks have much longer seasons and steadier attendance, but if you compare indoor and outdoor water parks, the outdoor water parks can have more than double the capacity for the same investment.

Holiday World's business model works partly because the US has a fairly long summer vacation. In the UK we have around 20 water parks, but most of them are primarily indoors, although often with small outdoor sections. I can only think of two water parks in the UK that are totally outdoors, and neither of them are particularly big. This is partly because the UK has a temperamental climate, but also because the school summer holiday is only about 6 ½ weeks. In the US the summer vacation is 10-11 weeks – about a month longer than in the UK. The US school holiday pattern makes it viable to concentrate a greater proportion of their attendance over the summer.

The mid-western states in the US and parts of Canada are able to have big outdoor water parks because of the long summer vacation. They don't need to have long seasons to be viable. If they're busy through the summer vacation, then that's enough to make them viable businesses. In the UK the summer holiday isn't long enough to sustain most attractions. To be successful they have to extend their season beyond the summer, and that's hard to do with an outdoor water park in the UK climate. The UK only really has about 3 months a year when the weather's good enough to support an outdoor water park, and that doesn't work with the UK school holiday pattern.

---

297   ZOOMbabwe, Holiday World official, https://www. holidayworld.com/rides/zoombabwe/#

Holiday World's biggest competitor, Kentucky Kingdom (Kentucky), opened their water park (Hurricane Bay) in 1992 - a year before Holiday World opened theirs. There are a lot of similarities between Kentucky Kingdom and Holiday World. Both parks have one admission price that includes the theme park and the water park. Both parks have short seasons, have built up a strong relationship with the enthusiast community and focus on getting the 'basics' right, including service, cleanliness and efficiency. They seem to have found a formula that works well in that area.

The relationship between Holiday World and Kentucky Kingdom is an interesting one. Kentucky Kingdom opened in 1987. It went bankrupt at the end of its first season and re-opened in 1990, spear headed by entrepreneur Ed Hart. From this point on Holiday World and Kentucky Kingdom grew very quickly. We've already looked at Holiday World's growth. Kentucky Kingdom followed a similar strategy, and they got nearly 1.4 million visitors in 1998. Then Kentucky Kingdom was sold to Six Flags and Kentucky Kingdom's attendance went into decline. This was the time when Six Flags were turning Geauga Lake into the world's 'biggest' theme park. It's also the point when they were spending over $80 million on a 'war on lines' and a new water park for Great Adventure. It's not completely clear when Six Flags' eventual bankruptcy became inevitable, but probably around this time.

By 2009 Kentucky Kingdom's attendance had fallen to under 600,000[298]. It's hard to know for certain whether Kentucky Kingdom was directly losing visitors to Holiday World, but there probably was an element of this. Holiday World were able to grow in this period, partly because they were better than their competition. As the old adage goes, if you don't look after your customers, someone else will. In 2007 Kentucky Kingdom had an accident, which contributed to their decline.

Trip Advisor was founded in 2000. From 2004 onwards we start to see growing numbers of reviews for Holiday World. Quite a few of them comment that Holiday World was very busy, but they still give it 5 stars. Often, they're impressed that the park was still very clean, despite being so busy. Although Holiday World was getting very crowded, guests could generally see that they were doing their best. The rides were reliable, the park was well staffed, and the park was investing as much money as they could into building more rides. Unlike a lot of parks, Holiday World has never charged people to skip the queues. In peak season the theme park rides are open 10am – 8pm/9pm. This gives people plenty of time to get on a decent number of rides. In the UK a similar sized park would be open for more days, but with shorter opening hours.

There are four things that might have been challenging for Holiday World as they expanded:

- Offering a high-quality experience when visitor numbers were rising very quickly

---

298   Bedraggled Kentucky Kingdom theme park gets a multimil-
lion dollar redo, Brady Macdonald, Los Angeles Times

- Giving the guests a positive experience, when the attendance is so heavily clustered around a small number of days

- Offering a strong experience when the park's capacity was so high relative to the number of major rides. There were quite a few smaller rides aimed at young children.

- Staffing a theme park that has such a short season. In 2020 they advertised for 2,000 seasonal staff[299].

We can imagine that the speed at which Holiday World's attendance grew might have caused them some challenges. The fact that they kept on growing and scooping up awards suggests that they dealt with those challenges pretty well. There are different pitfalls depending on where a theme park is in its cycle. For a park that's growing quickly, the challenge is to make sure its capacity can keep up and that overcrowding doesn't stifle the growth. You also want to make sure you don't concentrate so much on increasing the park's capacity, that you end up with quantity over quality. For parks with a stable attendance, you've got to give people reasons to keep on coming back without significantly increasing your overheads. For a park with a falling attendance, you're trying to cut costs without getting stuck into a downward spiral. Theme parks often struggle to adjust to these different modes of development.

2002 marked a big rise in attendance for Holiday World. The water park had been very popular ever since it opened in 1993, and advertising the world's biggest enclosed slide no doubt appealed to people. The park also started offering free sun cream. This became a symbol of how much the park cared about their guests. Following the September 11th terrorist attacks there had been a big fall in visitors to Disney and Universal. Perhaps more people were visiting their local park instead. Attendance was also declining at Kentucky Kingdom, presumably because people didn't like their new direction under Six Flags. Holiday World recognised that they'd struggled to cope with the influx of extra visitors in 2002 and added a package of three new rides the following year: Zinga (a big funnel slide in the water park), HallowSwings (A wave swinger) and Liberty Launch (a shot tower).

Holiday World communicated with their guests and were honest about the challenges they were facing. They concentrated on increasing their capacity as quickly as possible and did everything they could to keep the lines as short as they could. This not only allowed them to carry on winning the awards, but also to keep on growing their attendance. Imagine if instead of reinvesting their profits back into the business, the Koch family had given themselves a juicy dividend, or used the money to buy a second park. People are more forgiving of a crowded park, when it's doing everything in its power to offer them a good experience. Although Holiday World has a distinctive and unusual theme, their brand is based around strong service, cleanliness, maintenance, and thrilling rides. They're not known so much for their theming, storytelling or innovative ride systems.

---

299   Job alert: Holiday World to fill 2,000 jobs for the 2020 season, Witz FM, https://www. witzamfm.com/news/job-alert-holiday-world-to-fill-2-000-jobs-for-the-2020-season

Holiday World has an unusual theme, but traditionally it's been done in what they call 'a stylised way'. Each area has music from that 'holiday' and there are little details that capture the theme of the ride. Legend is a wooden coaster in the Halloween area. It's inspired by The Legend of Sleepy Hollow. The ride is meant to mimic a fateful journey being chased by the headless horseman. The station is built in the shape of a school house and as the train reaches the top of the lifthill there is the sound of a wolf howling. But they weren't a heavily themed park, and they invested most of their money into ride hardware. Holiday World is a good example of doing 'the basics' very well.

There is a clear difference between the types of park that are open daily from April – October (around 210 days), or maybe longer, and those that just open for weekends and holidays. The parks that are only open for weekends and school holidays include Holiday World, as well as most of the Six Flags and Cedar Fair parks. It's unusual for them to have onsite accommodation, even if their annual attendance is very high. They might get good occupancy when the park's open, but it's not enough for them to justify the investment. Cedar Point is something of an anomaly in that it does have quite a lot of accommodation and a relatively short season. In 2019 it was open for 138 days.

Parks that are only open for around 120 days a year or less don't make it economical to invest much money into building and maintaining theming. They invest most of their money into physical rides that are based around giving their guests a thrill. This is because they need a high capacity relative to their investment, something that theming doesn't necessarily give you. What's made Holiday World so successful, is that they've really exemplified this type of park. The regional American parks that are based more around themed experiences are the ones with a much longer operating calendars. Chiefly these are Knott's Berry Farm (California), Dollywood (Tennessee), Silver Dollar City (Missouri) and Busch Gardens Williamsburg (Virginia). Because these parks aren't so focussed on thrills, they're able to attract a broader audience including more adults who will visit during term time.

Because Holiday World's attendance has now plateaued, they no longer face the same challenge of constantly trying to improve their capacity. It is also a growing problem trying to recruit increasing numbers of staff for a park so far away from any major centre of population. Recently Holiday World has shifted some of their attention away from building more big rides and started putting more effort into improving the theming around the park[300]. In 2014 they added new themed facades to some of their buildings[301] and in 2019 they rethemed Christmas' Kringle Café into Santa's Merry Marketplace. Parks with such a short season don't normally have masses of theming. However, Holiday World is a park that has often punched above its weight, so it'll be

300   Interview: Holiday World - #1 for family fun! – Leah Koch (director), Ride Review, https://www.youtube.com/watch?v=1jcPvaoz3GQ

301   Holiday World amps up theming – Magic Partners with St Louis design firm, Holiday World official blog, https://www.holidayworld.com/holiblog/2014/03/07/holiday-world-amps-theming-magic-partners-st-louis-design-firm/

interesting to see how they develop in the future. This is a sensible change in direction, and doesn't make their future any less exciting.

A lot of smaller parks expand by adding more rides. Their attendance grows, they add more rides, their attendance grows and so it continues. However, most parks reach a stage where this cycle of development no longer works. It might be that they're struggling to hire more staff as the park expands. It might be that that they've run out of land. It might be that the roads into the park are getting jammed. All of these problems aren't insurmountable, but they are challenging and they do require a change in direction. They say that in business you have to adapt or die. Successful theme parks spot these challenges coming, and make sure they're prepared.

A park's ability to spot these problems coming relies on a couple of things. Firstly, it helps if the managers are experienced with the industry and understand the kinds of cycles that we go through. Secondly, it's beneficial if you have a culture where managers feel able to raise concerns. I've worked at parks where everyone's worried about people shooting the messenger. There's a strong belief in positive thinking and problems get brushed under the carpet. Once you see a challenge coming down the tracks, the sooner you can tackle it, the easier it will be.

It might be that you accept that your attendance is going to plateau, but you develop your attraction by improving the quality of what you've already got. It might be that you need to find ways to squeeze more capacity out of your existing staff count or acreage. Or that if you can't raise the park's capacity, you're going to have to extend the season. At some point every park hits a roadblock that either stifles its growth, its profitability or its guest satisfaction. None of these things are new problems that no park has ever faced before. This is part of my motivation for writing this book. There's an opportunity here for parks to learn from each other. Successful parks shouldn't be complacent, but if managers work together as a team and plan ahead, then they'll find a way to overcome the hurdles.

There are quite a few parks that look at what's being successful elsewhere, and then try to copy it. There's nothing wrong with doing research and looking for inspiration, but it's important to understand not only what other parks are doing, but why they're doing it. What works in one context doesn't always work in another. Once you start to understand why certain principles work, you can take the essence of what another park's doing, but reinvent the idea. This keeps your park imaginative and unique. I've seen quite a few parks copy ideas without understanding the theory behind what they're doing. This can lead to expensive mistakes. Holiday World, Dollywood and Hong Kong Disneyland all exemplify different styles of park that work well in different markets.

Park under the spotlight: Dollywood

Dollywood (Tennessee) goes back to 1961 when Rebel Railroad opened, a steam railway with a blacksmith, general stores and saloon. The train ride had attacks from union soldiers, train robbers and native Americans. The train was protected by confederates who fought off the attacks.

In 1970 a new owner renamed it Gold Rush junction and added several rides including a log flume. In 1976 it was sold to the family owned Herschend Entertainment chain, who already ran the Silver Dollar City park in Missouri. In 1986 Herschend Entertainment sold a stake in the park to country singer Dolly Parton and it was re-named Dollywood. It has been co-owned by Herschend Entertainment and Dolly Parton ever since.

Dollywood features a mixture of Tennessee history, including historic buildings and craft demonstrations, live shows such as musicals, themed areas, freshly produced food with a local flavour, and big roller coasters. These include Mystery Mine, a partly enclosed coaster, Wild Eagle, a wing coaster where the seats hang on the side of the track rather than above it, and Lightning Rod, a steel and wooden hybrid coaster with an uphill launch. Dolly Parton frequently visits the park and helps to launch new attractions.

By 2018, when they announced Wildwood Grove, the park was getting around 2.7 million visitors a year[302], and their attendance had increased six years in a row[303]. The rising attendance was driven by Wild Eagle (opened 2012), Fire Chaser Express (2014), Lightning Rod (2016), bigger events and the DreamMore resort with its 307 rooms[304].

The park was becoming increasingly crowded on big holidays like July 4th. It was decided that they needed a whole new area, which would increase the capacity of the park by about 20%[305]. Craig Ross, the Dollywood Company's president, said, "It is rare in our industry that a park adds a completely new land in its entirety, and as we continue to grow and set attendance records, we needed to add more area to give guests more room to spread out and explore"[306].

The sequence of events is important here. Dollywood's attendance kept on rising, so they decided to increase the park's capacity. They didn't take a build and they will come attitude. Their attitude was, if people keep on coming, we need to expand. I've seen quite a few parks expand in anticipation of extra visitors who don't come, and it's left them with rising costs and a flat revenue.

It's very difficult to turn around a theme park that's losing money by enlarging it. Theme parks don't tend to fail financially because they're too small, unless they lose their visitor base to a larger, more appealing park. You might get a park that's losing money, where people also complain about the length of the queues. That's probably because the park's poorly designed,

302   Dollywood by the numbers, Dollywood Insiders, https://insiders.dollywood.com/dollywood-by-the-numbers/

303   Dollywood announces largest park expansion in history with new land named Wildwood Grove, Business Wire, https://www.businesswire.com/news/home/20180803005051/en/Dollywood-Announces-Largest-Park-Expansion-History-New

304   Dolly Parton opens new resort after $300 million investment, Jenny Cosgrave, CNBC News, https://www.cnbc.com/2015/07/24/dolly-parton-opens-new-resort-after-300m-investment.html

305   Dreamer in Chief, Scott Fais, Fun World Magazine, IAAPA, https://www.iaapa.org/news/funworld/dreamer-chief

306   Dollywood opens $37 million Wildwood Grove, it's largest ever expansion

inefficient and badly managed, or perhaps because their price point is too low. From a business point of view, too much surplus capacity can be a massive problem. One of the significant issues for Disneyland Paris when it opened was low room occupancy, partly caused by too much capacity at their hotels.

To achieve the 20% increase in the park's capacity, the new area needed to accommodate about 5,000 guests. It would be built in two stages of roughly equal sizes. The first phase of the Wildwood Gove expansion opened in 2019 and cost $37 million. This area is primarily for children, but not exclusively so, and features six rides. The area's art director Patrick Brennan said, "We also really worked hard to create a space that is broad and wide and not congested. There's a lot of areas in Dollywood that sometimes get congested. We want you to feel a little bit of freedom coming into this space."[307].

The first phase of the area was six acres[308] and would accommodate about 2,500 guests. This gave it a density of about 417 guests per acre. Typically, the regional parks do have lower densities compared to the Disney or Universal parks. The 417 figure is similar to the general estimation for crowd density given by the Park Database[309]. According to the park's marketing director, Pete Owens, there are plans to expand Wildwood Grove by another 7 acres[310]. Dollywood plans further ahead than many regional parks, allowing them to make sure that areas flow together both thematically and logistically.

The centrepiece of the area is the 50ft tall Wildwood Tree, which has 650 LED butterflies which light up during a nighttime show including music, narration by Dolly Parton and projection mapping. There are four different versions of the show, one for each season[311]. Children's areas often tend to be quiet in the evenings, as parents start to leave as they want to get their children home to bed. The night show and table service restaurant helps to keep the area busier during these times.

Like most children's areas, it wasn't a through route to anywhere. However, they did place the main ride, the Dragonflier coaster, at the back of the area. This helps to draw people through it, so the crowds aren't concentrated just inside the entrance. You enter the area through a giant hollowed out log, and as soon as you're inside you see the Wild Wood Tree. This gives you a visual icon to head for. At Disney they would call this a 'weenie', for example like the castles, or the Tree of Life in Animal Kingdom. Wildwood Grove finds a compromise. In some ways it doesn't feel quite like a traditional children's

307   Dollywood's new land, Wildwood Grove, is opening Friday. Here are five things to know, Maggie Jones, Knox News,
https://eu.knoxnews.com/story/entertainment/2019/05/08/
dollywood-wildwood-grove-opens-5-things-know-dolly-parton-pigeon-forge/3629989002/

308   My first look at Wildwood Grove, Justin Marion, Dollywood Insiders, https://insiders.dollywood.com/my-first-look-at-wildwood-grove/

309   How to correctly size an attraction (of any kind), The Park Database,
https://www.theparkdb.com/blog/how-to-size-an-attraction-of-any-kind/

310   Wildwood Grove – Pete Owens interview Dollywood, Coaster Force Youtube channel, https://www.youtube.com/watch?v=9312r6T832w

311   Elation shares in magic of Dollywood Wildwood Grove tree, Mondo, https://
www.mondodr.com/elation-shares-in-magic-of-dollywood-wildwood-grove-tree/

area, in that it isn't based around a mascot, and that some features like the Wildwood Tree light show appeal to adults as well as kids. At the same time, they've also made it clear that this isn't somewhere for teenagers and adults to go for thrill seeking.

The area includes several activities for children to do without waiting in line, including a Wildwood Creek with a splash area, an outdoor play area and giant musical instruments. There's also a 4,000 sq ft indoor soft play area called Hidden Hollow, to make sure there's somewhere for people to go when the weather's bad. The area included snack carts selling popcorn and butterfly shaped pretzels, a takeaway unit called Sweets and Treats selling fried chicken, churros and ice cream sundaes, and the Till and Harvest table service restaurant. According to Pete Owens, it's "like a park within a park"[312].

Dollywood describes Till and Harvest as 'Smoky Mountain Mexican', and it doesn't look like the kind of restaurant you'd often find in a children's area. In fact, whilst the rides and play areas are clearly aimed at younger guests, the colour palette and theming will appeal to all ages. When an area of the park appeals exclusively to one audience, it does mean there are likely to be times when it's quiet, if that demographic isn't visiting the park. It does also make the park feel smaller, because there will be areas that some groups don't ever visit, because it isn't for them. On the other hand, you don't want groups of thrill seekers charging through an area full of small kids. There's a delicate balance to get right.

Aside from the fairly short Dragonflier roller coaster (1,486ft), there are four standard kids rides and a pirate ship themed as a leaf. I suspect a relatively small percentage of the $37 million budget went on the rides, and most of it went on the infrastructure and setting.

I estimate that the combined throughput of all six rides would be under 2,000 guests an hour. Dragonflier only had one train with 20 seats. As with other similar Vekoma family coasters it uses the station track as the brake run to stop the train. This makes the coaster more compact and cheaper to build, as you've saved on the cost of a separate brake run, a second train and a storage shed, however it does give the ride a low throughput. An extra hourly capacity across all of your rides of around 1,800 isn't bad for a single year, but clearly the rides weren't the only part of Wildwood Grove that was helping to raise the park's capacity.

The $37 million price tag is very high for a children's area. That reflects the quality of the theming. A lot of the signage is 3D and they've used scenic artists rather than cheaper vinyls. Many of the fences are themed and they've used materials from the local area. The queuelines have fans for the summer and heaters for the winter. Because Wildwood Grove is unique to Dollywood, there were more design costs compared to a 'cookie cutter' children's area. Parks in the US and Europe have generally reached the limits of their footprint, meaning that new areas re-use existing paths and facilities. Wildwood

---

312   Wildwood Grove – Pete Owens interview Dollywood, Coaster Force Youtube channel, https://www.youtube.com/watch?v=C14wCrjVKn0

Grove expanded the park's footprint onto fresh land. This increased the cost, because it wasn't re-using any existing infrastructure. It also reflects a significant investment in flattening the land. While a rugged terrain can make an area more interesting, they presumably wanted it to be easy to navigate with pushchairs, wheelchairs and young children.

Dollywood has gradually increased their capacity as they've started to feel too busy, although they've also used a succession of events to spread their attendance more evenly through the year, including: The Festival of Nations, the Flower and Food Festival, Harvest Festival (Halloween) and Smoky Mountain Christmas. At some parks events are organsied by the entertainments team. At Dollywood they've got a dedicated events team who presumably work in conjunction with the entertainments team. Their events team has six full time members, but there can be up to 100 workers rigging events up and taking them down[313]. Events aren't an afterthought, but a core part of their business plan.

Judging from interviews, they've grown in a fairly conservative way since their opening in 1961. They haven't splurged out on new rides and areas in a build it and they will come mentality. They've grown fairly slowly, but steadily, often adding new attractions as much in response to gains in attendance, as to generate them. Adding lots of rides quickly can work in an underserved market, but in mature markets like Western Europe or the United States, adding too many rides too quickly tends to increase your costs quicker than the revenue, leaving a park unprofitable. This partly explains why Six Flags accumulated so much debt, taking over parks and rapidly expanding them. Because Dollywood is co-owned by singer Dolly Parton and family owned Herschend Entertainment, they're able to plan further ahead than many of the corporate parks. Their developments aren't necessarily as focused around branding and marketing as some other parks. Instead they're able take a more holistic view, looking at how a development like Wildwood Grove affects the broader guest experience.

In the theme park industry, it isn't easy to be both commercially successful and to receive strong guest feedback, but Dollywood has consistently achieved both of those. In 2019 Trip Advisor's algorithm ranked it as the 13th best theme park in the world[314] and in 2010 it had received the Applause Award, recognising it as one of the most admired theme parks by the industry. Dollywood gets strong guest feedback, because they're able to keep their wait times reasonable and prevent the park from feeling unpleasantly crowded. But they're able to remain profitable by growing carefully and keeping a good ratio of rides to guests. This makes them a good park to study, for those struggling to find the right balance.

There is a challenge here for parks. We've established that if your queues become too long, like at Geauga Lake, then that lowers guest satisfaction and

313   Behind the scenes with Dollywood's special events team, Dollywood Youtube channel, https://www.youtube.com/watch?v=2S343aVKW0E

314   Top 25 amusement parks – world, Trip Advisor, https://www.tripadvisor.co.uk/TravelersChoice-Attractions-cAmusementParks-g1

stifles growth. We've also established that part of the success of Dollywood is making sure that they don't grow too much. If a park is too large and has too many rides for the visitors you're getting, then your expenses outstrip your income and you haven't got a viable business. However, it's also a well-known fact in the industry that you need to keep on providing new experiences for your guests, otherwise the experience becomes stale. Dollywood continues providing new experiences partly by running regular events and shows that can be changed. Show type attractions such as 4D cinemas and simulators can lend themselves to new offerings. Parks can also keep their experiences fresh by re-theming attractions and 'plussing' attractions, which means taking what's already there and making it better, for example adding a new tunnel to a roller coaster or upgrading animatronics with more sophisticated ones.

Thank you so much to Wes Ramey for his support with this chapter. Wes is the public relations manager at Dollywood.

Park under the spotlight: Hong Kong Disneyland

We've looked at Geauga Lake and Six Flags to see what happens when visitors rise beyond what a park can handle. We've compared this to Paultons Park and Island of Adventure to understand when a park's attendance can suddenly leap up without the guest satisfaction falling. We've gone back in time at Coney Island to discover how parks handled large crowds in the early days of the industry. We've visited Dollywood to find out how a major regional park balances its capacity and attendance. This allows Dollywood to maintain its strong guest feedback, in a way that's financially viable. So far, this section hasn't considered Disney. The Walt Disney Company has been perfecting the art of managing huge crowds since 1955. This makes them a master of their trade.

Compared to most parks, there is a lot of information about how Hong Kong Disneyland's capacity has grown since the park opened in 2005. I can't be completely sure that all the statistics are accurate, but readers can dig into my sources. They sound plausible and are the most reliable information available, taken from the park itself, trade associations and mainstream newspapers. They give us a rough idea of how the park has developed and grown its capacity. Hong Kong Disneyland is a particularly good park to research: partly because it's majority owned by the Hong Kong government and partly because its capacity is set by the Food and Environmental Hygiene Department[315], rather than the park itself. These two factors mean there's more transparency than there is for most parks. It's a fun story about a park's growth, rising attendance and capacity, as well as something that will practically help you run a theme park.

I'm going to include a lot of dates, statistics about attendance and capacity, and names of rides that were added. For those less familiar with the park, it

---

315   Disney ups intake for the New Year, Carrie Chan, The
Standard, http://thestandard.com.hk/news_detail.asp?pp_cat=11&art_
id=34507&sid=11427047&con_type=1&d_str=20061220&sear_year=2006

could be confusing. For this reason, I will give a narrative about the park's growth, and then finish with a table summarising the information. If people get confused by all the figures, feel free to skip forward to the table. Once we've followed the growth of Hong Kong Disneyland from 2005-2020, we'll compared their capacity to Disney's other Magic Kingdom style parks. Before we start looking at Hong Kong Disneyland's capacity, I want to spend a few paragraphs looking at the origins of the resort.

Hong Kong Disneyland was Disney's fifth resort, after Anaheim (California), Orlando (Florida), Tokyo (Japan) and Paris (France). It was their second resort in Asia, and the first in the Chinese market. Hong Kong currently has a population of 7,482,000 (2018 figure), while China has a population of 1,427,647,786 (2018 figure). Hong Kong Disneyland would therefore bring a Disney resort to the massive Chinese market. At the time China had a young theme park market, a rapidly growing economy and a rising middle class. There was a big opportunity for the theme industry to grow here, and Hong Kong wanted to tap into that. Hong Kong itself already had the well-established Ocean Park, which opened in 1977. They hoped that a Disney park would bring in more people from further afield.

The Chinese government had been relaxing the rules about foreign businesses and brands moving into China, meaning that there was a huge opportunity for Disney to grow in this market, both with its theme parks, but also with its films and other properties. Arguably Disney was already close to saturating the European and North American market, so China offered Disney their best opportunity for growth.

Disneyland Hong Kong was built and owned as a partnership between the Walt Disney Company and the Hong Kong government. This arrangement is more curious when you realise that Hong Kong is characterised by low taxes and low public spending. The low taxes encouraged companies to locate their headquarters there. In 2016 the public sector accounted for less than 10% of the economy[316]. Yet the government owned one of Hong Kong's theme parks (Ocean Park) and provided most of the capital for the other. Why did the Hong Kong government want to finance Hong Kong Disneyland?

Hong Kong has very little land for farming and few natural resources. This means that the economy is heavily focused on a few sectors. It has the 7th largest container port in the world and various financial services including insurance and banking. A lot of people visited from mainland China for the shopping malls, although recently these have been threatened by online shopping[317]. In the late nineties the Hong Kong government was keen to diversify their economy. This would spread the risk. For the Disney Company, Hong Kong Disneyland was an opportunity to dominate the Chinese market and introduce people to their brands and characters. For the Hong Kong

---

316   Hong Kong as a service economy, Hong Kong government report, https://www.gov.hk/en/about/abouthk/factsheets/docs/service_economy.pdf

317   No more only shopping: Hong Kong to diversify tourism offerings for long-term growth, Simon Chung, Kwun Tong, SCMP, https://www.scmp.com/comment/letters/article/2135478/no-more-only-shopping-hong-kong-has-diversify-tourism-offerings

government, it was a chance to diversify their economy into tourism, including for families and international tourists from China, but also from other parts of Asia and the world. China's economy has been tremendously successful over the last twenty years, but the Hong Kong government wanted to make their economy less dependent on importing and exporting goods to and from mainland China. As part of this diversification scheme, in 2003 they introduced the 'individual visit scheme', making it easier for people from mainland China to visit Hong Kong. In 2005 Hong Kong Disneyland opened.

Hong Kong is mountainous with the flatter areas being very densely populated. Disneyland used land reclaimed from the sea, making it a particularly expensive project to develop. Michael Eisner was CEO of Disney from 1984-2005, so this came right at the end of his tenure. It had been a period of exceptional growth for the company, fueled by a combination of rising ticket prices at the parks, a focus on thrill rides, the success of Disney's Cruise Line, releasing their back catalogue of animations on video and creating new blockbusters like The Little Mermaid, Aladdin and The Lion King. Towards the end of Eisner's tenure, their films had been less commercially successful, and they lost ground to rivals including Pixar and Dreamworks. Eisner was very good at using the Disney brands to create synergy between the different areas of the business. Hong Kong Disneyland helped to seal Disney's place as a global brand.

When the resort opened in 2005 their capacity was 28,000 guests. The park attracted 5.2 million guests in its first year[318]. This means an average of 14,247 guests a day – about half the park's capacity, which was below their expectations. Most parks would be very happy if they were averaging about 50% of their capacity each day. Why did Disney have such high expectations for their Hong Kong park? Disney parks typically have a high level of public funding, either directly into the park, who through improvements to the transport and infrastructure around it. Cynics might wonder whether Disney can be overly ambitious with their projections, partly to encourage governments to be generous with their support. However, there's no evidence to suggest that, and over the years Disney parks have been remarkably successful. A year after opening Hong Kong Disneyland increased its capacity to 34,000 and their attendance dropped to around 4 million. That's an average of 10,960 visitors a day, meaning they used about 30% of the park's capacity on an average day. If Disney were disappointed with the park's first year, they must have been more disappointed with the second.

I'm going to draw a comparison between Hong Kong Disney and Alton Towers, a park I used to work at. Hong Kong Disney's 28,000 capacity was similar to what Alton Towers (UK) had at the time, although Alton Towers was seasonal, had shorter opening hours and its attendance is bunched up over fewer days. Alton Towers has generally been considered the United Kingdom's biggest theme park. The Themed Entertainment Association suggests its attendance has recently been overtaken by Legoland Windsor,

---

318   Hong Kong Disney crowds disappoint for second year, Reuters, https://www.reuters.com/article/idINIndia-31029920071218

although other sources dispute that". It's set in about 500 acres of park land with a gothic mansion at its centre. It features 10 roller coasters, including the inverted coaster Nemesis, the vertical drop coaster Oblivion and the 14 inversion Smiler. It has several non-coaster attractions including Duel - a shooting ride, and Hex - a themed experience. Aside from the theme park is a water park and a considerable range of accommodation.

For Hong Kong Disneyland to open with just 10 rides, but a similar capacity to the well-established Alton Towers, can therefore seem like a curious statistic. It might also seem odd that a Disney resort would open with a similar capacity to a regional park like Alton Towers, although in the course of the year it would attract double the visitors. Compared to Alton Towers, Hong Kong Disneyland were able to spread their visitors more evenly through the year.

The only real E Ticket (headline) rides were Space Mountain and The Jungle Cruise. There was also a Buzz Lightyear's interactive omnimover (a ride consisting of a chain of vehicles in a continuous loop), a Winnie the Pooh dark ride, Mickey's Philarmagic 4D cinema (a 4D cinema has 3D glasses and physical effects like wind and water) and the Disneyland railroad, plus a few roundabouts (Cinderella Carousel, Dumbo the Flying Elephant, Mad Hatter Tea Cups, Orbitron). There was a Tarzan's Treehouse walk through, various meet and greets and two live shows (The Lion King and The Golden Mickeys musical). They had very ambitious projections for a park with only 10 rides, including one roller coaster, two modest dark rides and no water rides.

In this section we're going to explore several questions:

- How did they achieve such a high capacity relative to the number of attractions?
- How did they achieve such a high attendance relative to the capacity?
- Why was this still not enough to make the resort profitable?
- Were Disney's projections realistic?
- Why did nearby Ocean Park get more visitors, and to what extent were queues a factor?
- How has the park developed since it opened?

Some fans felt that 10 rides simply weren't enough for a park. They were also disappointed that all the attractions were copies of rides at other Disney parks, and it had the smallest castle of all the Magic Kingdoms, except the original. This became a symbol of the park's relatively low budget, and was eventually corrected in 2020 when the castle was significantly expanded. According to The Imagineering Story[319], the park was originally going to only have a façade of the castle front, but after California Adventure (opened 2001) and the Disney Studios in Paris (opened 2002) were criticised for feeling cheap, they increased the budget for Hong Kong Disneyland.

At the end of 2006 they put in extra seating, dining and supporting facilities which gained them permission to increase the park's capacity to 34,000,

---

319   Official Disney documentary on Disney Plus

helping them to take advantage of the big rush of people wanting to visit for Lunar New Year in February. Earlier in 2006 (July) they had also added Autopia, Stitch Encounter and UFO Zone. Stitch Encounter was a digital puppetry attraction where guests interact with CGI characters, like Monster Inc Laugh Floor and Turtle Talk with Crush (at Disney World, Orlando). It's different to the Stitch's Great Escape attraction in Magic Kingdom. The UFO Zone was a little water themed play area. According to Jim Hill Media, Autopia wasn't originally going to open so soon - just 10 months after the park. The plan was for a more elaborate version to open further down the road themed to Pixar's Cars film[320]. However, before Hong Kong Disneyland even opened it was being criticised for having too few attractions, so they bought forward the opening date for Autopia, but produced something simpler on a lower budget. The new rides undoubtedly helped to increase the park's capacity. Autopia was the main attraction in the expansion and that had a theoretical throughput of 1,600 guests an hour[321]. To increase the park's capacity by 6,000 with these upgrades was hugely ambitious.

Both Hong Kong Disneyland and Disneyland Paris had rides quickly rushed through the development process shortly after the parks opened; Autopia (Hong Kong) and Indiana Jones and the Temple of Peril (Paris). But they were for different purposes. One was to boost a low capacity and because people felt there wasn't enough to do. The other was partly to increase the park's offering, but also specifically to target a more thrill inspired audience. We talked in more detail about Indiana Jones and the Temple of Peril in the section on redistributing crowds between days and 'The problem with Disneyland Paris'.

In 2008 Hong Kong Disneyland increased their capacity again when they added a version of It's a Small World. This is one of the most iconic Disney rides, based on the ride Disney originally planned for the 1964 World's Fair. While it didn't solve all the park's problems, it did mean it now had a major dark ride. With the overall ride count being boosted to 16 (including round-abouts and a 4D cinema) it was starting to feel more like a complete park. The TEA (Themed Entertainment Association) estimates that in 2008 Hong Kong Disneyland had a 7.9% increase in visitors to 4.5 million, although that was still behind the 5.2 million they got in their opening year and fewer than the 5,030,000 visitors that nearby Ocean Park got[322]. According to Hong Kong Extras, after the 2008 additions the park's capacity rose by another 3,000 to 37,000[323]. This meant there were getting an average of around 12,330 guests a day – still about one third of the park's capacity. Since 2006 their attendance

---

320   Autopia on the road to Hong Kong Disneyland, Jim Hill, Jim Hill Media, http://jimhillmedia.com/editor_in_chief1/b/jim_hill/archive/2004/10/25/484.aspx

321   Disneyland Paris ride capacity list, Discovery Arcade, Medium, https://medium.com/@DiscoveryArcade/disneyland-paris-ride-capacity-list-192800281551

322   2008 attraction attendance report, Themed Entertainment Association, http://www.teaconnect.org/images/files/TEA_23_503031_140617.pdf

323   Hong Kong Disneyland, Hong Kong Extras, http://www.hongkongextras.com/_hong_kong_disneyland.html

has roughly expanded in line with their capacity, so on average the park still uses about a third of its capacity each day.

Although Hong Kong Disneyland quickly boosted their capacity, their first year's attendance wasn't surpassed until 2011 (based on figures from the Themed Entertainment Association). It isn't unusual for a new park to have a 'difficult second season', as often a new park has a certain amount of pent up demand and people visiting out of curiosity. However, it took a while and the addition of Autopia, It's a Small World and Toy Story Land for attendance to recover. In contrast, Hong Kong's original theme park, Ocean Park (opened in 1977), repeatedly drew more visitors than the Disney park nearby. Ocean Park had started as a botanic garden, petting zoo and a few rides, but expanded into a major marine park. It's about a 35km drive from Hong Kong Disneyland to Ocean Park. Here is a table comparing the attendance at Hong Kong Disneyland and Ocean Park.

Year	Hong Kong Disneyland	Ocean Park
2006	5,200,000	4,280,000
2007	4,150,000	4,920,000
2008	4,500,000	5,030,000
2009	4,600,000	4,800,000
2010	5,200,000	5,100,000
2011	5,900,000	6,955,000

The story of Hong Kong Disneyland vs Ocean Park is a fascinating one. Some people expected Ocean Park to close when Disneyland opened nearby, but instead Ocean Park managed to grow its attendance and for a time it was the only case where a Disney park was attracting fewer visitors than a nearby rival. Why did Ocean Park outperform Disneyland?

There are no doubt numerous factors. Despite their international appeal, Disney parks typically rely on local annual passholders visiting frequently to boost attendance. Hong Kong Disneyland lacked the attractions to encourage many people to buy annual passes[324]. In contrast Ocean Park had a much higher attraction count. The Hong Kong currency is tied closely to the US dollar, and as that rose it became more expensive for visitors from mainland China to visit[325]. This affected Disneyland more, because Disneyland was more expensive than Ocean Park. Hong Kong Disneyland's responses to the press were run past Disney's HQ in America, whereas Ocean Park's CEO appeared in person for interviews and developed a strong relationship with the media[326]. Ocean Park started forming packages with local hotels, ready to compete with Disney for the tourist dollars[327]. Ocean Park began focusing more on conservation. They stopped selling shark fin soup, added a

---

324   Hong Kong Disneyland turns a profit, Brooks Barnes, New York Times

325   Hong Kong Disneyland celebrates its birthday as analysts worry about its future, Robert Niles, Theme Park Insider.

326   Disney comes to China, Sheridan Prasso, Fortune Magazine

327   Approach of a new era, Doug Meigs, April 2011, Fun World Magazine, IAAPA

conservation message to their displays and set up a conservation fund. One dollar from each ticket sold went to the fund, and guests could scan their ticket on machines inside the park to decide which project their dollar was spent on.

It also seems that some visitors were put off coming back to Disneyland by the crowding when the park opened. In contrast Ocean Park put in a plan based around managing queues. Ocean Park's CEO Tom Mehrmann says, "I wanted to offer two attractions per guest, per an hour at peak times. We were offering less than one, so wait times were longer than they should have been"[328].

In another interview he told Park World, "Before the MRP [Master Redevelopment Plan] we were not even offering one entertainment unit per guest per hour during peak periods; we were offering maybe 0.7. That meant guests were waiting between an hour and maybe two hours for attractions during peak conditions. We wanted to take that metric to a different level and increase our instantaneous capacity in the park to 36,000 people who, even under the most extreme conditions, could enjoy two entertainment units per hour. This became a critical driver for us as we chose new attractions and examined capacities and throughput. I can say very confidently we are now looking at about 80,000 entertainment units per hour"[329]. In 2020 Ocean Park listed their 'normal' capacity as 36,000, indicating that they had reached their goal[330]. During the Coronavirus pandemic, their capacity was reduced by 50%.

Part of this plan to increase their capacity involved big events at Halloween, Christmas and Chinese New Year[331]. It also involved putting in more rides, which Ocean Park could do a lot more cheaply than Disney, but still offer something special by using the park's mountainside setting. They extended the park's hours and built up a strong evening trade, partly by bringing the park's dining in house and offering higher quality restaurants[332]. In 2011 they introduced the night show Symbio. It used a 360-degree water screen with projection, LED fountains, flame jets and pyrotechnics.

Three more areas were added to Disneyland in quick succession in 2011, 2012 and 2013. Toy Story Land came first, which contained several meet and greets and three flat rides. Toy Story Lands have been added to the Walt Disney Studios in Paris (2010), Hong Kong Disneyland (2011) and Shanghai Disneyland (2018). By Disney standards they are generally seen as cheap areas that can be added to parks quickly when there's a need to bulk the park out with more attractions. The year Toy Story Land opened in Paris the visitors fell by

328   Tom Mehrmann interview, Park Scope podcast, http://www.parks-cope.net/2017/05/immersive-irony-experience-theme-park.html

329   Transforming Ocean Park, September 2012, Park World Magazine

330   Hong Kong Disneyland and Ocean Park set to re-open, Alice Sarsfield-Hall, Bloo Loop, https://blooloop.com/news/hong-kong-disneyland-and-ocean-park-reopen/

331   Ocean Park, Paul Wiseman, USA Today

332   Transforming Ocean Park, September 2012, Park World Magazine

2.6% to 4.5 million[333]. In contrast, the year it opened at Hong Kong Disneyland visitors rose by 13.5% to 5.9 million[334]. When it opened in Shanghai it was the park's first expansion and lifted attendance by 7.3% to 11,800,000[335].

Why did almost exactly the same area have two completely different effects on the resorts in Paris and Hong Kong? Both parks already had a copy of Buzz Lightyear Lazar Blast, so neither area was the first Toy Story attraction at their resort. I think it shows that there are a lot of factors affecting attendance, including the economy, the weather, how high-profile Disney's films are that year and what competing parks do. The Paris resort was bigger by the point it added Toy Story Land, probably making it harder to push up the attendance, as each addition adds a relatively small percentage to the resort. Europe is generally a more mature theme park market, although Hong Kong Disneyland does compete with the well-established Ocean Park. It is fascinating though to see the different effect that three almost identical attractions have had on different parks.

In 2012 they opened Grizzly Gulch, a smaller version of other Frontierlands, with just one ride. Big Grizzly Mountain Runaway Mine Cars was a cross between Big Thunder Mountain and Expedition Everest. It was the park's first unique ride. This was the first time that Disney fans around the world started to dream of visiting. This year the resort had a marginally bigger 13.6% attendance increase to 6,700,000. In 2013 they added the third new area in as many years, Mystic Point. The area is set in the rainforest of Papua New Guinea and is home to one ride, Mystic Manor. Mystic Manor is a trackless dark ride that has often be compared to the Haunted Mansion rides at other Disneylands. Attendance rose once again. This time by 10.4% to 7,400,000336. This worked out at an average of 20,274 guests a day.

These new areas increased the park's capacity from 37,000 to 42,000. An increase of 5,000 visitors. Or an increase of 14,000 over the park's original capacity when it opened in 2005. On an average day Hong Kong Disneyland was using 48% of its capacity. The park was using more of their capacity than at any point since their first year and far more than most theme parks in the world, including Parc Disneyland Paris. In 2012 they recorded their first profit – a modest $14.06 million[337].

The park's plan was to carry on increasing the park's capacity to 50,000 by 2020[338]. According to Disney's projections, this would be enough capacity for

333   2010 Themed Index, Themed Entertainment Association, http://www.teaconnect.org/images/files/TEA_25_134960_140617.pdf

334   2011 Themed Index, Themed Entertainment Association, http://www.teaconnect.org/images/files/TEA_26_543179_140617.pdf

335   2018 Themed Index, Themed Entertainment Association, https://aecom.com/content/wp-content/uploads/2019/05/Theme-Index-2018-5-1.pdf

336   2013 Themed Index, Themed Entertainment Association, http://www.teaconnect.org/images/files/TEA_28_915227_140617.pdf

337   Hong Kong Disneyland turns a profit for first time, AFP, Gulf News, https://gulfnews.com/business/tourism/hong-kong-disneyland-turns-a-profit-for-first-time-1.1148073#

338   Hong Kong Disneyland, The Disney Fandom Wiki, https://disney.fandom.com/wiki/Hong_Kong_Disneyland

them to attract 10 million guests a year, if the demand was there. 10 million guests a year would work out as an average of 27,400 guests a day, although they wouldn't be distributed evenly across all the days in the year. It would mean that on average the resort would be using 55% of its capacity each day. This would be higher than any point in the resort's history, including its first year when the park was criticised for being too busy and in 2012 after three consecutive years of double-digit growth. It would be substantially higher than Parc Disneyland Paris, but marginally lower than Tokyo Disney and lower than their American parks. We've questioned whether Hard Rock Park's projections were realistic. One has to ask the same questions about Hong Kong Disneyland.

By 2020 The Park Database estimated that Hong Kong Disneyland's capacity was 54,000[339] - slightly more than they'd announced in their development plan. Park Database estimates capacities for hundreds of theme parks around the world. Unsurprisingly their figures look more accurate for larger parks than for some of the smaller ones. For the few parks I've worked at their figures are a bit off, but not wildly so. It is hard researching capacities for parks, because so few of them release official figures and there are so many variables that affect a park's capacity. I suspect 48,000 – 50,000 would have been a fair assessment of the park's capacity in 2020, pandemic aside.

In theory 10 million guests a year for a park that's open every day and has a capacity of 50,000 sounds ambitious, but possible, assuming the demand if there. To boost capacity from the 42,000 when Mystic Point was added, they opened Fairy Tale Forest in 2015. This was a garden with animatronic sets depicting fairy tales. It was a Disneyfied version of the Fairy Tale Forest at Efteling (Netherlands) and featured gardens with Tangled, Snow White, Beauty and the Beast, Cinderella and The Little Mermaid. It's the sort attraction that guests can just wander in and out of while they're waiting for their next Fast Pass slot. In 2017 the first phase of a new Marvel area opened with The Iron Man Experience, a ride similar to the Star Tours simulators. In 2019 they opened the second attraction in the area, Ant Man and the Wasp: Nano Battle. This is was a re-theme of their Buzz Lightyear ride. At this point they theoretically had the capacity they needed for 10 million guests a year, although they weren't yet hitting this figure, partly because attendance dropped by 10.3% the year that Shanghai Disney opened and they lost some of their visitors from mainland China[340].

Aside from adding extra rides, Hong Kong Disney has looked at other tricks to increase their capacity. At a charity event (4th September 2005) before the park opened, wait times for rides went up to two hours and wait times for food reached 45 minutes. The Hong Kong government had a 57%

339   Hong Kong Disneyland, The Park Database, https://www.theparkdb.com//results/in/name/739

340   2016 Themed Index, Themed Entertainment Association, http://www.teaconnect.org/images/files/TEA_235_103719_170601.pdf

stake in the company[341]. This was later reduced to 52%, when Disney injected more money into the business to help fund the park's expansion.[342]. The government wanted Disney to reduce the park's capacity, but Disney declined. A maximum capacity had been set by the Food and Environmental Hygiene Department, but they were purely looking at the safety. The politicians wanted to limit the capacity further to improve the guest experience. Disney balked at this. Although the government had a 57% share in the resort, their contract gave Disney the power to make executive decisions about how things were managed.

Disney knew what capacity they needed to make the business profitable. It's worth noting that while two-hour queues might sound bad to some people, it isn't out of line with what other major theme parks get on a peak day. It was far behind some of the most extreme queues we've heard about, such as the 7 hour wait to ride Slinky Dog Dash at Hollywood Studios on opening day[343], and a similar 7 queue for Escape from Gringotts at Universal Studios Florida on opening day[344]. Although some fans have suggested that 5 hours would have been a more accurate estimate for Gringotts.

Hong Kong Disneyland had 17 rehearsal days before the official opening, where they could test the park with different crowd levels, and make sure the staff had developed a certain level of competency before they were hit with large crowds buying full price tickets[345]. It's normal for Disney to spend a lot of time testing and soft opening new parks and attractions, rather than just throwing open the gates and seeing what happens.

Following negative publicity from the charity day, Disney spokesperson Esther Wong said she was, "confident we [Disney] can manage peak day attendance in the future and have designed our marketing and sales plan to manage attendance at Hong Kong Disneyland throughout the year."[346] In other words, she didn't think it would hit capacity very often. Nonetheless, for the park's opening day on 12th September 2005 they did only use half the

---

341   Business: the economy Disney comes to Hong Kong, BBC News, http://news.bbc.co.uk/1/hi/business/502371.stm

342   Disney will add new attractions in expansion of Hong Kong Park, China Daily, https://www.chinadaily.com.cn/bw/2009-11/09/content_8930180.htm - the expansion included Toy Story Land, Grizzly Gulch and Mystic Point.

343   Photos: Toy Storyland reaches capacity on opening day, WDW Magic, https://www.wdwmagic.com/attractions/toy-story-land/news/30jun2018-photos---toy-story-land-reaches-capacity-on-opening-day.htm

344   Harry Potter Escape from Gringotts ride has 7.5 hour wait, NBC News, https://www.nbcnews.com/business/travel/new-harry-potter-escape-gringotts-ride-has-7-5-hour-n151641

345   A trial run finds Hong Kong Disneyland much too popular for its modest size, Keith Bradsher, The New York Times, https://www.nytimes.com/2005/09/08/business/media/a-trial-run-finds-hong-kong-disneyland-much-too-popular-for.html

346   HK Disneyland won't cut maximum capacity, China Daily, http://www.chinadaily.com.cn/english/doc/2005-09/08/content_476154.htm

park's capacity and capped it at around 15,000 guests[347]. Incidentally, this was similar to the number of people invited to the opening of the original Disneyland in 1955, except that then, 30,000 people turned up, half of them with counterfeit tickets.

Hopefully I've managed to chart how the park's capacity grew from 28,000 in its opening year to around 50,000 in 2020. There wasn't anything particularly surprising about it. They added more rides, and that increased their capacity. It doesn't explain why the resort has been seen as a commercial failure.

In 2019 Hong Kong Disneyland attracted 5,695,000 visitors. Most parks could only dream of attracting so many people, so why was it such a problem for Disney? Hong Kong Disneyland had hoped to attract 10 million visitors a year by 2020, so they were far short of their target. They were only getting about 500,000 visitors more than in their first year, despite investing over a billion dollars in expanding the park. This investment was split between the Walt Disney Company and the Hong Kong government, and Disney has carried on earning royalties and management fees despite the resort losing money[348]. We can learn more about the problem by comparing Hong Kong's two parks.

Park	2019 attendance	2019 average daily attendance	2019 park capacity	Average attendance as a % of capacity
Hong Kong Disneyland	5,695,000	15,603	48,000	32.5%
Ocean Park	5,700,000	15,616	36,000	43%

In terms of the last box, there is no magic percentage that a park has to pass to be viable. Although Disney parks are unusually expensive to visit, they are also particularly costly to operate because of their long opening hours, high staffing levels, big nighttime shows and international advertising campaigns. Despite the loses and the disappointing returns on their investments, the park is currently building an Arendelle area themed to Frozen, which will have a boat ride and a sleigh ride roller coaster. There are also plans for an E ticket thrill ride in the Marvel area[349]. However, the Hong Kong government has removed the resort's option to build on a piece of land set aside for a second park[350]. At the time of writing it's not clear what the land will be used for instead.

347   Disneyland opens in Hong Kong, Don Lee, Los Angeles Times, https://www.latimes.com/archives/la-xpm-2005-sep-13-fi-disney13-story.html

348   Hongkongers will have to pay HK$5.45 billion for major expansion of Disneyland, Nikki Sun, South China Morning Post, https://www.scmp.com/news/hong-kong/economy/article/2092336/hongkongers-will-have-pay-hk545-billion-disneyland-facelift

349   Marvel – Frozen – and castle expansion at Hong Kong Disneyland, Tom Bricker, Disney Tourist Blog, https://www.disneytouristblog.com/new-castle-frozen-land-marvel-land-hong-kong-disneyland/

350   No new theme park for Hong Kong Disneyland, Robert Niles, Theme Park Insider, https://www.themeparkinsider.com/flume/202009/7741/

Hong Kong Disneyland had an exceptional first season caused by the pent-up demand and the media attention that comes with a new park. Most parks do find that their attendance falls after the first season, although there have been exceptions to that. Hong Kong Disneyland lost over 20% of their visitors, which may have been a particularly bad fall caused by lackluster reviews. From the second season onwards, attendance has mostly grown proportionately to the park's capacity. It grew a little faster 2011-2013 when they added a new area each year. Since then, the attendance dropped in 2016 when Shanghai Disneyland opened and it dropped again in 2019, possibly caused by the riots following the government's controversial 'extradition bill'. The questions the government and Disney had to ask themselves were:

- If they carry on growing the resort, will attendance carry on growing proportionately to the capacity?
- If they did lose visitors to Shanghai Disneyland, could they win them back?
- If the attendance carries on rising at about 30%-35% of capacity, is that enough to justify the investment?

As we saw with Holiday World, it isn't economical to keep on expanding your capacity when the attendance is either flat or going up at a much lower rate than your capex (capital expenditure) and opex (operating expenditure). The decision to cancel plans for a second park wasn't entirely commercial. The government also felt their contract with Disney was unfair, as it meant that Disney could make profits from its management services and royalties while the government just shouldered a loss. Some people thought it was unfair that Disney went ahead with Shanghai Disneyland when Hong Kong Disneyland wasn't profitable.

If the resort does stop expanding, the challenge will be to keep on offering something fresh and new. There are various options for doing this including new events, changing live entertainment (shows and parades), 'plussing' (upgrading) existing attractions, re-theming attractions and demolishing rides to free up space for new developments.

Every park is different, so we must be cautious about using generalisations. Very broadly, if a park is at less than 25% capacity, I wouldn't expect there to be much in the way of queues. Although irregularities might still cause them, for example if everyone rushes to an indoor attraction when it rains, or several big rides close due to high winds. Or perhaps a ride near a show gets deluged with guests when they all flood out the theatre, or one ride gets a big surge in demand when another one breaks down. If it's normal for a park to get much in the way of queues when it's at less than 25% capacity, then something's wrong. You've either been overly ambitious with your capacity, or there's some kind of significant design flaw in your attraction.

Less than 15% capacity and the atmosphere will start to decline. It's always worth knowing what your break-even point is, once you factor in the cost of staff, electricity and the wear on the rides. It's impossible to calculate an exact figure, as it depends on things like what percentage of guests are using promotions, annual passes, buying food etc. Some parks have high fixed costs (such as parks with animal areas) and relatively low variable costs, while other parks have much higher variable costs. I suspect for a lot of parks it's somewhere around the 7% mark. As a park you're often aiming for a sweet spot of around 50% - 60% capacity each day. This gives you enough guests to make a healthy profit and a strong atmosphere, but it doesn't cause too much stress to the guests or the staff.

Once a park goes over 25% of its capacity it's normal for queues to start forming. However, below 50% capacity and most people should feel that the queues are fairly reasonable. Once you go over 50% capacity guest satisfaction will start declining because of the waiting times and the number of complaints will increase, not just because there's more people to complain, but it'll go up exponentially because people are less happy. This exponential rise in the number of guest complaints can put pressure on the Guest Services. When a park's at less than 75% capacity queues should still be in the realms of what most of your staff and guests feel is reasonable. Once you go over 75% capacity, then that's when queuing can really start to spoil people's day. Successful parks are bound to have some days each year around big public holidays when their attendance goes over 75% of the capacity. However, if it's common issue, then your park has a capacity problem. You might want to actively discourage people from visiting on these really busy days, because in the long run it's not good for your business if people come and have a bad time.

If you're looking at putting on an event to shift attendance from a peak day to quieter day, a day where you're currently hitting around 30% of the park's capacity is often a good time to choose for a new event.

Although Disney didn't agree to lower Hong Kong Disneyland's original capacity, they did extend each day by an extra hour to give people more time to experience the park, and they introduced promotions to encourage more people to visit on quieter week days[351]. As we know, they also fast tracked Autopia through production so that they could extend Tomorrowland.

They didn't do Halloween in the first 2005 season, but in 2006 they introduced Disney Halloween Time to attract more visitors in October. It was a free event, rather than the hard ticket Mickey's Not so Scary Halloween Party. In 2007 the Disney Halloween Time was expanded with the Glow in the Dark Halloween Parade. Hong Kong has become the only Disney resort to feature Halloween scare mazes.

Hong Kong Disneyland had always had a firework show (Disney in the Stars) to encourage people to visit in the evenings. In 2014 they also introduced the Paint the Night Parade to give people another reason to visit later on in the day.

From a commercial standpoint, Hong Kong Disneyland has had a lot of financial problems, and a whole range of criticism from them serving shark

---

351   Innovation project management: methods - case studies – and tools for managing, Harold Kerzner p. 486.

fin soup, culling stray dogs who lived on the site before construction, poor working conditions and the small castle being a symbol of cost cutting. Before it opened the park had been politicised within the company. Critics of the then CEO Michael Eisner, including Walt's grandson Roy E Disney, saw Hong Kong Disney's small scale and lack of original attractions and innovation, as a sign that Eisner was taking Disney in the wrong direction. They thought he was cheapening the brand and trying to make a quick buck. There was talk of a hostile takeover from Comcast, which arguably could have destroyed the heart of the company. Many executives didn't want to be part of a big conglomerate, although ironically Disney's subsequent acquisitions of Pixar, Marvel, Lucas Film, The National Geographic Channel and Fox have made them that. Despite certain problems, the resort gave the Walt Disney Company a physical foothold in China. This was an important strategic step.

Despite all of these difficulties, the fact that Disney were able to achieve a 28,000 capacity with 10 rides, including 4 roundabouts, does tell us something about Disney's ability to move large quantities of people. If the visitors were distributed evenly between the rides, then that would be 2,800 guests per ride. Whether it's the efficiency of omnimovers (Buzz Lightyears Astro Blasters), of a large 4D cinema where guests enter and exit on each side of the theatre through a multitude of doors, or a roller coaster that you take your bags on and just has simple lapbars, we can see how fairly straightforward attractions are moving large volumes of people.

There isn't just one factor that gives the rides at Hong Kong and other Disney resorts their high hourly capacities. It's not just because they have staff at the entrance to each ride height checking, and don't height check in the station where it slows things down. It's not just because disabled guests often use the Fast Pass entrance, rather than entering from the exit where it slows things down. It's not just because Space Mountain can transfer trains on and off the track, so that disabled and elderly guests can spend longer loading without slowing down the flow of vehicles through the ride. It's all of these things and more.

Theme park fans around the world were disappointed that all of the rides at the opening in 2005 were copies of rides at other resorts, generally using relatively basic tried and tested technology. However, it did mean that the rides were relatively reliable. When you've only got 10 rides, if just one of them is unavailable due to a technical issue, then that's quite a problem. When Universal Studios Florida opened in 1990 it only had a few attractions, and three of those were so cutting edge they had a lot of downtime. Since then theme parks have been wary of having too many advanced rides in a new park. Although even by modern standards Hong Kong was quite conservative with its technology.

It also tells us something about how Disney is able to use Fast Pass and non-ride attractions, including a parade, fireworks show, two stage shows, a walk through, numerous shops and meet and greets, to keep at least a reasonable percentage of guests away from the rides. Disney might well have made mistakes, but Hong Kong was also a culmination of the company's expertise built up over half a century. There is a lot that other parks can learn from the resort's growth, its failures, but also its achievements.

There are perhaps two sides to the wonder of Hong Kong Disneyland. The first is how a park with so few attractions had such a high capacity and entertained over 5 million visitors in its first year. The second, is how a park with just 10 rides and over 5 million visitors in a year, still lost money. It took 7 years before the resort made its first profit, a rather modest $14 million[352]. Extending each day by an extra hour, 365 hours over the course of a year, had its cost. As did doing a discount of mid-week tickets. Disney aren't known for discounting and rely on strong 'price integrity'. But it can still seem remarkable that a park with so many visitors and so few rides can lose money.

Clearly a Disney park is a very expensive park to operate. They're open every day of the year for long hours. They have a daily fireworks show. They have a lot of staff. This includes a big entertainments team for the two live shows, numerous meet and greets and a parade. It also includes a big operations team with a lot of cleaners, and a large rides team. They always have a greeter at the entrance to each ride and someone manning all the merge points for Fast Pass. There might also be a batcher on the platform directing people to their seats. A ride at a Disney park could easily use several extra staff compared to a similar ride at a regional park. Hong Kong has a population of under 7.5 million, so Disneyland was always going to need to attract a lot of visitors from 'mainland China'. This meant a big advertising campaign. Just as Disneyland Paris sunk a lot of money into advertising all over Europe, Hong Kong Disney spent a lot of money on advertising to China.

Disneyland Hong Kong was its own company, and paid the Walt Disney Company a royalty of between 5% - 10% of revenue for using the Disney brands[353]. They also paid the Walt Disney Company a management fee, and had to pay Walt Disney Imagineering for any attraction they wanted. When you add up the royalties to Disney and tax, that's a significant percentage of their income. With Disneyland Paris and Hong Kong Disneyland we have learned that Disney parks are expensive to operate, maintain and market. Once Disney has taken their slice out of the revenue, there might not be any money left for the other investors (in this case the Hong Kong government) to take a profit. For managers studying Hong Kong Disneyland, there are certainly quite a few lessons for us to think about, in terms of how we manage and grow our own parks.

In the case of Wildwood Grove at Dollywood and Hong Kong Disneyland's initial offering, it's clear that there's more to a park's capacity than how many rides it's got and their combined hourly throughputs. In the case of Hong Kong Disneyland, it's also clear that a park's capacity isn't always a great indicator of what its annual attendance will be.

---

352   Hong Kong Disney ends seven year itch to make money,
Bernie Lo, CNBC, https://www.cnbc.com/id/100468535

353   For Disney, it's a small world after all, Paul r. La Monica, CNN Money,
https://money.cnn.com/2005/09/12/news/fortune500/hongkongdisney/

Year	Attractions	Park Capacity	Average Daily Attendance	Daily attendance as a percentage of capacity	Yearly Attendance
2005	Opening year	28,000	Partial year	Not applicable	Partial year
2006	Autopia/Stitch Encounter	28,000	14,247	51%	5,200,000
2007	-	34,000	11,370	34%	4,150,000
2008	It's a Small World	37,000	12,329	33%	4,500,000
2009	-	37,000	12,603	34%	4,600,000
2010	-	37,000	14,247	39%	5,200,000
2011	Toy Story Land	38,500	16,164	42%	5,900,000
2012	Mystic Point	40,000	18,356	46%	6,700,000
2013	Grizzly Gulch	42,000	20,274	48%	7,400,000
2014		Unknown	20,548	-	7,500,000
2015	Fairy Tale Forest	Unknown	18,630	-	6,800,000
2016		Unknown	16,712	-	6,100,000
2017	Iron Man Experience	Unknown	16,986	-	6,200,000
2018	Antman and the Wasp	48,000	18,356	38%	6,700,000

How does Hong Kong Disneyland compare to other Disney parks?

Let's compare the most recent figures to some of the other Disney parks. I will shortly provide a table summarising this information. I will explain my methodology first. All estimations of attendance are taken from the Themed Entertainment Association, and capacity figures use the most accurate I can find. For example, in the Coronavirus it was widely reported that Disneyland Shanghai was running at 30% of its 80,000 capacity[354]. All attendance figures are for 2018. I've chosen 2018, because in 2019 the attendance for Hong Kong Disneyland might have been distorted by protests against the 'fugitive offenders amendment bill'. This law allowed people to be extradited to Taiwan and mainland China. Critics, including human rights groups, feared that the new law would be used to stifle free speech and political opponents of China. The protests might explain why Hong Kong Disneyland's attendance dropped by 15% in 2019. However, Ocean Park's attendance only dropped by 1.7%, so there might have been another reason.

It is a little subjective what counts as a ride. For example, is a 4D cinema a ride or a show? Do walk through attractions like a maze count as a ride? I've been reasonably generous with what I've counted as a ride, although some attractions like upcharge shooting galleries and splash zones haven't been included.

---

354   Shanghai Disneyland to re-open on May 11th, Theme Park Insider, https://www.themeparkinsider.com/flume/202005/7433/

What counts as a headline ride is no doubt contentious, and I haven't been to every Disney resort, so I'm categorising attractions I haven't personally ridden. To give a rough idea, Pirates of the Caribbean, Star Tours, Haunted Mansion, Jungle Cruise and Big Thunder Mountain have all been counted as headline rides. Buzz Lightyear's Space Blast, Peter Pan's Flight and Journey of the Little Mermaid haven't been. Hopefully this will give a rough flavour of the parks.

Park	Annual attendance	Acres	Avg daily atten-dance	Daily atten-dance as % of capa-city	Number of rides	Number of head-line rides	Capacity
Hong Kong Disney	6,700,000	68	18,356	38%	21	6	48,000
Disne-yland Shanghai	11,800,000	100	32,329	40%	21	6	80,000
Parc Dis-neyland Paris	9,843,000	126	26,967	34%	25	7	80,000
Magic Kingdom	20,859,000	105	57,148	64%	32	8	90,000
Disney-land Park California	18,666,000	99	51,140	60%	37	13	85,000
Tokyo Disneyland	17,907,000	114	49,060	58%	30	9	85,000
Epcot	12,444,000	300	34,000	38%	15	5	90,000

Collecting capacities for Disney's American parks is challenging as Disney have never publicly released figures. During the coronavirus pandemic they talked about limiting parks initially to 25% capacity, but they didn't quantify this by the number of guests. In 2019 the Orange County Register (OCR) estimated that Disneyland (California) had a capacity of 75,000[355]. This estimation was given after Galaxy's Edge opened, but before Rise of the Resistance, the main ride in the area. Around the same time Las Vegas Weekly estimated 80,000[356]. The LA Times believes it was 80,000 before Galaxy's Edge opened[357]. In consultation with Touring Plan, the Orange County Register estimates a 90,000 guest capacity for Magic Kingdom[358]

---

355   Disneyland closes gates as holiday crowds fill the park, Brady Macdonald, OCR, https://www.ocregister.com/2019/12/27/disneyland-closes-gates-as-holiday-crowds-fill-the-park/

356   Disneyland fans: go now before you're forced out, Geoff Carter, Las Vegas Weekly, https://lasvegasweekly.com/ae/2019/jan/06/disneyland-star-wars-galaxys-edge/

357   Disneyland hits capacity – temporarily stops selling tickets,

358   What an attendance cap could mean for crowded Disney parks in the Cor-navirus era, Brady MacDonald, OCR, https://www.ocregister.com/2020/05/22/what-an-attendance-cap-could-mean-for-crowded-disney-parks-in-the-covid-19-era/

and this is generally echoed by other sources. Disneyland Paris seems to have more variance than others depending on the source. On the Disney Central Plaza forum people are pitching in with estimations between 60,000-90,000[359] while DLP Today suggests 85,000[360].

Interestingly, the best way to predict the capacity of a Disney park is by its acreage, rather than the number of rides or the number of headline rides. This might tell us that the capacities are set more by safety requirements rather than experiential requirements. Over time there has been a change in Disney's approach to designing areas. Disney's expansions have had a falling density of rides per acre, with more space being given over to paths, theming, landscaping and infrastructure. Before the Galaxy's Edge development, the original Disneyland had 35 rides in 85 acres. This includes Main Street which doesn't have any rides, aside from the railroad station. Galaxy's Edge had just two rides in 15 acres. If the whole of Disneyland had the same ratio of rides to space that Galaxy's Edge has, then Disneyland would have just 13 rides.

Disneyland has a particularly low capacity relative to the number of rides. This is mainly because the paths are relatively narrow and some of the facilities are quite small. It's also because Disneyland often has the original versions of rides which sometimes have lower throughputs than new versions, for example It's a Small World and Splash Mountain at Disneyland both have smaller boats.

We've already said quite a lot about Disneyland Hong Kong (opened 2005). Shanghai Disneyland (opened 2016) was both the next Disney resort and the next Disney park to be built. I expect it'll be a while before we see another Disney resort, if ever. Not least because of the coronavirus. The US and Europe are now both well covered, and another resort would cannibalise the parks they've already got. China might have the population to support another Disney resort, although Hong Kong Disneyland's attendance declined when Shanghai Disney opened. India has a large population, although its infrastructure has often seemed lacking to support a Disney sized project. South Americans often visit Disney World, which might put them off opening a park in Brazil, although the same could have been said of a European park. According to the TEA, in 2018 157,311,000 people visited a Disney park[361]. Worldometers says that the world's population is currently 7.8 billion. This meant that about 2% of the world's population visited a Disney park in 2018[362]. As the world's population continues expanding and economies like China and India grow, perhaps one day there will be demand for another Disney resort.

359   Quelle est la capacité maximum des parcs?, Disney Central Plaza, https://www.disneycentralplaza.com/t17404-quelle-est-la-capacite-maximum-des-parcs

360   Warning: Sunday 21st December will be full, DLP Today, https://forum.dlpguide.com/index.php?topic=11066.0

361   2018 Theme Index, TEA, https://aecom.com/content/wp-content/uploads/2019/05/Theme-Index-2018-5-1.pdf

362   Current world population, Worldometer, https://www.worldometers.info/world-population/

It's interesting that by my calculations Shanghai Disney and Hong Kong Disneyland have the same number of rides, but Shanghai has an extra 32,000 people in its capacity. These are reliable attendance figures as they've been officially released by the parks. Is this partly because the Food and Environmental Hygiene Department in Hong Kong has more stringent rules? How significant is it that that Disneyland Shanghai is roughly 32 acres bigger than Hong Kong Disneyland? Disneyland Shanghai has the largest hub of any Disney park at 11 acres. Called the Gardens of Imagination, this area features seven Chinese themed gardens. It also includes the Flying Dumbos and Fantasia Carousel – making it the only hub at a Magic Kingdom style park to include rides. There is also an amphitheater in front of the castle. This means that guests watching the nighttime show don't block the hub and Mickey Avenue (Shanghai's answer to Main Street), like they can at other resorts. Mickey Avenue itself is short and wide compared to the original Main Street and doesn't have any curbs. It's clearly been designed to more or less guarantee that it doesn't become a bottleneck. Likewise, the structure at the entrance to each area is really big with a very wide arch that spans the full length of the path. This means that that the path doesn't have to narrow at all, so there's no pinch point. Shanghai Disneyland was planned from the start with the kind of features that Project Stardust has retrospectively fitted into the original Disneyland (California).

Looking at the overall infrastructure for the different Disney parks, Disney have gradually geared them up to handle bigger crowds, with Hong Kong Disneyland being an exception. Perhaps that's partly because it's built on land reclaimed from the sea, making it one of the most expensive pieces of theme park real estate anywhere in the world. Disneyland Shanghai covers a similar footprint to the original park in California, despite having roughly half the number of attractions. Like Hong Kong Disneyland, the park has been designed with expansion in mind. Nonetheless, I wouldn't want to be there when the park's at capacity. It works out as about 3,810 guests for every ride. Even with Disney level throughputs, Fast Pass, a parade and a couple of shows, that's a 'tough crowd to handle'.

A group of theme park designers visited the park sooner after opening, and wrote this comment on Mice Age, "A tremendous amount of time and money have gone into this park. The bones are all there for a great park in the future, but that seems distant at the moment. It's clear that this resort is designed to scale. One day, this could be the WDW [Walt Disney World] of Asia. But, at the moment, this park has a long climb to be a major tourist destination. We are looking forward to returning in a couple of years to see how Disney fills in the blanks"[363].

Most parks aren't planning to have an 80,000 capacity with 21 rides, but there are still lessons for the smaller parks. One of the evolutions of the Magic Kingdom parks is to limit paths getting blocked by crowds watching

---

363   A theme park designer look at Shanghai Disneyland, Mice Chat Staff, Mice Chat, https://www.micechat.com/127863-shanghai-disneyland-theme-park-designer-look/

shows. First, Disneyland Paris added an open-air theatre next to the castle, for the smaller daytime shows. Disneyland Shanghai goes further with an amphitheatre in front of the castle for their night-time firework show.

The Thinkwell Group designs theme parks and manages their planning and development. They estimate that in a crowded space such as firework viewing or watching a parade, the average person needs 5 square foot (0.46 sq metres)[364]. Presumably this figure is based primarily on research at American parks. Guests with wheelchairs, ECVs (Electric Convenience Vehicle), push-chairs/strollers will take up more space. This would mean that for 15,000 to watch a firework show in front of the castle you'd need 75,000 sq ft, or 6,900 sq metres. That's about 1.72 acres of pathway.

Small parks have smaller crowds and rarely anything on the scale of a Magic Kingdom style firework show. However, paths might get blocked by pop up food stalls, face painting and portrait stands, sideshows and upcharge games like 'aqua balls', street theatre and things for events like scare mazes. As a park grows buildings can get extended and outside seating areas can get added or enlarged in front of restaurants. Paths can get temporarily closed off to create a construction site for a new project. Often paths are deliberately blocked, because people are more likely to notice something like a face painting stand, if it's blocking the path. However, parks should think about pinch points and guest flow, considering the worst-case scenario on a peak day. Over time there can be a slow creep of development across the midways, which can cause problems and be a risk, particularly if it's near the entrance where the crowds tend to be the thickest.

Disney often try to create a sense of intimacy and development while maintaining the width of paths, by building over the top of them. This can include arcades that have a building extending overhead, which has the double benefit of keeping guests dry when it's raining, while also maximising the width of the path. Balconies and signs hang over the edge of paths, big arches or bridges span them, as well as things like long washing lines, and strings of flags, lanterns or bunting. All these things help to keep a wide path at the bottom, without having a big expanse of asphalt with no theming. Mickey Avenue doesn't have any curbs, removing a possible trip hazard, however they have coloured the centre of the street red and the edges grey, to give the impression of a pavement (sidewalk). The path around the hub has a kind of mosaic effect. If you do have wide paths to accommodate a heavy guest flow, it's more obvious when it's all the same colour, like a big sea of grey.

Whilst Disneyland Shanghai is one of the most visited parks in the world, the problem with congestion is certainly not unique, and compact amusement parks at the seaside or in urban areas will have a particular problem making sure that all the crowds can be accommodated safely.

---

364   Designing a physically distanced theme park, Thinkwell, https://thinkwellgroup.com/2020/07/22/what-if-we-designed-a-theme-park-with-physical-distancing-and-health-safety-as-a-guiding-principle/

Growing a Disney park

We looked at the growth of Hong Kong Disneyland and how its capacity expanded roughly in line with its visitor numbers. We talked about why this wasn't enough to make it successful and how the numbers compared to rival Ocean Park. We then looked at how the statistics for Hong Kong Disneyland compared to Disney's original park (opened in 1955) and their newest park (opened in 2016). Over time the ratio of rides to acres has gone down. The paths and rides have got bigger and there's more infrastructure in between. Disney parks now have a higher capacity relative to the number of rides they've got. As Disney expanded beyond California, they've had to adapt to wetter and colder climates, and find new ways to weather proof their attractions. The way that Disney parks are designed has changed.

The way that they're operated has also changed, from the early days of ride tickets, the introduction of POP (pay one price) and the addition of Fast Pass followed by My Magic Plus and tiered pricing. These days Disney parks are more expensive to build and operate than the original Disneyland was. To make them economical they have to be less seasonal than Disneyland was in the 1950s. What has changed very little is the basic principle behind how the Disney parks grow and develop.

When Disney build a new park, it's typical for them to spend a relatively big chunk of the money on the infrastructure. Although new areas can be added over time, it isn't common. Hong Kong Disneyland was unusual in adding three new areas in quick succession. Disney parks are built with expansion in mind, and grow in a more controlled way than some regional parks. At a new park, the infrastructure is built to last, and is designed to accommodate expansion by adding more rides around the edge of the park, often into existing areas. As for the rides, Disney prioritises quality over quantity. This is partly because Disney knows that the number of rides isn't as strongly related to the capacity as you might imagine. Disney attractions are built to last. In the long run it's better to get things right the first time around. They don't want to put in a load of cheap rides to make up the numbers, and then have to remove them a short way down the line. Disney also know that they need to set themselves apart from the many regional parks, and that it'll be hard to do this if they start using too many cheap filler rides.

New Disney parks are often criticised for not having enough rides, although this was a bigger criticism at the Disney Studios (Paris), California Adventure and Hong Kong Disneyland than it was at Parc Disneyland Paris and Shanghai Disneyland. We will discuss whether the parks built after Disneyland Paris did suffer from the budgets being too small, but I will also argue that all of Disney's parks have grown in a similar way, regardless of their funding.

You could see Disney parks as being the art of how to squeeze the most capacity possible out of the smallest number of rides. They use every trick in the book: single rider queues to fill all the seats, virtual queuing and rides that are designed around having the highest possible throughputs. You have long opening hours, nighttime entertainment and a year-round business model aided by events (particularly Christmas and Halloween) and promotions (free Dining plans etc) to spread out attendance. You also have a big base of local annual pass holders who will visit at the quiet times of year, either because they know the parks will be quieter then, or because their annual pass is blocked out on peak days.

Hong Kong Disney was criticised for its small size when it opened, often said to be in response to the financial failure of Disneyland Paris. But how different was the early Hong Kong Disneyland compared to other Disney parks when they were new? The standard narrative is that Disneyland Paris was a financial disaster after it opened in 1992. After that Eisner (then CEO) and the executives became more cautious and built future parks on tighter budgets. In interviews Eisner himself has accepted that they were more cautious after Disneyland Paris.

There certainly were differences between Parc Disneyland Paris and some of the more recent Disney parks, for example Hong Kong had a smaller castle and California Adventure didn't have a berm to shield it from the outside world. After Disneyland Paris new parks had less money spent on big pieces of theming and fewer E ticket rides. Tokyo Disney, Epcot and Parc Disneyland all placed a lot of emphasis on dark rides when they were new. Dark rides are a Disney staple. They have no height restrictions (minimum height for the guests to ride), they're accessible for guests in wheelchairs and they can achieve very high throughputs. The Disney Studios, Hong Kong Disneyland and California Adventure all placed less emphasis on dark rides, although all them have added at least a couple of dark rides since they opened. But the basic principles of developing and growing a Disney park haven't changed.

You build things to last. You put in the infrastructure you need to cope with a large volume of people. You squeeze as much capacity as you can out of everything you've got. You leave plenty of room around the edge for future attractions. New Disney parks always receive a lot of publicity when they open, regardless of their size and budget. This initial burst of excitement is difficult to sustain. New parks are quickly followed by a major expansion. Sometimes this is planned in advance. If it isn't, there's a quick scramble to pull something together. When you plan a new park, you should assume that there's going to be a come down when the initial buzz dies off. Ideally you should have budget and plans set aside for an expansion. This can be easier for a major company like Disney than it is for an independent project, where they've often managed to scrape together just enough money to get the park built and open.

We will now consider several parks in turn: Animal Kingdom, Hollywood Studios, Disneyland Paris, Epcot and Shanghai Disneyland. For each park, we will look at how big they were when they first opened.

Animal Kingdom (opened 1998) is generally seen as a high-quality park, although when it opened it had just two big attractions: Kilimanjaro Safaris and Dinosaur, plus the Legends of the Lion King show, It's Tough to be a Bug 4D cinema and various animal enclosures. A Beastly Kingdom area themed to mythical creatures was cut from the final plan. Some of the imagineers later went on to work for Universals and some of the ideas from Beastly Kingdom ended up in the Lost Continent at Islands of Adventure (Universal Orlando). Unusually for a Disney park, they didn't initially try to attract people for the evening, because the animals couldn't be seen in the dark and a firework show could distress the animals.

The following year (1999) Animal Kingdom added the Tarzan Rocks stage show (later replaced with Finding Nemo the musical) and Kali River Rapids. Despite the low number of attractions, Animal Kingdom hasn't had the same level of criticism that Disney's next three parks had, perhaps partly because all the attractions were new, rather than copies of attractions at other parks. When it opened Kali River Rapids was better received by Disney fans, compared to Indiana Jones and the Temple of Peril (Paris) or Autopia (Hong Kong). Having a significant expansion coming in 1999 helped to distract people from the park's initial small size. With Animal Kingdom guests had the ability to park hop to one of Disney World's three other parks if they got bored, something guests couldn't do at Hong Kong Disneyland.

When it opened many visitors saw Animal Kingdom more as a safari park with a few other attractions, rather than a standard theme park. This made direct comparisons with other theme parks less relevant. The same principle might have applied to Hollywood Studios when it opened in 1989. At the time the park had just two attractions: The Great Move Ride and the Studio Tram Tour. However, Hollywood Studios was probably compared more to studios tours in the real Hollywood, and particularly to Universal's Tram Tour, rather than to other theme parks. In fact, Disney World had one traditional theme park (Magic Kingdom), a permanent World's Fair (Epcot), a Movie Studio tour (Hollywood Studios) and a safari park/zoo (Animal Kingdom). Slowly these have all added more theme park elements, and while Animal Kingdom still has its safari, Epcot's downplayed its World Fair elements and Hollywood Studios removed its tram tour in 2014, to make way for Star Wars: Galaxy's Edge. With a straightforward theme park, it's easier for people to compare the number of attractions. Furthermore, I suspect people's expectations of a new theme park have increased since Hollywood Studios opened.

Disney's parks in the early 2000s might have been scaled back because of the problems at Disneyland Paris. However, Hollywood Studios (then called MGM Studios) was perhaps equally cautious, if not more so. Epcot had cost double the projected budget, and this had threatened to derail the company. Disney also wanted to get the park open before Universals opened their own park nearby, meaning the project had to be delivered quickly. Universal Studios Florida opened a year later in 1990.

The Walt Disney Studios Paris (opened 2002), California Adventure (opened 2001) and Disneyland Hong Kong (opened 2005) were all built on relatively tight budgets. But it must be remembered that Disney parks have always tended to open with only a small number of attractions. The real difference between these three parks and earlier projects like Epcot, Tokyo Disney, Disneyland Paris, or even Animal Kingdom, wasn't about the number of attractions, but perhaps the scale of them, their originality and the quality of the theming between the rides. For instance, when California Adventure first opened, it didn't have a 'berm' (border), meaning you could see the city outside the park. Part of the reason they built Radiator Spring Racers (The Cars ride, opened 2012) was to create a big mountain that hid the outside world. California Adventure cost $650 million, which isn't cheap compared to some other parks, and still almost triple the cost of Hard Rock Park. However, it was a lot less than the $3 billion they estimated Westcot would have cost[365]. Let's compare Hong Kong Disneyland to Disneyland Paris.

When Disneyland Paris opened it only had 12 rides, 7 of which were built by budget manufacturer Zamperla[366]. That's two more rides than Hong Kong Disneyland had in its first year, but not a significantly higher number. Paris had a bigger more impressive castle and a longer Main Street. Sleeping Beauty's castle at Disneyland Paris was 167ft compared to the 77ft castle at Hong Kong Disneyland. The Paris resort had a lot more hotel rooms, although considering the low occupancy in its early days, it made sense to start with a much lower number for Hong Kong. More of the rides had unique elements rather than being direct copies, and more of the rides were headline attractions. So overall Hong Kong Disneyland did feel lower budget than Parc Disneyland Paris, even though both had low ride counts to start off with.

Opening rides at Disneyland Paris included Big Thunder Mountain, Phantom Manor, Pirates of the Caribbean, Star Tours and It's a Small World. By contrast, Hong Kong Disneyland only had two major rides when it opened: Space Mountain and The Jungle Cruise. Big Thunder Mountain was the biggest version of the ride, with two tunnels taking trains to and from an island. It's 4,921ft long[367], which compares to 2,671ft (Disneyland California) and 2,780ft (Magic Kingdom). Incidentally, Big Grizzly Mountain (Hong Kong) is 3,609ft long. Of course, longer isn't necessarily better, but it gives you a sense that Parc Disneyland Paris was trying to 'plus' what they'd done elsewhere. The Paris version of Pirates of the Caribbean has a duration of roughly 10.5 minutes, which is longer than the 8.5 minutes at Disney World, and a long ride time for this kind of scenic attraction. Phantom Manor (Paris) is a bit shorter than Haunted Mansion at Magic Kingdom, with about 785ft of track[368] compared to 960ft[369]. It does, however, have a more elaborate storyline. There clearly was an issue with Hong Kong Disneyland only having two E ticket rides when it opened, and some fans might dispute whether The Jungle Cruise really is an E ticket.

In its opening year (1982) Epcot was closer in scale to Parc Disneyland Paris, Tokyo Disneyland and Shanghai Disneyland, than it was to Disney's

365   The history of Disney California Adventure, Jack Spence, All Ears, https://allears.net/2012/12/10/the-history-of-disney-california-adventure/

366   History, Zamperla, https://www.zamperla.com/zamperla-world/company/

367   Statistics from RCDB, Roller Coaster Database

368   Phantom Manor, Disney Parks Fandom, https://disneyparks.fandom.com/wiki/Phantom_Manor

369   Haunted Mansion, All Ears, https://allears.net/magic-kingdom/haunted-mansion-liberty-square-magic-kingdom/

other subsequent parks. Original E ticket rides were Spaceship Earth, World in Motion and Universe of Energy. There were also two smaller boat rides (Living with the Land and El Rio del Tempo), two animatronics shows (Kitchen Kabaret and American Adventure), a 4D cinema and 3 circle-visions. That's a similar number of attractions to Hong Kong Disneyland, but no roundabouts and more E ticket rides. In the section on Bench Marking Against Disney we talked about why Epcot was so expensive to build. It's partly because of the research and development they did, the scale of the infrastructure and the cost of importing authentic props. But it also reflects the fact that Epcot was a fuller and more ambitious park than some of the other Disney parks were when they first opened. The year after opening Epcot expanded with Horizons (omimover) and Journey into Imagination (omnimover).

In the first 15 years after opening Hong Kong Disneyland's capacity almost doubled with three new areas and Autopia, It's a Small World, Big Grizzly Mountain, Mystic Manor, and the Iron Man Experience. Disneyland Paris initially expanded fairly quickly with Indiana Jones and the Temple of Peril (1993), the Casey Jr Circus Train (1994) and Space Mountain (1995), but since then the park has developed little, as almost all the attention has gone on the sister Disney Studios park. The development of Disneyland Paris and Hong Kong Disneyland is a bit like the story of the hare and the tortoise. Once the Arendelle area opens, Hong Kong Disneyland and Parc Disneyland Paris will have roughly the same number of rides, although Parc Disneyland Paris will still have a bigger acreage.

Disney's strategy for designing parks works for multiple reasons. They're able to handle large volumes of visitors with limited numbers of rides, which means they can focus on quality over quantity. Because they don't lumber their parks with poor quality attractions to make up the numbers, their rides stand the test of time. This means that they can grow by maintaining what they've got and slowly adding more rides, rather than building rides and then ripping them out to add better rides, which is an inefficient way of growing a park. When Disney has built parks on a lower budget, their design principles and approach to operations hasn't changed. What has changed is the number of attractions and headline rides, but not the type of attractions and the way they're put together. Even for the relatively low budget parks like California Adventure and the Disney Studios in Paris, they could have built a lot more rides than they did, if they'd created something more like a regional park. Disney would have known that some of their parks would be criticised for not having enough rides and they could have done something about it. But they also knew that in the long run quantity isn't a great way to get a high capacity, nor does it create a park that's likely to be popular in the winter.

There are plenty of things that the Disney parks do that don't translate well to other regional parks. Most parks are never going to attract the critical mass of visitors needed to make a Disney park viable. However, the basic principle of focusing on infrastructure (even if it isn't as marketable as a ride), focusing a little more on quality over quantity, and having a long-term strategy, are all values that other parks can benefit from.

I've heard people say that there's no point in a theme park having a long-term plan, because the technology changes too quickly. You don't necessarily need to come up with specific ride plans, but you need to have some objectives and a direction of travel. Are you trying to make your park less dependent on good weather? Is there a quiet area of the park you want to attract more people to? Are the lines too long at the restaurants? Unless you've got a humungous budget, you're going to have to prioritise a few areas. If you don't have a long-term plan that moves you towards a goal, developments are likely to get decided on by the marketing department. The marketing department should have a good understanding of branding and demographics, but they don't necessarily appreciate the concepts we've discussed in this book. Marketing also tends to be fickle, thinking more about the next publicity hit, rather than long term progress.

In this section I have focused very heavily on Disney, so I apologise to those of you who aren't fans of the Mouse. I have thrown around a lot of statistics, and some people's brains might now be swimming like a big bowl on number soup. Hurling around a lot of numbers doesn't in itself make a park more efficient, but there are a lot of numbers to think about. Ride capacities, hourly throughputs, average wait times, ride availability, the ratio of staff to guests, park capacities, peaks and troughs in attendance... to understand how efficient a park is you need to try to master all of these statistics. By focusing on all of these things, we can understand the bigger picture, see what our park's capable of and work out where to focus our efforts and resources to make it more successful. To grow our park, we have to find new audiences and increase our appeal, but we also have to make sure that when they do come, they have a safe and pleasant stay. You might be able to increase your attendance with a cool marketing campaign or an impressive ride, but if they don't have a good time when they're there, they won't come back.

Wrapping things up

In Summary

It occurred to me that for a book about efficiency, this has been a long read. Here are the main points in brief.

Queues are the biggest source of complaints about the theme park industry. They're frequently discussed on Trip Advisor and other guest feedback. Enthusiasts are passionate about efficiency, and have made Youtube videos about dispatch times, websites presenting data on queue times and apps for measuring a ride's efficiency. Staff generally hate queues too. They find them stressful, it makes the guests irate and leads to problems like queue jumping. If we can find ways to make our queues shorter, it will give us a massive competitive edge. There is a significant interest in operational efficiency, however it is often misunderstood. Too many managers only know how to walk around with a clipboard telling everyone to work faster.

Queues are as old as the industry. In 1884 Coney Island's Switchback Railway was getting 3 hours queues. Leading parks do everything they can to keep the waiting times as short as possible. There is always more work to do, and parks should never stop trying to be more efficient.

It's very difficult for a park to cope with big peaks and troughs in attendance, and even if the park can, the roads, transport infrastructure and accommodation around the park might not. Successful parks level off their peaks in attendance so that visits get shifted from busier days to quieter days. The regular public often don't realise how big the fluctuations in attendance are, so they'll attend on a particularly busy day and assume the park always has long queues. They also assume that the park's making more money than it is.

Big peaks and troughs in attendance aren't good for the guests. On the busiest days queuing spoils their day. On the quietest days the park can lack atmosphere. It's also not good for the staff who have times of year where they're working lots of hours and getting burned out, and other times of year when they're getting little work and small pay checks.

There are various things a park can do to encourage people to shift their visits to the quieter days. You can use crowd calendars and social media to clearly communicate how busy the park's likely to be on each day. You can use events to drive attendance at quieter times of year. For example, October used to be a quiet month for the theme park industry, but Halloween now makes it busy. Universal created Mardi Gras to drive attendance in the quiet period before Easter. Events can be expensive to put on, so they need careful planning and management. You need to think about how to market the event. What's the USP (unique selling point) and how do you summarise the event? Who's the audience? What's the capital investment? What are the running costs for each day it's on? If you're using events to spread out attendance, then you're often best running them when the queues are short, but the park isn't empty. Events are more cost effective when they take advantage of assets that your park's already got. Christmas events can help a seasonal theme park extend their season. If you're managing your queues by opening on extra days, then this has a significant price tag and it makes it harder to manage your winter maintenance programme.

Encouraging guests to plan their visits around birthdays rather than public holidays helps to spread out those peaks.

You can use pricing to direct guests towards the quieter days. This can include peak/off peak pricing. Dynamic pricing is where prices go up as more people buy tickets. Promotions can include giving people free meals at a quiet time of year, or allowing annual pass holders to bring a free guest on quiet days. When you do discounting and promotions it's important to make sure that even the most expensive tickets are seen as reflecting a fair price. Dynamic pricing has been successful at some parks including Leolandia, but when pricing becomes too complex it puts people off.

Parks generally struggle to cope with the demand for a major new ride, particularly on opening day. Demand for a new ride can be spread out, for example by having annual pass holder previews and soft openings. Parks often do any filming with the press before opening day, so that the operations can flow smoothly when there's a long queue waiting to ride. Plenty of testing before the ride opens reduces the amount of downtime and teething problems when the guests are waiting to ride.

Parks tend to busiest when people expect the weather to be good. This is particularly problematic for parks in poor or unsteady climates. Weather proofing by design includes having plenty of undercover rides, queues, shows and areas. Paths should have good drainage so that large puddles don't form. It means picking rides that aren't significantly affected by adverse weather. Rides with tyres have problems in wet weather because the tyres get wet and lose their grip. Tall roller coasters can struggle in high wind. We can get around this partly by making sure they have plenty of excess energy as they go over hills and high points in the layout. Areas with dark colour palettes can feel depressing when the weather's grey and miserable.

Once you've weather proofed, the park's marketing should support the message that it's still fun when the weather's poor. You can also use rain checks, where if it rains for a certain period in a guest's stay, they can come back for free. When the weather's poor customer service is vitally important. Staff need to stay upbeat, empathise with guest's disappointment and communicate clearly about why rides are closed and how the park will decide when they re-open them.

If your park has long queues at weekends and school holidays, then try to grow your attendance by attracting more guests who will come on week days during term time. This can include school trips, parents with pre-school toddlers and adults without school aged children. Older guests often want higher quality food and opportunities to sit down, including benches around the park, shows and restaurants. Part of the reason why Disneyland Paris had significant financial issues in its early days, was big peaks and troughs in attendance. This particularly affected their hotels, which had low occupancy. Most of their guests had school age children and it wasn't in the French culture to take children off school to visit a theme park. They picked Paris rather than a site near Barcelona with a steadier climate. The Europeans are more weather sensitive than the Japanese, who still pack into Disneyland Tokyo during the winter.

As well as distributing guests evenly between days, you want to make sure they're spread out around the park and not bunched up in a few areas. The layout of the park helps to disperse guests. The hub and spoke layout is arguably the most successful way of doing this, as it sends guest straight to the centre where they're equidistant from each area. Having an entrance in the corner of a park is least effective. Circular patterns of pathways are generally good for guest flow, while dead ends are avoided. The exception to this rule are areas for very young children, where you don't want guests rushing through it on their way to other areas.

If you want an efficient layout, it's important to plan ahead with future expansions in mind. If there's an area of the park that's noticeably quiet, then that's a good area for an upgrade or a new attraction. Parks might deliberately place their biggest rides at opposite sides of the park or space them out around the edge.

Virtual queues are when guests reserve a time slot and return to the attraction so that they can ride it with a reduced waiting time. Europa Park uses this for Voletarium, because it's by the park's entrance and gets hit particularly hard at the beginning of the day. Disney's Fast Pass allows guests to experience low key attractions, shops and shows while they're waiting for their reservation on a ride with a long waiting time. Often you get a surge of guests at the beginning of a time slot, so you want to have lots of time slots moving forward in small increments, e.g. 10:00-10:30, 10:05-10:35, 10:10-10:40.

Some parks have a whole range of options for spending time away from the rides. Retail is one of the less obvious ones, where it has been estimated that the average guest at some Disney parks spend 15% of their day shopping. Silver Dollar City has 44 shops, Europa Park has 45 and Epcot has 53 - as many as a mid-sized shopping mall. How much time guests spend shopping is partly based on the size and range of the shops, but also on the types of shop. Shops based around impulse buys, promotions and upselling will typically have shorter dwell times than shops based around theming and 'merchantainment'.

Theme parks with shorter, faster moving queues tend to have strong cooperation and a sense of people pulling together. Everyone takes responsibility for making the lines shorter. Blame isn't shifted onto one or two departments or individuals.

If you advertise the waiting times, the guests can make better informed decisions about what they're willing to wait for and move towards attractions in quieter areas of the park. Wait times can be communicated by staff at the entrance to lines, through announcements to the queue, on screens at the entrance to the queue, on screens at central locations in the park and on mobile apps. You can make this information clearer by colour coding waiting times as red, amber or green depending on how long the wait is. It's important to make sure that the waiting times are accurate. This can be helped with the right system where different parts (like the mobile app and screens in the park) talk to each other, and where operators can easily update their waiting time. The more consistent a ride's throughput is (the number of people who can ride it each hour), the easier it is to accurately predict the waiting time. Information about waiting times can be used to manage staff, for example sending cleaners and entertainers to busy areas.

If your park has a pay per ride model, you distribute guests partly by charging more for more popular rides, or by selling ticket books, where guests effectively get cheap tickets for less popular rides along with a ticket for a more popular attraction.

You want to encourage guests to plan their visit around avoiding queues. This means giving them the information to make informed decisions. As well as providing waiting times, you need to make it clear what the rides are. This can include drawings of the ride on signposts and posters capturing the name and essence of each ride as people enter the park.

If a park's open for long hours, you want to stagger guests. Instead of most of the guests being there for the middle period, it's better if more guests get there for the opening and leave earlier in the day and others arrive later in the day and stay until it closes. You encourage guests to get there early or stay later by having an opening ceremony and some kind of show at the end of the day, like a firework or fountain show.

A park's capacity is determined by safety factors and ensuring an acceptable guest experience. Safety factors include the ratio of toilets and wash basins to guests. The ability to serve them food and drink in a timely manner, particularly water. There must be reasonable first aid and security provisions for the number of guests, and the ability to get emergency vehicles to areas of the park in a timely manner. Fire regulations are important, particularly for indoor areas, where there must be sufficient fire exits for the number of people. Pathways must be able to cope with the crowds. Bottle necks can be a particular problem here, for example if the path narrows as it enters an area. A seamless crowd flow is especially important around the park's entrance. Parks should have the ability to control crowds, often involving a central command point with CCTV (cameras) that can monitor the situation, and PA (public address systems) that allow management to communicate with guests in a big crowd. Busy parks should have strong crisis management plans and training. Parks normally allow queues to become long before they limit things to improve the guest experience. However, there comes a point where you're not giving people any value for their money. You can get a rough idea of whether a park's got a fair capacity by doing an audit on a peak day. Are bins overflowing? Are eateries running out of many items? Do the toilets have soap in most of the dispensers? How long are the lines?

We looked at some case studies of parks to see how they used the lessons in this book. We saw how Geauga Lake struggled when they pulled in more visitors than they could cope with, and that the gains were short lived. We also saw how Paultons Park and Islands of Adventure were able to sustain big gains in attendance. This was because they had surplus capacity before adding popular new attractions.

We took a trip back to Coney Island to see how parks coped in the early days of the amusement industry. We saw how quickly the industry evolved the practices that leading theme parks still use.

We saw how Holiday World rapidly grew their attendance by concentrating on fun, thrilling, high capacity rides, cleanliness, value and customer service, with modest amounts of theming. Outdoor water parks can entertain a lot of people using wave pools, lazy rivers and sunbeds. Holiday World has very big peaks and needs a lot of staff on short contracts to cope with this. Eventually, finding enough staff who want this kind of contract becomes a challenge.

We looked at Dollywood and the fine balance they must strike to be commercially successful and achieve enviable guest satisfaction. Dollywood increased their capacity by investing in their infrastructure as well as in more rides.

We looked at how Disney grow their parks, and how they entertain huge numbers of people while keeping their ride counts fairly low. This is done through high throughput attractions that are designed for efficiency and optimised with single rider lines and simple restraint systems. They design parks with efficient layouts, Fast Pass, phone apps and queue time boards to distribute guests evenly around the site. They put on shows and parades at peak times and encourage people to visit in the evening with big night-time shows. They also use events to encourage people to visit at slower times of year.

Parks that are good at managing their queues tend to be the ones that plan further ahead.

Conclusion: A final word before I go

Shortly before I finished writing this book, I was trying to explain what it was about to someone I worked with. When I finished, they said, "Do you think you might be on the spectrum?" I was like, "What, the spectrum of completely awesome people?" "No, the autistic spectrum". Aside from confirming that my colleague was a rude ****, I do accept that getting excited about efficiently operated roller coasters isn't completely normal.

Knowing a lot about operational efficiency doesn't necessarily get you invited to many parties. But I hope you'll agree, that there's a lot more to this operational efficiency than most people realise. When you put down the clip board and stop shouting at people to work faster, it's a remarkably fascinating subject. Customers might imagine employees sitting around in the staffroom cackling about how long the queues are, before shoving a suitcase full of cash into the back of their car. In reality, managing the queues can be a tough exercise. Theme parks aren't easy to make money out of.

Some of the factors in this book might seem inconsequential, but collectively they can have a profound effect on how crowded parks feel and how much people enjoy their day. A lot of the concepts in this book are straightforward, and it isn't difficult to prove that they work. At the same time, parks can get bogged down in short term thinking and hitting the next month's numbers. Real efficiency takes long term thinking and forward planning. One of the biggest causes of inefficiency is workplace politics, which leads to poor team work, blame getting passed around and unhelpful rivalries, which all distract people from solving the genuine problems.

People sometimes ask me whether theme parks really care about the queues. "Once you're in, they've got your money", they tell me. But the industry has worked hard to keep on evolving, and to find new ways to manage queues more effectively and to reduce waiting times. I'd like to think that this book is a testament to that.

I've wanted to write a book for a long time. When I was eighteen, I went to university to study creative writing. My Mum said to me, "Isn't one of the problems with a creative writing degree, that everyone's young and hasn't got a lot of life experiences. Do you have much to write about?". I was defensive and pointed out that there are a lot of books with fantasy and science fiction themes that the writers can't have experienced themselves. But now

I'm older, I understand what she meant. When you sit behind a computer trying to come up with a story for your next assignment, it's unlikely to be your best writing. Your best work comes from ideas that force their way into your mind. I think that's what they mean when they say that everyone's got a book inside them. We all have something we're passionate about. We all have something interesting that we know about. Every time a manager came around with their clip board and shouted at everyone to work faster, I knew I had to do something. Every time a British park closed, I wasn't happy just to blame extraneous factors like rising taxes and fuel costs or poor weather. I felt there had to be something the theme parks could do to increase their chance of survival - like making themselves more efficient. In the end this book just came tumbling out.

This is the first book about operational efficiency in the theme park industry, but I hope it won't be my last. There are plenty more aspects to managing queues other than the areas I've covered in this book, and it will take another book to do them justice.

In the meantime, if you've got any views you want to share, pleasure get in touch: forneilwilson@gmail.com

If you run a theme park and you need any support with reducing your waiting times or improving other aspects of the guest experience, I would love to hear from you.

Glossary

For the most part I've tried to explain acronyms and technical terms as we're going along. I want this book to be accessible to as many people as possible. I hope this glossary also makes it easier to read.

4D cinema: The '4th dimension' in a 4D cinema are physical effects, such as water jets, fans, smells, vibrating seats and leg ticklers. 4D cinemas can play temporary films to support events. They're also good for parks looking to add more undercover attractions.

Annual pass/Season ticket: An annual pass normally lasts for 12 months from the moment you first use it. If you first use it in September, it'll expire in September the following year. A season ticket is for the current season. If the season runs from March to October and you buy a season ticket at the beginning of October, you'll only get to use it for one month.

Backstage: Disney encourage their staff (known as cast members) to think of themselves as putting on a show. They're part of the performance. When the guests can see them, they're on stage. When the guests can't see them, they're backstage. A theme park has to find space for backstage areas, such as staffrooms, storage for food and merchandise, workshops etc. In some parks the backstage areas are integrated into the main park, for example having offices above the shops and restaurants. In other parks, the backstage areas are more separate.

Benchmarking: Comparing how you do something to the best in the industry. For parks looking to benchmark their operational efficiency, parks they're likely to look at include Disney, Universal, Europa Park, Dollywood and Efteling.

Concessions: When a theme park brings in a third party to run parts of their business, such as shops, restaurants or games. Often there's a revenue sharing agreement, where the concession has to hand over a percentage of its income (e.g. 20%) to the park.

Destination shops: Shops people choose to visit, rather than the ones people are channeled into, often at the exit to a ride. Destination shops tend to rely less on promotions and impulse buys, and more on creating a themed experience with high quality products.

Capex/Opex: Capex stands for capital expenditure and opex stands for operating expenditure. Let's say you're going to be put on a new event in September to shift visits from the busy summer to the quieter period that follows. You might spend £100,000 on theming. If this theming could be used every year, this would be capex. If it costs £10,000 each year to put the theming up, then that's opex.

Dark ride: An indoor ride where guests are entertained by scenery, animatronics and effects.

E ticket ride: These are headline rides. They're called E ticket rides, because when Disneyland was new you bought tickets for the individual rides you wanted to go on. The biggest rides, like the Matterhorn Bobsled and Space Mountain, needed an E ticket. The last ride at Disneyland to be given an E ticket status was Big Thunder Mountain (opened in 1979)[370]. After that Disneyland switched to a POP (pay one price) model. The term E ticket is most commonly associated with Disney, but it might also be used to describe major attractions at other parks.

Feasibility study: A report that looks at whether a project's feasible. The key questions are: will it make a profit (be viable) and will the investors get back the money they put into the project (a return on their investment)?

Flat rides: a style of ride on a flat platform that spins people around. They might also be called roundabouts, fairground rides or carnival rides.

Flying theatre: This is a kind of theatre where a suspended bench moves in front of a giant screen. The first flying theatre was Soarin' at Disney's California Adventure.

Guests: Another name for visitors or customers. Disney started referring to their visitors as guests, because they wanted their staff to be as welcoming as they would be to a guest in their own home.

Imagineering: Across between imagination and engineering. The word was coined by Disney to describe the team who design and develop their theme park attractions. Imagineer has now been adopted across the industry.

IPs (intellectual properties): These are brands that a park brings in from outside the business to theme its rides and areas to and increase their appeal. For example, attractions themed to a TV show or a film.

Merchantainment: A cross between merchandise and entertainment. It's about finding ways to make shopping into a fun experience. At some parks the shops are seen as a core part of a guest's visit. If people spend more time shopping, the queues for the rides get shorter. If a park has a virtual queuing system, guests can be encouraged to look at the shops while they're waiting for their time slot.

Meet and greet: When you meet a costume character for a photo opportunity, for example having your photo taken with Mickey Mouse. There might be other kinds of interaction, for example the character might sign your autograph book or do a dance with you.

Omnimover: Omnimover is a word coined by Disney Imagineer Bob Gurr and fuses the words omni (meaning everywhere) and people mover. It's a

---

370   Can you name all 15 E ticket rides still at Disneyland – it's not as easy as you think, Brady Macdonald, Orange Country Register, https://www.ocregister.com/2019/08/05/can-you-name-all-15-e-ticket-rides-still-at-disneyland-its-not-as-easy-as-you-think/

type of 'dark ride' where a continuous chain of vehicles move slowly along a circular track, which takes them passed various scenes, normally with animatronics. Disney originally patented the concept for the Adventures Thru Inner Space ride in Tomorrowland at Disneyland. It operated from 1967 to 1985. Omnimovers are known for their exceptionally high throughputs.

Plussing: is about finding ways to improve an attraction, without changing the basic essence of it. You might improve the lighting, upgrade animatronics or add more rockwork. It's about taking what you've already got, and then adding something extra to make it better.

POV videos: Point of view videos. When someone films a ride from the perspective of someone riding it, this is called a POV video.

Practical throughput: The number of people who actually experience an attraction each hour. This is different from the theoretical throughput, which might assume that every seat is occupied, and doesn't account for delays, such as staff changing positions, people trying to take bags on with them, disabled guests etc. The theoretical throughput is always higher than the practical throughput.

Price integrity: Strong price integrity is when your customers feel that the full price of a product represents value for money. They don't expect a discount. Poor price integrity is when people feel that the full price is too expensive. You offer a discount for visiting at a quiet time, but your guests see the discounted price as being what the park is actually worth. You don't want the people visiting on your peak days to feel like they're being ripped off. Disney wants to encourage more people to visit at quieter times. They offer hotel guests free meals rather than a discount, to help maintain their price integrity. Liseberg wants to encourage guests to book in advance. They do this by offering them free fast track tickets to skip the queues, rather than a bigger discount. Businesses with strong price integrity are more likely to be referred to as 'premium brands', whereas a theme park with poor price integrity might be called a 'discounter'.

Primary Spend/Secondary Spend: Primary spend is the money guests spend on their entry fee. Secondary spend is all the money they spend inside the park, like on food and merchandise.

Regional theme park: When we talk about 'regional theme parks', we're excluding the big international resorts - chiefly Disney and Universal. However, over the past 25 years a lot more theme parks have added accommodation and 'second gates', like water parks. The line between an 'international resort' and a regional theme park has become blurred. Parks like Port Aventura (Spain) and Europa Park (Germany) may also be considered international resorts.

Resorts: Resort theme parks are generally those with accommodation, such as hotels and holiday villages. They might also include 'second gate' attractions, such as water parks.

Ride availability: This can also be known as uptime. It's the amount of time that rides are 'available' for. When they're closed it's called downtime. Rides can be closed for a range of reasons including technical problems (either mechanical, electrical or structural), adverse weather (including heavy rain, high winds or thunder and lightning), guest action (including a guest throwing up on the ride) or staff action (for example if the operator becomes ill). The better the ride availability, the shorter the queues will be.

Root cause analysis (RCA): Looking at the original source of a problem. For example, you might identify that the throughputs are lower than they should be because the staff are too slow. The root cause would be why the staff are slow. It might be that they're not getting enough breaks or water, leading to fatigue. Or it might be that you have high turnover and a lot of them are inexperienced. Alternatively, you might find that the queues are getting really long because everyone's trying to visit when the weather forecast is good. The root cause might be that there's not enough undercover attractions for when the weather's poor.

Service recovery: This is a gesture to win back customers who've had a bad experience. Strong service recovery techniques can encourage guests to visit even when they know that the weather's likely to be poor.

SBNO: Standing but not operating. If a ride is unavailable for a sustained period of time, we might refer to it as SBNO. For example, a ride that's closed for several weeks waiting for a spare part could be described as SBNO.

Seasonal theme parks: Some theme parks are open all year round. This includes the big resort parks (all the Disney and Universal parks), as well as some smaller parks in hot climates, such as Australia or California. Seasonal parks have a period each year when they're closed.

Single rider queue: Guests who are on their own, or don't mind splitting up from their group, can use the single rider queue to fill up empty seats on a ride.

Streetmosphere: Short for street atmosphere, this is about creating entertainment in the midways around the park. It's non linear entertainment that you can join and leave at any point, often without being specifically advertised with a time and location. It can be moved around the park to busy locations, so if a major ride breaks down, you could establish some nearby streetmosphere to mop up some of the crowds who would have queued for the big attraction. If a park has a ride reservation system where guests get a timed ticket for an attraction, they can watch some streetmosphere while they're waiting for their time slot to come up. Because it isn't advertised and has a lot of flexibility, more streetmosphere can be added on busy days to draw crowds away from the rides.

TEA (Themed Entertainment Association): The TEA was founded in 1991 and represents creators, designers and producers of themed entertainment. Every year, they publish a report showing how many people visited the major parks around the world. In this book, I've generally taken my attendance figures from the TEA reports.

Throughput: The throughput is the number of people who can ride an attraction each hour. In America this is often referred to as an hourly capacity. For the purposes of this book, when I use the word capacity, I'll be talking about the number of riders who can fit on an attraction at one time and I'll use the term throughput to describe the number of people who can experience it each hour.

Virtual queue: Instead of waiting in a physical line to ride an attraction, you're either given a time when you can ride it or you're summoned to the ride via a pager or phone app. While you're waiting for your slot you can wander around the park, shop, eat and experience the other attractions.

Weenie: A weenie is a big visual icon that guests see and head for. The weenie could be at the back of a park, to encourage guests to keep on moving through it. For example, the Wildwood Tree at Dollywood. Or it could be in the centre, like Spaceship Earth or the Tree of Life at Disney.

Printed in Great Britain
by Amazon

71615948R00159